Industry Milestones

Englisch für Industriekaufleute

Ruth Feiertag

Dr. Richard Hooton

Nicole Wichmann

Ilona Wildemann

Ernst Klett Verlag
Stuttgart · Leipzig

Industry Milestones
Englisch für Industriekaufleute

Autoren: Ruth Feiertag; Dr. Richard Hooton; Nicole Wichmann (Fachteile Industrie);
Ilona Wildemann (Fachteile Industrie)

Berater: Robert Kanzog, Münster; Asiye Sezgin, Duisburg; Margrit Meyer, Haan (Fachteile Industrie)

Die Videos auf Seite 103 und 130 wurden von der Firma lingua tv *we watch languages!*
http://www.linguatv.com/ lizenziert.
Bei den Videos handelt es sich um Auszüge aus der LinguaTV-Reihe Business English.

Werkübersicht:
Schülerbuch, 978-3-12-808262-2
Lehrerhandbuch, mit Lehrer-Service-DVD-ROM und 3 Audio-CDs, 978-3-12-808267-7
Workbook mit 1 Audio-CD-ROM, 978-3-12-808265-3
Workbook mit Prüfungsvorbereitung KMK-Fremdsprachenzertifikat und 1 Audio-CD-ROM 978-3-12-808266-0
Industry Milestones Online-Ergänzungen unter www.klett.de/online

1. Auflage

1 6 5 4 3 2 | 17 16 15 14 13

Alle Drucke dieser Auflage sind unverändert und können im Unterricht nebeneinander verwendet werden.
Die letzte Zahl bezeichnet das Jahr des Druckes.

Projektleitung: Matthias Rupp
Redaktion: Volker Wendland; Dr. Birgit Reinel, Tübingen
Herstellung: Angelika Lindner

Gestaltung: Marion Köster, Stuttgart
Umschlaggestaltung: Ulrike Wollenberg; Angelika Lindner
Grafiken: Jörg Mair, München
Satz: Marion Köster, Stuttgart
Reproduktion: Meyle + Müller Medien-Management, Pforzheim
Druck: Druckhaus Götz GmbH, Ludwigsburg

Printed in Germany
ISBN 978-3-12-808262-2

Das vorliegende Lehrwerk **Industry Milestones** für die Englischklassen in den kaufmännischen Berufsschulen, Berufsfachschulen und Fachschulen sowie für industriekaufmännisch ausgerichtete Englischkurse in der Erwachsenenbildung zeichnet sich insbesondere durch folgende Elemente aus:

- Berücksichtigung von Fertigungsprozessen, Warenbeschaffung, Marketing, umweltpolitischen Aspekten sowie der Incoterms® 2010 (gültig ab 01.01.2011)
- Einbeziehung neuester Entwicklungen in der beruflichen Praxis, z. B. durch realitätsnahe Arbeitsaufträge, Rollenspiele und Recherchen im Internet
- Konsequente Berücksichtigung neuester Lehrpläne (Lernfelder) sowie durchgängiges Sprachkompetenztraining nach dem Gemeinsamen Europäischen Referenzrahmen (Sprachstufen B1/B2).
- Möglichkeit zur Binnendifferenzierung durch gekennzeichnete Aufgaben mit höherem Schwierigkeitsgrad
- Umfangreiches Seh-/Hörverstehenstraining durch u. a. Originalvideos von der BBC sowie zahlreiche Audios
- Vokabelarbeit mit der „Word Bank" sowie mit den Vokabellernlisten, dem unit-begleitenden Vokabular und Glossar über Online-Link
- Vertieftes Vokabel-, Grammatik- und Hörverstehenstraining im Workbook 1 und 2, inklusive Audio-CD-ROM mit allen Schülerbuch- und Workbook-Audios
- Gezielte Prüfungsvorbereitung auf das KMK-Fremdsprachenzertifikat im Lehrwerk und im Workbook 2

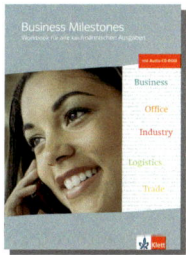

Workbook 1:
Business Milestones Workbook mit Audio-CD-ROM,
978-3-12-808265-3

Workbook 2:
Business Milestones Workbook mit Prüfungsvorbereitung KMK-Fremdsprachenzertifikat und Audio-CD-ROM,
978-3-12-808266-0

Lernhilfen	Symbole	
WORDBANK Schlüsselvokabular	◎ A 1.27	Audioverweis
Info-Box Faktenwissen	◎ V 4	Videoverweis
Communicating across cultures Interkulturelle Kompetenz	Phrases ▶	Verweis auf Phrases
Language and grammar Grammatik	P, M, I, R	Produktion, Mediation, Interaktion oder Rezeption
Video lounge authentische Videos	Example:	z. B. Beispieldialoge
	Online-Link	Vokabellernlisten, unitbegleitendes Vokabular und Glossar über Online-Link
	KMK	Aufgaben zur Vorbereitung auf die Prüfung zum KMK-Fremdsprachenzertifikat Englisch
	🌐🔍	Internet-Recherchen
	✱	„Advanced"-Aufgaben

1 Introducing yourself 6

TOPICS / SKILLS Introducing yourself • Talking about your (future) profession
COMMUNICATING ACROSS CULTURES Introducing and greeting people
LANGUAGE AND GRAMMAR Introducing yourself
INDUSTRY EXPERT Talking about your traineeship • Describing different departments

2 Taking care of visitors 16

TOPICS / SKILLS Greeting visitors • Making conversation • Giving directions • Taking foreign visitors to a restaurant
COMMUNICATING ACROSS CULTURES Small talk • Describing German dishes • Going to restaurants in Britain
LANGUAGE AND GRAMMAR Will-future • Explaining rules and regulations
INDUSTRY EXPERT Explaining the company to visitors • Explaining safety regulations

3 The company and its products and services 36

TOPICS / SKILLS Describing a firm and its history • Describing products and services
COMMUNICATING ACROSS CULTURES Joint stock companies in the USA and Britain
LANGUAGE AND GRAMMAR Simple past and present perfect • Since and for
VIDEO LOUNGE BBC: Sport and leisure
INDUSTRY EXPERT Different types of production processes • Product description

4 The office 49

TOPICS / SKILLS Describing the office / Computer terms • Catering in the office • Describing departments and responsibilities
COMMUNICATING ACROSS CULTURES Addressing people
LANGUAGE AND GRAMMAR Infinitive, gerund
INDUSTRY EXPERT Working in the marketing department • Checking costs

5 Telephoning 61

TOPICS / SKILLS Appliances • Receiving and redirecting calls • Taking messages / Spelling • Making telephone calls • Messages for the answering machine
COMMUNICATING ACROSS CULTURES Telephoning in an English-speaking country
LANGUAGE AND GRAMMAR Tricky prepositions

6 Making arrangements 80

TOPICS / SKILLS Booking flights, hotel rooms and exhibition stands / Hiring cars • Making appointments • Preparing a meeting • Taking the minutes
COMMUNICATING ACROSS CULTURES Tips for visitors to the UK
LANGUAGE AND GRAMMAR Continuous form
VIDEO LOUNGE BBC: Hospitality
INDUSTRY EXPERT Practising telephone language • Making room reservations • Preparing for a trade fair

7 Making presentations 98

TOPICS / SKILLS Preparing and delivering presentations • Describing graphs
LANGUAGE AND GRAMMAR Line graphs
VIDEO LOUNGE Lingua TV: Presentations
INDUSTRY EXPERT Climate change • Production and sustainability • Choosing a factory location

8 Form of written communication 110

TOPICS / SKILLS Layout / Components of business correspondence • Writing e-mails, faxes, letters
COMMUNICATING ACROSS CULTURES The tone of English business correspondence
LANGUAGE AND GRAMMAR Typical mistakes in business correspondence

9 Enquiries 126

TOPICS / SKILLS Making enquiries • Discounts
LANGUAGE AND GRAMMAR Adjectives, adverbs
VIDEO LOUNGE Lingua TV: General enquiries

10 Offers 136

TOPICS / SKILLS Making offers • Incoterms® 2010
LANGUAGE AND GRAMMAR Some and any
INDUSTRY EXPERT Enquiry • Comparing offers

11 Orders 153

TOPICS / SKILLS Placing orders
LANGUAGE AND GRAMMAR Capital letters
VIDEO LOUNGE BBC: Manufacturing

12 Transport and logistics 163

TOPICS / SKILLS Modes of transport • Packing • Dispatch advice • Documents in foreign trade
LANGUAGE AND GRAMMAR False friends
VIDEO LOUNGE BBC: IT
INDUSTRY EXPERT Outsourcing

13 Payment and reminders 176

TOPICS / SKILLS Invoice • Means and terms of payment • Reminders and replies
LANGUAGE AND GRAMMAR How to translate "sollen"
INDUSTRY EXPERT Documentary letter of credit (L/C) • Documents against payment (D/P) and acceptance (D/A)

14 Complaints and adjustments 192

TOPICS / SKILLS Making / Adjusting complaints
COMMUNICATING ACROSS CULTURES Complaining about products or services
LANGUAGE AND GRAMMAR Conditional clauses
INDUSTRY EXPERT Complaints in industry

15 Marketing products and services 211

TOPICS / SKILLS Product life cycle and market research • Distribution channels • Advertising and public relations
LANGUAGE AND GRAMMAR Comparatives and superlatives
VIDEO LOUNGE BBC: Retailing
INDUSTRY EXPERT The instruments of marketing • Market research and distribution policy • Communication and price policy • Marketing mix

16 Job applications in Germany and the EU 227

TOPICS / SKILLS Job ads • Letters of application, CVs and job interviews • Employment in the EU
COMMUNICATING ACROSS CULTURES Job applications
VIDEO LOUNGE BBC: Travel and Tourism
INDUSTRY EXPERT Applying for a job in industry

Appendix 248

Role cards **248**
Alphabetical word list • Glossary • Acronyms • False friends • Countries, nationalities, languages • Weights and measures • World map **253**
Unitbegleitendes Vokabular und Glossar zum Herunterladen über Online-Link 808262-0000

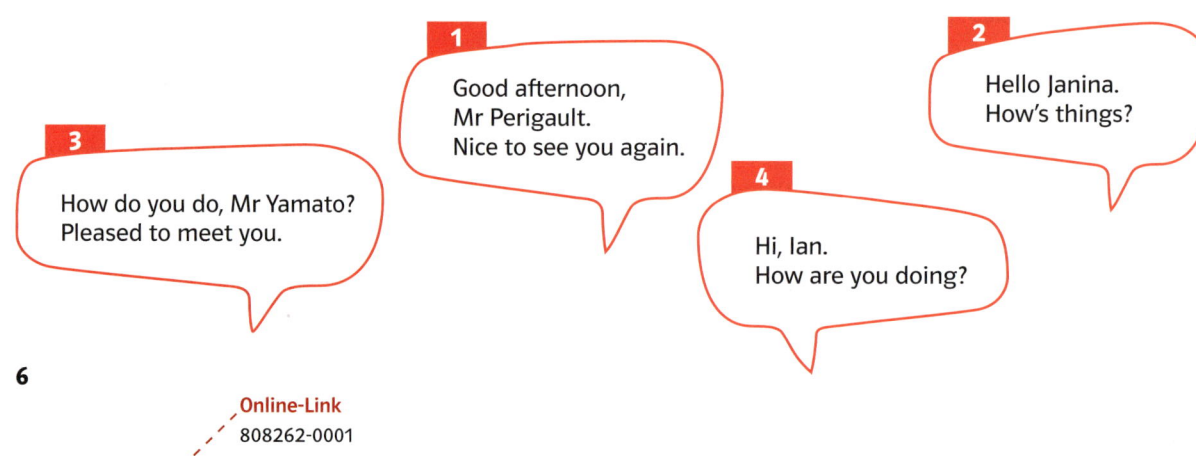

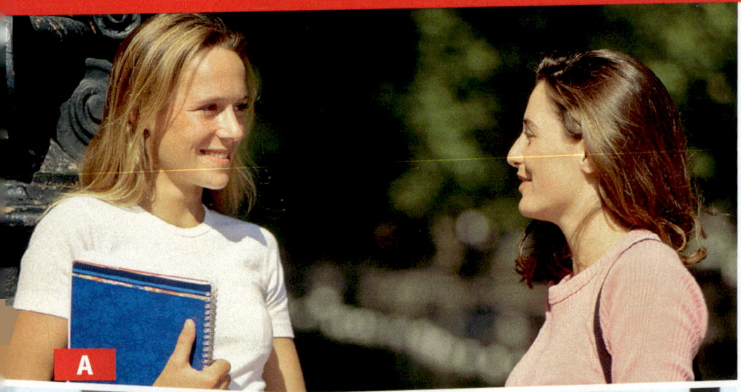
A

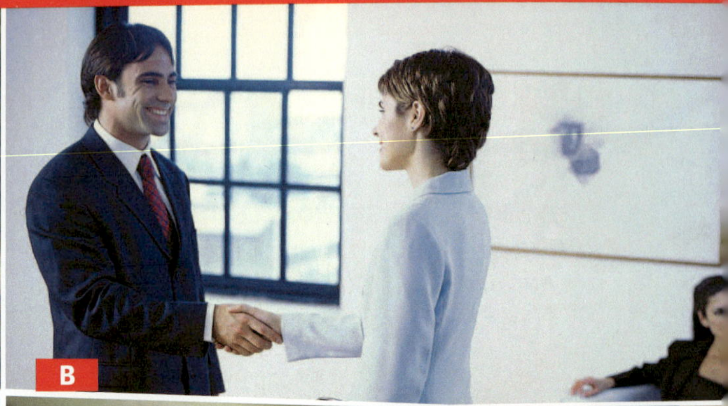
B

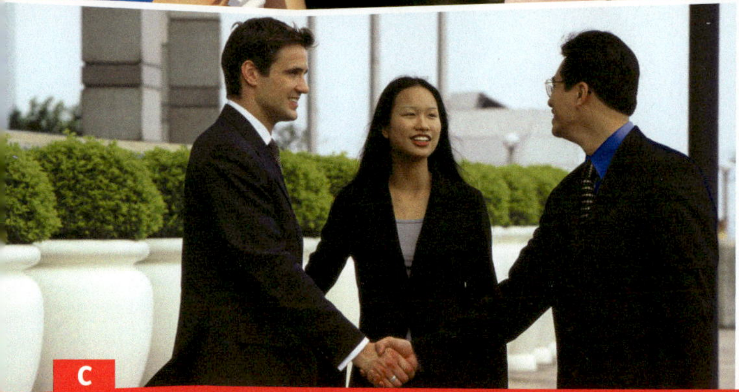
C

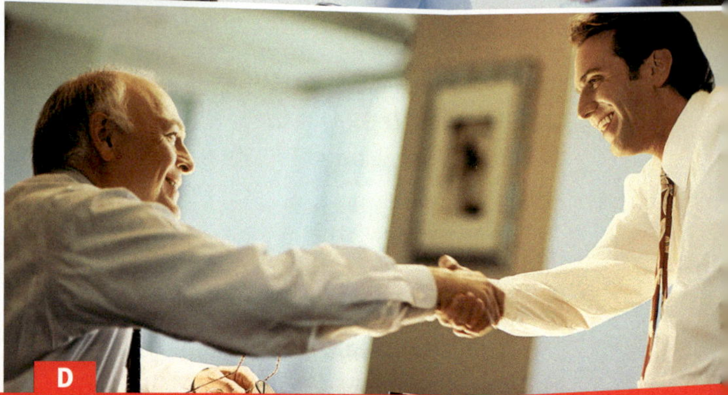
D

Unit 1
Introducing yourself

WORD BANK

I'm / my name is • I'm from • I was born in / on • to work as a … • to be a … • to work at / with / for … • to be interested in • to be into • trainee • apprentice • traineeship / apprenticeship • vocational school • to attend school • to be on a programme • to take part in • to train / to be training as a … • to train to be a … • to be training to become a … • to do a traineeship as a … • to qualify as a … • clerk • management assistant • consultant • specialist

In business it is often necessary to introduce yourself. It is therefore important to know what to say and what information to include. You may, for instance need to explain your professional role or duties in the firm. In a business situation introductions and greetings are often more formal than those among friends in a casual situation. It is important to choose the right style.

Decide which of the following phrases would be used in a formal and which in a casual situation. Match the phrases with the photos above.

1 Good afternoon, Mr Perigault. Nice to see you again.

2 Hello Janina. How's things?

3 How do you do, Mr Yamato? Pleased to meet you.

4 Hi, Ian. How are you doing?

Online-Link
808262-0001

A Talking about yourself

Students at a vocational school in Germany are asked to introduce themselves to a new English assistant who is to spend half a year at their school.

1 **Take the roles of the assistant and the students and read the introductions.**

Rona: Good morning. I'm Rona Mansfield. I come from Dulwich in South London and I'll be working here as an assistant teacher for the next six months. It would be good if a few of you could introduce yourselves so I can begin to learn your names. Perhaps you could tell me briefly what job you're training for and what your interests are. Hello, what's your name?

Stefanie: Hello. I'm Stefanie Krieger. I'm from Cologne but I was born in Hamburg. I'll be 17 next Monday. I'm doing a traineeship at Kabel AG in Leverkusen to become an office administration clerk. I'm very interested in computers and enjoy designing websites. I do quite a lot of sport, including aerobics and badminton.

Rona: Thank you, Stefanie, I'll remember the birthday! And what's your name?

Haris: Hi. My name's Haris Akbar. I'm from Cologne. I am 19 years old. I'm training at Schulz und Schmalenbach as an export clerk. I am very interested in football and support Werder Bremen. I work out regularly at a local gym. I love music. "The Devils" are my favourite group.

Rona: Thank you, Haris. My taste in music is a touch more traditional. Can you tell me something about yourself?

Antonella: My name is Antonella Piccolino but my friends call me Nella. Like Stefanie, I also work at Kabel AG but I'm training to be an Industrie-kauffrau, that's an industrial clerk or industrial business management assistant. I was born in Bergheim in 1992. Originally my family comes from Sicily. I'm very interested in the Italian language and Italian cooking. I also go to a fitness centre three times a week because I'm into body-building.

Rona: Gosh, I can see we'd better watch what we say. Right, we can continue with the introductions later. Could you make a plan of the classroom where everybody's sitting with names – first names and family names.

2 Say whether the following statements from page 7 are TRUE or FALSE.

R

1. Stefanie Krieger was born in Cologne.
2. She is training to be an office administration clerk.
3. She doesn't like working with a computer.

4. Haris Akbar is doing a traineeship to become an industrial clerk.
5. He is between 20 and 30 years old.
6. He supports a football club from Bavaria.

7. Antonella Piccolino is at the same firm as Haris Akbar.
8. Her hobby is cooking Italian dishes.
9. She tries to keep fit.

3 Complete the following introduction using the words from the box.

at • from • in (3x) • near • to • on

I was born **1** Garforth **2** 23 March 1964. Garforth is a small town **3** Leeds **4** the UK. My family comes **5** the West Indies. I work **6** an advertising agency and I'm taking part **7** a training programme for advertising assistants. I regularly go **8** a gym for a work-out.

4 Listen to the following introductions and answer the questions.

R

◎ A1.1

Thorsten

1. Where does Thorsten come from?

2. What is he training as?

3. What is his hobby?

Ludmilla

1. How long has Ludmilla been living in Germany?

2. How old is she?

Ayshe

1. When was Ayshe born?

2. What is she training to become?

3. What does she do in her free time?

5

P Work in groups and make up similar introductions with the help of the following hints.

Phrases ▶

Training or working as:	industrial clerk/industrial business management assistant, office administration clerk/office management assistant, wholesale and export clerk/management assistant in wholesale and foreign trade, bank clerk/bank business management assistant, management assistant in advertising, freight forwarding and logistics services clerk/management assistant in freight forwarding, IT specialist, management assistant in retail business, publisher's assistant/management assistant in publishing, insurance clerk/insurance business management assistant
Firms:	ENKA AG, Schuster & Schneider, Taufrisch OHG, Kohlhaas & Söhne, Globistik-Transport KG, Sportsmarketing GmbH, Online-Consulting
Hobbies:	Swimming, reading fantasy novels, cycling, volleyball, Sci-Fi films, buying clothes, computer games, horses, snowboarding, clubbing

Language and grammar
Work in groups of four. Introduce yourself briefly in writing.
You may use imaginary details if you wish. Read the introduction out to your group.

Phrases ▶

Language and grammar: Introducing yourself	
Antonella sagt: I **was** born in Bergheim in 1992.	Auf Deutsch hätte sie gesagt: Ich **bin** 1992 in Bergheim geboren.
Im Englischen werden Geburtszeitpunkt und Geburtsort mit simple past angegeben:	
My father **was** born in Italy. Haris **was** born on 7 July 1992.	Mein Vater ist in Italien geboren. Haris ist am 7. Juli 1992 geboren.
Außerdem wird im Englischen erst der Ort genannt und danach der Zeitpunkt: I was born **in Bergheim in 1992**.	Im Deutschen ist die Reihenfolge umgekehrt: Ich bin **1992 in Bergheim** geboren.
Haris sagt: I'm training as **an** export clerk. She's **a** travel consultant. He works as **a** programmer.	Auf Deutsch hätte er gesagt: Ich mache eine Ausbildung als Exportkaufmann. Sie ist Reiseverkehrskauffrau. Er arbeitet als Programmierer.
Im Englischen steht zur Angabe des Berufes der unbestimmte Artikel: **a travel consultant.** Im Deutschen steht kein Artikel: **Reiseverkehrskauffrau.**	
I am **a** publisher's assistant. I am training as **a** bank clerk or bank business management assistant.	Ich bin Verlagskaufmann. Ich mache eine Ausbildung als Bank-kaufmann.

In English-speaking countries people often give only their first name when introducing themselves - "Hi, I'm Jonathan". In more formal contexts they give their first name and surname but never just their surname as is usual in Germany - "I'm Jennifer Ashton". Often people add; "Please call me Jennifer".
"How do you do" is a formal greeting which is nowadays rarely used. The other person also says "How do you do" and will probably add "Pleased to meet you".
A usual greeting is "Hello, how are you?" The other person says something like "Fine, thanks / not so bad / so-so" and immediately adds "How are you?" Friends usually say something like "Hi, Justin. How are you doing?" or "Hello, Sarah, how's things?"
Sarah might reply: "Fine, how's things with you?"

B Young people talk about their (future) professions

Rona Mansfield meets more students at the vocational college and asks them to introduce themselves and tell her what training programme they're on:

Oliver: Hello, I'm Oliver: I'm training to become an office management assistant.

Jeannine: My name's Jeannine: I'm on the trainee programme of a high street bank.

David: I'm David: I'm an insurance business management assistant.

Jennifer: Hi, I'm Jennifer: I want to train as an advertising assistant.

Antje: I'm Antje: I hope to be a restaurant manager.

Rosa: Hi, I'm Rosa: I am interested in qualifying as a foreign language correspondent.

Dennis: I'm Dennis: I want to get on to a training programme for retail management assistants.

Niko: I'm Niko: I want to train as an event management assistant.

Simone: Hi, I'm Simone: I'm applying to train as an IT specialist.

Janina: Hello, my name's Janina: I work for a wholesaler in the electrical goods industry.

Mike: I'm Mike: I'm a trainee export clerk.

Dragan: I'm Dragan: I'm training to be a management assistant in publishing.

Hasan: Good morning. I'm Hasan: I am planning to train as an industrial clerk or industrial business management assistant.

> My name's Samira.
> I am taking part in an ITC programme.

> Hello, I'm Sabrina.
> I'm training to be a travel consultant.

1 Read the introductions on page 10 and match the German occupations with their English paraphrases.

1. Kauffrau für Tourismus und Freizeit	a. advertising assistant/management assistant in advertising
2. Kaufmann im Einzelhandel	b. bank clerk/bank business management assistant
3. Fremdsprachenkorrespondentin	c. automobile sales management assistant
4. Kaufmann für Spedition und Logistikdienstleistung	d. management assistant in event organisation
5. Veranstaltungskauffrau	e. management assistant for freight forwarding and logistics
6. Industriekauffrau	f. industrial clerk/industrial business management assistant
7. Automobilkaufmann	g. insurance clerk/insurance business management assistant
8. Kaufmann für Bürokommunikation	h. IT consultant/management assistant in informatics
9. Kauffrau für Marketingkommunikation	i. management assistant in office communication
10. Kaufmann im Groß- und Außenhandel	j. retail business management assistant
11. Kauffrau für Versicherung und Finanzen	k. secretary with foreign languages/foreign language correspondent
12. Informatikkaufmann	l. management assistant for tourism and leisure
13. Bankkaufmann	m. wholesale and export clerk/management assistant in wholesale and foreign trade

2 Übertragen Sie die folgenden Aussagen ins Englische.

M

1. Ich habe eine Ausbildung als Industriekaufmann gemacht.
2. Ich möchte eine Ausbildung als Automobilkaufmann machen.
3. Ich möchte als Fremdsprachenkorrespondentin ausgebildet werden.
4. Ich will Versicherungskaufmann werden.
5. Ich nehme an einem IT-Weiterbildungsprogramm teil.
6. Ich bewerbe mich um einen Ausbildungsplatz als Bürokauffrau.
7. Ich mache eine Ausbildung als Kauffrau im Einzelhandel.
8. Ich arbeite bei einem Großhändler.
9. Ich möchte gerne eine Ausbildung als Werbekaufmann machen.

Industry expert

1 Talking about your traineeship

1 Use the mind map to talk about yourself and present your talk in class.

P

Phrases ▸

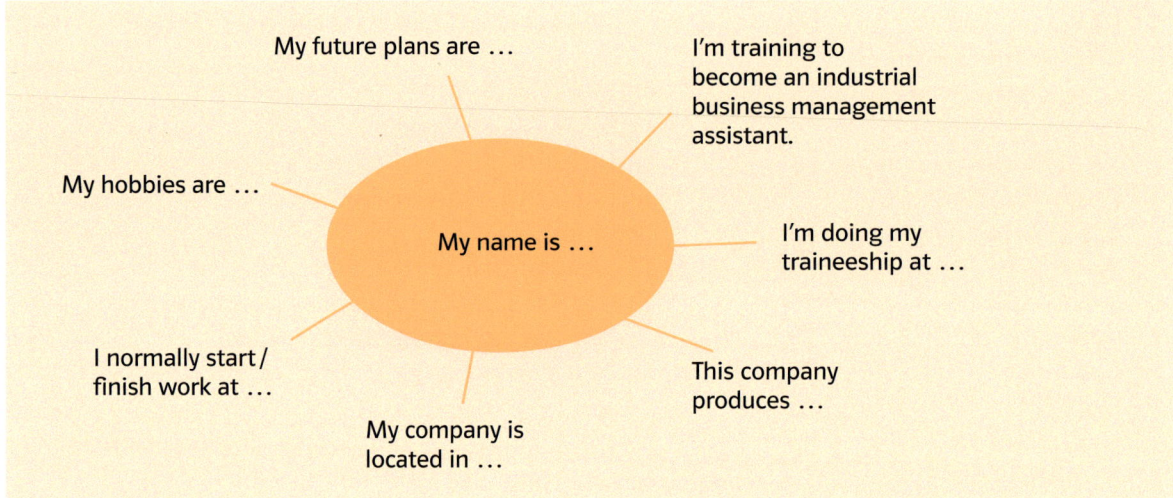

My future plans are …

I'm training to become an industrial business management assistant.

My hobbies are …

My name is …

I'm doing my traineeship at …

I normally start / finish work at …

This company produces …

My company is located in …

2 Match the school subjects (1.–9.) with their German equivalents (a.–i.).

1. information technology
2. English
3. commercial management and controlling
4. business studies
5. economics
6. social studies
7. German
8. religious education/ethics
9. physical education

a. Steuerung und Kontrolle
b. Gesamtwirtschaft
c. Deutsch
d. Gemeinschaftskunde
e. Betriebswirtschaft
f. Informationsverarbeitung
g. Sport
h. Englisch
i. Religion/Ethik

3 Use the subjects in Exercise 2 and complete your own school timetable.

P

Monday	Tuesday	Wednesday	Thursday	Friday

2 Describing different departments

1 During your traineeship you go through the different departments of your company. Use the words in the box and match them to the numbers (1.–6.) in the company organisation chart.

> Accounts • Finance • Human Resources/Personnel Department •
> Managing Director/CEO • Marketing • Production • Purchasing • Sales

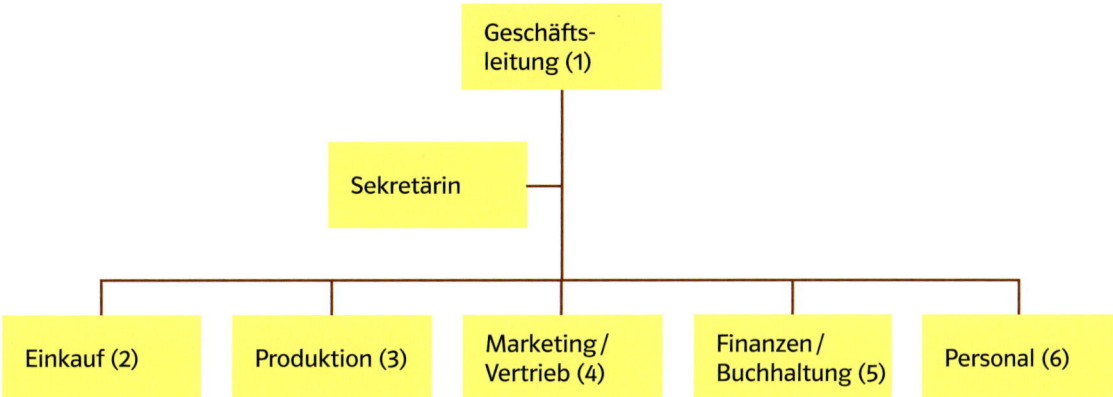

Geschäfts-leitung (1)

Sekretärin

Einkauf (2) | Produktion (3) | Marketing/Vertrieb (4) | Finanzen/Buchhaltung (5) | Personal (6)

2 Find out which of the departments above are described in texts A.–E.

R

A. All financial matters are managed in this department. Special software is used in order to do the bookkeeping and to invoice customers. This department prepares statistics and the annual statements. The cost-performance analysis is carried out here, too.

B. This department is in charge of selling the goods produced. Sales and marketing strategies are worked out. Further activities comprise negotiations with customers and after-sales service.

C. This department is responsible for making the payrolls and keeping the personnel files. Additionally, it conducts interviews and arranges work contracts.

D. This department is responsible for providing the materials for production, including raw materials and semi-finished products. It is necessary to calculate the exact quantity and time when the materials are needed. This department also compares offers.

E. This department is concerned with the planning, controlling and production of the goods.

✳ 3 Take notes about the departments which your company has and present them in class.

P

Phrases ▶

Phrases: Introducing yourself and others

To introduce yourself

I'm Peter./My name is Henry Myers.	Ich heiße Peter./Ich heiße Henry Myers.
Please call me Henry.	Nennen Sie mich doch Henry.
My surname is Hillary, my first name is Tom.	Mein Familienname ist Hillary, mein Vorname Tom.
How are you? (How are you doing?)	Wie geht es Ihnen/Dir? (informelle Begrüßung)
I'm from Berlin, and I am 20 years old.	Ich stamme aus Berlin und bin 20 Jahre alt.
I'm British/Irish.	Ich bin Brite/Ire.
I **was** born in Cyprus on 7 August 1982.	Ich bin am 7. August 1982 in Zypern geboren.
Have you met Mr Martens?	Kennen Sie Herrn Martens?
May I introduce Dr. Bolt to you?	Darf ich Ihnen Herrn Dr. Bolt vorstellen?
Pleased/Nice to meet you.	Ich freue mich, Sie kennen zu lernen.
And how are you?	Und (wie geht es) Ihnen?
Didn't we meet at the Boat Fair?	Haben wir uns nicht schon auf der Boot-Messe kennen gelernt?
I've heard a lot **about** you **from** Mr Winter.	Herr Winter hat mir schon viel von Ihnen erzählt.

To talk about your hobbies and interests

I am interested in computers.	Ich interessiere mich für Computer.
I love travelling more than anything else.	Ich reise schrecklich gern.
I like to go clubbing.	Ich gehe gern in die Disco.
I'm **into** body-building.	Ich interessiere mich für Bodybuilding.
I do a lot of diving.	Ich gehe oft tauchen.

To talk about your training or your work

I'm a trainee export clerk.	Ich mache eine Ausbildung zum Exportkaufmann.
I'm training to become	Ich mache eine Lehre als
an industrial clerk/industrial business management assistant	Industriekaufmann/-frau
a wholesale and export clerk/management assistant in wholesale and foreign trade	Kaufmann/-frau im Groß- und Außenhandel

an office administration clerk/office management assistant	Kaufmann/-frau für Bürokommunikation
a freight forwarding and logistics services clerk/management assistant in freight forwarding and logistics	Kaufmann/-frau für Spedition und Logistikdienstleistung
a bank clerk/bank business management assistant	Bankkaufmann/-frau
a retail clerk/management assistant in retail business	Kaufmann/-frau im Einzelhandel
a management assistant for tourism and leisure	Kaufmann/-frau für Tourismus und Freizeit
a publisher's assistant	Verlags-/Medienkaufmann/-frau
an insurance clerk/insurance business management assistant	Kaufmann/-frau für Versicherungen und Finanzen
a management assistant in advertising	Kaufmann/-frau für Marketing-kommunikation
a management assistant in event organisation	Veranstaltungskaufmann/-frau
an automobile sales management assistant	Automobilkaufmann/-frau
I'm taking part in an ITC programme.	Ich nehme an einem ITC-Ausbildungsprogramm teil.
I'm in the catering **industry**.	Ich bin in der Cateringbranche.
I work **at** SITCOM Ltd.	Ich arbeite bei SITCOM Ltd.
I **attend** vocational school.	Ich besuche die Berufsschule.
What are you doing job-wise, Nina?	Nina, was machst du beruflich?
What are you training to be, Timo?	Was machst du für eine Ausbildung, Timo?
What do you like **about** your job?	Was gefällt dir an deiner Arbeit?
What industry are you in?	In welcher Branche arbeitest du?

To say what you like or dislike about your training or your work	
I like my job because I get on well with the people I work with.	Ich mag meine Arbeit, weil ich mich mit meinen Kollegen gut verstehe.
I can work **on** my own.	Ich kann selbstständig arbeiten.
There are good prospects **of** promotion.	Die Aufstiegschancen sind gut.
I have to key in data all day long.	Den ganzen Tag muss ich Daten eingeben.
I have to work a lot of overtime.	Ich muss viele Überstunden machen.

A

B

C

D

Unit 2
Taking care of visitors

Greeting visitors to your company and making them feel welcome may be an important part of your job. You should always be friendly and helpful as first impressions are often very important. You may have to entertain them until the person they want to see appears. The language in which both you and they can communicate will often be English, even when the visitors do not come from an English-speaking country. English is rapidly becoming a lingua franca in Europe.

1 Match the phrases with the photos above.

1 Welcome to Schneider GmbH. Did you have any trouble finding us?

2 Have you met Ms Reuter? She is our marketing manager.

3 Go along the corridor. The conference room is the second door on the right.

4 Did you have a pleasant flight?

Online-Link
808262-0002

2 Translate the following statements from the introductory text into German.

M

1. Greeting visitors may be an important part of your job.
2. First impressions are often very important.
3. You may have to entertain visitors until the person they want to see appears.
4. The language in which both you and they can communicate will often be English.

A   Greeting visitors

Marcel Krenz, an export clerk at International Snacks GmbH, a German food processing company, has been asked by his boss, Markus Diepholz, to receive Kirsty Burnham and Kevin Sears who represent a major British catering chain. They are interested in the wide range of snacks and lunch boxes the company produces.

1 Read the above text, listen to the dialogue and answer the following questions.

R

A1.3

1. Who is Marcel Krenz?
2. What are his visitors from Britain interested in?
3. What refreshments do Kirsty Burnham and Kevin Sears prefer?
4. What is Kevin's position?
5. What is Frau Wieland in charge of?
6. Where have Kirsty Burnham and Frau Wieland met before?
7. Why has Marcel Krenz been asked to receive the visitors?

2 Match the expressions on the left with those on the right.

1. a food processing company	a. a large assortment of snacks
2. a major chain	b. she is responsible for sales to the EU
3. a wide range of snacks	c. a few minutes
4. I'll let him know you're here	d. we already know each other
5. a couple of minutes	e. water with gas bubbles
6. a sparkling mineral water	f. a company using raw materials to make food products
7. she's on the export staff	g. an important company with many branches
8. she's in charge of sales to the EU	h. I would like to introduce you to Frau Wieland
9. I'd like you to meet Frau Wieland	i. she is a member of the export sales personnel
10. we've already met	j. I will inform him that you have arrived

B Making conversation

Marcel and the visitors from Britain chat while waiting for Herr Diepholz.

1 Listen to the CD and complete the following dialogue on a separate sheet of paper.

R
A1.4

Marcel: Did you have a pleasant flight?

Kirsty: Oh yes, the flight was very straightforward – **1** . There was a bit of turbulence, though. I'm afraid I don't like that.

Marcel: **2** does the flight from Manchester take?

Kevin: It only takes about one and a half hours. But we **3** as a result of the time difference.

Marcel: Of course. What was **4** in Manchester? Was it as good as it is here?

Kirsty: Surprisingly, yes. We have been having **5** lately. It's almost like summer. But generally Manchester gets a lot of rain. From the Atlantic – it's on the west side, you know.

Marcel: Yes, I've heard it gets a lot of rain. **6** is Manchester United doing?

Kitsty: No idea, I'm afraid. I'm **7** a football person. Kevin is, aren't you? Ask him.

Kevin: They're still among the top teams and **8** in the Champions' League quarter finals.

Marcel: I know, they may be playing Bayern Munich next … ! I've heard that Manchester is a very vibrant place.

Kirsty: It certainly is. It's become a **9** city. Lots of gigs and clubs. All the old industry has gone and the old buildings have been renovated. You'd like it. You ought to come some time.

Marcel: I'd like to. Are there any **10** ?

Kevin: Definitely. It's amazing how cheap they are if you book **11** . If you search the internet you can save a lot of money.

Marcel: Well, that's really … Ah, here comes Herr Diepholz …

2 Complete the following conversations with the words from the boxes.

Dialogue 1

afraid • doing • flight • like • proud • time

You: How was your **1** ?

Visitor: Rather bumpy, I'm **2** .

You: I'm sorry to hear that. What was the weather **3** in Glasgow?

Visitor: Oh, it was the same as here, overcast and windy. But that's nothing unusual for this **4** of the year.

You: How are Glasgow Rangers **5** ?

Visitor: They play in the UEFA Europa League, we're rather **6** of them. I support Celtic, though.

Dialogue 2

apart • by • for • from • how • there

You: Where do you come **1**, Miss Spears?
Visitor: I'm from South Africa. Just now I've come from Berlin **2** train.
You: **3** was the train ride? Was the train punctual?
Visitor: Actually, the train was 10 minutes late, **4** from that the ride was quite
         pleasant, though.
You: South Africa must be a wonderful country. At least that's what
         everybody here says who's been **5**.
Visitor: You should come and see **6** yourself. There's a lot to see and do for
         tourists.

3 Match the questions with the answers.

1. Can I offer you a cold drink?
2. Is this your first visit to Germany?
3. Did you have a good flight?
4. Would you like something to read?
5. What was the weather like in Portugal?
6. May I take your coat?
7. Do you take milk and sugar?
8. Are you interested in tennis?

a. No, thank you. I'll keep it on. I'm cold.
b. No, thanks. I'm on a diet.
c. Yes, please. Perhaps your company brochure?
d. Very sunny. We could do with some rain.
e. No, it's not my thing. I prefer cycling.
f. Yes, it is.
g. Oh no. There was a lot of turbulence.
h. Thank you. An apple juice would be fine.

4 Restore the correct order of this jumbled dialogue.

1. Barmaid (in pub): Yes, it's freezing, isn't it? And this awful drizzle.
2. Customer: It's not like June at all.
3. Barmaid: They say its going to improve for the weekend, though.
4. Customer: Isn't the weather dreadful!

Communicating across cultures: Small Talk

In Britain the weather is very changeable, which makes it a constant topic of conversation:

The weather is wonderful, superb, lovely, very good. The weather is awful, ghastly, dreadful, terrible.

Example:
Newsagent: Good morning. How are you today?
Customer: Fine. Isn't it a beautiful day?
Newsagent: Wonderful. Let's hope it stays like this.
Customer: I'm afraid the weather forecast says rain.

5 Role play: Work in pairs. Make up dialogues using the following prompts and the phrases at the end of the Unit.

Phrases ▶

> Student A:
> How was your trip?

> Student B:
> Rather tedious, there was a tailback on the motorway from Frankfurt.

Student A asks about:		**Student B replies using these expressions:**
flight/trip/ journey	⟶	pleasant, rather tedious, lots of turbulence, tailback on the motorway, long delay at the airport, etc.
weather	⟶	sunny, overcast, slight drizzle, fog, gale-force winds, snow, is going to improve, cold for the time of the year, quite warm, pouring rain, windy, etc.
first visit to ...	⟶	oh yes, many times, once before, but not much time to see anything, no never, long been wanting to visit ..., etc.
hotel	⟶	nice and quiet, service first-class, a bit far from the exhibition centre, rather noisy, excellent restaurant, etc.
visitor's home town	⟶	small place in Wisconsin, has changed a lot in recent years, many tourists visit it, has vibrant business centre, scenic village in the mountains, busy port in India, etc.
sports events	⟶	not very interested in golf, watch as many tournaments as possible, would like to see the match, support XYZ club, etc.

C Giving directions

Kirsty Burnham has lost her way in the office building. She is standing at the reception desk. The receptionist directs her to Herr Diepholz' – the managing director's – office.

1 Take the role of the receptionist. Use the floor plan, the phrases below and the phrases at the end of the unit.

Phrases ▸

> Herr Diepholz' office is on the right / left hand side.

> The ladies' room / restroom is on your left / right.

> Go down the stairs.

> Go up the stairs.

> Take the lift to the first / second floor.

> Go down to the ground floor.

> Go along the corridor.

> If you turn left / right you will see Mr / Ms … office on your right / left.

> Take the first entrance to the right / left.

> Go across the hall.

Second floor, Advertising Department

Assistant	Managing Director	Stairs	
Secretary			Conference Room
Advertising Assistants	Storage	Kitchen	
Lift	Open Plan Office	Advertising Manager	
Storage		Assistant	
Gents		Secretary	
Ladies			

First floor, Marketing and Sales Department

Secretary	Assistant	Sales Manager	Stairs	Data Processing
Secretary				
Assistant		Storage	Secretary	Research Manager
Marketing Manager	Open Plan Office			
Lift		Secretary	
Kitchen		Marketing Assistants	
Gents		Sales Assistants	
Ladies			

Ground floor, Finance and Personnel Department

Company Training Manager	Chief Accountant	Secretary	Stairs
			Canteen
Secretary	Lounge Area	Stationery Room	Post Room
Kitchen			
Lift			Main entrance
Medical Room			
Gents			
Ladies	Receptionist		

2 **Work in pairs. Explain to each other the way to certain rooms.**

I

1. Your partner is at the main entrance. He asks you: "Could you tell me the way to the Sales Manager's office?"

2. You are in the canteen. You ask your partner:" Where is the conference room, please?"

3. Your partner is leaving the Advertising Manager's office. He asks you: "Would you mind telling me where the medical room is?"

4. You are in the Marketing Assistants' room. You ask your partner: "I need to freshen up a bit. Could you tell me the way to the ladies'/the men's toilets/restroom (Am)?"

3 **The visitors from England want to see some of the famous sights in Munich.**

P **Use the map on page 23 and direct them from the station (Hauptbahnhof) to the following destinations:**
Hofbräuhaus [1], Frauenkirche [2], Englischer Garten [3].

Phrases ▶

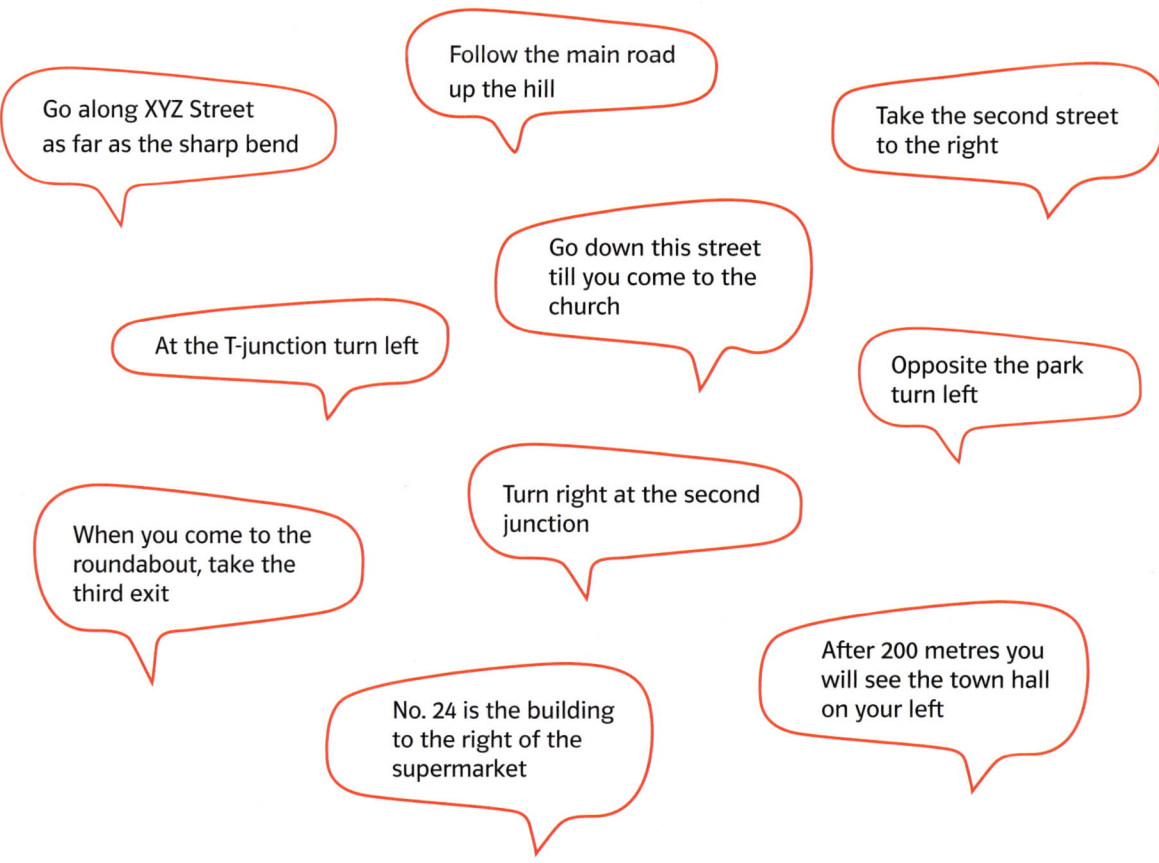

Go along XYZ Street as far as the sharp bend

Follow the main road up the hill

Take the second street to the right

Go down this street till you come to the church

At the T-junction turn left

Opposite the park turn left

When you come to the roundabout, take the third exit

Turn right at the second junction

After 200 metres you will see the town hall on your left

No. 24 is the building to the right of the supermarket

4 **R** **A1.5** Listen to the explanations given by the Tourist Information assistant and find out which famous sights the visitors will be seeing during their stroll through the town centre of Munich.

[Map of the town centre of Munich]

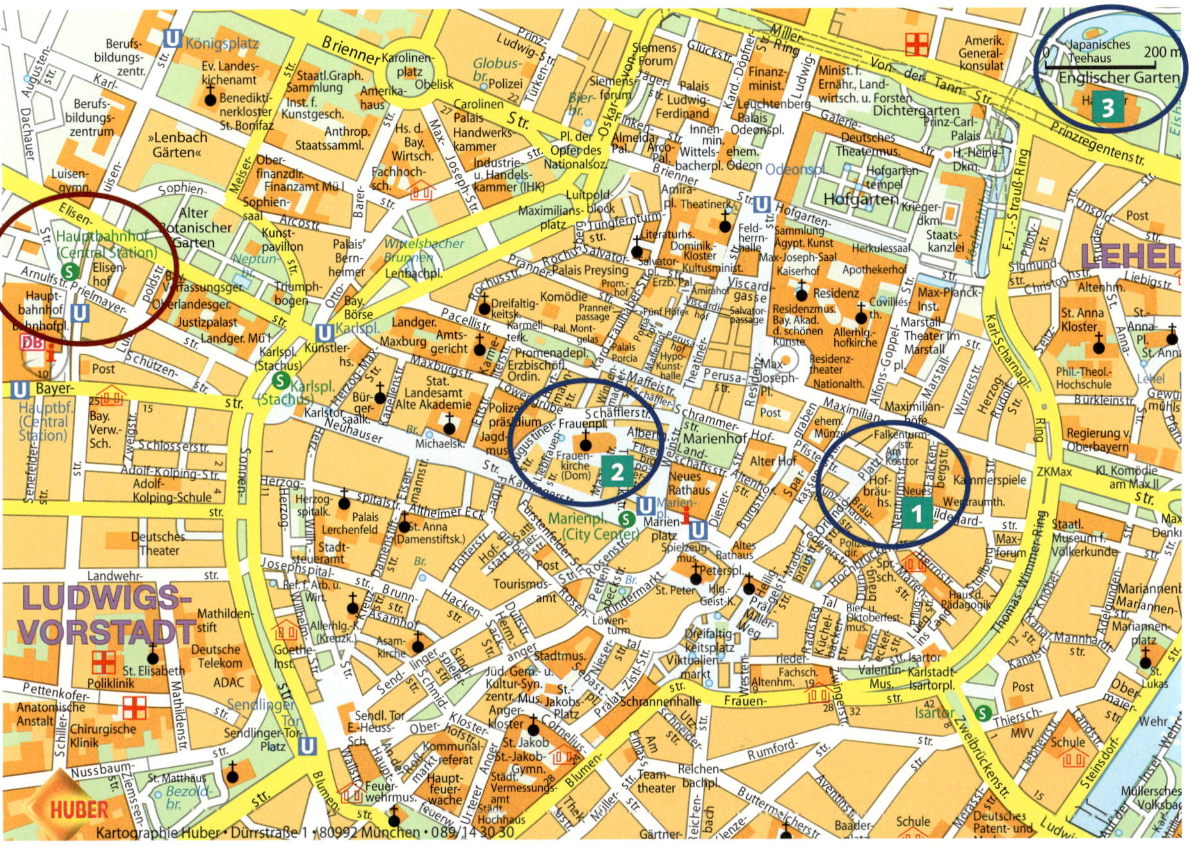

5 David Stedman has been visiting your headquarters in Berlin. He now has an appointment at your offices in Inselstraße, Düsseldorf. He has been told that the office is within walking distance of the main station. As he has some time on his hands before his appointment he would like to have instructions how to get there on foot.

Click on to a map of Düsseldorf on the internet and e-mail the instructions to him (davidstedman@aol.com).

D Describing the layout of the premises and carrying out a tour of the firm for visitors

Markus Diepholz and Marcel Krenz take Kirsty Burnham and Kevin Sears on a tour of the company's premises.

1 Listen to the dialogue and decide whether the following statements are TRUE or FALSE.

R
⊚ A1.6

1. All the administrative work is dealt with at the offices.
2. The senior staff also work in the open-plan offices.
3. Marcel Krenz' office has a nice view of the surrounding countryside.
4. The canteen also provides vegetarian snacks.
5. Herr Diepholz and his visitors cross the car park to reach the kitchen facilities.
6. Freshness and hygiene are the most important considerations.
7. International Snacks are planning to do some market research on what people feel about their packaging.

2 You are Kevin Sears. Write a memo in English on the tour of the premises of International Snacks.

P

Remember: A memo has to be brief, clear and to the point.

+ + MEMO + + MEMO + + MEMO + + MEMO + + MEMO + +

To:	Michael Kent, General Manager
From:	Kevin Sears, Assistant to Kirsty Burnham
Date:	Wednesday, 23 March 201_
Subject:	Our tour of the Premises of International Snacks, Düsseldorf

3 Sie sind Marcel Krenz. Verfassen Sie eine kurze Aktennotiz in Deutsch über die

KMK Betriebsbesichtigung und die Reaktionen der britischen Besucher.

MEMO

Für:	Geschäftsleitung
Von:	Marcel Krenz, Exportsachbearbeiter
Datum:	20.03.201_
Betreff:	Betriebsbesichtigung mit Kirsty Burnham und Kevin Sears von Global Catering, Manchester, UK

E   Taking foreign visitors to a restaurant

Herr Diepholz invites Kirsty and Kevin to lunch
and asks Marcel to join them and interpret.

1   **Listen to the dialogue and write down what**
R   **Kirsty and Kevin order (starter, main course,**
◎ A1.7 **dessert, drinks).**

Speisekarte

Vorspeisen

Pikante Brokkoli-Pastetchen
Gefüllte Steinpilze
Kraftbrühe mit Ei
Lauchcremesuppe
Avocado-Kaltschale

Hauptgerichte

Schweinebraten mit Rotkohl und Salzkartoffeln
Rinderrouladen mit Blumenkohl und Kartoffelpüree
Rheinischer Sauerbraten mit Rotkohl und Kartoffelklößen
Wiener Schnitzel mit Pommes frites und Salat
Wildgulasch mit Speckknödeln und Preiselbeeren
Forelle Müllerin-Art
Lauch-Soufflé
Gemüsebratlinge

Nachspeisen

Gemischtes Eis
Rote Grütze mit Sahne
Bayerische Creme
Käseplatte

2 Find the correct equivalents.

1. Bockwurst
2. Bratkartoffeln
3. Bratwurst
4. Erbsensuppe
5. Frikadellen
6. Gurkensalat
7. Kartoffelbrei
8. Kartoffelsuppe
9. Pommes frites
10. Rinderbraten
11. Rindfleischbrühe
12. Schokoladenpudding
13. Schweinebraten

a. beef broth
b. chocolate pudding
c. cucumber salad
d. French fries
e. fried potatoes
f. grilled sausage
g. mashed potatoes
h. meatballs
i. pea soup
j. potato soup
k. roast beef
l. roast pork
m. large frankfurter

Communicating across cultures: Describing dishes

For a number of typical German dishes there are no direct translations. You will have to describe them to your visitors from abroad. These expressions may help you:

Which part of the meal is it?
It's a starter.
It's the main course.
It's a dessert.
What kind of food is it?
It's meat (pork, beef, veal, lamb).
It's poultry (chicken, turkey).
It's fish (salmon, trout, plaice, haddock).
It's game (venison, rabbit).
It's a sort of pasta (spaghetti, noodles).
It's a vegetable (peas, beans, carrots, green peppers, cauliflower, cabbage, Brussels sprouts, asparagus).

How is it made?
It's made of mashed potatoes, ground / minced meat, chopped onions.
It's filled / stuffed with (rice, minced meat, vegetables).
It's boiled (baked, stewed, grilled, fried, smoked).
What does it taste like?
It's hot / spicy.
It's sweet / sour.
It's tart.
It's savoury.
It tastes a bit like (yoghurt, veal, mousse au chocolat).

3 Study the explanations and find out which of the German dishes
R   they refer to.

> Jägerschnitzel • Kopfsalat • Rote Grütze • Semmelknödel •
> Spätzle

1. It's a dessert. It's a jelly made of red berries thickened with
   corn starch. It's not too sweet. Quite tart, in fact.
2. They go with a main course. They're dumplings made of
   white bread with eggs and parsley. They're rather filling,
   though.
3. It's a schnitzel, a sort of pork escalope with sauce and
   mushrooms.
4. It's a kind of home-made pasta, typical of the South West of
   Germany.
5. It's lettuce with oil and vinegar dressing.

✱ **4** Ask the amateur chefs among you to explain two of the   Phrases ▶
M   following dishes in English to your group. Use the expressions at
     the end of the unit.

> Zigeunerschnitzel • Sauerkraut • gemischter Salat • gefüllte
> Paprikaschoten • Milchreis • Hackbraten • Linseneintopf

✱ **5** Choose a starter, a main course and a dessert from the menu on   Phrases ▶
M   page 25 and explain it to a foreign visitor. Use the phrases at the
     end of the unit.

✱ **6** Work in groups. Explain your favourite dishes to the group.
P

**Communicating across cultures:
Going to restaurants in Britain**

You may have to wait to be seated. A waiter will ask how many you are and indicate a table.
Of course, you can say something like: "Couldn't we sit over there in the window?"

The waiter / waitress may ask you whether you want to order drinks straight away. After you have
had time to study the menu, the waiter or waitress will say: "Are you ready to order, madam?"
If you are not, you could say: "We're not quite ready. We need a moment or two."

When the food comes, he / she will probably say: "Enjoy your meal" or sometimes just "Enjoy!"
However, there is nothing like "Guten Appetit" that you can say to your companions / guests.

Complaining is very difficult. You should at all costs avoid being aggressive or loud – this will not
get you anywhere. Be nice, understanding, humorous if possible.

Finally, when you want to pay, you say: "Could I have the bill, please."

Language and grammar 1
Choose the correct form of the verbs.

1. I `give` you a ring towards the end of the week.
2. We `let` you `know` as soon as possible.
3. If you `wash` the dishes, I `dry`.
4. I `ask` Joanna if she `want` to come.
5. You `chop` the mushrooms and I `cook` the pasta.
6. I `pass` on the message when I `see` her on Friday.
7. I `pick` him up at the station if you `want`.
8. He `help` you with your move if you `give` him a ring on Wednesday.
9. I `give` you a lift if you like.
10. David `stand` in for you if necessary.

Language and grammar 2
Translate the following text.

Wir übergeben die Sendung morgen früh der Spedition Fuhrmann Logistik und hoffen, dass die Ware übermorgen wohlbehalten bei Ihnen ankommt. Wir helfen Ihnen gerne, wenn Sie noch weitere Fragen haben. Wir sind sicher, dass unsere exquisiten Schuhe Ihren Kunden gefallen und dass sich diese Artikel in Großbritannien gut verkaufen lassen.

Language and grammar: Will-future

Die "will"-Zukunftsform (meistens in der abgeschwächten Form I'll, we'll) wird im Englischen bei spontanen Entscheidungen benutzt und entspricht dem Präsens im Deutschen.

Marcel Krenz says:	I'll give Herr Diepholz a ring and let him know you're here.
Kevin Sears says:	I'll have black coffee.
Marcel Krenz says:	I'll just ring through and order them.
Sit down and I'll make some coffee.	= Setz dich hin. Ich koche Kaffee.
You keep an eye on the spaghetti and I'll make the salad.	= Pass du auf die Spaghetti auf. Ich mache den Salat.

Allerdings wird "will" nicht in Nebensätzen der Bedingung und der Zeit verwendet.

I'll fetch the newspapers if you make the tea.	= Ich hole die Zeitungen, wenn du Tee machst.
I'll tell him as soon as he arrives.	= Ich sage es ihm, sobald er ankommt.

Industry expert

1 Explaining the company to visitors

Marie Peters is training to become an industrial business management assistant at ICR Chemicals Ltd., a company that produces cleaning agents. Her boss has asked her to show two trainees from their French branch around the company.

1
R
◎ A 2.1

Marie explains the company's premises. Listen and find out where the different departments are on the plan below. Use the numbers (1.–10.).

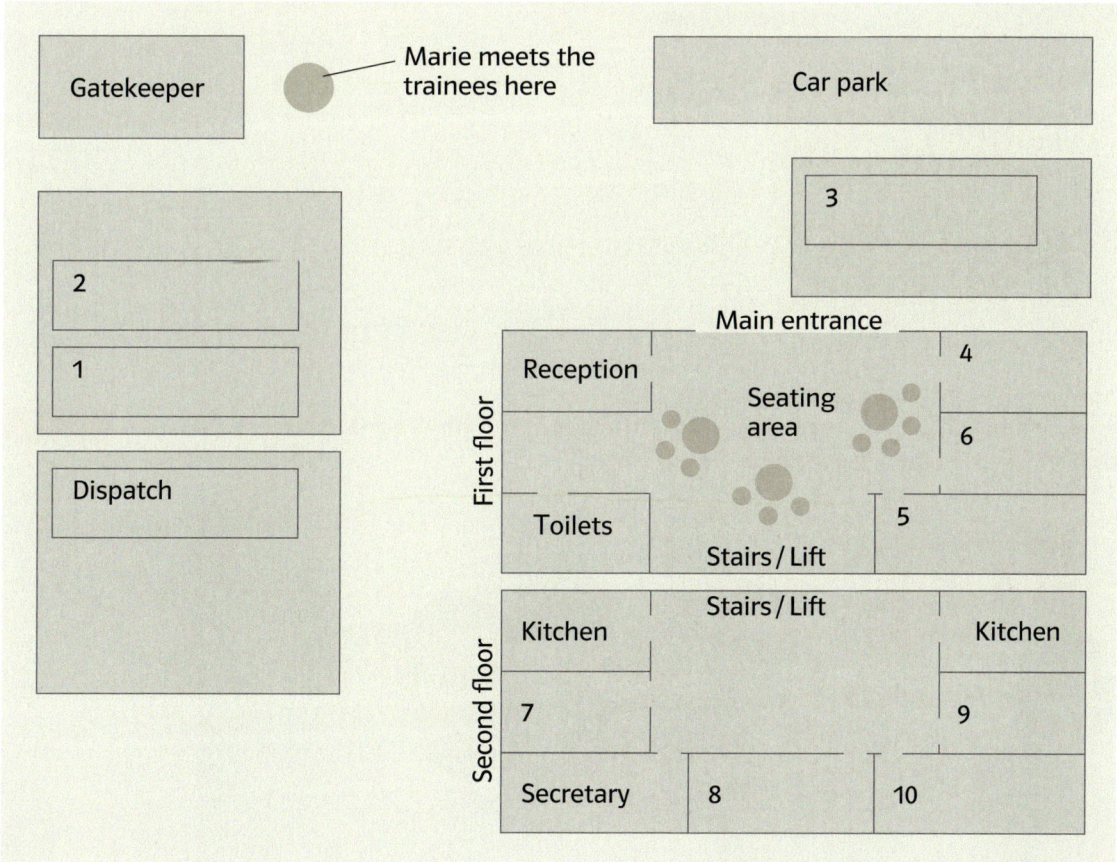

2
P

Draw a plan of the company you work for and present it in class.

Phrases

29

3 Marie has now reached the production department with Gabrielle and Luc.
P She offers them some drinks and then presents the organisation chart of
ICR Chemicals Ltd. Describe the organigram.

Phrases ▸

Example: Mr Wilder is the managing director. Mrs Just is his secretary.

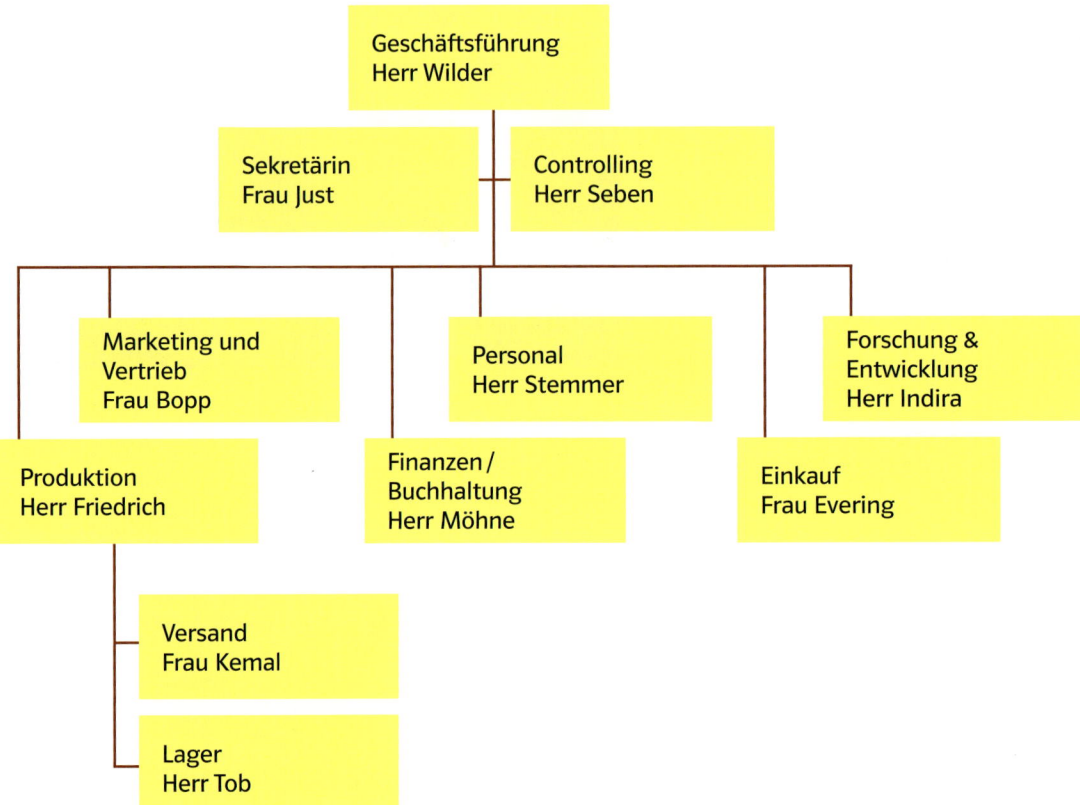

4 Zeichnen und beschreiben Sie das Organigramm der Firma für die Sie arbeiten,
KMK und stellen Sie es in der Klasse vor.

Phrases ▸

2 Explaining safety regulations

1
R
Before entering the production hall Marie explains the safety signs which are used there. Decide which types of signs (a.–e.) the following signs (1.–16.) are.

a. rescue signs
b. mandatory signs
c. prohibitory signs
d. warning signs
e. fire protection signs

2
R
Match the meanings (a.–p.) to the appropriate signs above (1.–16.).

a.	compressed gas	i.	hard hat
b.	corrosive	j.	no eating
c.	ear protection	k.	no mobile phones
d.	escape route	l.	no smoking
e.	eye protection	m.	protective footwear
f.	fire extinguisher	n.	respiratory protection
g.	first aid	o.	risk of explosion
h.	hand protection	p.	toxic

3
P
Work in pairs. Choose two signs and explain the meaning of these signs.

Language and grammar: Explaining rules and regulations

Verbote und Anweisungen werden mit dem **Imperativ** oder mit **must /
mustn't, to be allowed to / not to be allowed to** und **do not** ausgedrückt.
Achtung: „**mustn't**" heißt „**nicht dürfen**"!

Do not smoke. Wear eye protection.
Take care. This warning sign means that this is highly corrosive.
You mustn't use your mobile here.
You are not allowed to use your mobile.

---

* 4 Sie erhalten die Aufgabe für das Intranet Ihrer Firma die geltenden Sicherheits-
KMK bestimmungen zum Verhalten in der Produktionshalle sinngemäß ins Englische
zu übertragen.

Generelle Sicherheitsbestimmungen bei Betreten der Produktionsanlagen

1. Tragen Sie beim Betreten der Produktionsanlagen folgende Schutzkleidung:
   - Schutzhelm
   - Mundschutz
   - Hörschutz
   - Augenschutz
   - Sicherheitsschuhe
2. In der Produktionshalle besteht ein generelles Rauch- und Verzehrverbot.
3. Beachten Sie die Arbeitsanweisungen und Hygienepläne für die Produktionsanlagen.
4. Waschen Sie nach dem Verlassen der Produktionshalle Ihre Hände mit den speziell
   dafür vorgesehenen Desinfektionsmitteln.
5. Trennen Sie gebrauchte und saubere Schutzkleidung in die jeweiligen Behälter.
6. Das Tragen der benutzten Handschuhe außerhalb der Produktionsanlagen ist verboten.
7. Im Notfall Nummer 0-112 wählen.

---

5 Match the English regulations (1.–6.) to their German equivalents (a.–f.).

1. Law on Safety and Health at Work	a. Arbeitsschutzgesetz
2. Law on Safety at Work	b. Arbeitssicherheitsgesetz
3. Ordinance on Hazardous Material	c. Arbeitstättenverordnung
4. Radiation Protection Ordinance	d. Betriebssicherheitsverordnung
5. Working Reliability Regulation	e. Gefahrstoffverordnung
6. Workplace Ordinance	f. Strahlenschutzverordnung

---

6 Work in teams. Choose one of the regulations in Exercise 5 and prepare a short
P presentation on it. Use the internet to find relevant information.

Phrases ▶

Phrases: Taking care of visitors

To welcome visitors

Good afternoon. Can I help you?/What can I do for you?	Guten Tag. Was kann ich für Sie tun?
Please take **a seat**.	Bitte nehmen Sie Platz.
Can I offer you some refreshments?	Darf ich Ihnen etwas anbieten?
Coffee with milk and sugar, tea, herbal tea, fruit juice, sparkling/still mineral water, coke?	Kaffee mit Milch und Zucker, schwarzer Tee, Kräutertee, Fruchtsaft, Mineralwasser mit/ohne Kohlensäure, Cola?
Frau Sievers **is expecting** you.	Frau Sievers erwartet Sie.
I'm afraid, Frau Sievers is still in a meeting.	Frau Sievers ist leider noch in einer Besprechung.
She will be **with** you in a few minutes.	Sie wird in ein paar Minuten da sein.

To make conversation

Did you have a pleasant flight?	Hatten Sie einen angenehmen Flug?
How was the **journey**?	Wie war die Fahrt?
Have you ever been to Oldenburg before?	Waren Sie schon einmal in Oldenburg?
Where do you come **from**?	Wo kommen Sie her?
What was the weather **like** in Belfast?	Wie war das Wetter in Belfast?
Would you like to see something **of** Bonn?	Möchten Sie in Bonn etwas besichtigen?
Are you satisfied with your hotel?	Sind Sie mit dem Hotel zufrieden?
I'll have an orange juice.	Ich nehme einen Orangensaft.
No thanks, I don't take milk or sugar.	Nein danke, ich nehme weder Milch noch Zucker.
The flight was rather bumpy.	Der Flug war ziemlich unruhig.
The trip was very pleasant. Thank you.	Danke. Die Fahrt war sehr angenehm.
Actually, I have been to Oldenburg twice, in 1999 and in 2002.	Ich war tatsächlich schon zweimal in Oldenburg, 1990 und 2002.
The weather was fine. Not a cloud **in** the sky.	Das Wetter war schön. Kein Wölkchen am Himmel.
We've had a lot of rain lately.	In der letzten Zeit hat es bei uns viel geregnet.
I'd like to visit Beethoven's house.	Ich möchte mir gerne das Beethoven-Haus ansehen.

The hotel will do. It's **on** a rather noisy street, though.	Das Hotel geht einigermaßen. Es liegt allerdings an einer ziemlich lauten Straße.
The hotel is excellent. Very quiet.	Das Hotel ist ausgezeichnet. Sehr ruhig.

To give directions

GB	USA	**Germany**
second floor	third floor	2. Etage
first floor	second floor	1. Etage
ground floor	first floor	Erdgeschoss
basement	basement	Untergeschoss/Keller

Take the lift to the third floor.	Fahren Sie mit dem Aufzug in den dritten Stock.
Go up/down (the stairs) to the 2nd floor.	Gehen Sie (die Treppe) hinauf/hinunter zum 2. Stock.
Herr Diepholz' office is on the **right hand** side.	Das Büro von Herrn Diepholz ist auf der rechten Seite.
At the junction **turn** right/left.	Gehen/Fahren Sie an der Kreuzung nach rechts/links.
Go **straight ahead** to …	Gehen/Fahren Sie gerade aus bis …
Go down this street till you come to the …	Gehen/Fahren Sie auf dieser Straße weiter bis Sie zu … kommen.
When you come to the roundabout, take the 3rd exit.	Am Kreisverkehr nehmen Sie die dritte Ausfahrt.
Follow the main road up the hill.	Fahren Sie die Hauptstraße weiter bergauf.
After 200 yards you will see the church **to** your left.	Nach (ca.) 200 m sehen Sie die Kirche auf der linken Seite.

To take visitors on a tour of your firm's premises

We would like to show you **round** the company's premises.	Wir möchten Ihnen unsere Firma auf einem Rundgang zeigen.
We have two open-plan offices.	Wir haben zwei Großraumbüros.
These are our production facilities.	Hier sehen Sie unsere Fertigungsanlagen.
We'll go through this door which leads to the canteen.	Wir gehen durch diese Türe, die zur Kantine führt.

The canteen looks very modern and airy.	Die Kantine wirkt sehr modern und luftig.
We leave this building and **cross** the car park.	Wir verlassen jetzt dieses Gebäude und gehen über den Parkplatz.
I think we had better be getting back to our office now.	Ich glaube wir sollten jetzt lieber ins Büro zurückgehen.
Our visit has certainly been very interesting.	Unser Besuch war wirklich sehr interessant.

To take visitors to a restaurant

This is a typical German restaurant.	Das ist ein typisch deutsches Restaurant.
Let's have a look **at** the menu?	Wollen wir uns die Speisekarte ansehen?
What **about** you? What are you having?	Wie ist es mit Ihnen/Dir? Was nehmen Sie/was nimmst Du?
Are you having a starter?	Nimmst Du/Nehmen Sie eine Vorspeise?
I think I'll just have a main course.	Ich nehme nur ein Hauptgericht.
Could I have a starter as a main course?	Kann ich eine Vorspeise als Hauptgericht nehmen?
It's a sort of pasta.	Es sind Teigwaren.
It's cabbage stuffed with minced meat.	Es ist Kohl mit einer Hackfleischfüllung.
It tastes a bit like mushrooms.	Es schmeckt ein bisschen wie Pilze.
I'm not hungry enough for a 3-course meal.	Ein Menü mit 3 Gängen ist mir zuviel.
I'd like a German beer.	Ich möchte ein deutsches Bier.
Would you like a salad as a starter?	Möchten Sie einen Salat als Vorspeise?
I'll have the lamb cutlets with beans.	Ich nehme die Lammkoteletts mit Bohnen.
I prefer chicken **to** fish.	Ich esse lieber Geflügel als Fisch.
I'm **a** vegetarian.	Ich bin Vegetarier/in.
My wife would like the trout with almonds.	Meine Frau möchte die Forelle mit Mandeln.
What about some ice cream as a dessert?	Wie wär's mit Eis als Nachtisch?
I'd **rather** have some cheese.	Ich hätte lieber etwas Käse.
It was delicious but I'm afraid I can't eat any more.	Es hat sehr gut geschmeckt, aber ich bin leider schon satt.
I'm going to do without a dessert.	Ich verzichte auf eine Nachspeise.

A

B

Unit 3
The company and its products and services

When companies describe themselves in their sales literature they generally attempt to create a particular image. They may refer to the firm's history to emphasise qualities such as experience and reliability. If they do not have a long history behind them, they may prefer to emphasise that they are a young, dynamic, forward-looking company, providing new products and services.

WORD BANK

image • history • range of products • company brochure • global player • start-up business • family-owned firm • workforce • manufacturing • provision of services • business idea • stock corporation • public limited company • private limited company • to found • to establish • to manufacture • to provide • old-established • modern • traditional • leading • small • medium-sized • state-of-the-art

1 **List the adjectives and expressions from the box under the categories given below:**

old-established • flexible • dynamic • reliable • with many years' experience • young • forward-looking • taking advantage of the new media • solid • state-of-the-art

Example:

traditional	modern
old-established	state-of-the-art

Online-Link
808262-0003

2 Find examples of traditional and young companies in Germany and other countries.

3 Choose the adjectives from the box on page 36 which best describe the company you are training at. Is it a traditional or a young company? Give details.

A Introducing a firm and giving a brief history

While waiting for an interview at Herkules AG, Sandra Kohl studies the company brochure in English. It begins with an article on the history of the firm.

Herkules
the global sports brand

Back in 1922 the shoemaker Heinrich Schuster made the first sports shoes for the local sports club, the TSV Neustadt. Very soon sportsmen from neighbouring clubs ordered sports shoes from Mr. Schuster and two years later he employed a staff of 25. In 1927 he rented a factory building and bought the machinery required for industrial manufacturing. The company continued to prosper until World War II. In 1948 Heinrich Schuster's son Helmut took over and changed the company's name to Herkules. At the Olympic Games in Melbourne in 1956 several of the athletes competing wore Herkules shoes.

A few years later Helmut Schuster added footballs and other types of ball to Herkules's range of products and in the early 70s took up the production of sports bags. Meanwhile Herkules employed 3400 people and its products featured in all the Olympic Games and World Championships.

Olympic Games

By 2010 the workforce had risen to 12,500 and Herkules had become the market leader in the EU and a global player with production sites in Germany, Portugal, Morocco, Malaysia and Taiwan.

1 Read the text on page 37 and ask the questions which would produce the
R   following answers.

Example:
Question:
1. Who founded the company?

Answers:
1. The company was founded by **Heinrich Schuster**.
2. Mass production began **in 1927**.
3. **Olympic Games and World Championships** are of particular importance
   for the company.
4. Apart from shoes the company produces **bags and balls**.
5. Herkules has got production sites in **Germany, Portugal, Morocco, Malaysia
   and Taiwan**.

2 Find the missing prepositions from the box with the help of the text on page 37.
R

> by • from • in (2x) • of • over • until • up • to (2x) • with

Back **1** 1922 Heinrich Schuster made the first sports shoes.
Sportsmen **2** neighbouring clubs ordered sports shoes.
Two years later he was employing a staff **3** 25.
The company prospered **4** World War II.
In 1948 Schuster's son Helmut took **5** and changed the name **6** Herkules.
In the early 70s Herkules took **7** the production of bags.
Herkules' products featured **8** all the Olympic Games.
9 1990 the number of staff had risen **10** 9,500.
Herkules is a global player **11** production sites in several countries.

3 Read the text on Herkules again and find words or phrases that mean the same as
R   the following expressions.

1. people employed by a firm
2. production on a large scale
3. an assortment of articles
4. the company that has a dominant position in a given market
5. a company that is active worldwide

∗ 4 Sandra Kohl informiert eine Freundin über die Firma Herkules.
KMK Verfassen Sie hierfür eine schriftliche Zusammenfassung der wichtigsten Fakten in
     Deutsch, die ca. 80 Wörter umfasst. Gehen Sie dabei kurz auf folgende Punkte ein:

• Entwicklung des Unternehmens
• Produkte
• gegenwärtige Stellung des Unternehmens

5

R

A1.8

Read the introduction below, then listen to Martha Dinsdale describing her firm and complete the following text.

Christian Kleine, an IT specialist, is interested in doing a short practical abroad. At a job fair he meets Martha Dinsdale, managing director of Smartmart Ltd, who describes the development of her firm.

"Our company, Smartmart Ltd., was **1** in 1999. Our business **2** was to provide an online market for private individuals or **3** companies with something to **4** who do not want to spend a lot of **5** online selling it themselves. This, as we all **6**, can be very time-consuming! It's not everybody's idea of an **7** way to spend an evening! Some people do not feel sufficiently secure with the **8** to do their own buying and selling. But, it is amazing how many **9** have things to sell and how many potential **10** there are. After we had completed a feasibility study, we **11** through the local chamber of commerce for financial and other **12** in establishing a start-up business. Our **13** expenditure was for designing and setting up an attractive and efficient **14** which would be capable of dealing with a large **15** of hits. There's no point in opening up **16** on the internet with an inadequate or badly designed website. We were quite overwhelmed by the amount of **17**. Our business has grown in line with the other big **18** marts. We charge a commission of 10% on sales completed, i.e. the **19** pays. We are now making a healthy **20** and in two or three years' time we will be thinking in terms of going public."

6   **Match the English expressions with their German equivalents.**

1. private individuals	a. 10 % Provision verlangen
2. time-consuming	b. Auslagen, Ausgaben
3. sufficient	c. ausreichend, genügend
4. amazing	d. bei der örtlichen IHK beantragen
5. feasibility study	e. erstaunlich
6. apply through the local chamber of commerce	f. finanzielle Unterstützung
	g. Machbarkeitsstudie
7. financial support	h. neugegründetes Unternehmen
8. start-up business	i. Online-Markt
9. expenditure	j. Privatpersonen
10. inadequate	k. sich in eine Aktiengesellschaft umwandeln
11. overwhelmed	
12. online mart	l. überwältigt
13. charge a commission of 10%	m. unzureichend, unzulänglich
14. go public	n. zeitraubend

7 Answer the following questions on Martha's talk.

R

1. When was the company founded?
2. What was their business idea?
3. Why did they think people would use their services?
4. What was their most expensive investment?
5. How does the company earn its living?

8 Christian Kleine fasst die Informationen, die ihm Martha Dinsdale über ihre Firma

KMK gegeben hat, auf Deutsch in einer Gesprächsnotiz für seine Personalabteilung
zusammen. Bitte übernehmen Sie seine Rolle.

Gesprächsnotiz

Empfänger: *Personalabteilung*

Verfasser: *Christian Kleine, IT-Support* Datum: _____

Gesprächspartner: *Martha Dinsdale von Smartmart Ltd.*

Betreff: *Vorstellung von Smartmart Ltd.*

＊ **9** Describe your own company in writing. Model your description on the

P descriptions of other companies in this unit.

Communicating across cultures:
Joint stock companies *(Kapitalgesellschaften)* in the USA and Britain

The British **Public Limited Company** (abbreviated to **PLC** or **plc** after the company name) and the American **Stock Corporation** (abbreviated to **Inc.** or **Corp.**) are roughly comparable to the German Aktiengesellschaft. The British **Private Limited Company** (abbreviated to **Ltd**) and the American **Closed Corporation** are approximately equivalent to the German GmbH. British and American joint stock companies are managed by a **Board of Directors** under the leadership of a Chief Executive Officer (CEO) (chairman of the board or managing director), who may also hold the title of Chairman or President. The head of a **Private Limited Company** is generally called the Managing Director.

10 Search the Internet for some of the following global players. Make notes on their products or services in English. Compare your notes with the group.

Tata Group • GlaxoSmithKline • Arcelormittal • Antofagasta • RWE Group •
Berkshire Hathaway • Verizon • De Beers • China Mobile • Rio Tinto Zinc • HSBC •
Selesio AG • Sir Robert McAlpine

B Describing products and services

At home Sandra Kohl looks at Herkules' homepage on the internet. Sandra clicks on the button "about us" to learn more about the company. The following website appears.

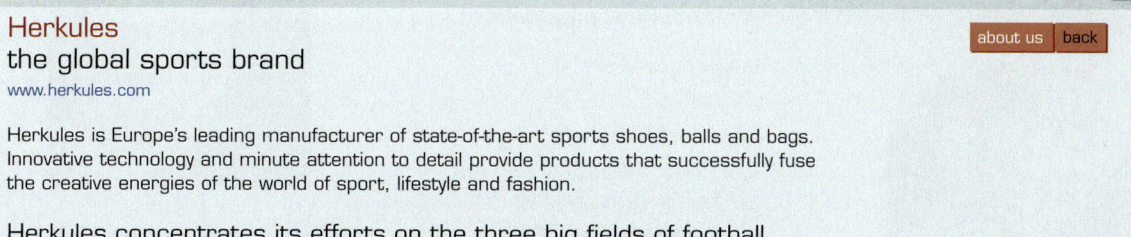

Herkules
the global sports brand
www.herkules.com

Herkules is Europe's leading manufacturer of state-of-the-art sports shoes, balls and bags. Innovative technology and minute attention to detail provide products that successfully fuse the creative energies of the world of sport, lifestyle and fashion.

Herkules concentrates its efforts on the three big fields of football, athletics and tennis. For decades our superb shoes, balls and bags have helped world-class athletes to win gold medals at Olympic Games and prestigious cups at World Championships and Tournaments.

1 **Which buttons do you click on if you want to find out more about the following?**

1. the firm
2. all their products
3. particular product groups
4. individual products
5. details about delivery
6. frequently asked questions
7. how to place an order
8. repairs

2 **Replace the adjectives in brackets with appropriate expressions from the box.**

excellent • the most modern • very careful • highly regarded

1. Herkules is Europe's leading manufacturer of (state-of-the-art) **1** sports shoes.
2. Innovative technology and (minute) **2** attention to detail provide products that fuse the creative energies of the world of sport, lifestyle and fashion.
3. For decades our (superb) **3** shoes and bags have helped world-class athletes to win gold medals at Olympic Games and (prestigious) **4** Cups at World Championships and Tournaments.

3
R/M Match the German statements on the next page with the following English statements.

Tatjana: The company I work for is a leading manufacturer of precision instruments.

Janine: I work for a small upmarket advertising agency. We specialise in media companies.

Patrizia: I work for a medium-sized company manufacturing organic cosmetic preparations.

Sinan: I work for a small family firm making a wide range of high quality furniture.

Markus: My company are IT consultants providing customised solutions for corporate clients.

Holger: I work for a small catering company specialising in providing lunches for local companies. We offer a lot of vegetarian dishes. We're basically a small start-up.

Jörg: My company is a whole-saler stocking a wide range of electrical products.

Claudia: The company I work for is a major retailer of food and some non-food products. I work in the admin section.

◎ V1 **Video lounge** Sport and leisure

BBC Motion Gallery

You are about to see a video on the sport and leisure industry. While watching the video, keep the following questions in mind:

1. How are the three presenters dressed? Which do you find most natural and convincing? Why?
2. Which different fitness club products does the video mention?
3. What does the first presenter mean when she says fitness has become a lifestyle business?
4. According to the video what is the overall economic situation of the fitness and leisure club industry?

Discuss your answers with the class.

1. Ich arbeite für ein mittelständisches Unternehmen, das Biokosmetik herstellt.
2. Meine Firma ist eine IT-Beratungsgesellschaft und bietet Firmenkunden maßgeschneiderte Lösungen an.
3. Die Firma, bei der ich arbeite, ist ein bedeutender Einzelhändler für Lebensmittel und Non-Food-Produkte.
4. Ich arbeite bei einem kleinen Partyservice, der sich auf Mittagessen für die Firmen in der Umgebung spezialisiert hat.
5. Meine Firma ist ein führender Hersteller von Präzisionsinstrumenten.
6. Ich arbeite bei einem Familienunternehmen, das hochwertige Möbel herstellt.
7. Ich arbeite bei einer kleinen exklusiven Werbeagentur.
8. Bei meiner Firma handelt es sich um eine Großhandlung mit einem breiten Sortiment von Elektroartikeln.

4 **Write similar descriptions of two firms' products or services with the help of the**
P **following hints.**

Types of firms	medium-sized enterprise, import/export company, large manufacturer, start-up company, wholesaler, retail chain, family-owned firm, IT consultancy, publishing house, advertising agency, catering firm, Public Limited Company, Private Limited Company, Stock Corporation
Products/services	household appliances, IT services, exotic fruit, steel tubes, creation of advertising material, groceries, silk fabrics, audio books, clocks and watches, cleaning services, office software
Descriptions	modern, upmarket, high-quality, fresh, in demand, excellent, unique, interesting, attractive, reliable, thorough, long-lasting, state-of-the-art, customised, inexpensive

We specialise in …

Our products/services are …

We are …

We offer …

I work for …

Example:
I work for a family-owned firm specializing in the manufacture of
state-of-the-art steel tubes.

5 **Work in groups. Describe the firm you are training at and its products and/or**
P **services to your group. Use the phrases at the end of the unit.**

Phrases ▸

6 Dolmetschen Sie folgende Aussagen:
M

1. „Ich arbeite bei einer mittelgroßen Werbeagentur. Wir stellen attraktives Werbematerial für eine Lebensmittel-Einzelhandelskette her."

2. „Meine Firma ist auf die Herstellung einzigartiger Seidenstoffe höchster Qualität spezialisiert."

3. „Wir bieten maßgeschneiderte Lösungen für Bürosoftware an."

4. „Wir sind ein junger Musik-verlag mit einem anspruchs-vollen Sortiment von Titeln."

✱ 7 Project work: Work together with two other students to set up your own
I/P company. See Exercise 5 for useful expressions.

Phrases ▸

Step 1: Discuss the following questions:
– What is your business idea?
– How can you find out whether your idea is any good?
– Where can you get help, financial or otherwise?
– What are the most essential investments to enable you to begin trading?
Step 2: Think up a good name for your company.
Step 3: Divide the work among yourselves:
– Student A creates an eye-catching logo.
– Student B designs a business card incorporating the logo.
– Student C designs a company letterhead also incorporating the logo.
Step 4: Present the result to the class.

6 Language and grammar 1
Find out whether the periods of time mentioned in the following sentences are entirely in the past or whether they continue to the present. Then choose the correct tense for the verbs in brackets.

1. It all (begin) in 1975.
2. Two years later he (launch) the new product.
3. The company (be successful) for many years now.
4. Since 2002 we (offer) these unique marketing services.
5. By now Herkules (become) a global player.
6. Last September Robert Hanks (start) a new business in the USA.
7. In the past there (be) a big demand for such systems.
8. But in the meantime they (be replaced) by faster systems.
9. So far we (have) no complaints.
10. I (speak) to him only yesterday.

Wird ein Zeitraum genannt, der vollständig in der Vergangenheit liegt, steht "simple past".

Back **in 1922** Heinrich Schuster **made** the first sports shoes.
At the Olympic Games several athletes **competed** wearing Herkules shoes.
A few years later he **added** footballs to the range of products.
Our company **was founded in 1999**.

Wenn ein Zeitraum genannt wird, der bis in die Gegenwart reicht, steht "present perfect".

For decades our superb shoes **have helped** athletes to win gold medals.
In the meantime ACE **has become** the market leader in Germany.
Since the beginning of the 90s **we have specialised** in real-time solutions.
I **have been** in my present department **for three months**.

Language and grammar 2
Decide which of the alternatives in brackets are correct.

1. I (am / have been) a trainee (for / since) 4 months.
2. We (see / have seen) a number of employees leave (for / since) 1998.
3. We (have specialised / specialise) in providing networking systems (for / since) more than a year.
4. She (wants / has wanted) to live in Berlin (since / for) she was 17 years old.
5. We (have known / know) the company (since / for) it was founded in 1983.
6. I (am thinking / have been thinking) of changing my job (since / for) a long time.
7. We (place / have placed) orders with this company (since / for) its foundation.

Language and grammar: "since" and "for"

"since" bezieht sich auf den Anfang des Zeitraums
since Christmas
since 24 June
since my last report

"for" bezieht sich auf den Zeitraum selbst
for 3 weeks
for several days
for a couple of years

Merke: **Im Deutschen wird „seit" mit der Gegenwart verwendet, "since" und "for" stehen im Englischen mit "present perfect".**

Ich **bin seit** drei Jahren bei Topline-Computers beschäftigt.
Seit Januar **bin** ich der Abteilungsleiter.

I **have been** employed with Topline-Computers **for three years** now.
Since January I have been head of the department.

Industry expert

1 Different types of production processes

1
R
Work with a partner. Find out if the different types of production processes are correctly explained in the following table. Copy the table and rewrite the information in the appropriate columns.

	1. Individual production	2. Series production	3. Batch production	4. Mass production
Main features	• special form of mass/series production • production of a limited number of identical products • production of different batches • standardised, mostly highly automated production process	• production of a unique product • different production lines are used • "batch" means the filling quantity of a container (e.g. bottles or cans) during a single production process	• production normally based on a direct contract • high costs per unit • this is the most popular production process • special customer requests cannot be considered	• the requirements of the customer can be individually fulfilled • a lot of different machines are needed • problems with retrofitting • different products occur because of the (natural) diversity of the raw materials

2 **Decide which process is likely to be used for the manufacture or production of the**
P **items shown in the photos and explain why.**

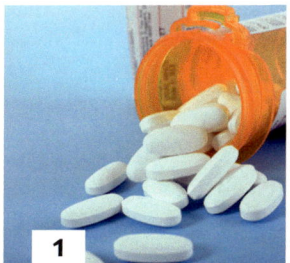   

1 2 3 4

3 **Manufacturing processes can also be defined by the degree of automation of**
R **production. Read the definitions and match them with the terms in the box.**

automated production • manual production • mechanical production

1. Machines and production lines are controlled by workers.
2. The work is normally done manually by highly qualified staff.
3. Machines take over all the work and operate completely automatically.

4 **Describe the manufacturing process of your company. Take notes and present**
P **your descriptions in class.**

Phrases ▶

2 Product description

✳ **Sie arbeiten für den Beleuchtungshersteller Ramo GmbH in Düsseldorf. Nächste**
KMK **Woche wird eine Produktschulung für Ihre europäischen Außendienstmitarbeiter**
angeboten. Sie werden damit beauftragt, die wesentlichen Informationen zu
diesem Produkt in die englische Sprache zu übertragen.

Neue dimmbare und energiesparende Tageslichtlampe (15 Watt)

Früher verbrachten die Menschen mehr Zeit im Freien und waren somit natürlichem Sonnenlicht ausreichend ausgesetzt. Nach einer langen, aber erfolgreichen Entwicklungsphase können wir nun eine neue dimmbare und energiesparende Tageslichtlampe anbieten. Diese Tageslichtlampe produziert eine Farbtemperatur (6000 Kelvin), die zu jeder Tageszeit ein Licht wie an einem Sonnentag liefert. Zudem verbraucht sie etwa 80 % weniger Energie als eine herkömmliche Glühlampe. Die Tageslichtlampe entwickelt kaum Hitze, so dass sie in allen Standardfassungen verwendet werden kann. Sie hat eine Lebensdauer von ca. 12 000 Stunden und ersetzt die herkömmliche 75 Watt Glühbirne.

Größe: 10 cm
Durchmesser: 5 cm
Lampenfassung: E 27
Energieeffizienzklasse: A
Verpackungseinheit:
5 Lampen pro Box

Phrases: The company and its products and services

To introduce your firm

Our company was founded in 1972.	Unsere Firma wurde 1972 gegründet.
Our business idea was …	Unsere Geschäftsidee bestand darin …
In 1998 we were taken over by …	1998 wurden wir von … übernommen.
We are a leading manufacturer **of** …	Wir sind ein führender Hersteller von …
I work for an upmarket advertising agency.	Ich arbeite bei einer exklusiven Werbeagentur.
We are a **medium-sized** family firm.	Wir sind ein mittelständisches Familienunternehmen.
We are a wholesaler **specializing in** …	Wir sind ein Großhandelsunternehmen und sind spezialisiert auf …
My company is a major food retailer.	Meine Firma ist ein bedeutender Lebensmitteleinzelhändler.
We are a start-up company offering customized solutions.	Wir sind ein junges Unternehmen, das maßgeschneiderte Lösungen anbietet.
We are a chain of organic cosmetics suppliers.	Wir sind eine Kette von Anbietern biologischer Kosmetikprodukte.
The legal form of our company is a public limited company.	Juristisch gesehen ist unsere Firma eine (britische) Kapitalgesellschaft, vergleichbar einer deutschen Aktiengesellschaft.
FastTrack Inc. is a stock corporation.	FastTrack Inc. ist eine (US-)Kapitalgesellschaft.

To describe your firm's products / services

We manufacture state-of-the-art solutions.	Wir bieten Lösungen nach dem neuesten Stand der Technik an.
Our high-quality products are well-known **all over** the world. They are unique.	Unsere erstklassigen Produkte sind weltbekannt. Sie sind einzigartig.
Our instruments are both reliable and long-lasting.	Unsere Instrumente sind zuverlässig und haben eine lange Lebensdauer.
The software we offer is carefully adapted to suit your requirements.	Unsere Software wird Ihren Bedürfnissen sorgfältig angepasst.
We make a wide range of high-quality furniture.	Wir stellen ein breites Sortiment hochwertiger Möbel her.
We import exotic fruit **from** South America.	Wir importieren tropische Früchte aus Südamerika.
The travel agency I work for **specialises in** upmarket package tours.	Das Reisebüro, bei dem ich arbeite, ist auf exklusive Pauschalreisen spezialisiert.

Unit 4
The office

Offices may be spacious open-plan, purpose-built areas in a major company, individual small rooms to accommodate two to three people, or elegant premises at a prestigious address in a converted building. They may be back offices where employees have no contact with the public, or front offices to which the public have access.

1 Match the following types of office with the pictures above.

1. front office
2. back office
3. manager's office
4. open plan

2 Tell your group in which type of office you would prefer to work and give reasons for your preferences.

> I'd like to work in a(n) … office because …

> I'd prefer to work in a(n) … office because …

49

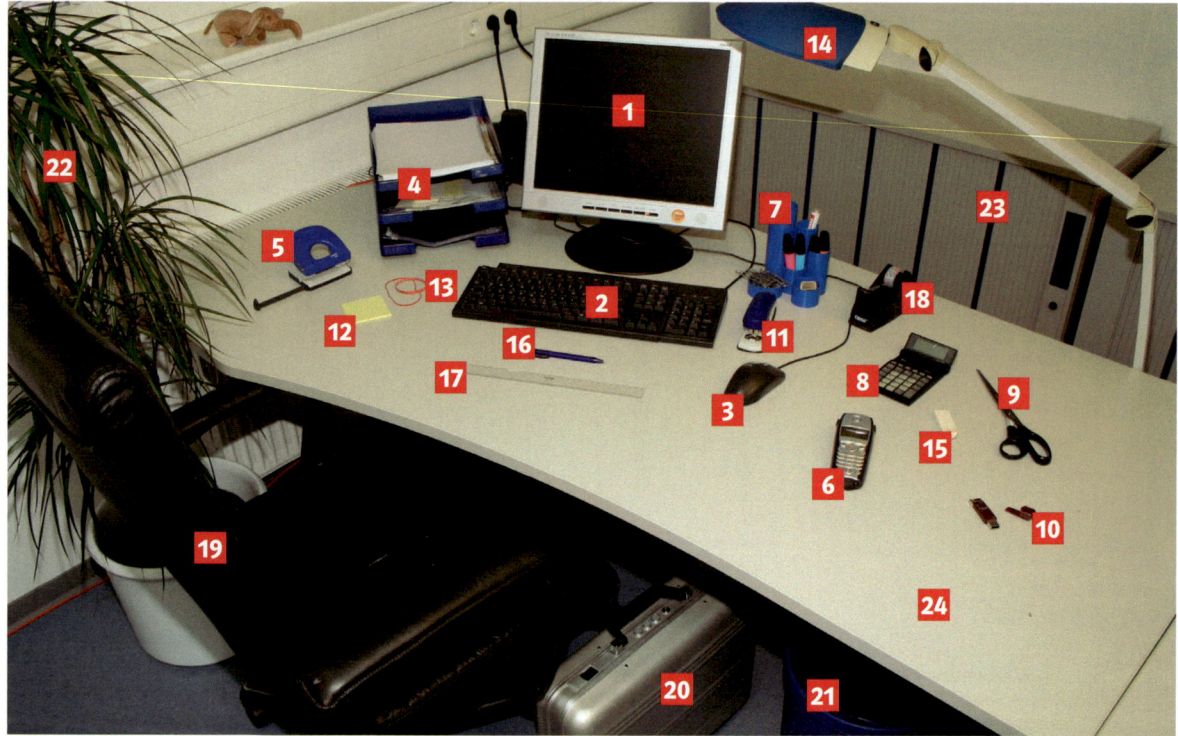

A The office environment

1 Match the following pieces of office equipment with the numbered items above.

a. calculator
b. scotch tape/sellotape
c. biro
d. desk
e. note pad
f. trays
g. filing cabinet
h. aluminium briefcase
i. keyboard

j. memory stick
k. monitor
l. desk tidy
m. pair of scissors
n. wastepaper bin
o. ruler
p. punch
q. rubber/eraser

r. pot plant
s. desk lamp
t. mobile phone
u. stapling machine/stapler
v. swivel chair
w. mouse
x. elastic band

2 Use the following prepositions and describe the position of the equipment you see in the picture.

The keyboard is The …	on • under • behind • between • in front of • next to • on the right of • opposite • near • on top of	the desk. the …

3 List the items shown on page 50 under the following categories:

Office supplies / Stationery	Furniture	Electrical equipment / Hardware
rubber	desk	computer

4 How many computer terms and abbreviations can you find in the puzzle below? Make a list. Compare your lists in class.

Computer terms puzzle

	A	B	C	D	E	F	G	H	I	J
1	I	B	M	O	D	E	M	Q	R	H
2	T	O	E	S	L	A	N	P	X	A
3	D	O	M	T	C	D	R	O	M	R
4	E	T	O	O	L	B	A	R	O	D
5	S	B	R	O	W	S	E	T	N	D
6	K	E	Y	B	O	A	R	D	I	I
7	T	E	R	M	I	N	A	L	T	S
8	O	S	C	A	N	N	E	R	O	K
9	P	C	C	C	U	R	S	O	R	M
10	D	O	W	N	L	O	A	D	X	B

5 Work in groups. Make up similar puzzles with other computer terms and abbreviations. Ask the other groups to find the terms and abbreviations.

P/I

6
R
A1.9

Listen to Anita, Ali and Nadine describing the office environment in which they work and take notes. Work in pairs and compare your notes.

7
R
A1.9

Draw a grid like the following. Use your notes and fill in the grid. Then listen to the dialogue again, complete the grid and answer the questions below.

	Office (front office – open plan or back office?)	**Office equipment** (PC? Photocopier? Scanner? …?)
Anita	…	…
Ali	…	…
Nadine	…	…

1. What does Anita like about her office?
2. What does Ali like about his office?
3. What does Nadine like about her office?

8
M

Translate the following statements from the dialogue into German.

1. I work in a large open-plan office with about 20 other people. It is spacious and airy with large windows. Fortunately, there is air-conditioning.
2. Our offices are situated in an old villa in the centre of Hanover. The office I work in is a front office.
3. The view from the windows is not very exciting – the office looks out on to the car park.
4. Our office has a wide range of equipment. We all have PCs with internet access.
5. I like the privacy of a small office – you don't get the feeling there's somebody looking over your shoulder the whole time. We all get on very well together.

9
P

Describe your own office.

10

Check out the latest products of three manufacturers of photocopiers and scanners, including any innovative features. Make notes and compare your findings with the group.

B Catering in the office

1 **Übertragen Sie die Aussagen von Anita, Nadine und Ali ins Deutsche.**

KMK

Anita We have a small kitchen attached to the office with a fridge and tea and coffee making facilities. Our official coffee break is a quarter of an hour at 10.30 am and 3 pm.
At lunchtime we go to the canteen. There is quite a good range of hot and cold snacks, some of them vegetarian. My friend Alexandra is a vegetarian so we usually have a fresh vegetable soup and a salad with fruit as a dessert. We both watch our figures and the canteen is very good about giving calorie counts.

Nadine We have a tea and coffee machine in the office and a kitchen at the end of the corridor with a microwave. We don't have a set coffee break but lunch is from 12.30 to 1.15 pm. Our company is too small to have a canteen so we either bring sandwiches or convenience food that we can warm up in the microwave. There is an upmarket supermarket nearby with an interesting range of good quality convenience food with things like fresh soups and Chinese and Thai dishes. We sometimes go out to a pub but the lunch break is really too short for that.

Ali We have a small kitchen with a coffee machine and fridge. Only Amelie is allowed to touch it. We have an hour lunch break.
We don't have a canteen either. So we usually bring sandwiches or go out. There's a snack bar nearby that has quite an interesting range of snacks and a pub with not very appetising meatballs and filled rolls. Quite often, when we're working to a deadline, we just eat a sandwich at our desks and an apple.

2 **Match the words on the left with the explanations on the right.**

1. calorie count	a. equipment for making coffee
2. coffee making facilities	b. pre-prepared food
3. convenience food	c. small restaurant/shop producing light/quick food
4. snack bar	d. high-quality supermarket
5. upmarket supermarket	e. energy content

3 What are the catering arrangements like at your firm? Work in pairs to produce a brief description in writing that you can read out to the other students.

Phrases ▸

C The company's organization chart

1 Study the organization chart below and complete the following text.

R

Nadine works for a car sales company. The **1** is Jochen Küppers who is one of the two owners of the firm. His personal assistant is his elderly **2** Eva Cebulla. Nadine's superior, Jessica Rathsmann, a trained accountant, is the head of the **3** Department, and a motor-car mechanic, Markus Nehring, is in charge of **4**. The **5** manager is Natalie Hoffmann, the managing director's sister-in-law. Eddy Gerstenberg, an engineer, is the head of the **6** Department. André Fontaine, who is training to become a car sales management assistant, reports to him.

The car sales company is organized like this:

Managing Director
Jochen Küppers

Secretary
Eva Cebulla

Administration and Finance	**Purchasing**	**Sales**	**Customer Service**
Jessica Rathsmann Nadine Boedeker	Natalie Hoffmann	Eddy Gerstenberg André Fontaine	Markus Nehring

Info: Large companies

The larger a company is the more complex its organisation tends to be. Large companies are headed by a chief executive officer (CEO) or a chairman of the board. They have many different business units and departments, such as a personnel, legal or marketing department. The scope of an individual employee's responsibilities will also be smaller and his or her duties more specialised in a large company than in a small one.

2 Study the above texts and find the equivalents of the German titles.

R

Geschäftsführer • Einkaufsleiter • Vorstandsvorsitzender •
Automobilkaufmann • Leiter des Kundendienstes • Personalchef •
Leiter des Rechnungswesens • Persönliche Assistentin

3 Work in pairs. Partner A asks Partner B about his/her current department.
I Then change roles.

`Phrases`

> Which department are you in?

> I work in the ... department.

Partner A	Partner B
Who is your boss?	The head of our department is ...
What is he/she responsible for?	She is in charge of ...
Who does she report to?	Her superior is ...
What's your general manager's name?	Our general manager is called ...
Who are your colleagues?	My colleagues are ...
What are you responsible for?	I process/I'm in charge of ...

4 Listen to five trainees describing to their friends what they or their colleagues do
R in the departments they are in. Find out which departments they are working in.
A1.10

	Christine	Harun	Annette	Simon	Christos
Department?	...	...	...	...	...

Language and grammar 1
Translate the following sentences.

1. Unsere Firma ist zu klein für einen eigenen Parkplatz.
2. Diese Frage zu beantworten ist für mich zu kompliziert.
3. Nun ist es zu spät für eine Bewerbung.
4. Es ist noch zu früh, darüber zu entscheiden.
5. Sie kam als Letzte zu der Besprechung.
6. Unser Unternehmen ist das einzige, das diese Lösung anbietet.

Language and grammar 2
Choose the correct form of the verbs in brackets.

1. We are having problems (find) qualified programmers.
2. We look forward to (get) your comments on this matter.
3. It is no use (buy) a new one, if it is still the same model.
4. They are having difficulties (meet) the deadline.
5. I am not used to (drive) big cars like this.
6. I object to (have) my work criticised when it's not justified.

Language and grammar: Infinitive and gerund

Nach "too ...", "the first", "the last", "the only one" steht im Englischen der Infinitiv:

Our company is	too small	**to have** a canteen.
This problem is	too difficult for us	**to solve** without help.
It is	too late for you	**to apply** for the job.
She was	the first	**to come.**
He was	the last	**to arrive.**
He was	the only one	**to take part.**

In folgenden Fällen sind deutsche Sprecher auch versucht, einen Infinitiv zu benutzen.
Es steht aber das Gerund:

I am looking forward **to receiving** your reply.
I am looking forward **to being shown** their new flat.
I am not used **to speaking** in public.
I object **to being forced** to work overtime.
I am having problems **understanding** him.
We had no difficulty **persuading** him.
It is no use **waiting** for the new regulations.

Communicating across cultures: Addressing people

In English-speaking countries hierarchical differences may be less pronounced than in German companies. Certainly, they are not so obvious from the way people address each other as first names are generally used. Immediate superiors are also usually addressed by their first name. Where there is a considerable difference in status the titles Mr / Mrs / Miss and surname may be used when addressing a superior.

In Britain or the USA business contacts will very quickly address you by your first name and try to establish an informal atmosphere. When introducing yourself to English-speaking people, always give both your first name and your surname. If they firstname you, you should, of course, do the same.

In schools students usually address teachers with the title (Mr / Mrs / Miss) and surname and in shops and restaurants customers may be addressed as sir / madam, e.g.: Are you ready to order, sir? Can I help you, madam? It is important simply to recognise this – you will not have to use it yourself.

Note:
As we have already seen there is often no one-to-one equivalent to German job titles. Similarly there is no direct equivalent to the much used German word "Sachbearbeiter". It may correspond to "the person dealing with the case / our order" or "the person in charge of ...".

Industry expert

1 Working in the marketing department

Phrases ▶

KMK **Sie arbeiten in der Marketing Abteilung des Süßwarenherstellers Horima. Ihre Abteilungsleiterin bittet Sie für einen Flyer anlässlich eines Sponsoringevents, die folgenden Unternehmensinformationen in die englische Sprache zu übertragen.**

- Das Unternehmen wurde 1918 von Horst Ritzel mit Hauptsitz in Mannheim gegründet. Horima steht für Horst Ritzel Mannheim.
- 1923 erfindet Horst Ritzel das Schokobonbon mit Karamellglasur.
- Bis zum 2. Weltkrieg floriert das Unternehmen.
- Nach dem Krieg übernehmen die beiden Kinder des Firmengründers, Susanne und Emil Ritzel, die Firma.
- Horst Ritzel war von 1948 bis 2010 für die Produktions- und Technikabteilung zuständig. Er stirbt am 4. August 2010.
- Das Unternehmen befindet sich noch immer in Familienbesitz.
- Horima hat 18 Fertigungsstätten und beschäftigt über 6.000 Mitarbeiter weltweit.
- Die Produkte werden in mehr als 100 Ländern verkauft.
- Jeden Tag verlassen etwa 100 Millionen Süßigkeiten die Produktionsanlagen.
- Somit ist Horima heute einer der weltweit erfolgreichsten Süßwarenhersteller.

2 Checking costs

1
P The management of Heit GmbH, a manufacturer of hydraulic filters, wants to find out if storage costs can be reduced. The finance and controlling department has been assigned the task of preparing an ABC-analysis for the next management meeting.

Prepare the ABC-analysis in teams. Copy the table below and complete it. Use a dictionary if necessary. Present your results in class.

	A	B	C	D	E	F	G	H
1	Warengruppe	Jahresabsatz [Stück]	Stückpreis [€]	Jahresumsatz [€]	prozentualer Anteil am Gesamtumsatz [%]	prozentualer Anteil an Gesamtmenge [%]	kumulierter Anteil an Gesamtmenge [%]	kumulierter Anteil am Gesamtumsatz [%]
2	B34-	134	9.900					
3	A32-	236	12.654					
4	D79-	97.875	98					
5	G45-	34.567	345					
6	E04-	5.876	3.010					
7	A24-	46.000	465					
8	M09-	92.134	234					
9	Gesamtwerte							
10								
11	Schrankenwerte							
12	A-Güter	70%						
13	B-Güter	90%						
14	C-Güter	100%						

2 Work in groups again and match the terms in the box with
R / P the appropriate column of the table below. Discuss your
results in class.

> delivery on demand • exact determination of material
> requirements • high stock levels • just-in-time delivery
> • long delivery periods • low stock levels • permanent
> check of the terms of delivery • regular delivery dates
> • short delivery periods • simplified order processing •
> these goods are in-between

A-goods	B-goods	C-goods
– delivery on demand – …	– …	– …

3   In the sales department

✳ ▮
KMK   **Die Verkaufsabteilung der Heit GmbH möchte ein neues Vertriebsbüro in Singapur eröffnen. Zu diesem Zweck bittet Sie Ihr Abteilungsleiter, eine E-Mail in Englisch an ein Immobilienbüro in Singapur zu verfassen. Verwenden Sie dazu die folgenden Vorgaben:**

`Phrases ▶`

- Das Gebäude sollte sich im Zentrum Singapurs befinden; ein moderner Büroturm wird bevorzugt.
- Wir benötigen ein helles Großraumbüro für etwa 6 Personen zur Miete, ein kleines Büro ohne Publikumsverkehr und ein weiteres mittelgroßes Büro mit Publikumsverkehr für 2 Personen.
- Die Ausstattung der Büros sollte zehn PCs mit Internetanschluss, einem Kopierer, ein Faxgerät und einen Aktenvernichter umfassen.
- Eine kleine Küche oder eine Kantine im Gebäude für die Mitarbeiter wären vorteilhaft.
- Wenn möglich möchten wir die technische Ausstattung in Raten bezahlen.

From:	(your name)@heit.de
To:	singapore.estate@org.com
Date:	201_-08-14 15:18
Subject:	Enquiry about new sales office

Dear Sir or Madam

Phrases: The office

To describe the office

I work in an open-plan office.	Ich arbeite in einem Großraumbüro.
I work in a small office for two people.	Ich arbeite in einem kleinen Büro für zwei Personen.
She works in the back office.	Sie arbeitet in einem Büro ohne Publikumsverkehr.
I prefer working in a front office.	Ich arbeite lieber in einem Büro mit Publikumsverkehr.
My office is spacious and airy.	Mein Büro ist geräumig und luftig.
The office looks **out on to** the car park.	Vom Büro sieht man auf den Parkplatz.
We all have PCs with internet access.	Wir haben alle einen PC mit Zugang zum Internet.
There is a photocopier, a fax machine and file shredders.	Wir haben einen Kopierer, ein Faxgerät und Aktenvernichter.
The senior staff use the computer projectors for presentations.	Die leitenden Angestellten verwenden die Beamer für ihre Präsentationen.

To introduce the people in the office

He is the overall **boss**, the managing director.	Er ist der oberste Chef, der Geschäftsführer.
Mr Kent is the chief executive.	Herr Kent ist der Vorstandsvorsitzende.
She is **head** of department.	Sie ist die Abteilungsleiterin.
He **reports to** Frau Niemeyer.	Er untersteht Frau Niemeyer.
Frau Niemeyer is our superior.	Frau Niemeyer ist unsere Vorgesetzte.
She is assistant/secretary **to** Mr Kent.	Sie ist Herrn Kents Assistentin/Sekretärin.
I am **in charge of** exports.	Ich bin Exportsachbearbeiterin.
I am responsible for sales to the EU.	Ich bearbeite/bin zuständig für den Verkauf in die EU-Länder.
He deals with/processes/handles complaints.	Er bearbeitet Mängelrügen.
He makes sure that instalments are paid **on** time.	Er kümmert sich um den pünktlichen Eingang der Ratenzahlungen.
Robert is one of the partners of our firm.	Robert ist einer der Partner in unserer Firma.
I hope to be **taken on** after I've finished my course.	Ich hoffe nach der Ausbildung übernommen zu werden.

To talk about catering in the office

Our official coffee break is a quarter of an hour.	Offiziell haben wir eine Viertelstunde Kaffeepause.
We have a small kitchen with a fridge, a coffee machine and a microwave.	Wir haben eine kleine Küche mit Kühlschrank, Kaffeemaschine und Mikrowelle.
At lunchtime we go to the canteen.	Zum Mittagessen gehen wir in die Kantine.
We either bring sandwiches or convenience food.	Wir bringen entweder belegte Brote oder ein Fertiggericht mit.
The canteen caters for vegetarians, too.	Die Kantine bietet auch Gerichte für Vegetarier.

To describe your company's organization chart

He is our **chief executive officer**.	Er ist der Chef unserer Firma.
The department Administration and Finance is subdivided into five units.	Die Abteilung Verwaltung und Finanzen besteht aus fünf Bereichen.
The Marketing Department is part of Sales.	Die Marketing-Abteilung gehört zum Verkauf.
IT Support is responsible for all our IT equipment.	IT-Support ist zuständig für alle IT-Anlagen.
We are an international company and our **personnel** department is called "human resources".	Wir sind ein internationales Unternehmen und unsere Personalabteilung heißt „Human Resources".
The head of our legal department is a lawyer specializing in company law.	Der Leiter unserer Rechtsabteilung ist ein Fachanwalt für Gesellschaftsrecht.
Our company is divided **into** five business units.	Unsere Firma ist in fünf Geschäftsfelder unterteilt.

A

B

C

D

Unit 5
Telephoning

WORD BANK

telephone • number • extension •
handset • landline • answering
machine • mobile / cell phone •
mailbox • text message •
telephone alphabet • symbols •
codes • to put through • to hold •
to catch • to spell • to repeat •
to take down • to read back •
slowly • clearly • precisely

The telephone has long been an essential tool of business communication but in the past few years it has been revolutionised by the privatisation of state telecom companies and the advent of mobile telephony. People can call and be called wherever they happen to be. Even if a person is not available to take calls a text message can be sent or a message can be left on their voice-mail.

1 **Read the text and match the expressions on the left with the explanations on the right.**
R

1. essential tool	a. telephoning without fixed lines
2. privatisation	b. arrival
3. advent	c. selling state-owned enterprises to the public
4. mobile telephony	d. mailbox
5. voice-mail	e. important instrument

2 **Describe the telephone situations above.**
P

Online-Link
808262-0005

A Appliances and components

1 **Read the following sentences and translate them into German. Use the words**
M **below.**

Handy

Telefonbuch

Festnetztelefonanlage

Hörer

Besetztzeichen

Onlineverzeichnis

Telefonauskunft

Anrufbeantworter

Freizeichen

Festnetzleitung

1. My fixed line handset includes an answering machine.
2. It is important to replace the receiver carefully otherwise anyone ringing will get the engaged signal.
3. When you pick up the receiver you hear the dialling tone.
4. The latest innovation is to combine landline and mobile phones – when you leave your home the landline becomes a mobile.
5. My telephone handset can also be used to send and receive fax messages.
6. Most people have a copy of the old-fashioned local telephone directory with a business section. Sometimes the Yellow Pages are in a separate book.
7. However, post offices no longer keep a complete nationwide set of telephone directories.
8. Many people have online directories.
9. The traditional Directory Enquiries has been replaced by a number of competing companies.
10. The applications of mobile phones/cell(ular) phones are increasing all the time.

2 **Work in groups. Describe to your group the telephoning equipment you have at**
P **the office, at home and for mobile communication.**

B   Receiving and redirecting calls

1 Restore the correct order of the two jumbled dialogues and write them out.

R

Dialogue 1

1. Receptionist:	Delphi Materials. Good afternoon. How can I help you?	
2. Caller:	No, thanks. I'll call back later.	
3. Receptionist:	Just a moment, Mr Martin. I'll put you through to Louisa Bates … Oh, I'm sorry, her extension is engaged at the moment. Would you like to hold?	
4. Caller:	Hello. This is Robert Martin from Komplettbau in Erfurt, Germany. I'd like to speak to someone in accounts, please.	

Dialogue 2

1. Receptionist:	May I ask what it's about?
2. Caller:	It's about the dreadful beds we had to sleep in. My back is still aching.
3. Receptionist:	Could you give me your name please?
4. Caller:	My name is Jakob Grailing and I need to speak to your general manager.
5. Receptionist:	Just a second. I'll connect you to Customer Relations.
6. Caller:	Hi. The reason I'm calling is …
7. Receptionist:	Florida Leisure Park. Good morning. What can I do for you?

2

R

A 1.11

Listen to the following telephone conversation between Marcel Krenz of International Snacks GmbH and Jennifer Glover, a receptionist at Global Catering in Manchester and say whether the following statements are TRUE or FALSE.

1. Jonathan Ashley works for Omnipolis Research Consultants Ltd.
2. Marcel Krenz wishes to speak to Jennifer Glover.
3. Jennifer Glover knows for certain that Kirsty Burnham is not in.
4. Marcel Krenz prefers to be put on hold.
5. Marcel Krenz has got Kirsty Burnham's mobile phone number.
6. Marcel Krenz does not want to be put through to Kevin Sears.

3

KMK

◎ A 1.11

Hören Sie sich die Dialoge noch einmal an und finden Sie heraus, wie Folgendes auf Englisch formuliert wird.

1. Was sagt Jonathan Ashley, als das Telefon klingelt?
2. Was sagt Marcel Krenz, als er sich verwählt hat?
3. Wie stellt sich Marcel Krenz bei Ms Glover vor?
4. Was sagt Jennifer Glover, während Sie Marcel Krenz durchzustellen versucht?
5. Was antwortet Marcel Krenz auf die Frage, ob er jemand anderen sprechen möchte?
6. Was sagt Jennifer Glover, als sie wissen will, ob Marcel warten möchte oder ob sie zurückrufen soll?
7. Mit welchen Worten schlägt Jennifer Glover vor, Kirsty auf ihrem Handy anzurufen?
8. Wie formuliert Marcel die Bitte, zu Kevin Sears durchgestellt zu werden?

4

KMK

Beantworten Sie die Fragen zu nachstehendem Text schriftlich auf Deutsch.

1. Warum schicken viele Menschen einem Geschäftspartner lieber eine E-Mail als ihn anzurufen?
2. Wovor haben wir Angst, wenn wir ein Auslandsgespräch führen sollen?
3. Welche Aspekte der Kommunikation fehlen bei einem Telefongespräch?
4. Was soll man tun, wenn man nicht versteht, was der Gesprächspartner sagt?

Info:
Telephoning in a foreign language

Telephoning in a foreign language can be rather frightening. No wonder people often prefer to send an e-mail where they can plan what they want to say and need not fear immediate comeback. However, a telephone call is sometimes unavoidable and one wonders: Will I understand what they are saying? What do I say if I can't? Can I just hang up in embarrassment? Will I be able to express what I want to say? Will they laugh if I make some awful mistake? We all know these kinds of fears when we have to ring someone abroad. And, to some extent, the fears are justified. The non-verbal side of communication is missing. We can't see the person's face, their lips and gestures. They can't see our gestures and the look of despair on our faces! It's best to remain calm and ask them to speak slowly and repeat anything that is not clear.

5 In her first week at Herkules Sandra Kohl finds herself alone in the office and it
R is precisely then that the telephone rings.

A1.12

**Work with a partner. Listen to the telephone conversation twice. Partner A makes
a note of the phrases Sandra uses to ensure that she understands what Jim
Farquhar is saying. Partner B makes a note of the strategies and phrases Jim
Farquhar uses to make Sandra understand him and feel good about her English.
Then compare your findings.**

6 **Complete the telephone phrases below using words from the box. Then translate**
R/M the phrases into German.

cut • get • line • repeat • slowly • speak • quite • what

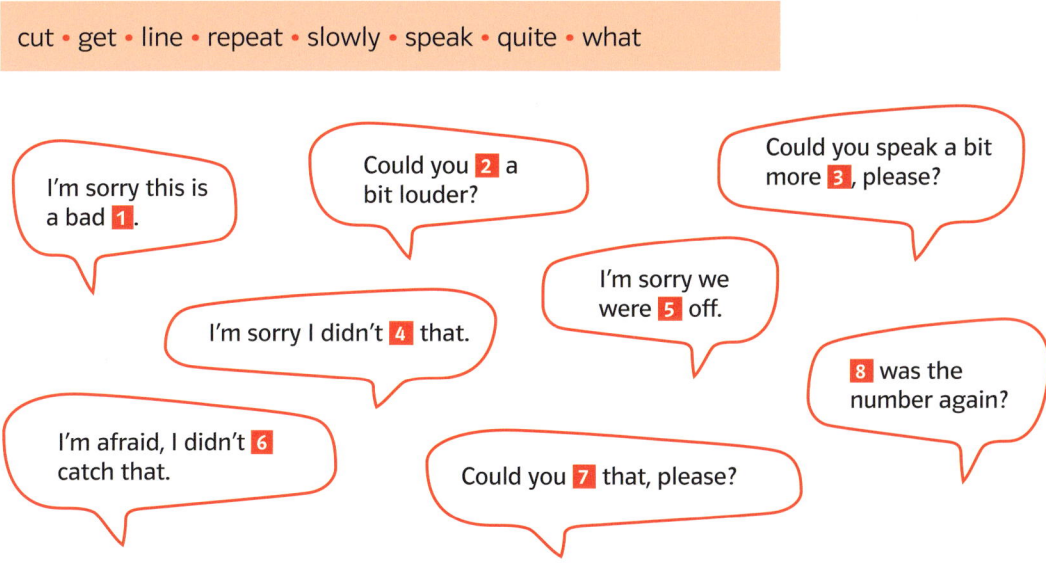

I'm sorry this is a bad **1**.

Could you **2** a bit louder?

Could you speak a bit more **3**, please?

I'm sorry I didn't **4** that.

I'm sorry we were **5** off.

I'm afraid, I didn't **6** catch that.

Could you **7** that, please?

8 was the number again?

7 Roleplay this telephone conversation with a partner. Use the phrases at the end of the unit.

Phrases ▶

Firma: Heinz GmbH, Dresden

Company: Baltic Car Supplies, Tallinn, Estonia

Nehmen Sie den Anruf entgegen.

Nennen Sie Ihren Namen und den Namen der Firma. Sie möchten Frau Lange sprechen.

Sagen Sie, dass Sie den Anrufer schlecht verstehen und bitten Sie ihn, etwas lauter zu sprechen.

Sprechen Sie etwas lauter und fragen Sie, ob Sie jetzt besser zu verstehen sind.

Es ist jetzt besser.
Fragen Sie, worum es geht.

Es geht um eine Rechnung.

Bitten Sie den Anrufer einen Moment zu warten und verbinden Sie ihn mit Frau Lange.

Bedanken Sie sich.

Sagen Sie, dass die Leitung leider im Moment besetzt ist und fragen Sie, ob der Anrufer warten möchte.

Sagen Sie, dass Sie lieber später zurückrufen möchten und fragen Sie nach der Durchwahl.

Die Durchwahl ist 23. Frau Lange wird bis 16 Uhr im Büro sein.

Sie haben das nicht richtig verstanden und bitten um Wiederholung.

Wiederholen Sie die vorherige Information.

Bedanken Sie sich und verabschieden Sie sich.

Antworten Sie und verabschieden Sie sich.

8 Work in pairs. Sit back to back. Use your notes from Exercise 5 and the phrases at the end of the unit. Then act out a similar dialogue.

Phrases ▶

C   Taking messages

✳ 1 Übertragen Sie den folgenden Text ins Deutsche.
KMK

Info: How to take a message

When taking messages it is important to make sure that you take down all the relevant details. You should first make sure that you take down the name of the caller. It is usually necessary to ask him / her to spell names and addresses. Be sure to get the postcode.

It is essential to note down telephone numbers accurately. Failure to do so will lead to a lot of problems. Read back telephone numbers to check that you have got them right. Telephone numbers are often read differently in different countries. In Britain numbers are simply given in the order they occur, eg: 0044 020 363 2991 = oh oh four four – oh two oh - three six three – two nine nine one. Instead of **oh** Americans usually say **zero**. People often say: double oh or: two double nine one. If necessary, ask the caller to repeat the number more slowly.

Get callers to spell e-mail addresses precisely. Even the slightest mistake results in e-mails being sent back. @ is pronounced at, (.) is read as dot, (cf "dotcoms" = internet companies), (/) is pronounced slash and (–) is read as hyphen or dash or minus.

Your company may have a special form for recording telephone messages.

2 There are different international telephone alphabets but people very often make
R up their own as they go along. Spell the following names and addresses using the
A1.13 international telephone alphabet on page 68. Then listen and check.

Brian Urquart • Jonathan McEwan • Trevelyan Networking Ltd • Peterborough • Heidi Schlösser • Detlev Jaegermeyer • Jörg Eyrich • Silberstein • Chemnitz • Ditzhuizen • Mbamali • Werchojansk • Ian McWhirter • Appletreewick in Wharfedale • Georg Süsterhenn • Bad Oeynhausen

3 Spell the following names and addresses using your own telephone alphabet.

Mississippi • Philadelphia • Rhondda • Le Havre • Eyjafiallajökull • Energize Ltd. • Joachim • Fort Myers • Wolfgang Somborn • Kiel • Mississauga Enterprises Inc. • Maldives Travel Lounge

International telephone alphabet

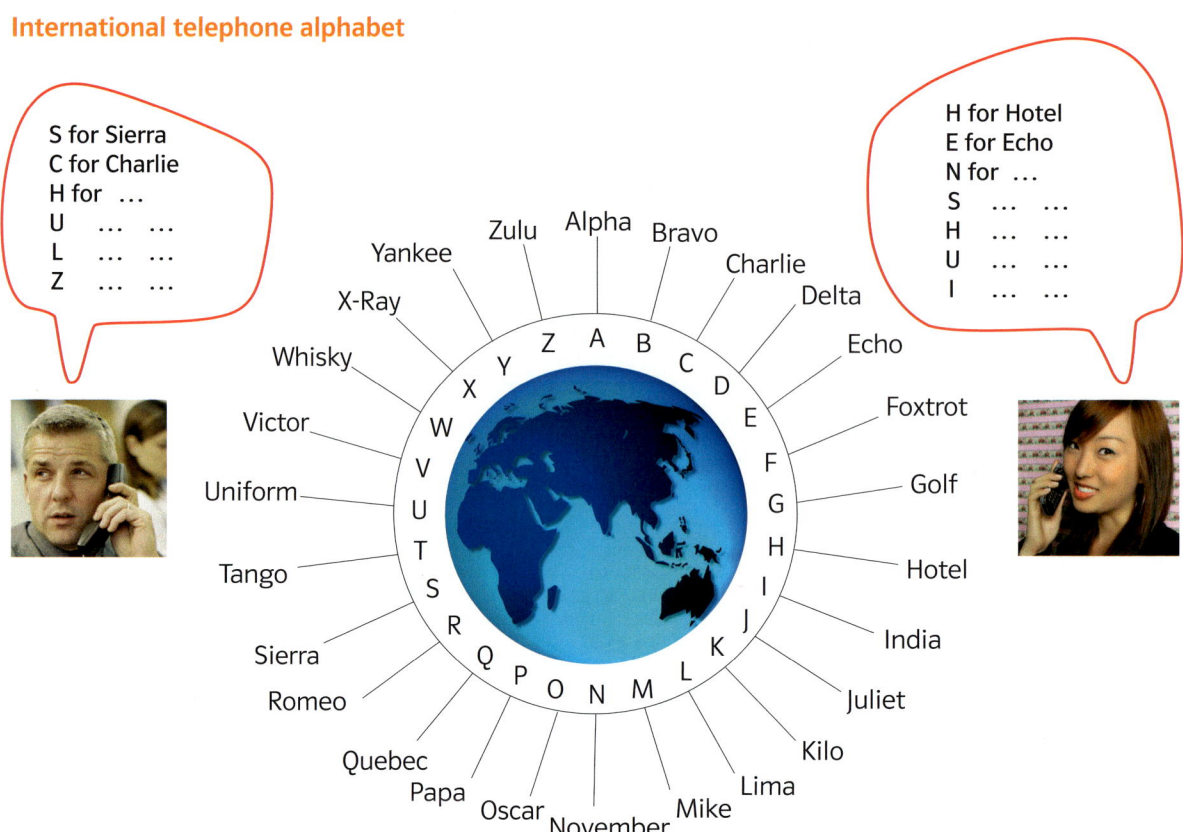

S for Sierra
C for Charlie
H for …
U … …
L … …
Z … …

H for Hotel
E for Echo
N for …
S … …
H … …
U … …
I … …

4 | Work in pairs: Sit back to back and spell your name and the name and address of your company using the international telephone alphabet. Then change roles and check the results.

Phrases ▸

Symbol:	Name:	Example:
'	apostrophe	O'Connor
@	at	info@
A/a	capital letters/small letters	USA/asap
-	hyphen/dash/minus	t-online
Ö	o-umlaut/oe/o with 2 dots	Möller
:	colon	http:
/	slash/stroke	org/gla/
\	backslash	\docs.nt\
.	dot	.de
_	understroke	tourist_org.

Codes / numbers:

+49	(0)711	664376-0	34
country code	**area code**	**office number**	**extension**
04275	Leipzig		
post / zip code	**city**		

5 Work in groups. Group A uses the role card below and dictates the following
KMK telephone numbers, e-mail addresses and websites. Group B uses the role card
on page 248 and dictates the information given there. Then check your results.

> **Role card: Partner A**   **Role card partner B ⇨ page 248**
>
> 1. +44 (1234) 687791
> 2. (0203) 4670976
> 3. (051) 27 81 13 - 12
> 4. (0171) 25333980
> 5. info@terstegen.com
> 6. dieter.wilhelmsen@abconsulting.de
> 7. www.mittelpunkt.de / abo
> 8. info@sykescottages.com

6 First copy the form below. Then listen to the conversation and take the message.
R / P
A 1.14

```
TELEPHONE MESSAGE

Message for:

Message taken by:              Date:

Caller:

Subject:
```

7 You are David Verhoeven. You receive a telephone call from the UK. See on
R / P page 70 for what you yourself say in the conversation with Mr Jones.
A 1.15

First copy the form below. Then listen to the conversation and make a note of the
message in German.

```
TELEFONNOTIZ

Nachricht für:

aufgenommen von:              am:

Anrufer:

Betreff:
```

David Verhoeven:	Anton Hein GmbH, Erkelenz, guten Tag.
David Verhoeven:	Good morning, Mr Jones. I'm afraid Mrs van Steuben is away on a business trip. She is not due back before the beginning of next week. Is there anyone else you'd like to speak to?
David Verhoeven:	Certainly. No problem.
David Verhoeven:	Right. Could you give me your name and your boss's name again, please?
David Verhoeven:	It's David Verhoeven. I'd better spell my second name: V for Victoria, E for egg, R for Richard, H for happy, O for ox, E for Egg, V for Victoria, E for egg and N for nice. I hope you got that alright.
David Verhoeven:	I'll make sure she gets your message. The name of your company was CyberWorld, wasn't it? I didn't catch the name of the town, though.
David Verhoeven:	Thank you and thank you very much for ringing. Goodbye.

8 Work in pairs. Copy the English and the German forms for telephone messages. Sit back to back. Partner A "rings" partner B and leaves a short message. Partner B takes down the message, either in German or in English – depending on the recipient. Then change roles. Use the role card on page 248.

`Phrases`

Example:

Partner A: "This is Pavel Banka speaking. I've got a message for Herr Meister, your purchasing manager. Please tell him that the MP3 Player C27 is again in stock and that I could ship them tomorrow morning. Ask Herr Meister to ring me as soon as possible."

Partner B takes down the message on a form.

TELEFONNOTIZ

Nachricht für: _Herrn Meister, Einkauf_

aufgenommen von: _(Ihr Name)_   am: _____

Anrufer: _Pavel Banka_

Betreff: _MP3 Player C27 wieder vorrätig_

Herr Banka könnte die C27-Player morgen früh absenden.

Bittet möglichst bald um Rückruf.

---

9 Work in pairs. Sit back to back and practise taking messages. Use the phrases at the end of the unit.

`Phrases`

D   Making telephone calls

Communicating across cultures:
Telephoning in English-speaking countries

It is important to use suitable polite phrases when ringing people in English-speaking countries. If you know the person you are ringing it is usual to ask how they are getting on etc. before you get down to business (Example: How are you doing? I haven't spoken to you for a long time etc.).

If you are about to mention a problem or difficulty, you should begin with "I'm afraid …"
A request often begins with "Could you possibly …?" (Could you possibly repeat the address?) or "I would be grateful if you would / could …".

When someone does you a service, it is usual to say something like: "Excellent!", or "Brilliant!"

When someone thanks you for your help you can say, "You're welcome" or "Not at all".

Don't just say "yes" or "no". Say: "Yes, I think so"; "No, I'm afraid not".

⚠ The problem for German speakers is that short answers which are NOT impolite in German come across in English as unfriendly or impolite.

1 **Listen to the conversation and note down the missing expressions on a separate**
R   **sheet of paper.**
A 1.16

Voice:	Good morning. Cardboard Box Company, John Hough speaking.
Nadine Pfeiffer:	Good morning. **1** your packaging materials. My boss **2** your sales literature.
John Hough:	Certainly, **3** you our literature. **4** the name and address of your company.
Nadine Pfeiffer:	The name of the company is Hülshoff GmbH.
John Hough:	**5**, please.
Nadine Pfeiffer:	H for Harry, **6**, L for lemon, S for sugar, H for Harry, O for Otto, double F for Frederick, and then G m b H. The street is Zülpicher Str 131, 50001 Köln, that's Cologne and it's spelt K for knock, O for Otto with two dots, L for lovely and N for nice.
John Hough:	Oh dear, **7** the street as well.
Nadine Pfeiffer:	Z for Zoe; U for ugly with two dots; L for lovely; P for princess; **8**; C for carrot; H for Henrietta; E for egg and R for Ritz.
John Hough:	Brilliant. I will send you the sales literature immediately and **9** you again. By the way, **10** name?
Nadine Pfeiffer:	Yes, Huff. **11**?

John Hough:	I'm afraid not. It's spelt H O U G H, that is H for Henry, O for orange, U for united, G for Green and H for Henry again. My first name's John **12** !
Nadine Pfeiffer:	Thank you very much. Goodbye.
John Hough:	Thank you. **13** the literature in a couple of days. Goodbye.

2 First copy the form below. Then listen to the telephone conversation between
R Lucy Batt and Chloe Stott and fill in the form Chloe has prepared for her boss's
◎ A1.17 information.

Contact person:

Days of arrival and departure:

Size and location of the cottage:

Charge per week:

Additional charges:

Half the total rent plus
booking charges to be paid by:

Balance to be paid by:

Modes of payment:

Mode of booking:

3 Roleplay this telephone conversation with a partner.

KMK

Phrases ▶

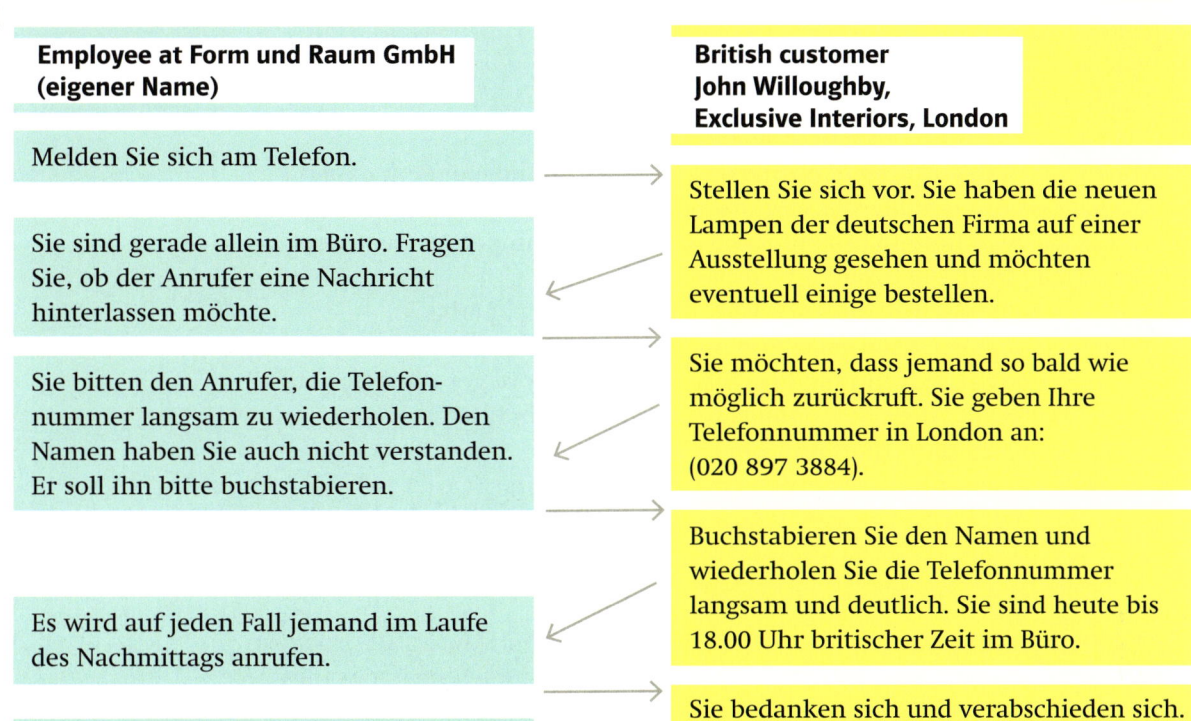

Employee at Form und Raum GmbH (eigener Name)	British customer John Willoughby, Exclusive Interiors, London
Melden Sie sich am Telefon.	Stellen Sie sich vor. Sie haben die neuen Lampen der deutschen Firma auf einer Ausstellung gesehen und möchten eventuell einige bestellen.
Sie sind gerade allein im Büro. Fragen Sie, ob der Anrufer eine Nachricht hinterlassen möchte.	Sie möchten, dass jemand so bald wie möglich zurückruft. Sie geben Ihre Telefonnummer in London an: (020 897 3884).
Sie bitten den Anrufer, die Telefonnummer langsam zu wiederholen. Den Namen haben Sie auch nicht verstanden. Er soll ihn bitte buchstabieren.	Buchstabieren Sie den Namen und wiederholen Sie die Telefonnummer langsam und deutlich. Sie sind heute bis 18.00 Uhr britischer Zeit im Büro.
Es wird auf jeden Fall jemand im Laufe des Nachmittags anrufen.	Sie bedanken sich und verabschieden sich.
Sie verabschieden sich ebenfalls.	

4 Work in pairs. Search the Internet for suggestions for role plays. (Search words: "Telephoning in English".) Sit back to back and practise telephone dialogues with your partner. Use the phrases at the end of the unit.

E Leaving a message on an answering machine

Kopieren Sie den Vordruck, hören Sie die Nachricht ab und fassen Sie sie
KMK auf Deutsch in einer Telefonnotiz zusammen.

A 1.18

```
TELEFONNOTIZ

Nachricht für:

aufgenommen von:                    am:

Anrufer:

Betreff:
```

Language and grammar
Choose the correct prepositions.

1. The meeting will be held from 2 pm (until/to) 4 pm.
2. Thank you for your letter (from/of) 9 December.
3. We are prepared to wait (until/by) next Friday.
4. We enclose a description of our facilities (by/of) an independent expert.
5. We have received numerous enquiries (of/from) start-up companies.
6. The tickets will have to be confirmed (by/until) the middle of next week.
7. We haven't heard (of/from) him recently.
8. The book (of/by) a well-known writer is available in paperback.
9. We expect to receive the consignment (by/until) Friday at the latest.
10. I've never heard (of/from) the firm. Are you sure you've got the name right?
11. It's a study (of/by) the CBI (Confederation of British Industry).
12. He has to get to the airport (until/by) 4 pm.

Language and grammar: Tricky prepositions –
getting the wrong one may change the meaning

by / until   bis
I need the report **by** Monday means that you must get it on Monday (or sooner) because from then on you will need it for your work. Example: The goods must reach us **by** the end of next week.

I need the report **until** Monday means that you need it only until Monday and will then be finished with it.
Example: The import licence is valid **until** 31 August. (You say: until **the thirty-first of** August.)

from ... to   von ... bis
This year's shoe fair will take place **from** 30 June **to** 4 August. (You say: ... from **the thirtieth of** June to **the fourth of** August.)
Wrong: from 30 June ~~until~~ 4 August

from, of, by   von / vom
The date of a communication is preceded by "of" or "dated":
Example: We refer to your offer **of** 2 November. (You say: ... of **the second of** November.)
Wrong: We refer to your offer ~~from~~ 2 November.

Where the communication came from is expressed by "from":
Example: We received a complaint **from** one of our customers.
Wrong: We received a complaint ~~of~~ one of our customers.

The author is introduced by means of the preposition "by":
Example: This is shown in a report **by** an independent study group.
Wrong: This is shown in a report ~~of~~ an independent study group.

Phrases: Telephoning

To make friendly remarks at the beginning of a telephone conversation

Oh, hello Nadine. Nice to hear **from** you. How are things **over there**?	Hallo Nadine. Schön von Dir zu hören. Wie geht's denn so?
Good morning Mrs Glover. I hope you had a pleasant holiday.	Guten Morgen Mrs. Glover. Ich hoffe, Sie hatten einen angenehmen Urlaub.
Good afternoon Mr McEwan. **What's** the weather in Scotland **like**?	Guten Tag Mr. McEwan. Wie ist das Wetter in Schottland?

Reactions

Fine, thank you. And how are you?	Gut, vielen Dank. Und wie geht es Ihnen?
Thank you, it was really very relaxing.	Danke, es war wirklich sehr erholsam.
We've had an awful lot of rain recently, I'm afraid. What's it like in Germany?	Es hat in der letzten Zeit leider schrecklich viel geregnet. Wie ist das Wetter in Deutschland?

To ask the caller to speak more slowly, to spell sth., to repeat sth.

Oh sorry. I didn't quite catch that. Could you repeat it more slowly, please?	Es tut mir Leid, das habe ich nicht verstanden. Könnten Sie es etwas langsamer wiederholen?
Could you possibly spell that? Is that the name of the town?	Könnten Sie das vielleicht buchstabieren? Ist das der Name der Stadt?
I'm afraid I didn't get the telephone number. Could you give me it again, please?	Leider habe ich die Telefonnummer nicht mitbekommen. Würden Sie sie bitte wiederholen?

To ask for somebody

Could I speak **to** Ms Burnham, please?	Könnte ich bitte Ms. Burnham sprechen?
Could you put me **through** to Mr Hough?	Könnten Sie mich mit Mr. Hough verbinden?
Could you give me his/her extension, please?	Könnten Sie mir bitte seine/ihre Durchwahl geben?
I'd like to speak to someone from the sales department.	Ich möchte gern jemanden im Verkauf sprechen.

To say that someone is not available

I'm afraid Kirsty Burnham is not in the office at the moment.	Kirsty Burnham ist z. Zt. leider nicht in ihrem Büro.
… is in a meeting.	… ist in einer Besprechung.
… has someone **with** her.	… hat Besuch.

… is **on** a business trip.	… ist auf Geschäftsreise.
… is out **at** lunch.	… ist zu Tisch.
… is no longer **with** the company.	… ist nicht mehr bei unserer Firma.

To offer to ring back or take a message

I'm afraid Mr Hough is speaking **on** the other line. Would you prefer to hold or shall I ask him to ring back?	Mr. Hough spricht leider gerade auf der anderen Leitung. Möchten Sie warten, oder soll er Sie zurückrufen?
Can he call you back this afternoon?	Kann er Sie heute Nachmittag zurückrufen?
Can I give him a message?	Kann ich ihm etwas ausrichten?
Would you like to leave a message?	Möchten Sie eine Nachricht hinterlassen?

Reactions

Thank you. I'll ring back later.	Danke sehr. Ich rufe später zurück.
I'm afraid I won't be in the office this afternoon. I'll give you my mobile number.	Ich bedaure, ich bin heute Nachmittag außer Haus. Ich gebe Ihnen meine Handy-Nummer.
Yes, please. Could you tell him that …?	Ja bitte. Könnten Sie ihm ausrichten, dass …?

To refer someone to someone else

I'm afraid … I don't know the details. … I am not familiar **with** this order. … I am not in charge of this transaction. I'll put you through to Mr Sears.	Leider … kenne ich mich damit nicht aus. … weiß ich über diesen Auftrag nicht Bescheid. … bearbeite ich diesen Vorgang nicht. Ich stelle Sie zu Mr. Sears durch.
Shall I put you through **to** his secretary?	Soll ich Sie mit seiner Sekretärin verbinden?
Would you like to speak **to** somebody in the accounts department?	Möchten Sie mit jemandem aus der Abteilung Rechnungswesen sprechen?

Reactions

Yes, please. She may be able to help.	Ja bitte. Sie kann mir vielleicht helfen.
No thanks, I really need to speak **to** the export manager.	Nein danke. Ich muss unbedingt mit dem Exportleiter sprechen.

To ask for / about something

Would you please let me know if …?	Ich möchte gern wissen, ob …?
I'd like to ask **whether** it would be possible to …	Wäre es möglich, dass …

Could you possibly …?	Könnten Sie/Könntest Du …?
Do you think you could …?	Könnten Sie/Könntest Du vielleicht …?
You'd be doing us a great favour if you could …	Sie täten uns einen großen Gefallen, wenn Sie …
Please **make sure** that …	Bitte sorgen Sie dafür, dass …
I would really appreciate **it** if you could …	Ich wäre Ihnen sehr dankbar, wenn Sie …

Reactions

Certainly.	Ja, natürlich.
I see no reason why not.	Natürlich. Warum nicht.
Certainly. No problem.	Klar. Kein Problem.
I will certainly do my very best.	Ich werde bestimmt mein Bestes tun.
Definitely. I'll see to it myself.	Ganz bestimmt. Ich werde mich selbst darum kümmern.

To refuse something

I'm afraid we can't agree **to** your proposal.	Leider können wir uns mit Ihrem Vorschlag nicht einverstanden erklären.
We find this level of service quite unacceptable.	Für uns ist diese Art von Kundendienst absolut inakzeptabel.
This is unfortunately not what we had in mind.	Leider hatten wir uns das nicht so vorgestellt.

Reactions

That is a pity.	Das ist wirklich schade.
That is most regrettable.	Das ist überaus bedauerlich.
I can quite understand. We are trying hard to improve things.	Das kann ich verstehen. Wir bemühen uns nach Kräften um eine Verbesserung.
There must have been a misunderstanding.	Hier muss ein Missverständnis vorliegen.

To apologise

I'm terribly sorry but …	Es tut mir schrecklich Leid, aber …
I really must apologise for the inconvenience we've caused you.	Ich möchte mich für die Ihnen entstandenen Unannehmlichkeiten vielmals entschuldigen.
I'm very sorry. Thank you for being so understanding.	Es tut mir sehr Leid. Vielen Dank für Ihr Verständnis.
I can only repeat that I'm very sorry **for** the delay.	Ich kann mich nur nochmals für die Verzögerung entschuldigen.

Reactions

It could happen to anyone.	Das hätte jedem passieren können.
It's a mistake that is very easily made.	So ein Fehler kommt oft vor.
Don't worry. The main thing is that the mistake has been rectified.	Machen Sie sich keine Gedanken. Hauptsache, der Fehler ist behoben.
Well, let's just hope it doesn't happen again.	Hoffen wir nur, dass es nicht noch einmal geschieht.
It has caused us a lot of embarrassment.	Es war für uns sehr peinlich.

To play for time

Can I ring you back? I need to look **at** the file.	Kann ich Sie zurückrufen? Ich muss erst die Unterlagen einsehen.
I'll have to have a word with the line manager.	Ich muss die Sache erst mit dem Bereichsleiter besprechen.
I'm afraid I can't access the file **on** my monitor at the moment. Can I ring you back?	Leider habe ich im Moment auf meinem Computer keinen Zugriff auf die Datei. Kann ich Sie zurückrufen?
I'm afraid I can't give you a definitive answer **at** the moment. I'll get back to you this afternoon if that's OK.	Leider kann ich Ihnen z. Zt. keinen endgültigen Bescheid geben. Wenn es Ihnen recht ist, rufe ich Sie deswegen heute Nachmittag zurück.

Reactions

I'm afraid you said that the last time I rang. I'm not prepared to be put **off** again.	Das haben Sie schon beim letzten Mal gesagt. Ich lasse mich nicht noch einmal so abspeisen.
Certainly, but please give me your extension so that I can ring you direct if necessary.	Natürlich, geben Sie mir aber doch bitte Ihre Durchwahl, damit ich Sie nötigenfalls direkt anrufen kann.
I wish to settle the matter now. I should be grateful if you would put me through to the person responsible.	Ich möchte die Angelegenheit jetzt klären. Bitte stellen Sie mich zu dem entsprechenden Sachbearbeiter durch.
Fine. I look forward to hearing from you. I leave the office **at** 4 pm your time.	Schön. Ich erwarte Ihren Anruf. Ich bin bis 4 Uhr Ihrer Zeit im Büro.

To insist that something is done by a certain date

We need the goods **by** Wednesday **at** the very latest.	Wir benötigen die Ware bis spätestens Mittwoch.
We definitely need the documents **by** 3 May.	Wir müssen die Unterlagen unbedingt bis zum 3. Mai erhalten.
Can we rely **on** that?	Können wir uns darauf verlassen?
Please make sure it arrives **no** later **than** the end of April.	Bitte sorgen Sie dafür, dass es spätestens Ende April eintrifft.
Monday 31 July is the final deadline.	Montag, der 31. Juli ist der letzte Termin.

To promise something

We promise you that …	Wir versprechen Ihnen, dass …
You have my word. The documents will reach you **by** Monday.	Ich gebe Ihnen mein Wort. Die Dokumente treffen spätestens Montag bei Ihnen ein.
We will certainly **ensure** that …	Wir werden bestimmt dafür sorgen, dass …
The goods will be definitely dispatched tomorrow.	Die Ware wird mit Sicherheit morgen abgeschickt.

To end the conversation

Goodbye Miss Pfeiffer. Thank you for calling.	Auf Wiederhören, Frau Pfeiffer. Vielen Dank für Ihren Anruf.
Thank you. Goodbye. Have a nice weekend.	Danke schön. Auf Wiederhören. Schönes Wochenende!
Sorry, I must have got a wrong number.	Entschuldigung, ich habe mich verwählt.

Reactions

Goodbye Mr Hough. You'll be hearing from us again soon.	Auf Wiederhören Mr. Hough. Sie werden bald wieder von uns hören.
Goodbye. You too.	Auf Wiederhören. Gleichfalls.

Unit 6
Making arrangements

WORD BANK

arrangements • booking •
reservation • flight • destination •
departure • arrival • hotel •
accommodation • ensuite
bathroom • diary • appointment •
conference • meeting • topic •
agenda • minutes • fair •
exhibition • application • stand •
to organise • to book • to hire •
to attend • to record

An important part of the job of secretarial or clerical staff is to make
arrangements on behalf of management. This may include managing
the boss's diary and making or rescheduling appointments, booking
flights or train tickets, making hotel reservations and hiring cars.
A secretary may be required to organise meetings and conferences and to take
part in order to keep a record of what is said and decided. It is her job to generally
facilitate proceedings, making sure that the participants have everything they need.
Many companies take part in trade fairs and exhibitions and it may be the task of
the secretary to book stand space and help organise the company's participation.
Finally, the secretary will be responsible for welcoming visitors, often from abroad.
Obviously, a good command of foreign languages is an absolute must.

Study the text and answer the following questions.

R / P
1. Why may a secretary be asked to be present at a meeting?
2. What are the various duties of a secretary as given in the text? Make a list and
   translate it into German.

Online-Link
808262-0006

A Flights and accommodation

1
R
A1.19

Global Catering in Manchester has meanwhile taken over a German company and renamed it Global Catering München GmbH. Executives from the German, British and American companies are to meet for a conference in Munich before flying on to Madrid to attend an international food fair.

Melanie Schmiedel, personal assistant (PA) to Udo Moersen, manager of Global Catering München GmbH, has been asked to organise the conference from 5th to 7th September at the company's premises in Munich. She decides to start by ringing her opposite number at the company's headquarters in Manchester.

Listen to the dialogue and complete the following sentences:

1. The conference is to take place in **1** on **2**
2. The sales manager is going **3**
3. Melanie Schmiedel will book rooms for **4** at **5**
4. Jackie Rowland asks whether the Munich hotel caters for **6**
5. Lunch will be provided by **7**
6. Jackie Rowland will book the flights from **8** to **9**
7. Jackie Rowland sends Melanie Schmiedel a copy of **10**

2
P
Taking the role of Melanie Schmiedel send two e-mails confirming the hotel reservation at Zum Goldenen Ochsen, Wittelsbacher Allee 57, 81220 München to Naomi Rodgers at the American company on Rodgers.GlobalCateringusa@aol.com and to Jackie Rowland on Rowland.GlobalCateringuk@aol.com answering Jackie Rowland's query and asking whether the Americans have any special wishes as far as catering is concerned. Executives will be picked up at the airport. You require flight times and the names of the American executives.

To:	Rowland.GlobalCateringuk@aol.com	Cc:	
From:	schmiedel.GlobalCateringmunich@aol.com	Date:	
Subject:			

3   Melanie Schmiedel then rings the Hotel Granada in Madrid to make arrangements
R   for the six executives attending the International Food Fair from 7 to 9 September.
A1.20

Listen to the conversation twice and answer the following questions:

1. What rooms does Melanie want to book?
2. What are the special features of the rooms she is offered?
3. What are the nationalities of the executives?
4. What meal will the executives receive automatically?
5. What arrangements are there for the evening meals?
6. What special catering arrangements are necessary for Kirsty Burnham?
7. How will the executives get to the exhibition grounds?
8. Why are they advised against hiring a car?

Flight	Departure Time	Arrival Time	Destination
ZY 207	8.45 am	11.30 am	Madrid
ZY 213	6.30 pm	9.15 pm	Munich

Melanie has meanwhile booked the flights from Munich to Madrid. The flight
ZY 207 leaves Munich at 8.45 am on 7 September and arrives in Madrid at
11.30 am. Return flight ZY 213 is at 6.30 pm on 9 September.

4   Taking the role of Melanie Schmiedel send an e-mail to the Granada Hotel
P   informing them of the flight number and times and giving the names of the
six executives. Ask them to confirm that the executives will be picked up at the
airport.

Phrases ▶

5   In your role as Melanie Schmiedel send an e-mail to Naomi Rodgers cc Jackie
P   Rowland giving information about the flight from Munich to Madrid and the hotel
booking in Madrid.

Phrases ▶

6 Work with a partner. Act out the following dialogue with the help of the prompts.

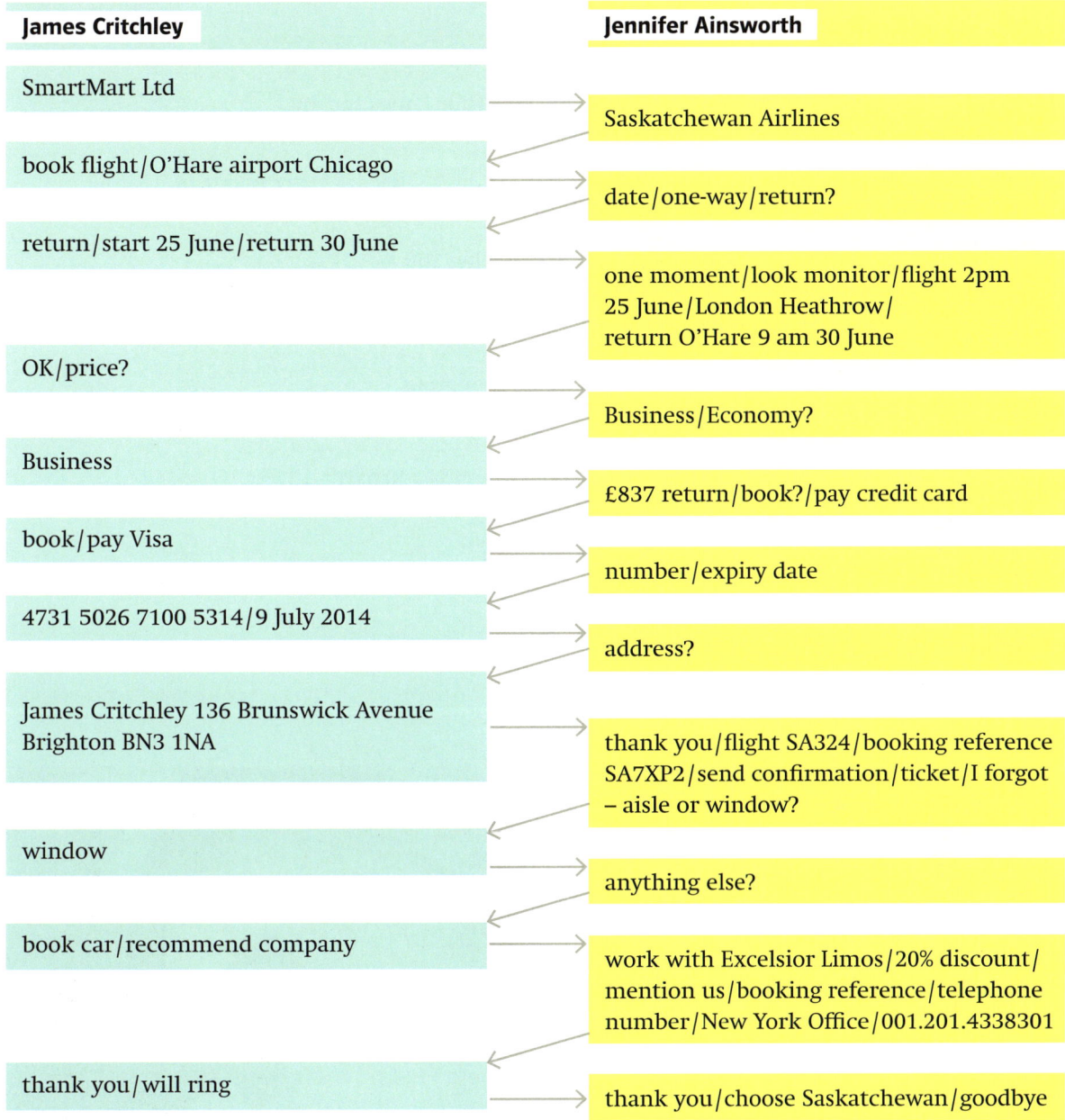

James Critchley	Jennifer Ainsworth
SmartMart Ltd	
	Saskatchewan Airlines
book flight/O'Hare airport Chicago	
	date/one-way/return?
return/start 25 June/return 30 June	
	one moment/look monitor/flight 2pm 25 June/London Heathrow/ return O'Hare 9 am 30 June
OK/price?	
	Business/Economy?
Business	
	£837 return/book?/pay credit card
book/pay Visa	
	number/expiry date
4731 5026 7100 5314/9 July 2014	
	address?
James Critchley 136 Brunswick Avenue Brighton BN3 1NA	
	thank you/flight SA324/booking reference SA7XP2/send confirmation/ticket/I forgot – aisle or window?
window	
	anything else?
book car/recommend company	
	work with Excelsior Limos/20% discount/ mention us/booking reference/telephone number/New York Office/001.201.4338301
thank you/will ring	
	thank you/choose Saskatchewan/goodbye

7 Your boss asks you to check out times and prices of business class flights to Mumbai, India (direct flights from your nearest airport). Make notes on the options.

* **8** **Work with a partner. Act out the following dialogue with the help of the role cards.**

Phrases ▶

Role card: Partner A   **Role card partner B ⇨ page 249**

Sie sind Ivor Friedmann von der Mietwagenfirma Excelsior Limos Inc. in Chicago und erhalten einen Anruf von James Critchley von der britischen Firma SmartMart Ltd. **Nehmen Sie den Anruf entgegen.**

- Mietwagen verschiedener Kategorien (Kompakt- bis Luxusklasse) zur Abholung am Flughafen bereit
- Preis für Kompaktklasse $200 pro Woche, Preis pro Tag $50
- keine Beschränkung der Anzahl der gefahrenen Meilen
- Versicherung im Preis enthalten, bei Unfall muss der Kunde allerdings 10 % der Kosten selbst tragen
- Zusatzversicherung zur Deckung der 10 % Selbstbeteiligung (excess coverage): $60 pro Woche
- 20 % Rabatt für Kunden der Saskatchewan Airlines
- Gesamtpreis: $200 plus $60 Zusatzversicherung minus $40 Rabatt = $220
- Zahlung per Kreditkarte erwünscht unter Angabe der Kreditkartennummer und des Verfallsdatums sowie der Adresse des Kunden

B Meetings, conferences and fairs

1 Making an appointment

Melanie Schmiedel's boss Udo Moersen is to go to Manchester for one day to discuss the integration of the German company into the group and the new product range with Kirsty Burnham. He asks his PA to arrange a day to fit in with Ms Burnham's agenda. He would arrive about 9.30 and stay till 2.45. He would prefer Wednesday.

Melanie Schmiedel has Herr Moersen's diary in front of her and rings Jackie Rowland, who likewise refers to Ms Burnham's diary. They try to decide which day it would be possible to meet. Kirsty Burnham would like to invite Udo Moersen out to a pub for a working lunch, if he would like that.

1 Sit back to back with your partner (Role card B) and act out the dialogue between them in which they arrange an appointment in Manchester and cover the other points mentioned.

Phrases ▶

Role card: Partner A	Role card partner B ⇨ page 249

Terminkalender von Udo Moersen

Montag   **13. Juni**
9 Uhr: Treffen mit Lieferanten Pauli & Co;
11.30 Ad.Slot Internetwerbung Frau Franzen

Dienstag   **14. Juni**
Einzelhändler im Großraum München ab 9 Uhr bis ca 15.30 Uhr

Mittwoch   **15. Juni**

Donnerstag 16. Juni
Geburtstag meiner Frau, 20.00 Uhr Tisch bei Da Pino reserviert

Freitag 17. Juni
11 Uhr: Besprechung der Produktplanung mit Xaver;
13–14 Uhr Mitarbeiterbesprechung

Communicating across cultures: Tips for visitors to the UK

Trains:
There are no supplementary charges for faster trains in Britain (the Eurostar to Brussels and Paris is more expensive!). Trains that stop at many stations are obviously slower than those that rarely stop. How often and where they stop is given on the indicator and timetables. It is very important to make sure that the train stops where you want to get off! Do not assume that all trains will stop at the same station on your return journey. Each train may stop at a different selection of stations.

Pubs:
Pubs are an important institution in Britain and are a popular venue at lunchtime for an informal meal. Many provide food at lunchtime, less often in the evening. As a rule there is no waiter service. You go to the bar to buy drinks where turn-taking is observed although there is no visible queue. If the pub is crowded it may be a good idea to discreetly wave a 10 pound note to let the barman/barmaid know you are waiting. Often English people buy rounds, saying things like "What's yours?" or "What are you having?".

Everybody is in principle expected to buy a round. If you don't, there may be an embarrassed silence. Food is also ordered and paid for at the bar and is brought to the table where you are sitting. All drinks and food are paid for straight away.

Tipping (taxis and restaurants):
In Germany you frequently tip by rounding up the amount of the bill. If the taxi fare is Euro 8.10 you might say Euro 8.50 or Euro 9.00. In Britain a taxi driver would not know what you meant. If the fare is £5.30 you could give the driver a £10 pound note and say "please give me change for £6". In restaurants the bill is generally brought on a little tray. You put enough money on the tray to pay the bill. The waiter returns, takes the tray away and comes back again with your change on the tray. You then decide what to put on the tray as a tip. It does not have to be a percentage of the bill.

2 **Ihr Chef muss geschäftlich zum ersten Mal nach England. Geben Sie ihm einige Tipps. Fassen Sie dazu die Informationen in der Box (Communicating across cultures) zusammen.**

KMK

2 Preparing the agenda

1 **Übertragen Sie die Agenda ins Deutsche.**

KMK

Melanie Schmiedel has now received the draft agenda of the conference in Munich on 6 and 7 September as drawn up by her boss.

> **Agenda**
>
> 1. Welcoming guests
> 2. Minutes of the last conference in Boston, USA
> 3. Report on the Munich company and its integration in the group by Xaver Ertl
> 4. Presentation by Kirsty Burnham on the development of Global Catering's sales
> 5. Report by Kevin Sears on the development of Global Catering's European business
> 6. Consumer health concerns – from obesity to organic food – recent market research presented by Jeanne-Anne Taylor
> 7. Presentation on the role of international trade fairs in Global Catering's marketing strategy by Udo Moersen
> 8. Other business

2 **In your role as Melanie Schmiedel send an e-mail to Jackie Rowland at Global Catering UK and Naomi Rodgers at Global Catering USA enclosing the above draft agenda as an attachment, requesting notification of any additions or modifications in the course of the following week.**

P

Phrases ▶

3 Preparing a meeting

Read the following text and make a list of the most important points.

R

As PA to Udo Moersen Melanie Schmiedel has been asked to assist at the conference in Munich.

This involves supervising the preparation of the room, making sure that there is an adequate supply of tea, coffee, soft drinks and mineral water (sparkling and still) available.

Any equipment required such as a computer projector, whiteboard or flip chart with a supply of board markers must be available and in working order.

Her boss may require files, additional information, or he may need to make telephone calls etc.

She must be on hand to provide any assistance necessary. Some of the German executives' English leaves much to be desired and so she may be asked to interpret or translate.

BBC Motion Gallery

⊚V2 Video lounge Hospitality

This video deals with the hotel and catering trade.
Keep the following questions in mind while watching the video:

1. Does Judith like her job? What are the disadvantages?
2. What problem does the sector face that is highlighted several times in the course of the video?
3. What – mentioned towards the end of the video – is the sector doing to solve this problem?
4. What is Wayne Spencer's job title? Describe his appearance.
5. What particular skills do people working in this industry require?

Discuss your answers with the class.

4 Taking the minutes

✳ **Translate the first three paragraphs of the following text.**

M

The minutes

It is important for an accurate written record of the transactions of a meeting or conference to be kept. It is essential for those involved to be able to refer back to the minutes and see what was said and, in particular, what was agreed. The minutes are evidence in law of the proceedings of the meeting.

The names of those present and any apologies for non-attendance must be recorded. In this case there are the six executives with Udo Moersen acting as chairman or chair and a number of other employees of the Munich company and finally, Melanie Schmiedel.

Especially in a discussion it is difficult to keep a word for word account of what is being said. The person taking the minutes may be able to note down only the most important points. It is particularly important that any figures or dates should be recorded accurately.

The minutes have to be presented to those present at a later date for approval or corrections.

Melanie Schmiedel has also been asked to take the minutes. As most of the topics on the agenda are presentations which will be available in written form her minute-taking will be largely restricted to the questions and answers following the presentations.

5 Booking an exhibition stand

Melanie now has to ring the exhibition authorities in Madrid to check that their order for a stand is OK. After checking her records she sees that she returned the application about two months ago.

Melanie Schmiedel:	Good morning. Melanie Schmiedel from Global Catering in Munich speaking. I'm afraid I don't speak Spanish. Do you speak English or German?
Exhibition authorities:	I do speak English. What can I do for you? By the way my name's Rosa de la Fuente.
Melanie Schmiedel:	I'd like to check our stand reservation for the International Food Fair. I sent off the application form two months ago but I have not received confirmation yet.
Rosa de la Fuente:	Just a second. Let me check my monitor. Yes, here it is. Global Catering. A corner stand, 25m^2, with kitchenette and conference area. Is that OK?
Melanie Schmiedel:	Excellent. When will you be sending out the confirmations?
Rosa de la Fuente:	In a couple of weeks at the latest, I should think. But you can assume that everything's OK.
Melanie Schmiedel:	We shall need an interpreter with English and German. Can you recommend anyone?
Rosa de la Fuente:	I would get in touch with the Multilingua Agencia by e-mail under multilinguaservices@aol.com or send them a fax. The telephone number is 0034 91 4022468 and the fax number is the same with a 9 at the end instead of the 8. I'm sure they'll be able to recommend someone suitable.
Melanie Schmiedel:	Brilliant. I'll get in touch with them right away. Thank you very much. Goodbye.
Rosa de la Fuente:	Thank you for ringing. Bye.

1 **Lesen Sie den Dialog, decken Sie den Text dann ab und drücken Sie Folgendes auf Englisch aus.**

R

1. Sie sprechen kein Spanisch.
2. Sie möchten die Standreservierung überprüfen.
3. Sie haben einen Eckstand von 25 m^2 mit Teeküche und Besprechungsraum gebucht.
4. Sie wollen wissen, wann die Bestätigungen herausgeschickt werden.
5. Sie brauchen eine Dolmetscherin für Englisch und Deutsch.

2
P

Write a fax as Melanie Schmiedel to the Multilingua Agencia (see page 89) giving details of your requirements. Set out your fax as in the form below.

TELEFAX TRANSMISSION
Global Catering München GmbH

Nymphenburger Allee 93
80335 München
Tel.: (0049) (0)89277183
Fax: (0049) (0)89277190

To:	Attention:
From:	Fax: (0034) (91)4022469
Date:	Pages (incl. this one):
Subject:	

Language and grammar
Translate the following sentences.

1. Als Anhang senden wir Ihnen unsere neueste Preisliste.
2. Gestern habe ich von 13:00 Uhr bis 16:30 Uhr auf Ihren Anruf gewartet.
3. Pro Woche versenden wir zwischen 20 und 30 Angebote.
4. Wir investieren regelmäßig 5 % unseres Gewinns in neue Technologien.
5. Leider warten wir noch immer auf Ihre Überweisung.
6. Zur Zeit versuchen unsere Mitbewerber eine Firma in USA zu übernehmen.
7. Wegen des Booms in China steigen die Stahlpreise weltweit.
8. Er organisiert die Konferenz, die nächste Woche stattfindet, und wir buchen die Hotelzimmer.

Language and grammar: Continuous form (Verlaufsform)

Die Verlaufsform (he is writing an e-mail) dient zur Beschreibung einer gerade vor sich gehenden Handlung sowie einer allmählichen Entwicklung, häufig markiert durch **now, just, still, when, while, since, for** etc.	Our competitors **are trying** to undercut our prices. They **are** still **waiting** for a reply. Prices **have been rising** in the last few months. We **are thinking** of buying a house.
Da die einfache Verbform (he writes 50 e-mails a day) ausdrückt, dass etwas immer so ist oder immer wieder geschieht, ist die Verwendung der Verlaufsform in bestimmten Fällen unerlässlich, um klar zu machen, dass etwas nur von vorübergehender Natur ist.	They **are having** problems with their suppliers (= at the present time). They **have** problems with their suppliers (= often / always). I **am living** with my parents at the moment (= but I'm looking for a flat of my own). I **live** in Dresden (= permanently).
Die Verlaufsform kann für feste Planungen und Abmachungen auch für die Zukunft benutzt werden.	He is giving a presentation at the conference. I am picking him up at the airport next Friday (= this has been arranged).

Industry expert

1 Practising telephone language

1 **Kopieren Sie die untenstehenden Vorgaben.**
KMK **Hören Sie aufmerksam zu und tragen Sie**
A 2.2 **die Informationen in die dafür vorgesehenen**
Felder ein.

Anrufer 1

Name

Telefonnr.

Anrufer 2

Name

Grund des Anrufes

E-Mail

Anrufer 3

Name

Liefernr.

Grund des Anrufes

Telefonnr.

2 Match the German expressions (1.–10.) with their English equivalents (a.–j.).

1. Anzahlung	a. basic charge
2. ausgebucht	b. booked (up)
3. Grundpreis	c. cancellation
4. Gültigkeitsdatum	d. deposit
5. Halbpension	e. ensuite room/private bath
6. Hoteleinrichtungen	f. expiry date
7. Messestand	g. full board
8. Stornierung	h. half board
9. Vollpension	i. hotel facilities
10. Zimmer mit Bad	j. stand/booth

3 Translate these sentences into appropriate English.

M

1. Unser Vorstand lädt um 13.00 Uhr zum Empfang am Stand ein.
2. Ich möchte einen Eckstand buchen. Er muss mit einem Internetanschluss und einem Beamer ausgestattet sein.
3. Ich möchte fünf Einzelzimmer mit Bad und Frühstück anfragen.
4. Ich möchte die Reservierung für den Konferenzraum stornieren.

`Phrases` ▶

2   Making room reservations

1 Role play: Room reservation

Phrases ▶

| Role card: Partner A | Role card partner B ⇨ page 250 |

Sie arbeiten für die Meiner GmbH in Mannheim. Ihre Chefin, Marita Peiler plant eine Geschäftsreise nach Edinburgh/UK. Rufen Sie im Caledonian Royal Hotel in Edinburgh an und reservieren Sie ein Zimmer sowie einen Konferenzraum.

- Stellen Sie sich vor und sagen Sie, dass Sie ein Einzelzimmer mit Bad auf den Namen Marita Peiler von der Firma Meiner GmbH buchen möchten.
- Datum: 4.–6. Dezember dieses Jahres
- Preis pro Nacht? (Preisvorstellung: bis £120,00 mit Frühstück.)
- Sie buchen mit Frühstück. Wie lange wird Frühstück serviert?
- Frau Peiler wird nicht vor 22.00 Uhr ankommen. Wie lange ist die Rezeption geöffnet?
- Ist ein Internetzugang vorhanden? Kostet dieser extra?
- Kann ein Konferenzzimmer für etwa 10 Personen für den 5. Dezember gebucht werden?
- Ist ein Cateringservice verfügbar? Was bietet das Hotel an?
- Welche Einrichtungen bietet das Hotel zur Entspannung an?
- Sie buchen auf den Firmennamen Meiner GmbH.
- Mastercard Nr. 5647 8776 3625 8674. Gültig bis 09/2016. Bitten Sie um eine Bestätigung der Buchung per E-Mail.
- Ihre Adresse: (Ihr Name)@meiner.de
- Bedanken und verabschieden Sie sich.

✳ **2** **Sie arbeiten in der Verkaufsabteilung der Weller KG in Düsseldorf. Ihr Chef bittet**
KMK **Sie, für die jährliche Vertreterkonferenz in Atlanta / USA Raumreservierungen vorzunehmen. Verfassen Sie ein Fax unter Berücksichtigung der Informationen unten und auf Seite 93.**

Phrases ▶

Weller KG | Karl-Arnold-Platz 5 | 40021 Düsseldorf
Tel.: +49 211 867439 | Fax: +49 211 867438

TELEFAX

To: Attention:

From: Fax:

Date: Pages (incl. this one):

Subject:

Regency Hotel Atlanta,
265 Pineapple Street NE,
Atlanta, Georgia, 30303, USA
Tel: +1 404 577 1234
Fax: +1 404 588 4137

Erbitten Sie um Angabe des Komplettpreises (Firmentarif) sowie Bestätigung per Fax!

Checkliste Veranstaltungen

Veranstaltung   Jährliche Vertreterkonferenz
Thema   „Neue Produkte – Neue Chancen"
von   15.05.201_   bis   17.05.201_
Teilnehmerzahl insgesamt   15
   Düsseldorf   4
   Inland   –
   Europäisches Ausland   6
   Übersee   5
Veranstalter   unsere Firma

1 Veranstaltungsräume	ja	nein	erl. am
Raumreservierung	X	☐	

1.1 Raumausstattung	ja	nein	erl. am
Bühne, Podest	X	☐	
Rednerpult	☐	X	
Schautafeln	X	☐	

Zahl   5   Erstellung u. Aufbau   vor dem Konferenzraum

1.2 Technische Ausstattung	ja	nein	erl. am
Overheadprojektor	☐	X	
Video	☐	X	
Mikrofone	X	☐	
Computer	☐	X	
Computer mit Internetanschluss	X	☐	
Beamer	X	☐	
Flipchart	X	☐	

2 Gastronomisches Angebot	ja	nein	erl. am
2.1 Mittagessen	X	☐	

Datum   15.–17.05.201_
Uhrzeit   12.30 Uhr
Ort   Hotelrestaurant
Anzahl Personen alle Teilnehmer

2.2 Kaffee / Teepausen	X	☐	

Datum   15.–17.05.201_
Uhrzeit   9.30 Uhr, 15.30 Uhr
Ort   Konferenzraum
Anzahl Personen alle Teilnehmer

2.3 Konferenzdinner	X	☐	

Datum   15.–17.05.201_
Uhrzeit   19.30 Uhr
Ort   Hotelrestaurant
Anzahl Personen alle Teilnehmer

3 Hotels	ja	nein	erl. am
3.1 Hotelzimmerbestellung	X	☐	

Anzahl   15
Extras   mit Bad und Frühstück

3.2 Teilnehmertransfer	☐	X	
Abholung vom Flughafen			
Busbestellung			

93

3 Preparing for a trade fair

1 Role play: Trade fair

KMK

Phrases

Role card: Partner A   **Role card partner B ⇨ page 250**

Sie arbeiten für die Firma DTG Verpackungen GmbH in Leipzig. Ihre Firma möchte auf der Pack Exhibition International in Chicago/USA einen Stand mieten. Rufen Sie das Buchungsbüro der Messeleitung in Chicago an.

- Stellen Sie sich vor und sagen Sie, dass Sie einen Stand für die nächste Pack Exhibition International in Chicago buchen möchten.
- Sie benötigen einen Stand von 6 m × 7 m.
- Wählen Sie den kleinsten Stand. Preis?
- Wie ist der Stand ausgestattet?
- Sie benötigen am Stand zudem: fließend heißes und kaltes Wasser, eine Sitzraumfläche, einen Beamer.
- Sind Sie für den Aufbau (installation) und den Abbau selbst zuständig?
- Ab wann können Sie den Messestand vorbereiten?
- Wie lange ist die Ausstellung täglich geöffnet?
- Wie viele Aussteller werden erwartet?
- Buchstabieren Sie Ihren Firmennamen. Ihre Fax-Nr. lautet: 0049-3413391544. Bis wann muss die Buchung bestätigt sein?
- Ist eine Anzahlung notwendig?
- Verabschieden Sie sich.

2 Verfassen Sie eine Rundmail an Ihre Kunden zur Information, dass die
KMK DTG Verpackungen GmbH auf der Pack Exhibition International ausstellen wird. Berücksichtigen Sie dabei die folgenden Angaben:

Phrases

- Laden Sie Ihren Kunden ein, Sie auf der Pack Exhibition International in Chicago/USA vom 9. bis 13. November dieses Jahres am Stand zu besuchen, um Ihre neuen Produkte und Dienstleistungen kennenzulernen.
- Ihr Stand ist in Halle B, Stand Nr. 3324.
- Ihr Geschäftsführer, Herr Dr. Reinhard, lädt am 9. November um 10 Uhr zum Empfang am Messestand ein.
- Sie würden sich freuen Ihren Kunden begrüßen zu dürfen.

3 Work with a partner and do the following tasks.

P

1. Why is it important for companies to attend trade fairs?
2. Give the advantages and disadvantages of trade fairs.
3. Which trade fairs does your company attend?
4. Search the internet for a website where you can design a trade fair stand. Create a stand. Your budget is €5,000. Be prepared to present your stand and its details in class.

Phrases: Making arrangements

To book flights or trains

Please reserve a window/aisle seat **on** the 8.30 am flight to Munich.	Bitte reservieren Sie einen Platz am Fenster/Gang für den Flug um 8:30 Uhr nach München.
Are you travelling economy or business class?	Fliegen Sie Economy- oder Business-Class?
I would like to reserve a window seat on the 9.15 ICE train to Hamburg.	Ich möchte einen Fensterplatz des ICE um 9:15 Uhr nach Hamburg reservieren lassen.
Is that first or second class, one way or return?	Erster oder zweiter Klasse? Einfach oder hin und zurück?
Is there a supplementary charge for the InterCity to Edinburgh?	Muss für den Intercity nach Edinburgh ein Zuschlag bezahlt werden?
There is no supplementary charge.	Es wird kein Zuschlag erhoben.
You are booked **on** flight no ZY 652 **on** 23 March, departing London Gatwick **at** 7.30 am, arriving Munich 10.15 am.	Sie sind am 23. März für Flug Nr. ZY 652 gebucht, Abflug London Gatwick um 7:30 Uhr, Ankunft München 10:15 Uhr.
You should check in two hours before departure to allow **for** security.	Sie sollten wegen der Sicherheitsüberprüfung zwei Stunden vor Abflug einchecken.

To book hotel or conference rooms

We require a single/double room with **ensuite** bathroom.	Wir benötigen ein Einzel-/Doppelzimmer mit Bad.
I should like to book an executive suite for three nights **from** 3 **to** 6 March with Internet access.	Ich möchte eine Prasidentensuite mit Internetzugang für drei Nächte vom 3. bis 6. März buchen.
We require a conference room **to seat** 25–30 people.	Wir brauchen ein Besprechungszimmer für 25–30 Personen.
For our annual general meeting we need an assembly hall **of** at least 500 square metres equipped with a stage and a big screen.	Für unsere Jahreshauptversammlung brauchen wir einen Versammlungssaal von mindestens 500 Quadratmetern mit Bühne und Großbildschirm.
I should be grateful if you could confirm the booking **in** writing/**by** e-mail/**by** fax.	Wir wären für eine Bestätigung der Buchung per Brief/E-Mail/Fax dankbar.
Is it possible to order a buffet lunch?	Besteht die Möglichkeit ein Mittagsbuffet zu bestellen?
We regret that we have to cancel the reservation. We realise that it is very short notice.	Wir bedauern, diese Reservierung stornieren zu müssen. Wir sind uns dessen bewusst, dass dies sehr kurzfristig geschieht.

I'm afraid I'm engaged all day on Wednesday.	Leider bin ich am Mittwoch den ganzen Tag besetzt.
Friday would suit me fine.	Freitag würde mir gut passen.
I'd prefer Thursday morning.	Donnerstag Morgen wäre mir lieber.
It's Monday **at** 11, then.	Also bleibt es bei Montag um 11 Uhr.
Could we meet **on** Monday 17 at 10 am?	Könnten wir uns am Montag, den 17. um 10 Uhr vormittags treffen?
– Certainly. Monday at 10 am is fine.	– Ja, sicher. Montag 10 Uhr ist o.k.
Would Tuesday suit you?	Würde Ihnen Dienstag passen?
– Not so good. My diary's full, I'm afraid. Wednesday would be better.	– Eigentlich nicht. Mein Terminkalender ist leider voll. Mittwoch wäre besser.
I'm free all day Wednesday.	Am Mittwoch geht es den ganzen Tag.

A draft agenda has already been drawn up.	Ein Entwurf für die Tagesordnung ist bereits erstellt worden.
Notification of any additions or changes is requested within a week.	Es wird gebeten, eventuelle Zusätze oder Änderungen innerhalb einer Woche anzugeben.

He/She is chairing the meeting.	Er/Sie leitet die Sitzung.
He is the chairman, he/She is the chairperson.	Er/Sie ist der/die Vorsitzende.
Perhaps you could each introduce **yourself** briefly indicating your role in the company.	Vielleicht könnten Sie sich kurz vorstellen und dabei auf Ihre Stellung in der Firma eingehen.
Has everyone got a copy of the agenda?	Haben alle eine Kopie der Tagesordnung bekommen?
We shall adjourn **for** lunch **at** …	Um … unterbrechen wir für das Mittagessen.
Lunch will be provided by our own caterers.	Unser eigener Versorgungsbetrieb wird das Mittagessen liefern.
Are there any further comments?	Gibt es noch Wortmeldungen?
Shall we take a vote?	Sollen wir nun abstimmen?
The proposal is accepted.	Damit ist der Vorschlag angenommen.

To book an exhibition stand

We are interested in displaying our products **at** the Madrid Motor Show.	Wir sind daran interessiert, unsere Produkte auf der Automobilmesse in Madrid auszustellen.
Our company wishes to reserve floor space for a stand **covering** 8 x 15 metres.	Unsere Firma möchte die für einen Stand von 8 x 15 Metern benötigte Ausstellungsfläche reservieren lassen.
We are interested in introducing our software solutions at this years's Computer Fair and would like to ask you to send us your information package with application forms.	Wir sind daran interessiert, unsere Software-Lösungen bei der diesjährigen Computermesse vorzustellen und möchten Sie bitten, uns Ihre Messe-Information mit Anmeldeformularen zu schicken.
We wish to book a stand in the main exhibition hall.	Wir möchten einen Stand in der Hauptausstellungshalle buchen.

To organise the necessary equipment

Our stand must have internet access and it must be equipped with telephone lines.	Unser Stand muss Internetzugang haben und er muss mit Telefonleitungen ausgestattet sein.
First-class catering services will also be required.	Wir benötigen ebenfalls erstklassigen Catering-Service.

To write invitations

The chairman will be pleased to welcome you **at** our annual dinner **at** the Park Hotel.	Der Vorsitzende gibt sich die Ehre, Sie zu unserem alljährlichen festlichen Abendessen im Park Hotel begrüßcn.
The reception will be held in our main hall **between** 10 am **and** 3 pm.	Der Empfang findet zwischen 10 und 15 Uhr in unserer Haupthalle statt.

To have a stand built and dismantled

Are you in a position to design an eye-catching stand for us and erect it before 15 March?	Sind Sie in der Lage, für uns einen ins Auge fallenden Stand zu entwerfen und vor dem 15. März aufzubauen?
Can you help us remove the heavy exhibits and dismantle the stand?	Können Sie uns dabei helfen, die schweren Ausstellungsstücke zu entfernen und den Stand abzubauen?

Unit 7
Making presentations

WORD BANK
presentation • audience •
delivery • content • prompt
cards • key words • points •
introduction • main body •
conclusion • visual aids • eye-
contact • body language •
handout • to prepare • to
rehearse • to deliver • statistics •
developments • degree •
percentage • comparisons •
rankings • graphs • diagrams •
bar chart • line graph • pie chart •
to visualise • to describe • to rise
• to fall • to remain unchanged •
to fluctuate • to account for •
slight • steady • dramatic

You may be required to present your company and its products –
either informally or on a more formal level. This may range from
the introduction of a specific product or products to presenting the
company as a whole. Although many may feel a bit scared of standing
up before an audience, the ability to make good oral presentations
is a key skill. However, it is a skill that can be acquired and improved
by practice. It is important, above all, to remember that the style and
manner of delivery is as important as the content.

Translate the following sentences into German.

M

1. You may feel scared of standing up before an audience.
2. Making a good oral presentation is a key skill.
3. This skill can be acquired and improved.
4. Style of delivery is as important as content.
5. You may be required to make a presentation on your company
   and its products.

Online-Link
808262-0007

A   Preparing a presentation

You have been asked to give a presentation of your company and its products. The presentation will be brief. You have a maximum of 5 minutes at your disposal. The following hints should help you to prepare.

Start by deciding what you want to include and what your objectives are. Remember that there are limits to the number of facts your audience can absorb. The following are intended as helpful hints:

How to make a presentation

- Do not write out your presentation in full. Use numbered prompt cards with key words. They are the best way to avoid forgetting important points.
- Your presentation should have an introduction, main body and conclusion.
- First give a brief overview of points to be covered.
- Divide up the main body according to the number of important points.
- Finish with a conclusion.

Use expressions like:

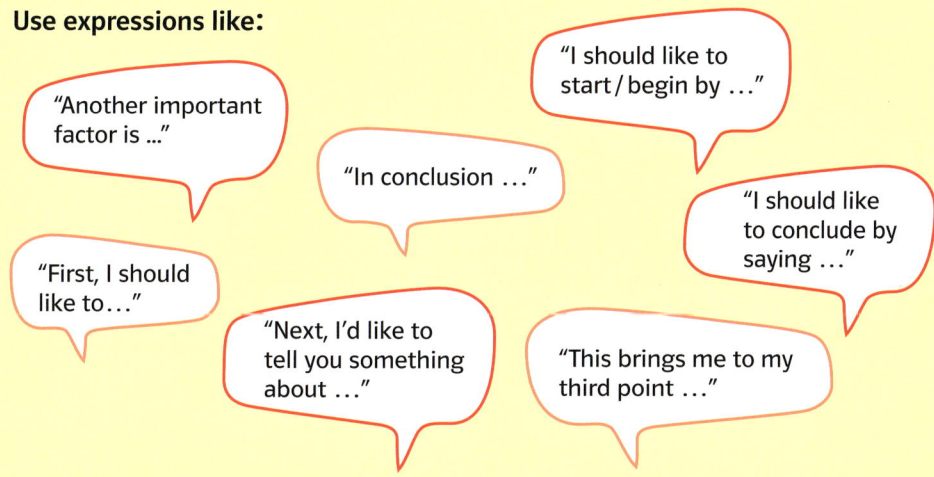

"Another important factor is …"

"I should like to start / begin by …"

"In conclusion …"

"I should like to conclude by saying …"

"First, I should like to…"

"Next, I'd like to tell you something about …"

"This brings me to my third point …"

in order to signal the different sections of your presentation.

Reinforce what you say by **visual aids**, such as PowerPoint slides. Visual aids help you to explain complicated ideas more easily and arouse and hold the interest of your audience and make your presentation look more professional. If you print them out they may double as a handout.

Visual aids may take the form of overhead transparencies or computer files showing graphs, pictures, flowcharts, brief statements/cues (e.g. the key words from your prompt cards). Here are a few helpful hints:

- Limit the text to six lines.
- Use no more than six words per line.
- Print the text in large letters, using upper and lower case letters.
- Use dark colours, such as black, red, blue or green.

1 Fassen Sie den Text über die Vorbereitung einer Präsentation unter Beantwortung
KMK folgender Fragen auf Deutsch zusammen.

1. Warum soll eine Präsentation nicht schriftlich ausformuliert werden?
2. Wie soll eine Präsentation gegliedert sein?
3. Welche Vorteile bietet Anschauungsmaterial?
4. Wie müssen Folien aussehen, damit sie wirken?

2 Now listen to a presentation by Udo Moersen from the German subsidiary of
R Global Catering and complete the following text.
◎ A1.21

Good morning, ladies and gentlemen. **1** a few words about our company. Since
last January we have been a part of Global Catering Manchester but we are an
old-established Munich company producing a range of Bavarian specialities.

We have now entered the rapidly growing market for convenience foods, **2** a
range of freshly prepared dishes to quality supermarkets and delicatessens and **3**
the catering for company board meetings, conferences etc.

In Munich and internationally **4** of young business people (male and female)
who do not have the leisure to cook but who still demand high-quality,
imaginative, prepared meals which they can quickly pop into their briefcases on
their way home.

Our sales figures show that this is a growth market (I don't want to bore you **5**
which I hope you have all received). We are also exporting Bavarian specialities
to Britain and the USA via Global Catering and its subsidiaries. At the same time
we are importing British and American specialities to Germany.

6 that we look forward to rapid growth in these markets. Catering is a modern
industry with massive potential whose importance is still underestimated in
Germany **7**.

3 Udo Moersen used the following prompt cards for his presentation.
R Listen again and restore the correct order of his jumbled prompt cards.
◎ A1.21

① conclusion: growth industry

② part of Global Catering but old Munich company. Bavarian specialities!

③ target group: busy young professionals

④ supermarkets / delicatessens / corporate catering

⑤ sales figures (see handout!) exports to USA/UK; imports

✳ **4** Having studied the above information, hints and examples now start preparing
P your presentation of your company and its products. Write your prompt cards and
decide which visual aids you are going to use.

Content of your presentation:
- size, type, location, activities of company
- products in general, selection of products, services
- main markets, domestic/export
- sales figures
- special features of products e.g. state-of-the-art, environmentally friendly

 5 As your British boss frequently has to give presentations at changing venues,
she has asked you to find information on the latest computer projectors. She is
especially interested in lightweight compact models that are easy to carry and
cost under $500. Use the internet to find this information and make notes for her
in English.

B Delivering a presentation

> ### Useful tips
>
> It is a good idea NOT to read out a prepared text. It is easy to bore your audience.
> You make a much more lively impression if you speak freely using prompt cards
> and visual aids to remind you of the various points. This also helps to ensure
> that your body language is natural. If you are planning to use equipment such
> as an overhead projector or a computer projector, make sure a) they are working
> and b) you know how to operate them. Practise and rehearse your presentation,
> preferably with real people as an audience.
>
> - Do not speak too quickly (in order to get the whole thing over as quickly as
>   possible!)
> - Speak clearly – make sure everybody can hear you.
> - Do not speak monotonously – you will sound as if you are boring yourself and
>   will bore your audience!
> - Do not wave your arms around mechanically – your gestures should be
>   appropriate.
> - Look at your audience, establish eye contact.
> - Look happy and confident. Smile.
>
> It is very helpful for the person making the presentation to be given constructive,
> concrete and detailed feedback. Only in this way can they become aware of
> how they come across and how this can be changed. This is a prerequisite for
> developing skills in oral presentation.

1 Ein Kollege muss eine Präsentation halten und hat Sie um Rat gebeten.
KMK Schreiben Sie ihm eine E-Mail auf Deutsch und geben Sie ihm Hinweise für eine
Präsentation unter Verwendung der Informationen in „Useful tips".

✳ **2**
P/I
Now give your presentation on your company and its products to your fellow students. The other students listen to the presentation and assess it according to the following evaluation scheme. The audience should award points out of ten under each heading (on a separate sheet of paper).

Evaluation of presentation/checklist:

		Points
Preparation	evidence of careful preparation	▪
Structure	introduction, main body – clear emphasis on small number of important points – conclusion	▪
Content	relevance, well-substantiated with facts and figures	▪
Visual aids	appropriate use of simple, easy-to-understand visual aids	▪
Delivery	not too fast, eye contact, appropriate body language, confident, relaxed	▪
Language	no jargon, straightforward, use of signalling expressions like: "I should like to begin/conclude by …"	▪
Overall impression	lively, humorous, easy to follow, right length	▪

✳ **3**
R
The following is an example of a more ambitious presentation using visual aids. At an investment seminar Daniela Webb gives a brief presentation on the Limpopo Mining Company and its products, using a computer projector. Make a list of expressions that would be useful in any presentation.

"Good morning, ladies and gentlemen. I should like to give a brief presentation on our company and its products in the context of this investment seminar.

I'll begin by showing you a graph illustrating the rising demand for zinc and copper worldwide and the development of production at our sites in Asia and Africa. As a result of the strength of the world economy and particularly rapid growth in China and India demand for our products has soared dramatically over the last two years.

At the same time we are investing strongly in the development of our sites. This is a photograph of construction work on our new site in Kazakhstan. As you can see from this graph, production there jumped by 20% last year. We are also spending a large slice of our profits on exploration.
The pie chart shows what proportion of our expenditure goes on the construction and development of sites and the exploration of new sites.

In conclusion, I should like to emphasise that demand for our products is expected to be strong in the foreseeable future. I am sure that this brief presentation will have shown you that Limpopo Mining shares will add some excitement to your investment portfolio.

Thank you very much indeed for your time. I shall be very pleased to answer any questions you may have."

Language and grammar: Describing graphs

Statistics are easier to read if they are presented in the form of bar charts, line graphs or pie charts. When making a presentation, you may have to describe graphs. The expressions given on the following page will be helpful.

Developments over time can be visualised by **line graphs**.

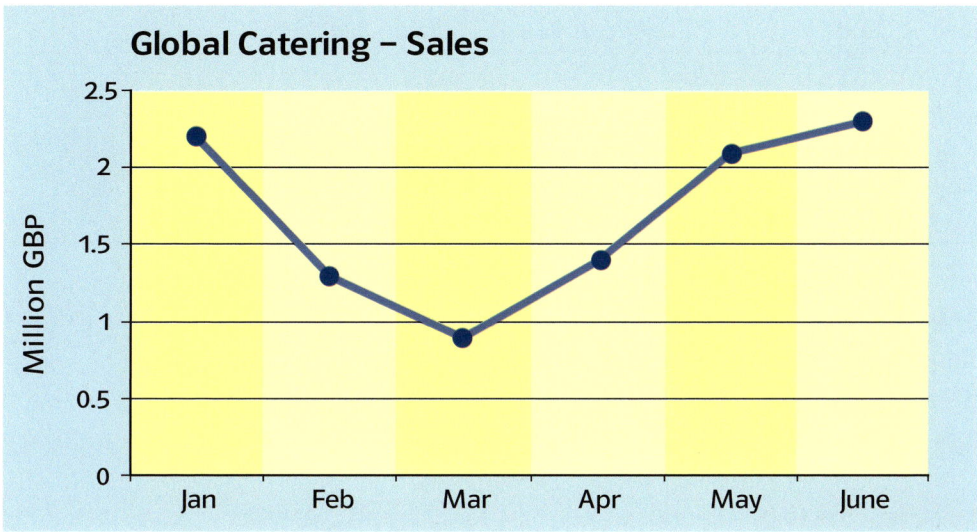

Global Catering – Sales

V3 Video lounge Presentations

lingua tv

This video shows a presentation given by a senior Purple Fashion executive. After watching it answer the following questions:

1. Does the presenter make a natural impression?
2. Do you find her gestures and smile convincing?
3. Why is it not necessary to take notes?
4. When does she plan to answer questions?
5. When and where was Purple Fashion founded?
6. Is this her actual presentation?
7. What in her view is Purple Fashion's "obsession"?

To describe developments

1. upwards to rise / increase / go up / jump **by … from … to …** to reach a peak / maximum of …	Between May and July exports rose by 5% from 10,000 units to 10,050 units. In June prices reached a peak of €75.	
2. unchanged to remain / stay unchanged / stable / flat **at …** to fluctuate **between … and …**	Sales remained unchanged at 750m units. In the second quarter oil prices fluctuated between 42 and 61 dollars per barrel.	
3. downwards to fall / decline / go down / drop / slump **by … from … to …** to reach a low / minimum **of …** / the lowest point **at …**	Last year the average price dropped by 2% from € 100 to €98. In March the lowest point was reached at 28 dollars.	

At a meeting Kirsty Burnham from Global Catering in Manchester presents her company to a gathering of potential customers. She refers to the last half year's sales and to the line graph on the preceding page.

4 **Read her description and find the correct prepositions from the box.**

> at • by • from • of • of • to • to • to

In January sales stood **1** 2.2 million pounds. Then there was a dramatic decline **2** GBP 1.3m in February. Sales continued to fall steadily and reached the minimum **3** 0.9m in March. Between March and May, however, sales jumped **4** 0.9m **6** 2.1m. In June sales had risen **7** around 9% **6** the peak **8** 2.3 million pounds.

5 **Choose the correct adjective or adverb.**
See *Language and grammar* in Unit 9.

1. In January imports fell (sharp / sharply).
2. Sales remained (constant / constantly) for three months.
3. A (slight / slightly) increase in prices had been expected.
4. There was a (gradual / gradually) fall in turnover.
5. Oil prices have been rising (dramatic / dramatically).

To describe the speed or degree of change

slight(ly)
slow(ly)
moderate(ly)
gradual(ly)
steady / steadily
significant(ly)
sharp(ly)
dramatic(ally)

In the second quarter there was a **dramatic** increase in sales. In June imports rose **sharply**.

Industry expert

1 Climate change – a challenge for the manufacturing industry

1 Nowadays, when watching the news you
P can see all kinds of climate catastrophes: floods, landslides, devastating fires. What do you feel about this? Discuss in class.

2 Read the text and summarize what
R manufacturing companies can do to reduce their carbon footprint.

Environmental policy expert Klaus Töpfer's anwer is simple and to the point: "There must be a clear vision that mother earth has a limited capacity. We have to use our brains to find new solutions to the existing problems. The differences between natural catastrophes and human-made catastrophes are becoming more and more indistinct."

It is an inconvenient truth that we risk causing climate change through the emission of greenhouse gases. According to scientists, changes in the way we behave are urgent. We must all reduce our carbon footprint.

For manufacturing companies this can be a challenge in several ways. First of all, they can invest money in renewable energies like wind and solar power or hydropower.

They can also do research in the field of e-mobility (e.g. on e-bikes and electric cars) to become market leaders in these emerging markets. Additionally, they can minimise their carbon footprint.

Most of our electricity is generated by fossil fuels like coal, oil or gas. Companies can reduce their consumption of electricity and use alternative energy sources. Wind power, for example, is produced without the carbon dioxide emissions which are destroying our ozone layer. Furthermore, they can reduce, reuse or recycle packaging. Partnerships with suppliers can be established to reuse materials. Finally, employees have to be made fully aware of the concept of the carbon footprint in order to encourage their environmental commitment.

3 Translate the following key words of the text and explain the meanings in your
M own words.

1. emission
2. greenhouse gases
3. carbon footprint
4. renewable energies
5. wind power
6. solar power
7. hydropower
8. e-mobility
9. fossil fuels
10. carbon dioxide
11. ozone layer
12. environmental commitment

✳ **4** Ms Carolin Bossi, Expertin für Nachhaltigkeit in Industrieunternehmen, spricht
KMK in einem Interview mit Susan Maier über Energieeffizienz. Beantworten Sie
◎ A 2.3 stichwortartig die folgenden Fragen auf Deutsch. Sie hören den Text zweimal.

1. Ms Bossi glaubt, dass wir eine Offensive für erneuerbare Energien benötigen. Welche vier Energiearten nennt Sie in diesem Zusammenhang?
2. Wie viel Prozent des Energiebedarfs wird heutzutage durch fossile Brennstoffe erzeugt?
3. Warum müssen Großstädte eine führende Rolle bei der Bekämpfung des Klimawandels einnehmen?
4. Welche Beispiele für eine nachhaltige Städteplanung werden von Ms Bossi genannt?
5. Wie kann sichergestellt werden, dass möglichst viele Leute Zugang zu erneuerbaren Energien haben?
6. Welche Maßnahmen sind notwendig, um einen Wandel in der Energiepolitik durchzuführen?
7. Welche Länder sind für mehr als zwei Drittel des weltweiten Schadstoffausstoßes verantwortlich?

2 Production and sustainability

1 Sie arbeiten bei dem Getränkedosenhersteller Can GmbH. Auf einer
KMK Handelsmesse möchte Ihr Unternehmen seine Leitlinien zur umweltfreundlichen
Produktion vorstellen. Ihre Aufgabe ist es, die wesentlichen Aussagen der
folgenden Unternehmensleitlinien in die englische Sprache zu übertragen.

Can GmbH und Nachhaltigkeit

→ Als globales Unternehmen sind wir uns bewusst darüber, dass unsere Aktivitäten Auswirkungen auf unsere Umwelt haben – dieses Umweltbewusstsein ist ein wichtiges Element der nachhaltigen Entwicklung.

→ Wir entwickeln umweltfreundliche Produkte mit modernster Technik. In unseren Fertigungsprozessen stellen wir sicher, dass die Umweltbestimmungen und Standards eingehalten werden.

→ Durch verschiedene Maßnahmen, wie z. B. einer verbesserten Energieausnutzung bei der Produktion, haben wir eine Materialverringerung von 40 Prozent erreicht.

→ Gleichzeitig konnte die Treibhausgasemission unserer Produktionsanlagen unter die im Kyoto-Protokoll festgelegten Ziele reduziert werden.

→ Zudem unterstützen wir seit Jahrzehnten Recyclingprogramme weltweit.

→ Wir arbeiten mit Organisationen zusammen, um für eine nachhaltige Entwicklung zu sorgen.

2 Work in teams of 3–4 students. Read the following e-mail from Anne Miller.
P/I Agree on one company you work for and prepare a PowerPoint presentation for it. Use the checklist below to make suggestions for supporting or introducing environmental standards in your company. Also use other sources to inform yourself more about this subject, e.g. internet, magazines, newspapers.

Phrases

From:	a.miller@future.com
To:	(your name)@future.com
Cc:	m.fyfe@future.com; d.pourramazan@future.com
Sent:	201_-03-18 11:59
Attachments:	
Subject:	Eco-friendly company

Dear Mr / Mrs …
The managing directors of our company have decided to become an eco-friendly company and to introduce environmental standards. In the long run we would like to achieve the internationally recognised ISO 14001 certification.
As a first step we would like to ask you to prepare suggestions of how we can minimise our environmental impact. We expect a PowerPoint presentation of your ideas by next week.
Best regards
Anne Miller
Assistant to the Managing Directors

Checklist
* air-conditioning
* biodiesel
* campaign for employees
* consumption
* customers
* distances
* generating power
* packaging
* rainwater harvesting
* suppliers
* waste disposal
* water, electricity, gas

Info: PowerPoint presentation

A PowerPoint presentation should be informative and entertaining with the focus on the speaker – **not** on the slides. A useful rule is: KISS – Keep it Straight and Simple. Other important aspects are:
* A presentation should consist of approximately ten slides.
* There should only be one message per slide.
* The sentence structure should be simple.
* Do not use more than two font types.
* The font size should be at least 16.
* Focus on colours of one family.
* Avoid special effects.

3   Choosing a factory location

1 There are many factors which can influence a company's decision about where to
P build a new factory. Depending on the industry or on the company's preferences, some factors are more important than others. Discuss the factors shown in the mind map in class.

Phrases ▶

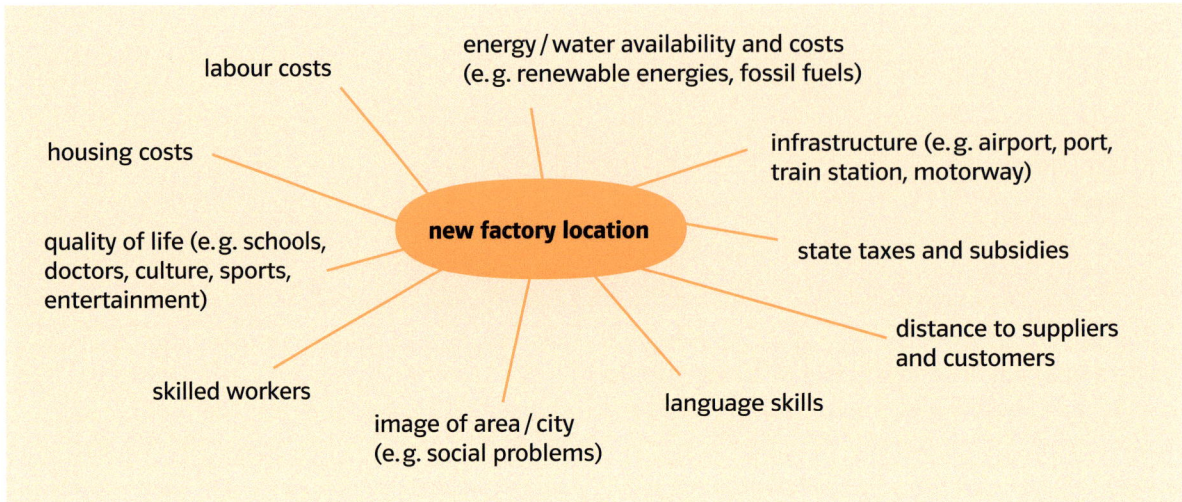

labour costs

energy / water availability and costs
(e.g. renewable energies, fossil fuels)

housing costs

infrastructure (e.g. airport, port,
train station, motorway)

new factory location

quality of life (e.g. schools,
doctors, culture, sports,
entertainment)

state taxes and subsidies

distance to suppliers
and customers

skilled workers

language skills

image of area / city
(e.g. social problems)

2 A Japanese car manufacturer wants to build a plant at which a new car model
I for the European market will be manufactured. The CEO, Hillary Simmons, has taken two different locations into consideration. The first one is in Stuttgart, Germany, and the second one in Cluj, Romania.

Work in teams of five students and prepare a meeting. Use the role cards below and coordinate your roles. Add more advantages and disadvantages to underline your standpoint. Then present the meeting in a role play in class.

Phrases ▶

CEO
- Organise the meeting
- Take the vote and reach a final decision
- Consider the company's carbon footprint (e.g. pollution, distance to suppliers)

Sales Manager
- You are undecided
- Romania: low costs → low sales price
- Germany: good infrastructure, short distance to customers

Finance Manager
- You are for Romania
- Cheap housing and labour costs
- Tax relief as incentive from state – unemployment is high

Personnel Manager
- You are undecided
- Romania: high unemployment rate, many skilled and semi-skilled workers
- Germany: a lot of skilled workers, high quality of life (e.g. schools, leisure facilities)

Marketing Manager
- You are for Germany
- Mostly German customers
- "Made in Germany" is a sales argument

Phrases: Making presentations

To make a presentation

I should like to start **by** telling you something about my company/organisation.	Zunächst möchte ich Ihnen etwas über meine Firma/mein Unternehmen sagen.
First, I should like to introduce my company briefly.	Als Erstes möchte ich Ihnen mein Unternehmen kurz vorstellen.
My presentation will deal **with** …	Meine Präsentation behandelt …
I intend to keep my presentation as brief as possible.	Ich möchte meine Präsentation so kurz wie möglich halten.
I would like to focus **on** the following points/areas/products/services:	Ich möchte mich auf folgende Punkte/Gebiete/Produkte/Dienstleistungen konzentrieren:
I would welcome any questions **at** the end of my presentation.	Ich wäre gern bereit, etwaige Fragen am Ende meiner Präsentation zu beantworten.
Has everyone received a copy of the handout?	Haben alle den Handzettel bekommen?
The handout summarises the main points and gives an overview of the relevant figures and statistics.	Der Handzettel enthält die Hauptpunkte und gibt einen Überblick über die entsprechenden Zahlen und Statistiken.

To structure the main part of your presentation

Now my second point is …	Ich komme nun zu Punkt 2 …
Thirdly, let me give you some basic statistics.	Drittens darf ich Ihnen ein paar grundlegende Statistiken zeigen.
The gist of the matter/central issue is …	Der Kernpunkt/die zentrale Frage ist …
I should now like to move **on** to the next topic.	Ich möchte nun gern zum nächsten Thema kommen.
An excellent example **of** this is …	Ein hervorragendes Beispiel dafür ist …
I should like to give you an example to illustrate this point.	Ich möchte diesen Punkt mit einem Beispiel erläutern.
A distinct trend emerges **from** the figures.	Aus den Zahlen geht ein deutlicher Trend hervor.
In this connection it is worth mentioning …	In diesem Zusammenhang sollte man erwähnen, …

To conclude your presentation

To sum **up** we can say that …	Zusammenfassend kann man sagen, dass …
I should like to finish **by** saying/thanking the organisers/pointing out …	Ich möchte schließen mit der Bemerkung/dem Dank an die Organisatoren/dem Hinweis …

Unit 8
Form of written communication

WORD BANK

e-mail • facsimile message • letter • sender • letterhead • addressee • recipient • attention line • reference line • date • attachment • subject • salutation • initials • complimentary close • signature • covering page • enclosure • structure • paragraph • style • linking words • to attach • to delete • to forward

Written communication plays an essential role in business in cases where documentation in writing is required. It may, for instance, also be used to ensure that misunderstandings cannot arise. However, in recent years the traditional letter has increasingly been replaced by new, quicker and frequently less formal media. In business correspondence the letter has now largely been replaced by e-mails and to a lesser degree by faxes.

1 Work with a partner. Make a grid for yourself like the one below. Then read the text that follows
R and fill in your grid. Compare the result with your partner's information in the grid.

	Advantages	Disadvantages
E-Mail		
Letter		
Fax		

Online-Link
808262-0008

The advantages of **e-mails** are too well-known to require explanation here. However, there are a number of disadvantages. Spam is a major time waster. According to one source 95% of e-mails sent worldwide are spam. Hence the need to install spam filters. Security is also a major issue. E-mails and attachments may be used to transfer spyware and other viruses. Privacy is also a problem – you cannot be sure that your e-mails are not being read by an unauthorised third party. Finally, authenticity – who is the e-mail really from? – is a further issue undermining the reliability and safety of e-mails which can be addressed by installing digital signatures. Sometimes one might feel it's safer to entrust one's important message to the old-fashioned snail-mail!

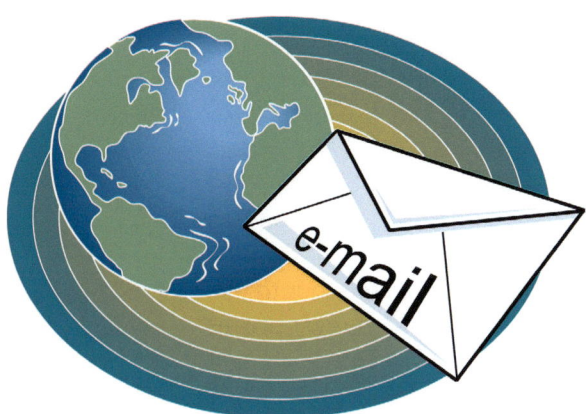

In international business transactions **faxes** are used to communicate with partners in countries where the e-mail system is still unsatisfactory or unreliable. Faxes are also preferred to e-mails whenever business people want their partners to have some written (and possibly signed) evidence of a transaction. Faxes, like e-mails, may also be used where speed is essential, e.g. for offers. Signatures on faxes are nowadays recognised as evidence even by the courts.

The business **letter** is still widely used in legal contexts, in connection with formal contracts and complaints. Such letters are often "faxed and posted", i.e. sent by fax and by post. Only a letter ensures that the communication is not read by an unauthorised person. Letters also serve as covering letters when a catalogue or similar enclosure is to be sent.

2 Translate the following English sentences into German.

M

1. Letters have largely been replaced by e-mails.
2. E-mails can be addressed to several people at the same time.
3. Worms and viruses may make it necessary to instal protective software.
4. It is a disadvantage that e-mails cannot easily be signed.
5. In some countries the e-mail system is unsatisfactory or unreliable.
6. It may sometimes be necessary to have written evidence of a transaction.
7. Business letters are still widely used in connection with formal contracts.
8. A letter is less likely to be read by unauthorised persons.

Layout and components of business correspondence

1 E-Mails*

From:	stella.starr@shineandsparkle-uk.com
To:	info@sunshineflights.co.uk
Cc:	f.pluto@shineandsparkle-usa.com
Sent:	201_-08-14 15:18
Attachments:	
Subject:	Package tours to the Dominican Republic

Dear Sunshine Flights — salutation

As an incentive we wish to offer a one-week package tour to the Dominican Republic to our most successful sales representatives. Please make us preliminary offers for at least three price categories. — body of e-mail

Kind regards — complimentary close

Stella Starr
Marketing Manager — signature block

Shine and Sparkle UK Ltd.
143 High Street
Starminster
BS34 1BU
Tel. 01420 562 265 — signature footer

* Both ways of spelling are acceptable, **e-mail** and **email**.

Info: E-mails

From:	Your e-mail address will appear automatically.
To:	Be careful not to make the slightest mistake when entering the recipient's address, or else the e-mail will be returned.
Cc:	The abbreviation stands for "carbon copy". With old-style typewriters copies used to be made by inserting carbon paper between the blank sheets of paper. This is where you enter the addresses of the persons to whom you wish the message to be forwarded.
Bcc:	Addresses listed under "Blind Carbon Copy" do not appear in the message header of the other recipients.
Sent:	Instead of "Sent" you may find the word "Date". The correct date and time will be entered automatically.
Attachments:	Any kind of file, such as word documents (.doc), excel sheets (.xls), pictures (e.g. .jpg), etc. can be attached to an e-mail.
Subject:	You should always mention the precise subject matter of your correspondence. Firstly it will help your business partner to deal with your mail and secondly it will prevent him / her from deleting it for fear of viruses.
Salutation:	Very formal salutations like "Dear Sirs" or "Gentlemen:" are not used in e-mails. Use "Dear …" instead. In the English-speaking world correspondence is personalised whenever possible: Dear Fiona Dear Ms Starr or even (to avoid "Dear Sirs"): Dear Sunshine Flights
Body of the e-mail:	Note that the first word starts with a capital letter.
Complimentary close:	There is a range of expressions to choose from, like: With best / kind regards Kind / Best regards Regards Best wishes or (very formal in e-mails) Yours sincerely
Signature block:	Write your title or department below your name. In Britain women often add (Miss) or (Mrs) in brackets after their name, e.g. Janine Smith (Miss), if they wish to be addressed in this way.
Signature footer:	Add your company's full name, address and telephone number to all e-mails you send to persons or companies who may not know you or your firm.

Do not use special characters like ß, ä, ö or ü. They may come out very strangely at the other end! Use ss, ae, oe and ue instead.

1   **Choose the appropriate alternative from the brackets.**

1. You may (enclose/attach) files to an e-mail.
2. You should always watch out for (viruses/germs).
3. Make sure that you (wipe out/delete) suspicious e-mails.
4. E-mails can be (passed on/forwarded) to third parties.
5. Do not forget to mention the (theme/subject) of your e-mail.
6. E-mails always start with the (complimentary close/salutation).
7. The recipient or (addressee/sender) is the person the e-mail is sent to.

2   **Study the example e-mail on page 112. Then restore the correct order of the jumbled elements below and rewrite the e-mail.**

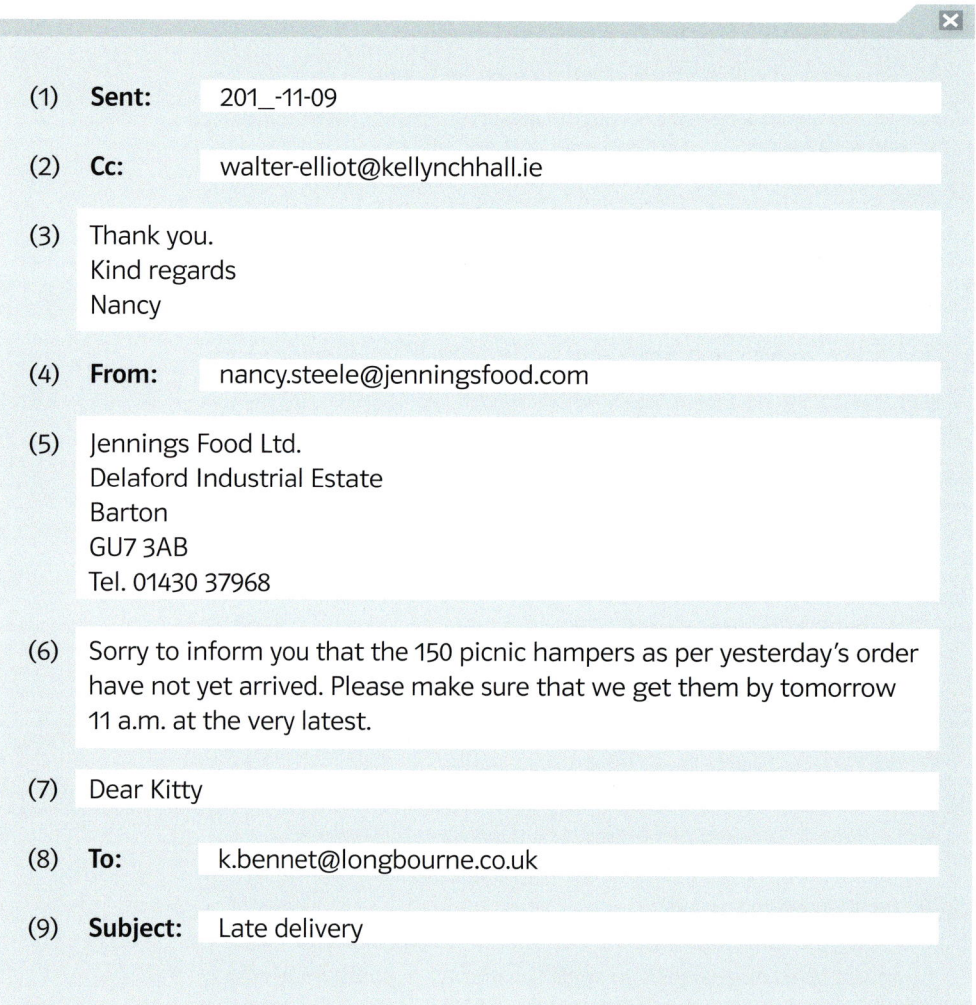

(1)   **Sent:**   201_-11-09

(2)   **Cc:**   walter-elliot@kellynchhall.ie

(3)   Thank you.
Kind regards
Nancy

(4)   **From:**   nancy.steele@jenningsfood.com

(5)   Jennings Food Ltd.
Delaford Industrial Estate
Barton
GU7 3AB
Tel. 01430 37968

(6)   Sorry to inform you that the 150 picnic hampers as per yesterday's order have not yet arrived. Please make sure that we get them by tomorrow 11 a.m. at the very latest.

(7)   Dear Kitty

(8)   **To:**   k.bennet@longbourne.co.uk

(9)   **Subject:**   Late delivery

3 Search the Internet and find out about "netiquette" and "texting abbreviations". Make notes and compare your findings with the group. Send a text message in English using appropriate abbreviations to one of your classmates.

Info: How to write e-mails

- Keep messages short and to the point.
- Focus on one subject per message and include a relevant subject title for the message.
- Include your signature footer when communicating with persons who may not know you personally.
- Capitalize words only to highlight an important point. Capitalizing is generally felt to be like SHOUTING!
- Be sparing in your use of exclamation marks.
- Never send chain letters through the Internet.
- Be professional and be careful what you say. E-mails are easily forwarded.
- Be careful when using sarcasm and humour.
- Never assume that your e-mails will be read only by you and the recipient.
- Emoticons like :-) for "happy" or ;-) for "only joking" should be reserved for communication with business partners with whom you are on a familiar footing.
- Use abbreviations sparingly as you cannot be sure that your partner in a foreign country is familiar with them.

4 Your colleague does not speak English. Explain the above information to him
M in German.

You might begin like this:
„Ich habe im Internet interessante Hinweise über das, was man bei E-Mails beachten soll, gefunden. Der Text beginnt mit der Ermahnung E-Mails kurz und präzise zu formulieren. Man soll sich auf ein Thema pro Mail beschränken und einen passenden Betreff wählen …"

2 Faxes

There is no established layout for faxes (facsimile messages). Firms are free to design their own covering page. A typical one could look like this:

Herkules
the global sports brand

Ziegelberg 8–12
89331 Neustadt
Tel. +49 8358 888-0
Fax +49 8358 88820
www.Herkules.com

Telefax Message

To: India Sports
112 Delhi Road, Meerut-250 001
Uttar Pradesh, India

Attention: Mr. Kunal Mahajan

Fax: +91 121 2512275

From: Laura Bayerle, Purchasing Department

Date: 1 Feb 201_

Pages: (incl. this page) 1

Subject: Our order No. ABF / 16 of 20 January

Dear Mr. Mahajan

If it is possible, we should like to increase our order for item 345 (plain navy T-shirts) from 1750 to 2000 units for the sizes L and XL.

Please let me know by return whether you are in a position to dispatch the extra articles together with the rest of our order.

Thank you very much.

Regards

Laura Bayerle
Laura Bayerle

If you do not receive all the pages, please advise us as soon as possible.

Info: Fax

The **names, addresses, telephone** and **fax numbers** of both the sender and the addressee should be recorded on the fax. The **date** is also essential as well as an appropriate **subject line**. As fax transmissions are sometimes interrupted, the **number of pages** is mentioned to show the recipient whether any pages are missing. If you send a business letter by fax, write the recipient's fax number below the inside address and refer to the total number of pages on the first page.

1 Use the fax on page 116 as an example and rewrite the following fax using the
P correct spacing and punctuation.

> Getränke König Am Sprudelbach 17 06122 Halle Tel. 0345 785634 Fax 0345 785635 Telefax To BIG Beverages Ltd 38 Cromwell Road Chipping OX7 5SR UK Fax +44 1608 647919 Attention Ms Maggy Lane From Nicole Sachse Import Department Date 31 Jan 201_ Pages incl. this one 1 Subject Our order for 500 bottles of Tropicana Fruit Juice of 28 Jan Dear Ms Lane I am sorry to cause you trouble but our client has just informed us that he needs the fruit juice as early as Friday next week I trust you will be able to bring forward delivery by three days Thank you for your co-operation Best wishes *Nicole Sachse* Nicole Sachse

2 Study the fax on page 116. Then restore the correct order of the jumbled elements
R/P below and rewrite the fax.

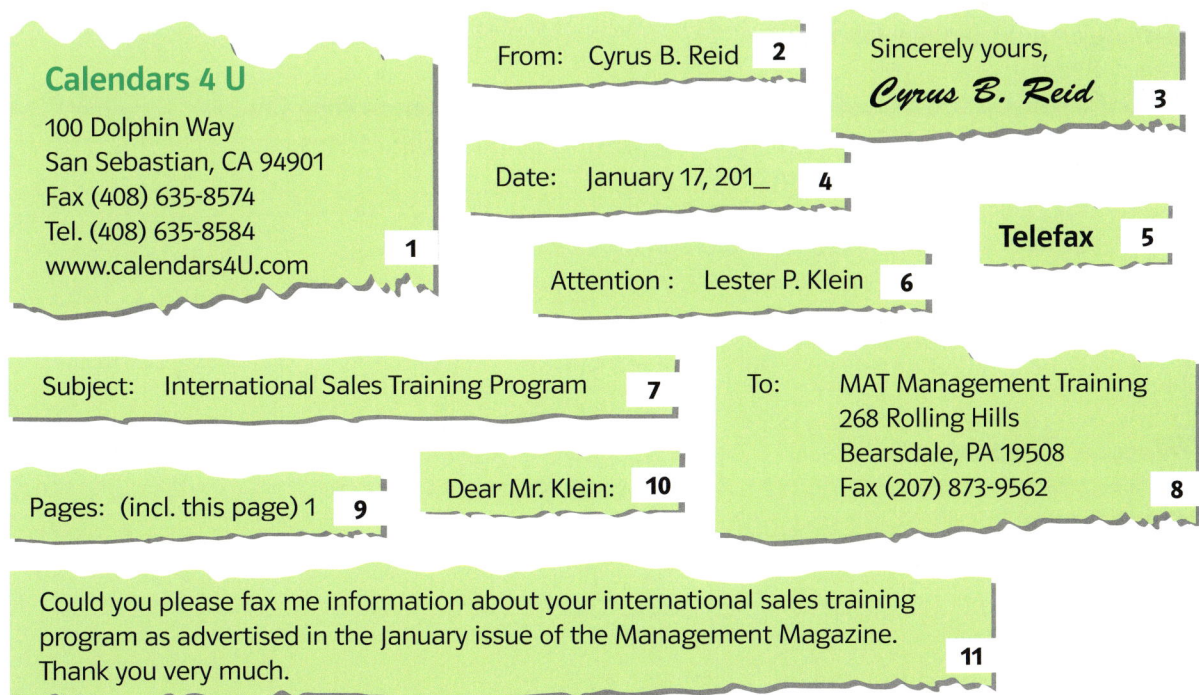

Calendars 4 U
100 Dolphin Way
San Sebastian, CA 94901
Fax (408) 635-8574
Tel. (408) 635-8584
www.calendars4U.com
1

From: Cyrus B. Reid   **2**

Date: January 17, 201_   **4**

Attention :   Lester P. Klein   **6**

Sincerely yours,
Cyrus B. Reid   **3**

Telefax   **5**

Subject: International Sales Training Program   **7**

To: MAT Management Training
268 Rolling Hills
Bearsdale, PA 19508
Fax (207) 873-9562   **8**

Dear Mr. Klein: **10**

Pages: (incl. this page) 1   **9**

Could you please fax me information about your international sales training program as advertised in the January issue of the Management Magazine. Thank you very much.   **11**

3 Business letters

1 Match the numbers (1–11) in the following business letter with the letters (A–K)
R   in the definitions given on the following pages.

International Snacks GmbH (1)

Fürstenstr. 19
40547 Düsseldorf
Tel. 0211 577563
Fax 0211 577566
E-Mail info@internationalsnacks.de
www.internationalsnacks.de

MD / rf   (2)

14 August 201_   (3)

Global Catering   (4)
17 Nelson Square
Manchester
MA17 3DF
UK

Attention: Ms Kirsty Burnham   (5)

Dear Ms Burnham   (6)

Brochure on rules and regulations   (7)

As promised on the occasion of your recent visit to our company I am sending you
enclosed the translation of the brochure on the German rules and regulations for
food processing in the catering industry.

May I take this opportunity of thanking you and Mr. Sears for your visit.
My colleagues and I greatly enjoyed meeting you in person.   (8)

Yours sincerely   (9)
International Snacks GmbH   (10)

Markus Diepholz

Markus Diepholz
Export Manager

Enc.   (11)

A Letterhead shows a company's logo, name and address, its telephone, fax and e-mail numbers and its Internet address.

B Reference line may show the initials of the signatory and the secretary or references to files or departments.

C Date

As 07/08/12 would mean 7 August 2012 for an Englishman and 8 July 2012 for an American, it is advisable to write out the month. The following ways of writing the date are recommended:

7 August 2012   or   7 Aug 2012   or   August 7, 2012

Note that the year is written out in full.

Giving the year first, then the month and then the day is rapidly becoming accepted worldwide: 2012-08-07.

D Inside address

British usage	North American usage
Messrs J. McDream & Co. 91 Malvern Road Ashford Kent CA3 6AH UK	Samantha Duvet The Mattress Corporation 1386 Munras Avenue Monterey, CA 93940 USA

Note that in British business letters Messrs, Mr, Mrs, Ms and Miss are written on the same line as the name. In the USA they are often omitted altogether. Messrs is only used for smaller firms, such as partnerships. Do not write Messrs if the company's name is followed by "Ltd", Plc", "Inc." or "Corp.". Ms should be used whenever the marital status of the female addressee is not known.

Note that in Great Britain the postal code is written on its own line below the place name, whereas in USA and Canada it is placed after the place name on the same line.

When letters are written to foreign countries, the name of the country should be shown on the final line of the inside address.

E Attention line ensures that the letter is dealt with by a specific person. You may write **Attention:**, **For the attention of …:**, or (less formal) **FAO:**
As an alternative the person's name may be included in the inside address. This is a must if the recipient is addressed by name in the salutation.

Global Catering
17 Nelson Square
Manchester
MA17 3DF
UK

Attention: Ms Kirsty Burnham

Ms Kirsty Burnham
Global Catering
17 Nelson Square
Manchester
MA17 3DF
UK

F Salutation (UK)

Dear Sirs, Dear Sir/Madam

Dear Ms Burnham
Dear Customer
Dear Margaret

G Complimentary close (UK)

Yours faithfully/sincerely
(Yours faithfully is rarely used now)
Yours sincerely, Kind regards
Yours sincerely
Best regards, Kind regards,
Best wishes

Salutation (USA and Canada)

(Ladies and) Gentlemen:
To whom it may concern:
Dear Mr O'Reilly:
Dear Sean:

Complimentary close (USA and Canada)

Sincerely, Very truly yours,
Sincerely, Sincerely yours,
Yours truly, Sincerely, Sincerely yours,
Regards, Cordially,

If at all possible you should address the person you are writing to by name. "Dear Sirs" or "Gentlemen:" is only used when you do not have a name to write to. Traditionally salutation and complimentary close should be in line with each other.

H Body of the letter

Note that in English the first word of a business letter starts with a capital letter.

I Subject line

may be preceded by the words "Subject" or "Re" and should be as specific as possible. Do not just write **"Your offer"** but **"Your offer for mouse pads of 23 May"**. In the UK subject lines are normally written below the salutation, in the USA above the salutation. They may be either underlined or typed in capital letters or bold type.

J Enclosure

Whenever enclosures are sent with a letter, a reference to the enclosure is required at the bottom of the letter. You may write "Enclosure(s)" or "Enc(s)".

K Signature block

In the UK – but not in the USA – the signature block often begins with the company's name. The signatory's name and title (or department) are typed below the signature. If somebody signs the letter on behalf of another person, the other person's name is typed below the signature, preceded by the word **"for"** or by the abbreviation **pp.** meaning "on behalf of".

NetOrbiter Ltd.

Maria Bertram

pp. Henry Crawford
Chief Information Officer

Fred Parry

for Betty Bickerton
Credit Manager

2 Work with a partner. Find the right order for these jumbled addresses. Then dictate them to your partner.

UK Woodbridge Messrs Frost & Winter 22 James Street Suffolk IP3 7KL Managerial Skills Training	Ultimate IT Solutions Inc. USA Denver, CO 80121 Barbara Goodyear 1280 Mayflower Drive	Attention: Tom Finch 4 Tamar Industrial Estate UK Finch Electronics Ltd. PL3 7CT Plymouth

3 Seven elements are missing from this traditional business letter. Copy the letter
R/P and add the missing elements using your own imagination for details.

Superdress GmbH

Fritz-Walter-Str. 28, 80469 München
Tel. +49 89 4677524, Fax +49 89 4677625
www.superdress.munich.de

TS / is

Mr Tony Shaw
Wilson and Thatcher Ltd.
2 Brook Lane
Bristol
BS9 2ET

We are pleased to enclose our Spring Catalogue showing our absolutely fabulous range of shirts. We feel sure that they will appeal to your young customers. If you place an order within the next two weeks, you will be granted 3% early order discount.

We look forward to welcoming you as a customer.

Resi Martl

Language and grammar 1
Decide which of the alternatives in brackets is correct.

1. I suggest (that you wait/to wait) for the outcome of the inspection.
2. We would appreciate (if you could/it if you could) let us have your confirmation by return.
3. We would appreciate (receiving/to receive) your prompt reply.
4. We would like to (excuse us/apologize) for not having reacted earlier.
5. Please (excuse/apologize) the inconvenience caused by this incident.
6. We look forward (to doing/to do) business with you.
7. We hope (to be entrusted/to being entrusted) with your order.
8. I would appreciate (to hear/hearing) from you soon.
9. We would suggest (to ring/ringing) Fisher's bookshop in Cambridge.
10. I would appreciate (it if you sent/if you sent) a driver to the airport.

* Language and grammar 2
Find the English equivalents of the following German phrases.

1. Wir möchten uns für die entstandenen Unannehmlichkeiten entschuldigen.
2. Wir sehen Ihrer baldigen Antwort mit Interesse entgegen.
3. Bitte entschuldigen Sie dieses Versehen.
4. Wir hoffen, bald wieder von Ihnen zu hören.
5. Wir schlagen vor, die Teile per Luftfracht zu schicken.
6. Wir möchten Ihnen vorschlagen, die Sache mit der Geschäftsleitung zu besprechen.
7. Wir wären Ihnen für eine ausführliche Beschreibung sehr dankbar.
8. Ich würde vorschlagen, ein Taxi zu nehmen.
9. Wir freuen uns, Ihren Auftrag in Kürze zu erhalten.
10. Für diese Verzögerung bitten wir um Entschuldigung.

Language and grammar:
Typical mistakes in business correspondence

Wer diese Verben korrekt verwendet, vermeidet die häufigsten Fehler, die Deutschen beim Verfassen englischer Geschäftskorrespondenz unterlaufen.

suggest (vorschlagen)
We suggest **repeating** the test.
We suggest **that you (we) repeat** the test.
falsch: We suggest to repeat the test.

appreciate (schätzen, begrüßen, dankbar sein, anerkennen)
(a) We would appreciate **it** if you could assist us.
(**"it"** is absolutely necessary here!)
(b) We would appreciate **receiving** the unit as soon as possible.
falsch: We would appreciate to receive the unit as soon as possible.

apologize (sich entschuldigen)
We **apologize for** the delay.
falsch: We ~~excuse us~~ for the delay.

excuse (verzeihen, entschuldigen)
Please **excuse** the delay.
falsch: Please ~~apologize~~ the delay.

look forward to (entgegensehen, sich freuen auf)
We look forward to **hearing** from you soon.
falsch: We look forward to ~~hear~~ from you soon.

hope (hoffen)
We hope **to hear** from you soon.
falsch: We hope to ~~hearing~~ from you soon.

Communicating across cultures:
The tone of English business correspondence

What is considered polite differs in different cultures. For example, one-word answers such as "ja", "nein" are not impolite in German. If I say: "Sollen wir ins Kino gehen?", you could answer "Ja" in German. In English people would be more inclined to say "Yes, that would be nice / great". Thus, German business correspondence tends to be factual and to the point. Polite phrases are often considered superfluous. While this abrupt tone is generally accepted in Germany, it may seem rude to English-speaking people or sound as though you are not interested. That is why you ought to aim to make frequent use of expressions like: **We would like to** (inform you); **I would be grateful** (if you could help me), **I am afraid** (the system is not running smoothly); **We are very sorry** (to inform you); **Would you be so kind as** (to inform us in time) in your English correspondence. Do not forget to insert the word **please** whenever you make a request, e.g.: If we can be of further assistance **please** do not hesitate to contact us.
Note: Please do not say: ~~We kindly ask you~~ …, say **We would like to ask you** … instead.

Phrases: Correspondence – E-mail, Letter, Fax

To refer to previous communication

Thank you very much for your letter **of** …	Wir danken Ihnen für Ihren Brief vom …
Many thanks for your e-mail/e-mail.	Vielen Dank für Ihre E-Mail.
We refer to your fax **of** …	Wir nehmen Bezug auf Ihr Fax vom …
Further to our discussion **on** 2 May …	Im Anschluss an unser Gespräch am 2. Mai …

To ask for something

Please let us have …	Wir bitten Sie um …
Would you please send us …	Bitte schicken Sie uns …
Please be so kind **as** to send us …	Wir bitten Sie höflich uns … zu schicken.
We **would** like to ask you for …	Wir möchten Sie um … bitten.
Please make sure that …	Bitte sorgen Sie dafür, dass …

To communicate good news

We are pleased to inform you that …	Wir freuen uns Ihnen mitteilen zu können, dass …
You will be pleased to hear that …	Sie werden sich bestimmt darüber freuen, dass …
It is particularly gratifying that …	Besonders erfreulich ist, dass …

To refuse something

I'm afraid I cannot agree **to** this proposal.	Leider muss ich diesen Vorschlag ablehnen.
I'm afraid that sounds quite unacceptable **to** us.	Das ist für uns leider völlig inakzeptabel.
Much as we regret it, we have to say no.	Zu unserem großen Bedauern müssen wir eine abschlägige Antwort geben.
We regret that we are unable to assist you.	Wir bedauern, Ihnen nicht behilflich sein zu können.

To apologize

We are very sorry but …	Es tut uns sehr leid, aber …
We **would** like to apologize for the delay.	Wir möchten uns für die Verspätung entschuldigen.

| Please accept our apologies for this. | Wir entschuldigen uns dafür. |
| Please excuse the mix-up. | Bitte entschuldigen Sie die Verwechslung. |

To make a suggestion

We would suggest that you send us a copy.	Wir schlagen Ihnen vor, uns eine Kopie zu schicken.
May we suggest that you inform the supplier.	Wir möchten vorschlagen, den Lieferanten zu benachrichtigen.
It would be advisable to send the details **by** fax.	Es wäre gut, wenn Sie uns die näheren Angaben faxen könnten.

To request that something is done by a certain date

We need the components **by** Friday **at** the very latest.	Wir benötigen die Teile spätestens Freitag.
Please make sure that they arrive **no** later **than** the end of April.	Bitte sorgen Sie dafür, dass sie spätestens Ende April ankommen.
Monday, 31 July, is the final deadline.	Montag, der 31. Juli, ist der letzte Termin.

To end a correspondence on a friendly note

We **look forward to hearing** from you.	Wir sehen Ihrer Antwort mit Interesse entgegen.
We **hope to hear** from you soon.	Wir hoffen, bald von Ihnen zu hören.
We look forward to a long and fruitful business relationship.	Wir freuen uns auf lange und lohnende Geschäftsbeziehungen mit Ihrer Firma.
We look forward to serving you again.	Wir freuen uns darauf, Ihnen wieder zu Diensten sein zu können.
We look forward to welcoming you as our customers.	Wir würden Sie gerne als neuen Kunden begrüßen.
We hope this proposal will be of interest **to** you.	Wir hoffen, dieser Vorschlag findet Ihr Interesse.
We hope this information **will** help you.	Wir hoffen, dass diese Auskunft hilfreich für Sie ist.
Thank you for your assistance.	Wir danken Ihnen für Ihre Bemühungen.

Unit 9
Enquiries

WORD BANK
enquiries • transactions •
supplier • source of information •
website • quotation • cost
estimate • brochure • price list •
terms and conditions • samples
• trade discount • quantity
discount • cash discount •
introductory discount

Business transactions often start with enquiries. **General enquiries** are requests for brochures, pricelists etc. and for information about business terms. **Specific enquiries** give particulars about the goods/ services requested and ask for detailed **quotations**.

The internet is now the most convenient way of locating possible suppliers and this is facilitated by the use of search engines. Traditional sources of information, such as chambers of commerce, yellow pages and trade associations have their own websites offering links to many potential suppliers. Trade fairs and exhibitions, visits by agents and advertising campaigns also provide information on new products.

Read the text above and translate the German sentences into English.

M

1. Die Suche nach Lieferanten im Internet wird durch Suchmaschinen sehr erleichtert.
2. Industrie- und Handelskammern, Gelbe Seiten und Branchenverbände geben auch über das Internet Auskunft.
3. Auch auf Messen und Ausstellungen sowie durch Werbekampagnen und den Besuch eines Vertreters werden neue Produkte bekannt gemacht.

Online-Link
808262-0009

A Enquiries in writing

Sarah Brookfield, purchasing manager at SPORTS ISLAND, a British sports equipment chain, is interested in the latest running shoes presented by Herkules, the German manufacturers, on their website. She decides to make further enquiries by e-mail.

1
R
Study Sarah's e-mail enquiry and say which of the prepositions in brackets are correct.

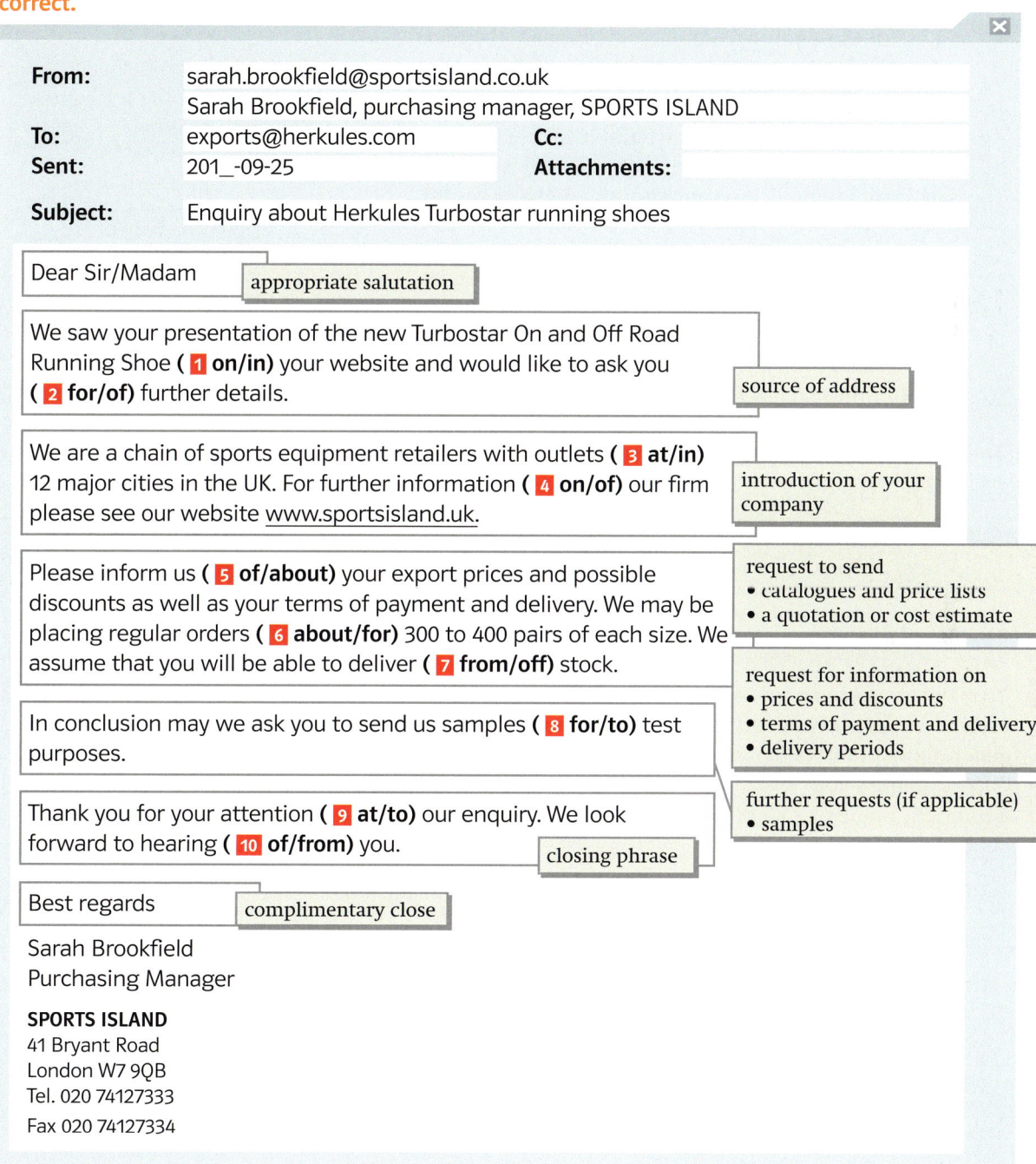

From:	sarah.brookfield@sportsisland.co.uk		
	Sarah Brookfield, purchasing manager, SPORTS ISLAND		
To:	exports@herkules.com	Cc:	
Sent:	201_-09-25	Attachments:	
Subject:	Enquiry about Herkules Turbostar running shoes		

Dear Sir/Madam   **appropriate salutation**

We saw your presentation of the new Turbostar On and Off Road Running Shoe (**1** on/in) your website and would like to ask you (**2** for/of) further details.   **source of address**

We are a chain of sports equipment retailers with outlets (**3** at/in) 12 major cities in the UK. For further information (**4** on/of) our firm please see our website www.sportsisland.uk.   **introduction of your company**

Please inform us (**5** of/about) your export prices and possible discounts as well as your terms of payment and delivery. We may be placing regular orders (**6** about/for) 300 to 400 pairs of each size. We assume that you will be able to deliver (**7** from/off) stock.

request to send
• catalogues and price lists
• a quotation or cost estimate

request for information on
• prices and discounts
• terms of payment and delivery
• delivery periods

In conclusion may we ask you to send us samples (**8** for/to) test purposes.

further requests (if applicable)
• samples

Thank you for your attention (**9** at/to) our enquiry. We look forward to hearing (**10** of/from) you.   **closing phrase**

Best regards   **complimentary close**

Sarah Brookfield
Purchasing Manager

SPORTS ISLAND
41 Bryant Road
London W7 9QB
Tel. 020 74127333
Fax 020 74127334

2 Cover up Sarah Brookfield's e-mail and complete these sentences on your own
R / P sheet of paper.

1. Sarah Brookfield saw a presentation of …
2. SPORTS ISLAND is a …
3. They would like to be informed about …
4. Their regular orders might comprise …
5. For test purposes they would like to have …
6. They look forward to …

3 Restore the correct order of these jumbled elements and rewrite the
R / P correspondence on your own sheet of paper.

1   We look forward to your early reply.

2   Please send us your price list and information on quantity discounts, terms of payment and delivery and indicate your shortest delivery time.

3   Subject: Topsweets Mint Bars

4   We are a German wholesaler specialising in confectionery for young people and are very interested in your Mint Bars as there is a rapidly growing market for British-type sweets here in Germany.

5   Yours sincerely
Zuckermann & Sacher GmbH

Dieter Sacher

6   We would appreciate it if you could send us samples for test purposes.

7   Dear Topsweets Ltd

8   We would then place a trial order. If the mint bars sell well, we expect to place regular orders in future.

9   We saw the advertisement for your Topsweets Mint Bars in the March issue of the International Confectionery Journal and our general manager tasted them at a reception in the British Embassy in Berlin.

4 Copy the e-mail form below. Use the above correspondence and the phrases at
P the end of the unit and write a detailed e-mail enquiry about the new innovative generation of tablet PCs. You saw their advertisement in the computer journal "IT. COM!". Address your e-mail to IT.COM, ITcom@aol.com, using your own name and a company name of your choice. Use your imagination for any details you may need.

Phrases

From:	
To:	Cc:
Sent:	Attachments:
Subject:	

✴ 5
KMK Sie arbeiten bei Getränke König, Am Sprudelbach 17, 06122 Halle, Tel. 03 45 78 56 34, Fax 03 45 78 56 35 im Einkauf. Ihre Firma möchte ihren guten Kunden zu Weihnachten ein besonderes Geschenk machen. Ihre Chefin, Nicole Sachse, hat auf der Hompage des irischen Glasherstellers Wexford Crystal plc, 1 Wexford Avenue, Sanditon, County Cork, Republic of Ireland, farbige Kristallgläser für Long Drinks im Geschenkkarton zu je drei Stück gesehen.

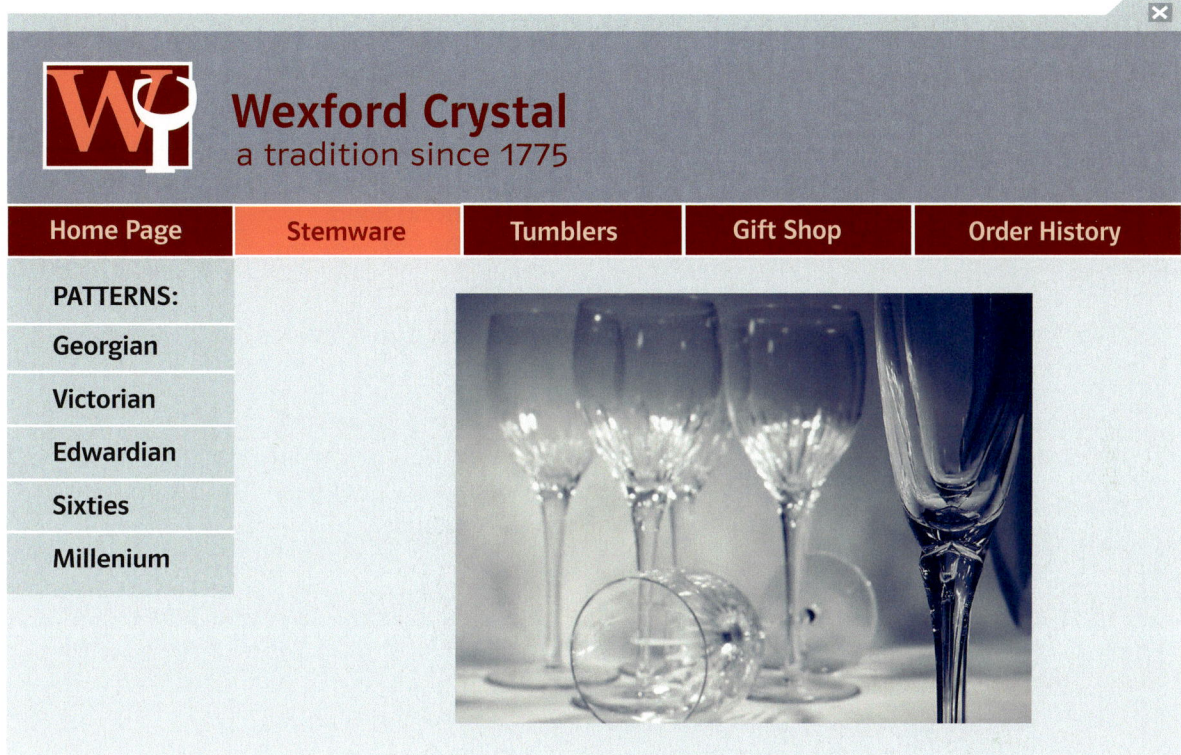

Sie bittet Sie eine Anfrage, die sie selbst unterschreiben wird, zu verfassen und dabei folgende Punkte zu berücksichtigen: `Phrases ▶`

- Datum 1. September
- Betreff
- Bezug auf Internetseiten von Wexford Crystal
- Vorstellung Ihrer Firma als einer führenden Getränkegroßhandlung, Firmenbroschüre liegt bei
- Grund Ihrer Anfrage
- Bitte um Zusendung von Prospekten und Preislisten
- Bitte um Angabe der Lieferzeit
- Bitte um Angabe der Liefer- und Zahlungsbedingungen
- Sonderwunsch: nur je zwei Gläser pro Geschenkpackung
- Umfang eines möglichen Auftrags: 3 000 Sets
- Bitte um baldige Antwort
- Anlage: Firmenbroschüre

6 Your stressed out boss, a Canadian, feels he is in desperate need of a wellness holiday on a Caribbean island. Check out wellness holidays on the Caribbean Commonwealth island of Santa (or Saint) Lucia and make notes for him in English. Your boss is very demanding and only the best is good enough for him.

B Enquiries by phone

1 Restore the order of this jumbled dialogue. Match the numbers with the letters.

1. Calendars 4 U. Michael Bennet speaking. How can I help you?

2. Certainly. Please let me have your address.

3. Thank you. I'll post it today.

4. Yes of course. And full details of our generous discounts for volume orders.

5. My pleasure. Thank you for calling.

a. That's good. Thank you.

b. It's 30, Netherfield Road, Winchester SO2 9LZ. And my name is Jonathan Denny.

c. I take it the brochure contains a price list?

d. Hello. My name is Jonathan Denny. I'm interested in your animal calendars. Could you send me a brochure?

e. Goodbye.

2 Listen to the dialogue and check your work.

R
◎ A 1.22

◎ V 4 **Video lounge** General enquiries

This video shows an enquiry by telephone. Look out for the answers to the following questions:

1. Compare the appearance of the two women. Which do you find more appropriately/appealingly dressed?
2. What seems to be the secretary's main activity apart from answering the phone?
3. What is Purple Fashion enquiring about?
4. What kind of order does she wish to place first?
5. What discount does the manufacturer offer her? What discount does she want?
6. What is the final discount offered?
7. What is the total amount of the invoice?
8. How long does delivery take?

3 Working with a partner now create and act out a similar dialogue along the
I/P following lines.

Phrases ▶

A

Linda/Larry Lawson from the British
language school Business Speak in
Brighton gets a call.

Linda/Larry Lawson offers to send a
detailed brochure and asks for the
caller's address.

Linda/Larry Lawson promises to send
the brochure by post the next morning
and thanks the caller for his/her
interest in their courses. He/she adds
that he/she is convinced that the caller
will find the appropriate course.

B

The caller introduces him/herself as
Stefan/Stefanie Merz from Rostock,
Germany. He/she is interested in crash
courses in business English in the
summer.

Stefan/Stefanie Merz spells his/her
name and address, Ostseeallee 27,
66123 Rostock, Germany.

Stefan/Stefanie Merz thanks Linda/
Larry Lawson and says Good-bye.

4 Work with a partner, sit back to back and act out the following telephone
I conversation with the help of the role cards.

Phrases ▶

Role card: Partner A   Role card partner B ▷ page 251

Torsten/Tanja Kirchner, Auszubildende/r bei Hammer Werkzeughandel,
Remscheid, ruft auf Bitten des Chefs bei Powertools plc, Cardiff, UK, an.
Torsten/Tanja bittet um Auskunft über die Werkzeugsätze für Heimwerker
(household tool kits) von Powertools.
Die E-Mail-Adresse lautet: imports@hammerwerkzeughandel.de. Vor allem
möchte man Näheres über Lieferzeiten und Mengenrabatte erfahren.
Torsten/Tanja beendet das Gespräch und dankt für die Bemühungen.

Info: Discounts

Granting discounts is an effective means of winning new or retaining old
customers.
Trade discounts are granted to retailers.
Introductory discounts are granted to facilitate the introduction of
new products or services.
Quantity discounts are granted for volume orders.
Early order discounts are granted for bookings/purchases made well in advance.
Cash discount is granted for early payment.

5 Copy the sentences and complete them on your own sheet of paper, inserting the
R   appropriate type of discount.

1. In view of the size of your order we are prepared to grant you a **1** of 15 %.
2. We are prepared to launch your new product on the Greek market, if you
   grant us a substantial **2** .
3. For payment within 7 days we grant 2 % **3** .
4. Only registered businesses qualify for a **4** .
5. On bookings made 3 months in advance you will be granted 10 % **5** .

6 Work with a partner. Partner A wishes to place an order with partner B, provided
I   he/she is granted a discount. Use the ideas from the grid below to negotiate the
    granting of a discount. Then change roles.

Phrases ▶

Example:

A

I'd be quite willing to introduce your
new software package CP36-97 to the
German market. But I'm afraid that won't
be so easy. There are a lot of competing
programs. That's why I'd have to offer
customers at least a 20 % introductory
discount.

I'm afraid we will have to offer **some**
incentive to our customers. What would
you say to 10 % introductory discount?

B

Well, actually the package isn't exactly
new. It's just an updated version of the
previous one. So there isn't any real
reason for granting an introductory
discount.

I'd have to get back to my boss for that.
I'll let you know in a few minutes.

Order for	Discount requested	Arguments	
		for	against
Hotel room for 3 nights	20 % early order discount	booking made 2 months in advance	granted on bookings made 3 months in advance
200 Topsweets Mint Bars	30 % trade discount	buyer is a retailer, has a small shop	quantity too small, trade discount only for business-size volumes
50 CD/radio/cassette stereo players	3 % cash discount	payment made within 10 days	normally only 2 %
75 kgs of Norwegian Smoked Salmon	5 % quantity discount	price high compared to competitors' prices	quantity discounts start at 100 kgs.

Language and grammar
Copy the sentences and fill in the correct form, either the adjective or the adverb, and underline the word the adjective or adverb refers to.

Example:
(clear) We wish to point out **1** that this is the deadline.
We <u>wish to point out</u> *clearly* that this is the deadline.

(prompt) We would be grateful for a **2** reply.
(prompt) Thank you for replying **3** to our inquiry.
(strict) This information is given in **4** confidence.
(relative) This is a **5** minor problem.
(immediate) We must insist on **6** delivery.
(immediate) Please contact our representative **7**.
(comparative) Last year they placed **8** small orders with us.
(high) We are **9** dissatisfied with your services.
(fair) Their customers receive updates **10** regularly.
(considerable) Prices have increased **11** in the last few months.
(considerable) They have **12** funds at their disposal.
(approximate) What is the **13** arrival date of the vessel?
(approximate) We have received **14** seventy enquiries.
(definite) This car is **15** too small for me.
(definite) We will let you have our **16** decision by Wednesday.

Language and grammar: Adjectives and adverbs

Mit Adjektiven werden Substantive und das Verb "to be" näher bestimmt.

We expect to place **regular orders** in future.
"regular" ist ein Adjektiv und kennzeichnet das Substantiv "orders".

We **will be glad** to receive information on your discounts.
"glad" ist ein Adjektiv und gehört zu "will be", einer Form von "to be".

Mit Adverbien (adjective +ly) werden Verben, Adjektive und Adverbien näher bestimmt.

We assure you that your order **will be executed promptly**.
"prompt**ly**" ist ein Adverb und kennzeichnet das Verb "to execute".

There is a **rapidly growing** market for British sweets in Germany.
"rapid**ly**" ist ein Adverb und kennzeichnet das Adjektiv "growing".

There is an **extremely rapidly** growing market for British sweets in Germany.
"extreme**ly**" ist ein Adverb und kennzeichnet das Adverb "rapidly".

Phrases: Enquiries

To mention the source of address

We saw your advertisement for laser printers in the October issue of PC World.	Wir haben Ihre Anzeige für Laserdrucker im Oktoberheft der Zeitschrift PC World gesehen.
We have obtained your address **from** the Anglo-German Chamber of Commerce.	Wir erhielten Ihre Anschrift von der Deutsch-Britischen Handelskammer.
Your services have been recommended to us **by** a business partner, …	Ihre Dienstleistungen wurden uns von einem Geschäftspartner empfohlen, …
We have visited your website and …	Wir haben Ihre Webseite angeklickt und …

To introduce your company

We are a young and rapidly growing firm **specialising** in …	Wir sind ein junges, rasch wachsendes Unternehmen und sind auf … spezialisiert.
We are well-established manufacturers **of** …	Wir sind ein gut eingeführter Hersteller von …
Our firm is a leading importer of tools with excellent contacts **all over** the EU.	Unsere Firma ist ein führender Importeur von Werkzeugen mit ausgezeichneten Kontakten in der gesamten EU.

To say what you require

We are interested in …	Wir interessieren uns für …
Could you please let us have a brochure and a price list **for** the services you offer.	Wir bitten um einen Prospekt und eine Preisliste für die von Ihnen angebotenen Dienstleistungen.
Please enclose a catalogue **of** your latest products.	Bitte fügen Sie einen Katalog für Ihre neuesten Produkte bei.
Please send us a quotation **for** …	Bitte machen Sie uns ein (Preis-)Angebot über …
We would be grateful for a cost estimate **for** …	Für einen Kostenvoranschlag für … wären wir dankbar.
Please quote your lowest prices for …	Bitte nennen Sie uns Ihre günstigsten Preise für …
We need a further shipment **of** …	Wir benötigen eine weitere Lieferung …

To ask for further information

We would be grateful for information **on** your terms of payment and delivery.	Wir bitten um nähere Angaben zu Ihren Liefer- und Zahlungsbedingungen.
Do you grant any quantity discounts? ... any early order discount? ... trade discount? ... introductory discount? ... cash discount?	Gewähren Sie Mengenrabatt? ... Frühbucherrabatt? ... Wiederverkaufsrabatt? ... Einführungsrabatt? ... Skonto?
Can you deliver ex stock?	Können Sie ab Lager liefern?
Please state your earliest delivery date.	Bitte geben Sie uns Ihr frühestes Lieferdatum an.
What is the minimum quantity **for** a trial order?	Was ist die Mindestmenge für einen Probeauftrag?

To ask for other services, if applicable

We would welcome a presentation of your services on our premises.	Wir wären dankbar für eine Präsentation Ihrer Dienstleistungen in unseren Geschäftsräumen.
A visit **by** your representative would be appreciated.	Wir wären dankbar für einen Besuch Ihres Vertreters.

To close the communication with a standard phrase

We look forward to hearing from you soon.	Wir freuen uns darauf, bald wieder von Ihnen zu hören.
If your prices are competitive, we may be able to place substantial orders in future.	Wenn Ihre Preise konkurrenzfähig sind, werden wir Ihnen bald größere Aufträge erteilen können.
If the goods **meet with** our customers' approval, your products should sell well in this market.	Wenn die Ware unseren Kunden zusagt, dürften sich Ihre Erzeugnisse auf unserem Markt gut verkaufen lassen.
We hope to hear from you shortly.	Wir hoffen, bald wieder von Ihnen zu hören.

Unit 10
Offers

WORD BANK

offer • quotation • cost estimate • catalogue • brochure • price list • stock • sample • terms of delivery • INCOTERMS • terms of payment • options • solicited • unsolicited • valid • to offer • to quote • to process • to enclose • to attach

Offers are sent either in reply to an enquiry **(solicited offers)** or on the seller's own initiative in the form of sales communications to individuals or companies likely to be interested in the goods or services offered **(unsolicited offers)**. Detailed, specific offers are often called **quotations**. Offers for work to be done take the form of **cost estimates**.

By making an offer the seller declares his willingness to sell certain goods or perform certain services at a certain price and on certain terms.

Offers are binding on the person or firm making the offer unless it is expressly stated in the offer that

- the prices are subject to change without notice or that the offer is either
- without engagement or
- valid until a certain date or
- valid as long as stocks last.

Note that all enquiries should be answered, even those for goods or services your firm does not provide. Where possible, recommend an alternative supplier.

Online-Link
808262-0010

1 Study the text on offers on page 136 and match the expressions on the left with their German equivalents on the right.

1. solicited offer	a. freibleibend
2. unsolicited offer	b. gültig bis 31. Mai
3. without engagement	c. Preisänderungen vorbehalten
4. valid until 31 May	d. Kostenvoranschlag
5. as long as stocks last	e. solange Vorrat reicht
6. prices are subject to change without notice	f. unverlangtes Angebot
7. cost estimate	g. verlangtes Angebot

2 Übertragen Sie folgende Sätze ins Englische.

KMK

1. Ein verlangtes Angebot wird als Reaktion auf eine Anfrage abgegeben.
2. Viele Firmen schicken unverlangte Angebote an mögliche Interessenten für ihre Produkte.
3. Ein Kostenvoranschlag ist ein Angebot für eine Arbeit, die ausgeführt werden soll.
4. Dieses Angebot ist freibleibend.
5. Unsere Preise gelten nur bis zum 31.07.201_.
6. Preisänderungen bleiben vorbehalten.
7. Solange der Vorrat reicht, bieten wir Ihnen wie folgt an: …

Info: Successful offers

Effective offers are decisive for the success of your business. When making an offer you should
• answer an enquiry promptly
• whenever possible personalise the salutation
• thank the enquirer for his interest in your goods or services
• if you cannot provide all the information right away let the prospective customer know that his enquiry will be processed as soon as possible
• be as helpful and polite as possible
• give all the information required
• provide additional information that might be useful
• refrain from making promises you cannot keep
• say something positive about your firm and / or your products
• conclude your offer with a phrase designed to make the customer feel positive towards your firm

---

3 Work in pairs. Close the book. Write down as many of the above recommendations as you remember. Then compare your list with your neighbour's list.

P

A   Offers in writing

In reply to her enquiry about running shoes Sarah Brookfield from SPORTS ISLAND
has received the following e-mail offer from Herkules.

1 Study the e-mail offer and find the missing nouns from the box.
R

> attachment • business • delivery period • discount • enquiry • orders • position • sample • stock

| From: | exports@Herkules.com, Philipp Schäfer, export department |
| To: | sarah.brookfield@sportsisland.co.uk, Sarah Brookfield, purchasing manager, SPORTS ISLAND |

| Cc: | | Attachments: | Price List, Test Report, |
| Sent: | 201_-09-26 | | Brochure |

Subject: Your enquiry about Herkules Turbostar running shoes

Dear Ms Brookfield   [personal salutation]

Thank you very much for your **1** of 25 September.   [expression of thanks for the enquiry]

We are sending our brochure and price list as an **2** . On
orders exceeding 200 pairs in one size we grant a quantity **3**
of 5 per cent. Our prices are quoted EXW Neustadt. For orders
exceeding 1000 pairs of one size each we require a **4** of
3 weeks. Smaller orders can be delivered from **5** .
   [description of goods / services offered]
   [prices (unit and total) and discounts]
   [terms of delivery and delivery period]

Normally we do business on the basis of cash with order for first orders. For regular **6**
we are prepared to grant open account terms with quarterly settlement.
   [terms of payment]

We are also attaching a Test Report, published by the British Consumers' Association,
which puts Herkules running shoes in top **7** in the categories of both comfort and
durability.
   [additional information]

Five **8** pairs of the new Turbostar have been despatched to you this morning and should
reach you in the next few days.
   [reference to samples, etc.]

We look forward to establishing regular **9** relations with you.   [goodwill phrase]

Yours sincerely
Herkules   [complimentary close]

   Philipp Schäfer
   Export Department

2 **Restore the correct order of these jumbled elements and rewrite the**
R/P **correspondence on a piece of paper.**

1 We look forward to welcoming you as our customers.

2 Topsweets Mint Bars

3 For first orders our terms of payment are cash with order.
For regular customers our terms are 30 days net.

4 Our prices are quoted DAP to your premises. On orders for more than 100 kgs
we grant 10 % discount. The mint bars can be delivered within 2–4 weeks
from receipt of order, depending on the volume of the order.

5 We are pleased to send you enclosed our brochure describing our whole
range of products and our special folder on Topsweets Mint Bars as well as
our latest price list.

6 Dear Mr Sacher

7 To enable you to convince yourself of the superior taste of Topsweets
Mint Bars we are sending you by separate post samples together with an
assortment of our other products. We are sure that you will be delighted
with our sweets that are very popular among discerning customers all
over the world.

8 Encls. Brochure, folder, price list

9 Yours sincerely
Topsweets Ltd.

Martha Creams

10 Thank you very much for your recent enquiry.

3
P You work in the export department of a German wholesaler for electronic equipment. Your boss, Cornelia Klinkenberg, has received the following e-mail enquiry. Reply to this enquiry taking your boss's notes into account.

Phrases ▶

From: james.leigh@leigh.co.uk
To: cornelia.klinkenberg@topelektronik.de
Cc:
Sent: 201_-08-02   **Attachments:**
Subject: SomeThing Mp3 Players

Dear Ms Klinkenberg

Please quote us your best prices for the following
SomeThing Mp3 players:

vorrätig, Stückpreis EURO 83,50

500 units   article No. 487-13, 8 GB,
                 with backlit LCD display

*nur 400 vorrätig, Stückpreis EURO 32,80
Lieferzeit für die restlichen 300 Stück 6 Wochen
als Ersatz Artikel 487-15 vorschlagen, gleiches Modell,
aber Lebensdauer der Batterie 30 statt 24
Stunden, Stückpreis EURO 45,90*

700 units   article No. 487-26, 16 GB 3D,
                 USB, extremely compact in size

300 units   article No. 487-45, 1.5 GB,
                 with SD-card slot

vorrätig, Stückpreis EURO 85,30

As the goods are urgently required for a new store to
be opened by the end of next month, we would ask
you to indicate your earliest date of delivery.

*20 % Mengenrabatt für gesamten
Auftrag einräumen*

We assume that the usual terms of payment and
delivery will apply.

*Versand kann drei Tage
nach Auftragseingang erfolgen*

richtig

Thank you for your prompt attention to our enquiry.

Yours sincerely

James Leigh
Leigh & Co. Ltd.
17 Camden Place   *bitte meinen Namen darunter setzen*
Bristol
BS6 6HR   *Danke Klinkenberg*
Tel. 0117 4430030

✳ **4**
KMK   Sie sind Susan/James Vernon und arbeiten im Verkauf bei Powertools plc, Snowdon Industrial Estate, Cardiff CA4 9ZB. Torsten/Tanja Kirchner von der Firma Hammer Werkzeughandel, Lehmkuhle 104, 42896 Remscheid, hat um eine schriftliche Bestätigung des Angebots gebeten, das Sie ihm/ihr heute früh telefonisch gemacht haben.

Verfassen Sie dieses Schreiben (in englischer Sprache) und berücksichtigen Sie dabei Folgendes:

- Datum von heute
- Betreff: Angebot Nr. TK/234
- Bezug auf Telefongespräch
- Angebot für 1000 Stück 9-teiliger Haushalts-Werkzeugsatz (9-piece household tool kit), Artikel Nr. HTK-9
- Listenpreis pro Stück: € 4,99, FCA Cardiff, Incoterms 2010, einschließlich Verpackung, abzüglich 30 % Händlerrabatt
- Gesamtpreis nach Abzug des Händlerrabatts: € 3.493,00.
- Zahlungsbedingungen: innerhalb von 30 Tagen netto, innerhalb von 10 Tagen 2 % Skonto (cash discount)
- Lieferzeit: 3 Wochen
- 2 Muster-Werkzeugsätze werden heute an Hammer Werkzeughandel zu Testzwecken geschickt
- Dank für das Interesse an den Produkten von Powertools plc
- Zusicherung sorgfältiger Ausführung des Auftrags

B   Offers by phone

1
R
A1.23
Edward Ferrars from Norland Industries in Southampton, Great Britain, gets a phone call from an overseas customer.
Read the statements first. Then listen to the dialogue and mark on your own sheet of paper whether the statements are TRUE or FALSE.

1. Tom De Boer is calling from South America.
2. He has no Norland colour printers left in his stock.
3. He wishes to order 200 units of the colour printer CP 150.
4. The terms of delivery are FOB Durban.
5. Last year's model CP 100 cost GBP 72.50.
6. There is increasing competition from Japan.
7. 30% trade discount will be granted on all future orders.
8. The customer asks for an offer in writing.

2
R
Copy Mr Ferrars' quotation and insert the missing expressions from the box.

from receipt of order • look forward to • pleased to • Referring to • within 30 days

---

Dear Mr De Boer

Norland Colour Printers CP 100 and 150 – Quotation no. CP-2024

1 your enquiry of 2 Feb. 201_ we are **2** inform you that we can quote as follows

Quantity	Description	Unit Price	Total
500	Norland Colour Printer CP 100	GBP 75.50	GBP 37,750.00
200	Norland Colour Printer CP 150	GBP 85.20	GBP 17,040.00
			GBP 54,790.00
	less 30 % trade discount		GBP 16,437.00
TOTAL			**GBP 38,353.00**

Delivery: within four weeks **3** , CIF Durban.

Payment: net cash **4** from receipt of invoice.

We **5** receiving your order.

Yours sincerely
Edward Ferrars
Norland Industries

C INCOTERMS® (Terms of delivery)

The Incoterms are a set of nationally and internationally accepted rules defining the obligations of the seller and the buyer as regards the tasks, costs and risks involved in the transport of goods. They were first drawn up by the International Chamber of Commerce in Paris in 1936 and were last updated in 2010.

The Incoterms 2010 are grouped in two categories:
- rules for any mode or modes of transport
- rules for sea and inland waterway transport

The Incoterms 2010 consist of 11 rules, two of which are new:
- DAT (Delivered at Terminal) replaces the former DEQ rule
- DAP (Delivered at Place) replaces the former rules DAF, DES and DDU

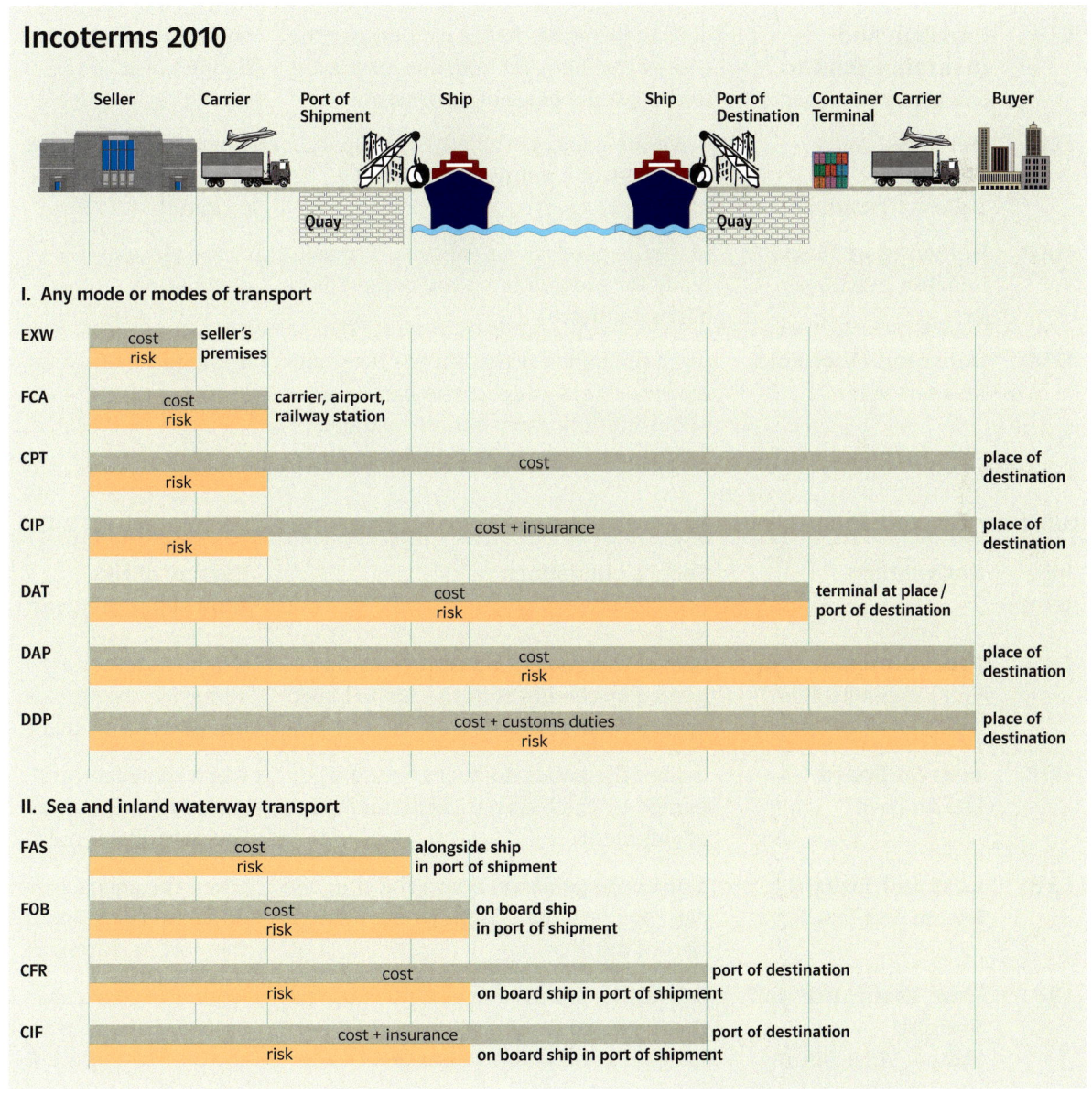

Incoterms 2010

® International Chamber of Commerce, ICC

Rules for any mode or modes of transport

Incoterms® 2010

Inco-term	Designation	Seller's obligations	Passing of risk from seller to buyer
EXW	**Ex Works** Ab Werk	place the goods at the disposal of the buyer at the seller's premises (factory, warehouse etc.)	at the seller's premises
FCA	**Free Carrier** Frei Frachtführer	deliver the goods to the carrier named by the buyer	when the goods are handed over to the carrier
CPT	**Carriage Paid to** Frachtfrei	deliver the goods to the carrier and pay the cost of carriage to the named place of destination	when the goods are handed over to the carrier
CIP	**Carriage and Insurance Paid to** Frachtfrei versichert	deliver the goods to the carrier, pay the cost of carriage and take out insurance to the named place of destination	when the goods are handed over to the carrier
DAT	**Delivered at Terminal** Geliefert Terminal	place the goods at the buyer's disposal, unloaded, at a named terminal at a named place/port	when the goods have been unloaded at the terminal
DAP	**Delivered at Place** Geliefert benannter Ort	place the goods at the buyer's disposal, ready for unloading, at the named place of destination	at the place of destination
DDP	**Delivered Duty Paid** Geliefert verzollt	place the goods at the buyer's disposal, ready for unloading, at the named place of destination, carry out all customs formalities and pay import duty, if any	at the place of destination

Rules for sea and inland waterway transport

Incoterms® 2010

Inco-term	Designation	Seller's obligations	Passing of risk from seller to buyer
FAS	**Free Alongside Ship** Frei Längsseite Schiff	deliver the goods alongside the ship named by the buyer at the named port of shipment	when the goods are alongside the ship in the port of shipment
FOB	**Free on Board** Frei an Bord	deliver the goods on board the ship named by the buyer at the named port of shipment	when the goods are on board the ship in the port of shipment
CFR	**Cost and Freight** Kosten und Fracht	deliver the goods on board the ship and pay the costs and freight to the named port of destination	when the goods are on board the ship in the port of shipment
CIF	**Cost, Insurance and Freight** Kosten, Versicherung und Fracht	deliver the goods on board the ship; pay the costs and freight to the named port of destination and take out insurance for the transport	when the goods are on board the ship in the port of shipment

® International Chamber of Commerce, ICC

Under all clauses the seller must deliver the goods to the buyer at the named place and the buyer must take delivery of the goods *(Ware abnehmen)*. The seller must procure *(beschaffen)* or help to procure the transport documents and pack the goods, if customary *(handelsüblich)*.

Note that under the Incoterms CPT, CIP, CFR and CIF the seller bears the risks only up to the place of delivery, i.e. until the goods are handed over to the (first) carrier or have been loaded on board ship in the port of shipment. Under these terms the seller must, in addition, contract *(Vertrag abschließen)* and pay for the carriage to the place or port of destination.

1 **Read the business transactions and complete them with the right Incoterms.**
R

1. Jennings Food Ltd. has bought five colour printers from Norland Industries. Jennings Food's driver picks up the colour printers at Norland Industries' production plant. The printers have been sold on the basis of …?

2. Powertools plc, Cardiff, has received a large export order from a Brazilian customer. Powertools plc pays for the goods to be taken to the docks in Cardiff and for the loading on board the vessel "Southern Cross". The terms of delivery are …?

3. International Snacks GmbH, a German food processing company, usually delivers its snacks by lorry to Global Catering's premises in Manchester, assuming all costs and risks for the entire transport and dealing with any border formalities that may arise. Their terms of delivery are most likely …?

4. Herkules is processing a major order for running shoes and tennis shoes from a Japanese customer. Herkules arranges and pays for the transport of two 20 ft containers to the container terminal at the Japanese port of Yokohama. Herkules delivers on the basis of …?

2 **Study the Incoterms 2010 on page 143 and 144 and find the English equivalents**
M **for the following German expressions.**

1. Geschäftsräume des Verkäufers
2. Frachtführer
3. vom Käufer benannt
4. Gefahrenübergang
5. Beförderungskosten
6. Versicherung abschließen
7. entladebereit
8. Bestimmungsort
9. dem Käufer zur Verfügung stellen
10. Verschiffungshafen
11. sich an Bord befinden
12. Einfuhrzoll

Language and grammar
Complete these sentences with "some" or "any".

1. He says he has lived in the UK for … years.
2. Fortunately we did not have … trouble getting an import licence.
3. When we finally managed to go the cafeteria there was hardly … food left.
4. I don't think he will complete … of these tasks in time.
5. Could you lend me … of your knives and forks for the party?
6. I couldn't think of …thing else to buy.
7. Scarcely …body turned up for the meeting.
8. …body must help me with this update.
9. We doubt that …body could have solved that problem without help
   from the experts.
10. We will send you … samples by parcel post.
11. Has …body seen my car keys?
12. …body must have copied the data.
13. I wonder whether …body will bother to return the questionnaire.
14. There are scarcely … funds left for this project.

Language and grammar: some and any	

"Some" steht
• in **bejahten Aussagen** und
• in Fragen, auf die eine **positive Antwort** erwartet wird.
	Examples:
	  Here are **some** brochures for you.
	  Can you give us **some** of these folders?

"Any" steht
• in **verneinten Aussagen** und
 	
• in Fragen, auf die eine **negative Antwort** erwartet wird,
 	
• bei **"hardly"**, **"scarcely"** oder **"barely"** (deutsch: kaum),
• in **Bedingungssätzen** und
• nach Ausdrücken des **Zweifels**.
	Examples:
	  I am afraid there aren't **any** mint bars among the samples TOPSWEETS sent us.
	  Are there **any** of those delicious ginger cookies left?
	
	  There can hardly be **any** doubt about it.
	
	  If you have **any** problems, let me know.
	  I wonder whether **any** of the students will be satisfied with this reply.

Industry expert

1 Enquiry

Alex and Clara are doing a traineeship as industrial business management assistants at the Karamba Health Food GmbH in Stuttgart. For the next two months they will be working in the purchasing department. As the supplier for cranberries has gone bankrupt, the head of department, Mr Miller, asks them to find a new supplier. On request, the chamber of commerce has sent them two addresses of potential suppliers in Massachusetts, USA.

KMK **Schreiben Sie unter Berücksichtigung der unten genannten Angaben eine höfliche Anfrage, die an beide amerikanischen Adressen verschickt werden kann.**

`Phrases ▶`

- Adresse: Karamba Health Food GmbH, Clara Schuster/Alex Berger, Wagenburgstraße 12, 70186 Stuttgart
- Wir haben Ihre Adresse von der IHK Stuttgart erhalten und suchen einen neuen Lieferanten in den USA.
- Unser Unternehmen ist bekannt für seine Säfte, Müsliriegel und Kuchen aus Cranberrys.
- Eine große Anzahl von Kunden in ganz Europa wird von uns beliefert.
- Es besteht nur Interesse an Cranberrys von hoher Qualität.
- Bitte schicken Sie uns ein ausführliches Angebot.
- Nennen Sie Liefer- und Zahlungsbedingungen sowie Lieferzeiten.
- Wir benötigen die Ware spätestens bis Ende Oktober.
- Bitte nennen Sie den günstigsten Preis.
- Ab welcher Menge gewähren Sie Mengenrabatte?
- Wenn die Preise und Konditionen konkurrenzfähig sind und das Angebot unseren Erwartungen entspricht, werden wir einen Probeauftrag erteilen.
- Wir freuen uns, bald von Ihnen zu hören.

RUBY RED
Cranberry Growers' Association

28 State Street
Boston
MA 02109
USA

**East Coast Cranberry
Farmers' Alliance**

10 Court Street
Plymouth
MA 02360
USA

2 Comparing offers

1
R/P
Two weeks later Clara and Alex receive two offers. Read the dialogue and the offers below and on page 149. Explain what Mr Miller means with his last question. What else must be taken into consideration?

Mr Miller: Good morning. Have we already received the offers for cranberries?

Clara: Yes, we got them yesterday.

Mr Miller: Great. Which one is more favourable?

Alex: Well, it depends on the amount we order.

Mr Miller: We urgently need 12,000 kilos.

Alex: Wait a minute … then will Ruby Red grant a discount of 10 % which means they are cheaper. So we should place an order with them.

Mr Miller: Is the decision really that straightforward?

RUBY RED
Cranberry Growers' Association
28 State Street • Boston • MA 02109 • USA

24 September 201_

Karamba Health Food GmbH
Ms Clara Schuster
Wagenburgstrasse 12
70186 Stuttgart
Germany

RE: Your inquiry about cranberries

Dear Ms Schuster

Thank your for your inquiry about our cranberries, which we received yesterday.

We are pleased to send you the following offer:
100 kilos of cranberries at $90, ex works our warehouse in Boston.
We grant a quantity discount of 10 % for orders of more than 5,000 kilos.

We guarantee delivery within 2 weeks after receipt of order. Our terms of payment for first orders are payment in advance. If you order regularly our terms of payment will be 30 days net.

Our cranberries are grown without using any pesticides and are of outstanding quality. Enclosed you will find a brochure on our growing and harvesting techniques.

We hope to hear from you soon.

Best regards

John Zarenko

John Zarenko
Sales Manager

Enc. brochure

From:	mandy.jones@eastcoastfarmers.usa
To:	a.berger@karamba.com
Sent:	201_-09-23
Subject:	Your inquiry about cranberries

Dear Mr Berger

Thank you very much for your interest in our naturally grown cranberries.

We are pleased to submit an offer as follows:
100 kilos of cranberries at a price of $84. We normally deliver CIF Hamburg at $120 per 100 kilos. As our prices have been calculated as low as possible we are unfortunately not able to grant any kind of discount. Delivery can be effected one week after receipt of order. Our terms of payment are 60 days net if you can provide references. Otherwise we must insist on cash with order.

Our cranberries are of first-class quality. A sample of our cranberries has been sent to you to convince you of their outstanding quality.

We would be pleased to receive an order from you. For further information we attach our current brochure about our environmentally friendly growing methods. If you have any further questions, please do not hesitate to ask.

Best Regards

Mandy Jones
Export Department

2 Work in groups and calculate the purchase price for 1,000 kilos (1t) for each of the two offers. Then present your results in class.

P

Quantity comparison

Supplier	Ruby Red	East Coast
List purchase price	900	840
– Discounts	150	—
= Target purchase price	9001	860
+ Transport costs to warehouse Stuttgart	710	1200
= Purchase price	1610	2060

149

Calculation of the transport costs

	Ruby Red	East Coast
Ex works Boston		
↓ cost and insurance		✕
CIF Hamburg		$1,200
↓ cost and customs duties		
DDP Stuttgart		

Price list of your forwarding agent (1 t)

1. Warehouse Boston to docks Boston	Cartage: $50
2. Boston quay to ship	Loading charges and port dues: $35
3. Boston to Hamburg (groupage)	Freight: $250
4. Ship to Hamburg quay	Loading charges and port dues: $40
5. Import customs	$80
6. Hamburg quay to warehouse Stuttgart	Cartage: $120
7. Insurance Boston to Hamburg	$75
8. Insurance Hamburg to Stuttgart	$60

3 **Find three further qualitative criteria which you consider important when**
P **choosing a supplier for the company and complete the table below. Present**
and discuss your results in class.

Quality comparison

Offer	Weighting	Ruby Red		East Coast	
	%	1–5 assessment points	Points × weighting	1–5 assessment points	Points × weighting
Purchase price					
Sum	100				

Assessment points: 5 = best, 1 = worst

Phrases: Offers

To say thank you for an enquiry

Many thanks for your enquiry **of** 2 October **about** our new range of …	Wir danken Ihnen vielmals für Ihre Anfrage vom 2. Oktober wegen unseres neuen Sortiments von …
We **were** pleased to hear that you are interested in our …	Wir freuen uns über Ihr Interesse an unseren …

To make an offer and to refer to prices and discounts

As requested, we are sending you enclosed our latest catalogue and price list.	Wie gewünscht, fügen wir unseren neuesten Katalog und unsere Preisliste bei.
We are pleased to quote as follows:	Wir freuen uns, Ihnen hiermit folgendes Angebot machen zu können:
We would now like to make the following quotation:	Wir möchten Ihnen nun folgendes Angebot unterbreiten:
… **at** a unit price of € …, including packing.	… zum Stückpreis von € … einschließlich Verpackung.
… less 30 % trade discount.	… abzüglich 30 % Händlerrabatt.
We can offer a 10 % quantity discount **on** orders **for** at least 500 units.	Für Aufträge über mindestens 500 Stück wird 10 % Mengenrabatt gewährt.
May we draw your attention **to** our special offer for …?	Dürfen wir Sie auf unser Sonderangebot für … aufmerksam machen?
We grant 2 % cash discount **for** payment within 10 days.	Für Barzahlung innerhalb von 10 Tagen gewähren wir 2 % Skonto.
We take pleasure **in** submitting the following cost estimate:	Wir freuen uns Ihnen folgenden Kostenvoranschlag zu unterbreiten:

To state your terms of delivery and payment

Our prices are quoted CIF Singapore.	Unsere Preise verstehen sich CIF Singapur.
Terms of delivery: EXW Neustadt	Lieferbedingungen: EXW (Ab Werk) Neustadt

Our usual terms of payment are:
 	
    cash **with** order
    cash **on** delivery
    30 days net, 10 days 2 %
    by irrevocable and confirmed letter of credit
	Normalerweise lauten unsere Zahlungsbedingungen:
	    Barzahlung bei Auftragserteilung
	    Barzahlung bei Lieferung
	    30 Tage netto, 10 Tage 2 % Skonto
	    durch unwiderrufliches und bestätigtes Akkreditiv

Regular customers are granted open account terms.	Unseren Stammkunden gewähren wir offenes Zahlungsziel.
We would request payment **by** bank transfer **to** our account **with** ABC bank.	Wir bitten um Zahlung per Banküberweisung auf unser Konto bei der ABC Bank.

To refer to the delivery time

The delivery period is 6 weeks.	Die Lieferzeit beträgt 6 Wochen.
Delivery can be made ex stock.	Die Lieferung kann ab Lager erfolgen.

To inform the customer how long the offer is valid

The offer is
    firm **until** 31 March.
    without engagement.
    valid **as long as** stocks last.
	Das Angebot ist
	    fest bis 31. März.
	    unverbindlich.
	    gültig solange der Vorrat reicht.

The prices are **subject to** change without notice.	Preisänderungen bleiben vorbehalten.
The offer is **subject to** prior sale.	Zwischenverkauf vorbehalten.

To create goodwill

I hope this quotation will find your approval.	Ich hoffe, dieses Angebot sagt Ihnen zu.
We look forward to welcoming you as our customers.	Wir freuen uns darauf, Sie als Kunden begrüßen zu dürfen.
We assure you that your order **will be** dealt with promptly and carefully.	Wir sichern Ihnen eine rasche und sorgfältige Erledigung Ihres Auftrags zu.
Should you have any further queries, our staff **will be** pleased to assist you **at any** time.	Sollten Sie nun weitere Fragen haben, stehen Ihnen unsere Mitarbeiter jederzeit gerne zur Verfügung.

Unit 11
Orders

WORD BANK

initial order • trial order •
standing order • repeat order •
order on call • order form •
quantity • description • item •
article • sample • pattern • terms
and conditions • unit price •
total price • to choose • to order •
to place an order • to process •
to deliver

Orders are placed either in response to an offer or on the buyer's own initiative. A first order is also called an **initial order**. A **trial order** is placed for a small quanitity to test the merchandise or service. **Repeat orders** cover goods or services ordered before. **Standing orders** ensure that identical quantities are supplied at regular intervals. **Orders on call** are placed for large quantities, called for at irregular intervals. They play an important role within the concept of just-in-time delivery.

1 **Read the text. Then cover it up and complete the sentences.**

R / P

1. A first order is also called …
2. A trial order is placed for a small quantity to test …
3. Repeat orders cover goods or services …
4. Standing orders ensure that identical quantities are supplied at …
5. Orders on call are placed for large quantities, called for at …

✳ 2 **Translate the text above.**

M

Online-Link
808262-0011

A   Orders in writing

Sarah Brookfield has studied Herkules' offer for Turbostar running shoes and has read the attached test report. As she is favourably impressed by this report and by the results of the durability tests Sports Island conducted on the sample pairs, she decides to place a trial order.

1 **Study Sarah Brookfield's order letter and the order form on the next page and choose the correct prepositions from the box.**
R

by • for • from • of • to • with (2x)

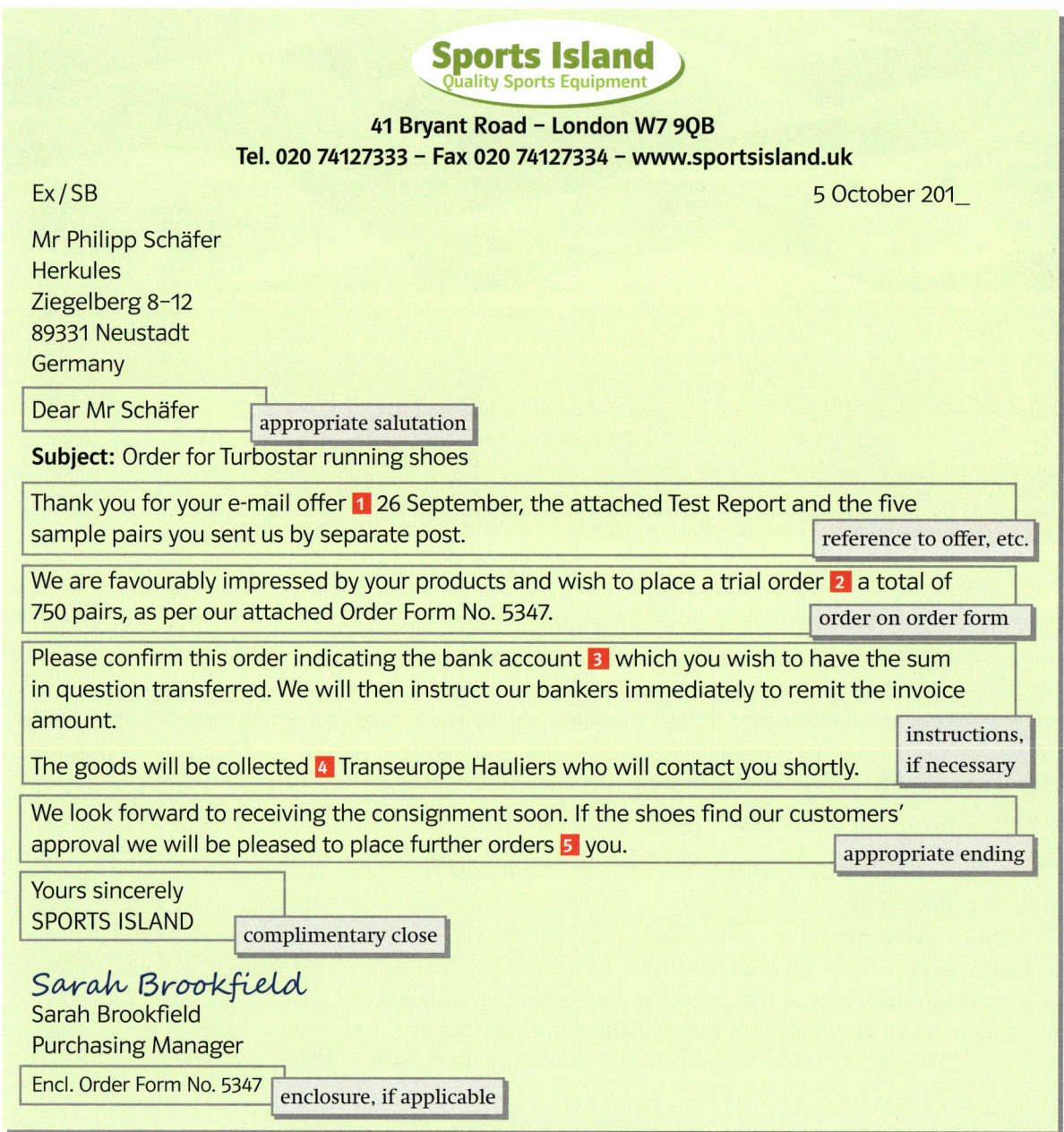

Sports Island
Quality Sports Equipment

41 Bryant Road – London W7 9QB
Tel. 020 74127333 – Fax 020 74127334 – www.sportsisland.uk

Ex / SB   5 October 201_

Mr Philipp Schäfer
Herkules
Ziegelberg 8–12
89331 Neustadt
Germany

Dear Mr Schäfer   [appropriate salutation]

Subject: Order for Turbostar running shoes

Thank you for your e-mail offer **1** 26 September, the attached Test Report and the five sample pairs you sent us by separate post.   [reference to offer, etc.]

We are favourably impressed by your products and wish to place a trial order **2** a total of 750 pairs, as per our attached Order Form No. 5347.   [order on order form]

Please confirm this order indicating the bank account **3** which you wish to have the sum in question transferred. We will then instruct our bankers immediately to remit the invoice amount.

The goods will be collected **4** Transeurope Hauliers who will contact you shortly.   [instructions, if necessary]

We look forward to receiving the consignment soon. If the shoes find our customers' approval we will be pleased to place further orders **5** you.   [appropriate ending]

Yours sincerely
SPORTS ISLAND   [complimentary close]

Sarah Brookfield
Sarah Brookfield
Purchasing Manager

Encl. Order Form No. 5347   [enclosure, if applicable]

Order form

Sports Island
Quality Sports Equipment

41 Bryant Road – London W7 9QB
Tel. 020 74127333 – Fax 020 74127334 – www.sportsisland.uk

ORDER NO. 5347   5 October 201_

Herkules
Ziegelberg 8–12
89331 Neustadt
Germany

Please supply

> order (on order form, if appropriate)
> – quantity
> – description (article No.)
> – unit price, total price

Quantity	Item	Sizes	Unit Price	Total Price
25 pairs each	Turbostar Running Shoes	5, 5 ½ ,11, 12	€ 40.50	€ 4,050.00
50 pairs each		6, 6 ½, 7, 7 ½, 10	€ 40.50	€ 10,125.00
100 pairs each		8, 8 ½, 9, 9 ½	€ 40.50	€ 16,200.00

Terms of delivery: EXW Neustadt   terms of delivery

Terms of payment: Cash **6** order   terms of payment

Delivery: **7** stock   delivery time

Sarah Brookfield

Sarah Brookfield
for Sports Island

155

2

R/P **Restore the correct order of these jumbled elements and rewrite the correspondence on a sheet of paper.**

1   We have studied the enclosed spring catalogue and have chosen two models:

2   Dear Ms Martl

3   I would like to stress that this is a trial order. If we are satisfied with your shirts you may expect regular repeat orders.

4   Thank you very much for your letter of 11 November.

5

Quantity	Article No.	Description	Colours	Sizes	Unit price
50 each	334 053 R	Sports Shirt	Canyon Red	L and XL	€ 17.50
50 each	334 062 T	Dress Shirt	White	L and XL	€ 21.70

6   We look forward to receiving the goods as soon as possible.

7   We would like to point out that this order qualifies for 3 % early order discount, as mentioned in your letter.

8   Yours sincerely
Tony Shaw

Wilson & Thatcher Ltd.

9   This order is placed subject to the terms and conditions specified in your catalogue.
Payment will be made by bank transfer on receipt of your invoice.

10   Subject: Trial order for shirts

3 You work in the purchasing department of the German stationery shop,
P Papier Gehrke, Bahnhofsallee 27, 19053 Schwerin, Tel. 0385 467095, e-mail m.gerke@papier-gehrke.de. Your boss, Martin Gehrke, has put this leaflet with his handwritten notes on your desk and has asked you to e-mail an order to Calendars 4 U.

Phrases ▸

Calendars 4 U

proudly presents its multilingual animal calendar range

Kittens
You're certain to be smitten
12" x 12" wall calendar

$11.99

*gehen besonders gut!
30 Stück bestellen*

Tigers !new!
Spectacular photos
12" x 12" wall calendar

$11.99

*sehr interessant,
20 Stück bestellen*

Puppies
Bright-eyed and
ready to romp
8" x 8" wall calendar

$9.99

*fragen, ob auch in
"12 x 12" erhältlich,
wenn ja 20 Stück,
sonst nur 10 Stück*

Horses
Superb photos
capture
their nobility
12" x 12" wall calendar
$11.99

nicht bestellen

*We offer special rates for orders of 200+ items.
Please call us: 800 / 752-3326.*

Calendars 4 U
100 Dolphin Way
San Sebastian, CA 94901
info@calendars4U.com
www.calendars4U.com

*auf sofortige Lieferung per
Luftpost drängen

Zahlung, wie üblich, durch Überweisung bei Erhalt
der Rechnung
um kurze Auftragsbestätigung bitten
E-Mail in meinem Namen an Cyrus B. Reid
senden: cb.reid@calendars4U.com*

✳ 4
KMK Sie arbeiten bei Getränke König, Am Sprudelbach 17, 06122 Halle, Tel. 0345 785634, Fax 0345 785635 im Einkauf. Ihre Chefin, Nicole Sachse, hat von der irischen Glashütte Wexford Crystal plc, 1 Wexford Avenue, Sanditon, County Cork, Republic of Ireland, ein Angebot über farbige Kristallgläser für Long Drinks im Geschenkkarton erhalten. Die Gläser sollen guten Kunden zu Weihnachten geschenkt werden.

Sie bittet Sie, das Auftragsschreiben, das sie selbst unterschreiben wird, zu verfassen und dabei folgende Punkte zu berücksichtigen:

- Datum 10. September
- Ansprechpartner: Sean O'Sullivan
- Betreff
- Dank für Angebot vom 5. September
- Bestellung: je 1000 Sets bestehend aus je 2 Kristallgläsern für Long Drinks in den Farben rot, blau und grün, im Geschenkkarton
- Gesamtauftragsvolumen: 3000 Sets
- Preis: € 12,50 pro Set zu 2 Gläsern
- Mengenrabatt: 10 %
- Lieferungsbedingung: DAP Am Sprudelbach 17, 06122 Halle, Germany, Incoterms 2010
- Zahlung: bei Erhalt der Ware durch Banküberweisung auf das Konto bei der Cork County Bank.
- Bitte um strikte Einhaltung der versprochenen Lieferfrist von vier Wochen
- Bestellung wird auf Grund unserer beiliegenden allgemeinen Geschäftsbedingungen erteilt
- Anlage: Geschäftsbedingungen

5 **Your boss wants "draper trestles" (Tischböcke) to furnish a factory outlet. Use the internet to find suppliers. Note down prices etc. in English and check that the supplier has an online ordering facility.**

B Orders by phone

Kirsty Burnham from Global Catering in Manchester has received an order from an upmarket chain of delicatessens. She rings International Snacks in Düsseldorf and places an order with them.

1 Kopieren Sie das Bestellformular und füllen Sie es aus,
KMK während Sie das Telefonat zweimal hören.
A1.24

Portionen	Code-Nr.	Artikel	Preis pro Portion
	PSF 135	Schwäbischer Wurstsalat	€ 0,55
	PSF 136	Schinkenröllchen mit Spargel	€ 0,45
	PSF 137	Salami-Aufschnitt auf Roggentaler	€ 0,60
	PSF 138	kleine Frankfurter Würstchen mit Senf	€ 0,45
	PSF 139	Mini-Frikadellen mit Kartoffelsalat und fettarmer Yoghurtsoße	€ 1,05
	PSG 234	Putencocktail in Melone	€ 0,85
	PSG 235	Geflügelsalat Hawaii	€ 0,75
	PSM 311	Räucherlachs auf Pumpernickel mit Meerrettich	€ 0,95
	PSM 312	Bismarckhering, gerollt mit Gürkchen	€ 0,35
	PSM 313	Matjesfilet mit Remoulade	€ 0,65
	PSM 314	Anchovisfilet, gerollt mit gefüllten Oliven	€ 0,85
	PSM 315	Eismeerkrabben-Cocktail	€ 1,15
	PSD 408	Früchtequark	€ 0,45
	PSD 409	Rote Grütze mit Vanillecreme	€ 0,45

Transportart:	Liefertag und -zeitpunkt:	Lieferort:	Rechnung an:

2 Schreiben Sie als Marcel Krenz die im Telefonat mit Kirsty Burnham angekündigte
KMK E-Mail als Auftragsbestätigung (siehe ausgefülltes Bestellformular) mit Versandanzeige.

Absender: marcel.krenz@internationalsnacks.de
Empfänger: burnham.globalcateringuk@aol.com
Sie haben inzwischen folgende Einzelheiten zum Versand geklärt:
- Versand per Luftfracht durch Spedition Fuhrmann & Söhne, Düsseldorf
- Flug-Nr. LH 3697, Abflug: Flughafen Düsseldorf, 13:05 Uhr deutsche Zeit
- Ankunft Manchester Airport, Freight Terminal, 13:25 Uhr britische Zeit

3 Work with a partner. Sit back to back and act out the following telephone
conversation. Then change roles.

Phrases ▶

A

Sie sind Nico/Nicole Sachse und arbeiten bei Getränke König in Halle. Sie hatten ihren britischen Lieferanten BIG Beverages gestern in einem Fax gebeten, einen Auftrag über 500 Flaschen Fruchtsaft, Marke Tropicana, drei Tage früher auszuliefern.

Sie nehmen den Anruf entgegen. Reagieren Sie angemessen auf die Frage, wie es Ihnen geht.

Drücken Sie Ihre Enttäuschung aus und erklären Sie, dass Ihr Kunde den Fruchtsaft spätestens nächsten Freitag für einen großen Empfang benötigt.

Fragen Sie nach dem Preis dieses neuen Fruchtsafts.

Machen Sie Ihrem Gesprächspartner klar, dass Sie nicht in der Lage sind, so viel mehr zu bezahlen.

Zeigen Sie sich erfreut über dieses Entgegenkommen und fragen Sie, wann die 500 Flaschen abgeschickt werden können.

Danken Sie Ihrem Gesprächspartner für seine Bemühungen und beenden Sie das Gespräch.

B

You are Max/Maggy Lane from BIG Beverages in Chipping, UK. Yesterday you got a fax from a German customer, Getränke König from Halle requesting you to bring delivery of their order for 500 bottles of Tropicana fruit juice forward by three days. You ring them up. Begin the conversation with a few friendly personal remarks e.g. asking how the person taking the call is.

Refer to yesterday's fax and tell your partner that you regret that it is absolutely impossible to dispatch this particular fruit juice earlier.

Suggest that you send a substitute, your new fruit drink, called Tropical Sunset. The taste is very similar to that of Tropicana fruit juice.

Tell your partner that you are sorry to say that the price is 5 p higher per bottle as Tropical Sunset contains no artificial flavouring.

To accommodate the customer offer 2.5 % introductory discount on this particular order.

Reply that the consignment will be handed over to the forwarders tomorrow morning and will reach the customer the day after tomorrow.

Close with thanks for the order.

■ **Language and grammar**
Rewrite the following text, using capital letters where necessary.

the organisation of petroleum exporting countries (opec) was formed in 1960 with five founding members: iran, kuwait, saudi arabia and venezuela. by the end of 1971 six other nations had joined the group: qatar, indonesia, libya, united arab emirates, algeria and nigeria. since then opec has been trying to control crude oil prices by setting quotas for production. some major oil exporting countries such as russia, norway and mexico have remained outside opec. the british analyst jonathan baker writing in the june edition of the trade journal "global oil" says that oil prices are highly cyclical and are supported by high demand from south east asia, especially china and india.

Language and grammar: Use of capital letters

Geographische Eigennamen werden groß geschrieben. Im Gegensatz zum Deutschen werden im Englischen auch geographische Adjektive groß geschrieben.

We have customers in **N**ew **S**outh **W**ales in **A**ustralia.
Our **B**ritish and **I**talian subsidiaries are quite successful.

Wochentage, Monate und Feiertage werden groß geschrieben.

The meeting will be held next **F**riday / in **S**eptember / before **C**hristmas.

Vorangestellte Titel, die Teil des Namens bilden, schreibt man groß. Nachgestellte Titel werden meist klein geschrieben.

The report was presented by **V**ice-**P**resident Brian Laurel.
John Hardy, chairman of Media Clusters, agreed to the proposal.

Die Namen von Ministerien, Behörden etc. werden groß geschrieben.

The **F**ederal **C**ommunications **C**ommission ruled that the deal was illegal.
The **D**epartment of **T**rade and **I**ndustry provides help for start-ups.

◉ V5 **Video lounge** Manufacturing   **BBC** Motion Gallery

You are about to see a video about a company based on the Isle of Wight (small island off the south coast of England). Watch the video, then answer the following questions:

1. What does the company manufacture?
2. What industry do orders for these products come from?
3. How are the products transported to customers?
4. What other industry on the Isle of Wight is mentioned?

Phrases: Orders

To refer to previous contacts and place an order

We have studied your quotation and enclose Purchase Order No. …	Wir haben Ihr Angebot genau durchgesehen und fügen unsere Bestellung Nr. … bei.
Please supply the following items **on** the terms stated below:	Bitte liefern Sie uns folgende Positionen zu den unten genannten Bedingungen:

To confirm prices and discounts

We would like to order model AC **at** the price of € … less 5 % introductory discount.	Wir möchten Modell AC zum Preis von € …, abzüglich 5 % Einführungsrabatt, bestellen.
We would like to confirm that the prices are taken **from** your price list **of** 1 September.	Wir möchten bestätigen, dass die Preise Ihrer Preisliste vom 1. September entnommen sind.

To confirm the method of payment and the terms of delivery and the delivery time

As agreed, we will effect payment **by** bank transfer 30 days **from** date of invoice.	Wie vereinbart werden wir die Zahlung 30 Tage nach Rechnungsdatum per Banküberweisung vornehmen lassen.
Payment will be made **by** irrevocable and confirmed letter of credit.	Die Zahlung erfolgt durch unwiderrufliches und bestätigtes Akkreditiv.
Your above-mentioned prices are quoted CIF Hamburg.	Ihre oben genannten Preise verstehen sich CIF Hamburg.
Delivery **is to** be made DAP Stuttgart.	Die Lieferung soll DAP Stuttgart erfolgen.
Complete delivery **by** … is a firm condition of this order.	Vollständige Lieferung bis … stellt eine feste Bedingung für diesen Auftrag dar.
Please note that the goods must reach us **by** 1 March at the latest.	Wir weisen darauf hin, dass die Ware bis spätestens 1. März hier eintreffen muss.

To give instructions and ask for confirmation

Please arrange for transportation **by** Eurotrans Ltd.	Bitte veranlassen Sie, dass der Transport von Eurotrans Ltd. durchgeführt wird.
Please make sure that the figurines are packed with the utmost care.	Bitte sorgen Sie dafür, dass die Figürchen äußerst sorgfältig verpackt werden.
Please acknowledge this order promptly.	Bitte bestätigen Sie diesen Auftrag umgehend.

To close the correspondence

We look forward to receiving the goods **in** time and to doing further business with you.	Wir sehen dem rechtzeitigen Eintreffen der Ware entgegen und freuen uns auf weitere Geschäfte mit Ihnen.

Unit 12
Transport and logistics

WORD BANK
transport • logistics • shipping • forwarding • cargo • freight • door-to-door delivery • modes of transport • types of packing • dispatch advice • waybill • consignment note • bill of lading • certificate of origin • packing list • insurance policy / certificate • to confirm • to acknowledge • to send • to ship • to transport • to pack • to wrap • to deliver

CONTAINER SHIPPING

World trade is forecast to continue growing strongly over the next decade. Today roughly 90 % of non-bulk cargo is transported in containers stacked on transport ships. Cargo is also transported via roll on/roll off (ro-ro) ferries that offer easy loading and unloading. New cars, for instance, are simply driven on and off massive car carriers that hold thousands of vehicles. Ports such as Felixstowe in East Anglia are being deepened to accommodate the new generation of massive container ships.

The fact that the average consumer appears to have no idea how running shoes, washing machines, coffee or tonnes of toys arrive in the shops from all over the world is a constant source of irritation to the shipping world. "The global economy only exists thanks to shipping, in particular container shipping," says one industry analyst. The long-term downward trend in shipping costs has facilitated economic growth worldwide.

At the present time China clearly dominates world trade flows both in terms of exports of finished goods and imports of raw materials. However, shipping is a highly cyclical business reflecting growth and stagnation in the world economy. Carriers, ship-owners and terminal operators have constantly to invest in new ships and facilities. But they do not have a good record of getting the supply/demand ratio right and have often ended up either with inadequate or excess capacity.

Online-Link
808262-0012

1 Beantworten Sie folgende Fragen zu vorstehendem Zeitungsartikel auf Deutsch.

R

1. Welches sind die größten und wichtigsten Transportmittel für den Welthandel?
2. Weswegen ist die Schifffahrtsbranche verärgert?
3. Wodurch wurde das rasche Wachstum des Welthandels erst ermöglicht?
4. Wie zeigt sich, dass die Schifffahrtsbranche von der Konjunktur abhängt?

✱ **2** Work in groups. Each group translates one paragraph from the text on page 163
M in writing. Present your result to the class.

3 Use the internet to find out the percentages of goods transported by a. road and
b. rail in the EU.

A Modes of transport

Tobias Krabbe from the German company Form und Raum GmbH has been asked to collect first-hand information on the various modes of transport. He interviews Marie Boucher from the freight forwarding company FranceTransports which handles most of Form und Raum's international shipments.

1 Listen to the interview with Marie Boucher twice and complete the grid on a
KMK separate sheet of paper. Then add whatever other advantages, disadvantages and
◎ A1.25 suitable cargoes you can think of. Compare your result with that of your neighbour.

	Road	Rail	Air	Sea / Inland Waterways
Advantages	door-to-door delivery, flexible timetables			
Disadvantages		unless a firm has its own private siding, goods must be transported to and collected from the station		slow; seaworthy packing required
Suitable cargoes			light, urgently required, perishable or valuable goods	

2 Work in groups. Choose one of the goods mentioned below and explain to your group which mode(s) of transport you would use, giving reasons for your choice. Use the expressions in the bubbles.

Example: "I'd send the wine by road from Spain to Poland because door-to-door delivery by lorry is probably faster than rail transport."

"I wouldn't transport … because …"

"I'd rather send …"

"It would not be a good idea to ship … considering that …"

"I'd definitely not use … as …"

"In my opinion it would be best to choose …"

"There's no doubt that … should be transported by …"

"I think it would be better to …"

"I suggest we send … either by … or by …"

"I'd suggest sending …"

Urgent medical supplies from Leipzig, Germany, to Wellington, New Zealand

Laptops from a port in South Korea to Berlin

A large printing press from Mannheim in Germany to the port of Jeddah in Saudi Arabia

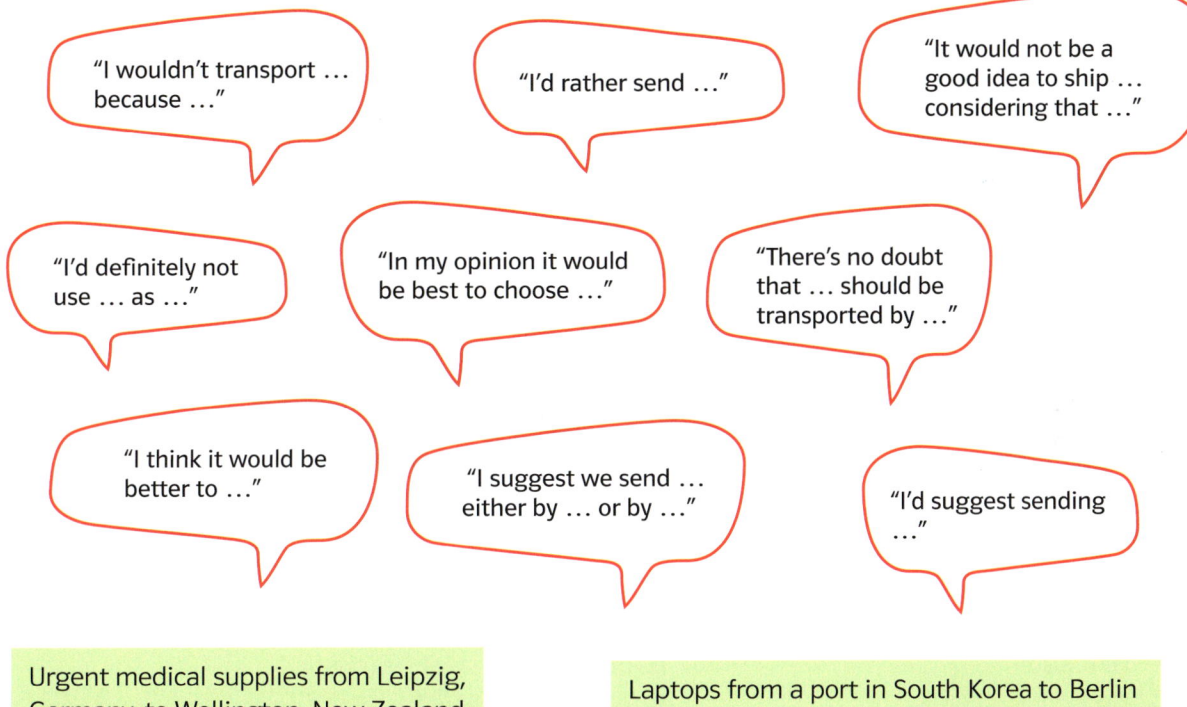

Tropical fruit from Brazil to Sweden

Designer shoes from Italy to Denmark

Furniture from a manufacturer in Westphalia to a hotel in Austria

Wine in bottles from Spain to Poland

50 cars from a plant in Munich to a car dealer in Lisbon, Portugal

B Packing

Adequate packing is essential to ensure that goods arrive in perfect condition, regardless of the distance they have travelled.

1 Match the German terms (see photos above) with their English equivalents.

1. Eisenfass, Trommel	a. bale
2. Holzkiste	b. bundle with steel strapping
3. Fass	c. coil on euro-pallet
4. folienumwickelter Karton	d. container
5. Rolle, Coil auf Europalette	e. crate
6. Kunststoffbox mit Formeinlagen	f. drum
7. Container	g. foil-wrapped cardboard box
8. Ballen	h. plastic box with mouldings
9. Bündel mit Stahlbandumreifung	i. one-way pallet
10. Lattenkiste, -verschlag	j. sack
11. Einwegpalette	k. wooden case
12. Sack	l. barrel

2 The following sentences do not make much sense. Rearrange the words to form
R/P meaningful sentences.

1. The fruit will be packed in 15 bundles with steel strapping.
2. The pure new wool will be sent in a crate.
3. The steel rods will be shipped in bales.
4. The replacement Mp3 player will come on a reusable pallet.
5. The printing machine will be packed in a cardboard box.
6. The engine will be sent in a plastic gift box with mouldings.

C Dispatch advice

As soon as the goods are ready for dispatch it may be necessary to inform the customer that the goods can either be collected at the seller's premises or that they have been handed over to the carrier – depending on the Incoterms agreed upon in the sales contract. Remember that you are communicating with a customer and be as friendly and helpful as possible.

1 Dispatch advice in writing

Topelektronik has received an order for a total of 1,500 SomeThing Mp3 players from the British company Leigh & Co. Ltd. Cornelia Klinkenberg, head of sales at Topelektronik, informs James Leigh that the goods have now been shipped to the UK.

1 **Complete Cornelia's e-mail using the verbs from the box.**

R

> accompanied • arrive • attached • delivered • given • packed • picked up • pleased • reach

From:	cornelia.klinkenberg@topelektronik.de		
To:	james.leigh@leigh.co.uk		
Cc:			
Sent:	201_-08-14	**Attachments:**	Invoice No. 149 / 08 / 1_
Subject:	Your order dated 7 August for 1,500 SomeThing Mp3 Players		

Dear Mr Leigh

We are **1** to inform you that the consignment has today been **2** by our forwarders, Transcontinental Logistik, to be **3** by road to your warehouse in Bristol.
The forwarders have **4** us the assurance that the goods will **5** you by Friday afternoon, at the latest.

The Mp3 players are **6** in 15 triple-walled cardboard boxes on one pallet.
The consignment is **7** by the required documents (consignment note, packing list and commercial invoice). A copy of the invoice is **8**.

Thank you once more for this order. We hope the goods will **9** safely and in good time. We look forward to serving you again.

Kind regards

Cornelia Klinkenberg
Topelektronik
Am Osthang 37
09114 Chemnitz
Tel. +49 371 460873
Fax. +49 371 460874

2
P Mr Kunal Mahajan, export manager at India Sports, has been processing an order
for T-shirts from the German firm Herkules. He now sends them a dispatch advice.
Write his fax, using the following prompts:

- reference to their order of 20 Jan. and their letter of 1 Feb.
- consignment packed in one 20 ft container
- markings on the container: HKS, 3479, Antwerp
- yesterday loaded on board MV Maharani in the port of Mumbai
- expected time of arrival at Antwerp: on or about 12 March
- friendly closing phrase

India Sports

112 Delhi Road, Meerut–250 001
Uttar Pradesh, India
Fax +91 121 2512275
Tel. +91 121 2512270

Telefax

To :	Herkules Ziegelberg 8–12 89331 Neustadt, Germany	**Attention:**	Ms Laura Bayerle
From:	Kunal Mahajan, Export Manager	**Fax:**	+49 8358 88820
Date:	15 Feb 201_	**Pages (incl. this one):**	1
Subject:	Your order No. ABF / 16 of 20 January and 1 February		

3
KMK Sie (eigener Name) arbeiten bei der Münchner Firma Superdress GmbH,
E-Mail: sales@superdress.munich.de. Ein britischer Kunde, Richard Knight,
Einkäufer bei der Warenhauskette Hamilton's, E-Mail: richard.knight@
hamiltons.co.uk, hatte bei Ihnen eine Sendung Herrenhemden bestellt, die
dringend für eine Modeschau benötigt werden.

**Schreiben Sie eine E-Mail als Versandanzeige und berücksichtigen Sie dabei
Folgendes:**

- Bezug auf Auftrag vom 18. August
- Sendung heute der Spedition Kleine zum Transport per Luftfracht übergeben
- British Airways Flug Nr. BA 777
- Abflug: Flughafen München, 22 August, 11:35 Uhr,
  Ankunft: Manchester Airport, 12:55 Uhr
- Erwartung, dass Hemden rechtzeitig für die Modeschau eintreffen
- nochmaliger Dank für den Auftrag

2 Order confirmation and inquiry concerning transport by phone

1

R

) A 1.26

Thomas Krabbe from Form und Raum has received an order from a British customer. He confirms the order and the transport arrangements by phone. Listen to the dialogue and answer the following questions.

1. What is the name of Jennifer Ashley's firm?
2. Has Tobias spoken to Jennifer before?
3. When did Jennifer place the order?
4. How many Hermes standard lamps, Odin uplighters and Bauhaus coffee tables were ordered?
5. What are the first and the last order numbers, the second being O160u?
6. When is the consignment expected to arrive?

2

I

Cornelia Klinkenberg from Topelektronic in Chemnitz had promised James Leigh from Leigh & Co. Ltd in Bristol, UK, that the Mp3 Players he had ordered would arrive by Friday afternoon at the latest. It is now 4 pm on Friday (local time) and the lorry has not yet arrived. James Leigh rings Cornelia Klinkenberg.

Act out their dialogue with your neighbour using the prompts below.

Phrases ▶

James Leigh	Cornelia Klinkenberg
	Topelektronik, Klinkenberg
James Leigh / Leigh & Co., Bristol / Mp3 players / not yet arrived / now 4 pm	
	Try to reach driver on his mobile phone / hold line? / ring back?
hold / urgent	
	spoken to driver / driver on motorway M4 / 20 miles away
here / next half hour?	
	driver confident / arrive before 5 pm / reason for delay / held up in Channel Tunnel / security check / false alarm / explosives in a van on the train / took almost 3 hours
glad to hear / arrive this afternoon / thanks	
	lucky still in office / 5 pm in Germany
e-mail / as soon as goods have arrived / nice weekend / Bye	
	too / Goodbye

D Documents in foreign trade

Waybills, also called **consignment notes, (Frachtbriefe)** are used in road, rail or air transport. They are contracts between the sender of the goods and the carrier (Frachtführer) and provide detailed information about the consignment and the transportation.

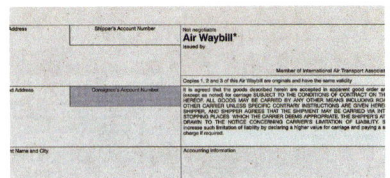

The **Bill of Lading** (B/L) **(Konnossement)** is the freight document in sea transport and when the transportation involves several modes of transport. It is a document of title (Eigentumsurkunde), which means that any lawful holder of the B/L is the rightful owner of the goods. Bills of Lading must be **clean (rein)**, that is to say the carrier (e.g. the captain of the ship) must have signed the B/L **without** making a note on it that the consignment shows signs of a defect or damage from the outside.

A **Certificate of Origin (Ursprungszeugnis)** shows the country of origin of the goods or the country where they were mainly produced. There is a common EU Certificate of Origin. Certificates of Origin are usually legalized by a chamber of commerce.

The **Packing List (Packliste)** is a detailed statement of the goods supplied in a particular consignment.

Commercial Invoice (Handelsrechnung) and Proforma Invoice (Proforma-Rechnung) see Unit 13.

Insurance Policy/Certificate (Versicherungspolice/-schein) see Info-Box on page 171.

Export documents are available as standard paper forms. Increasingly, however, such documents are created by computer software and forwarded via the internet.

1 Compare the translation with the above text on the Bill of
R Lading and find the missing words from the box.

> Beschädigung • Eigentümer • Kapitän • Seetransport • Sendung

Das Konnossement (B/L) ist das Frachtpapier für den **1** und für Transporte, bei denen mehrere Transportarten zum Einsatz kommen. Es ist eine Eigentumsurkunde, d.h. jeder rechtmäßige Inhaber der B/L ist rechtmäßiger **2** der Ware. Konnossemente müssen rein sein, das heißt, der Frachtführer (z.B. der **3** des Schiffes) muss die B/L unterschrieben haben, ohne einen Vermerk anzubringen, der besagt, dass die **4** äußerlich Zeichen eines Mangels oder einer **5** aufweist.

2 Edward Ferrars from Norland Industries in Southampton ships 700 colour printers
P to a customer in Durban, South Africa. Study his quotation in Unit 10 and fill in
the details missing from the B / L (on a separate sheet of paper).

SHIPPER Norland Industries, 39 Marchwood Industrial Park, Southampton SO11 3DG		CUSTOMER NO. MSA-24	REF. NO. CP 100 / 150	B/L NO. 428 379 421
CONSIGNEE		**LINER BILL OF LADING**		
NOTIFY De Boer Office Equipment Pty., 422 Drakens Road, Durban 4051, SA		568 HARBOUR STREET, SOUTHAMPTON, SO4 3DL UNITED KINGDOM		
LOCAL VESSEL	FROM Southampton	**GENERAL AGENTS WORLD WIDE** **WORLDCARGO**		
OCEAN VESSEL Santa Maria	PORT OF LOADING			
PORT OF DISCHARGE	FINAL DESTINATION	FREIGHT PAYABLE AT Southampton	NUMBER OF ORIGINAL B/L three	
MARKS & NUMBERS	NUMBER OF PACKAGES/DESCRIPTION OF GOODS	GROSS WEIGHT Kos.	MEASUREMENT Cbm.	
MOE, 18/18 Durban	18 pallets containing	6.1 t	600 x 1200 x 215 each	
FREIGHT AND CHARGES GBP 1145.30	Shipped on board in apparent good order and condition, weight, measure, marks, numbers, quality, contents and value unknown, for carriage to the port of discharge or so near thereunto as the Vessel may safely get and lie always a oat, to be delivered in the like good order and condition at the aforesaid Port unto Consignee or their Assigns they paying freight as per note on the margin plus other charges incurred in accordance with the provisions contained in this Bill of Lading. In accepting this Bill of Lading the Merchant expressly accepts and agrees to all its stipulations on both pages, whether written, printed, stamped or otherwise incorporated as fully as if they were all signed by the Merchant. One original Bill of Lading must be surrendered duly endorsed in exchange for the goods or delivery order. IN WITNESS whereof the Master of the said Vessel has signed the number of the original Bills of Lading stated above, all of this tenor and date, one of which being accomplished, the others to stand void.			
	PLACE AND DATE OF ISSUE **SOUTHAMPTON**			
	SIGNED FOR THE MASTER BY:			

Info: Insurance Policy / Certificate

Exports shipments are usually insured **"against all risks"**, which covers a wide
range of risks, from sinking to theft. The contract between the sender and the
insurance company is called a **policy**. Whenever an open policy, covering a
certain lump sum or valid for a certain period, has been taken out, the insurance
company issues an insurance **certificate** for an individual shipment. The **premium**
is the sum payable by the insured to the insurance company at regular intervals.

3 Translate the text above into German. Use the words from the box.
M

abdecken • abschließen • ausstellen • Diebstahl • Generalpolice •
Pauschalsumme • Police • Prämie • Untergang • Versicherungsnehmer •
Versicherungszertifikat

Language and grammar
Translate the statements into English.

1. Ich arbeite in einem Warenhaus und möchte Einzelhandelskaufmann werden.
2. Mein Chef ist leider ziemlich selbstbewusst und nicht sehr sympathisch.
3. Auf Seite 3 unseres Prospekts finden Sie Berichte unserer Kunden, die den Erfolg unserer Methode beweisen.
4. Ich bekomme ungefähr 50 E-Mails pro Tag.
5. Unsere Firma beobachtet die aktuellen Trends auf dem Markt sehr genau.
6. Diese Rechnungen müssen noch einmal geprüft werden.
7. Dieses System wird eventuell in unserem Büro eingeführt.

Language and grammar: False friends

Einige deutsche Wörter werden oft mit englischen Wörtern verwechselt, die etwas ganz anderes bedeuten

deutsches Wort	englische Bedeutung	nicht zu verwechseln mit	deutsche Bedeutung
aktuell	current(ly), topical	actual	tatsächlich, wirklich
bekommen	to get	to become	werden
Billion	trillion	billion	Milliarde
Chef*	boss	chef, chief	(Chef-)koch, Häuptling
eventuell	perhaps, possibly	eventual	schließlich
Fabrik	factory, works	fabric	Stoff
Gymnasium	grammar school	gym(nasium)	Sporthalle
Prospekt	brochure	prospect	Aussicht
Provision	commission	provision	Vorsorge
prüfen	to check, examine	to prove	beweisen
übersehen	to overlook	to oversee	überwachen
Warenhaus	department store	warehouse	Lagerhaus

*Ausnahme: Zusammengesetzte Begriffe wie chief accountant, chief executive officer

---

◎ V6 Video lounge IT

BBC Motion Gallery

This video illustrates important IT applications.
Look out for the answers to the following questions:

1. What are the duties of the three staff members shown in the video?
2. Give a brief description of any one of them.
3. Why is it important to check everything carefully?
4. What possible problems do they have to watch out for?

Industry expert

Outsourcing

1 **Lesen Sie den folgenden Text aus der *New York Times* aufmerksam durch.**
KMK **Entscheiden Sie, ob die Aussagen (1.–4.) auf Seite 174 richtig oder falsch sind und begründen Sie Ihre Entscheidung auf Deutsch. Beantworten Sie danach stichwortartig die offenen Fragen (5.–8.) auf Deutsch.**

In a sinking world economy, outsourcing proves resilient

The global downturn has slowed the rapid growth in Indian outsourcing, but because of the pressure on companies, and even governments, to cut costs, many outsourcing businesses are booming. And a mood that was deeply uncertain just six months ago has turned optimistic. Unemployment has risen in the United States, the highest in 26 years, increasing longstanding pressures to keep jobs in America. But managers of companies big and small, squeezed between political pressures and the necessity of slimming down to survive, are choosing the bottom line.

J. Brandon Black, president and chief executive of the Encore Capital Group, a debt collection company in California, said he planned to increase his staff in India in the next few years, in part because of the tough economic times. "The supply of well-trained, educated labour at reasonable prices is just too great to ignore," Mr Black said. "In India," he said, "we're hiring college-educated people." The company is not doing that in the United States, where it would incur greater infrastructure and health care costs. "Outsourcing is here to stay," Mr Black said.

Some of the biggest U.S. companies continue to invest in India, even as they trim costs at home. Last month, Honeywell International, the manufacturing company based in New Jersey, said it would invest 50 million USD in a research and development facility in Bangalore that would employ 3000 people. The move comes after Honeywell began a reorganization, closing plants and trimming hundreds of jobs in the United States. The company declined to comment for this article, but when it initially announced its India plans, its chairman and chief executive, David M. Cote, said about half of Honeywell's employees and half of its business were outside the United States. "Anything that creates any kind of protectionism, anything that stops the globalisation activity, will be harmful," he said.

Many Indians believe demographics are on their side in the long run. "In most developed economies, the workforce is aging," said Mr Tinaikar. The health care costs associated with employing those Western workers will continue to increase, he said, creating a "big opportunity" for India. Growth will slow this year at many of India's biggest outsourcing companies, however, because of the fall of some of their largest clients: banks and Wall Street firms. But that does not mean revenue is no longer growing. "People who have never looked at outsourcing before are saying they have to do it," Amitabh Chaudhry, the chief executive of Infosys BPO, said. He expects his unit to expand 25 percent to 30 percent this year, compared with 40 percent to 50 percent in the past.

But political pressures are making a difference in how business is done. One growing trend, many outsourcing executives say, is placing more Indian employees in offices in the client's home country. That way the job does not move abroad. But over the long term, many workers are likely to be moved across the globe.

"Our view is we start work onshore, then move it to Poland or Morocco, and then over time to India," said Sachdev Ramakrishna, director of marketing for Steria, an information technology and outsourcing company. Steria is based in Paris, but a quarter of its employees are in India and it has offices in Morocco and Poland. "Everyone recognizes that this is a changed world order, and the focus is more on preservation of jobs," Mr Ramakrishna said.

(Quelle: *New York Times*)

Aussagen (richtig/falsch, weil …)

1. Die Arbeitslosigkeit in den USA stieg auf ein Rekordhoch.
2. Einige der größten US-Firmen investieren weiterhin sowohl in Indien als auch in den USA.
3. Die Hälfte aller Mitarbeiter von Honeywell arbeitet in Indien.
4. Wir leben in einer veränderten Welt und das Ziel ist heute eher die Erhaltung von Jobs.

Verständnisfragen

5. Was ist für Mr Black der Hauptgrund mehr Arbeitskräfte in Indien einzustellen?
6. Viele Inder glauben, dass der demografische Wandel Vorteile für sie bringt. Nennen Sie zwei Gründe.
7. Warum wird sich das Wachstum vieler großer Outsourcing Firmen in Indien verlangsamen?
8. Welche Auswirkung hat politischer Druck auf Outsourcing?

2 **Some companies have decided to move production back to their home countries.**
P **Discuss the reasons in class.**

"A Steiff animal has to look cute, it has to look at you and say 'Take me in your arms and hug me, I'm here for you, I'm your friend.' If the symmetry is off and it looks like it's been run over by a car, it's not what we want. People don't pay for that."

Martin Frechen, managing director of Margarete Steiff GmbH, Giengen/Brenz

3 **Work in teams and think about companies that have outsourced their production**
P **or moved it back. Use the internet to find out why they have done so. Make a list**
   with pros and cons and present it in class.

Phrases ▶

Phrases: Transport and logistics

To give particulars about packing

The goods are packed in …	Die Ware ist verpackt in …
• polythene bags.	• Plastikbeutel.
• 20 bales weighing 50 kgs per bale.	• 20 Ballen zu je 50 kg.
• one 20 ft container.	• einem 20-Fuß-Container.
• fibreboard boxes with steel bands.	• Hartfaserkisten mit Stahlbändern.
The goods will be shipped …	Die Ware wird …
• **in** sturdy crates.	• in stabilen Lattenkisten
• **on** reusable pallets.	• auf Mehrwegpaletten
	versandt.

To say that the goods are ready for collection

We are pleased to inform you that the keyboards can now be collected **at** our plant in Leeds.	Wir freuen uns Ihnen mitteilen zu können, dass die Keyboards jetzt in unserem Werk in Leeds abgeholt werden können.

To give particulars about the transport

The consignment has today been handed over to the freight forwarders **for** transportation **to** Warsaw by lorry.	Die Sendung wurde heute der Spedition zur Beförderung nach Warschau per LKW übergeben.
Yesterday the machine was loaded **on board** MS Seagull in Bremerhaven.	Die Maschine wurde gestern in Bremerhaven auf die MS Seagull verladen.
The spare parts will be sent **by** air freight **on** Air Canada flight No. AC 442, arriving **at** Toronto airport at 11:55 **on** 25 September.	Die Ersatzteile werden per Luftfracht mit Air Canada, Flug Nr. AC 442 verschickt. Ankunft: Flughafen Toronto, 25. Sept., 11:55 Uhr.

To close on a friendly note

We hope the goods will arrive punctually and in good condition.	Wir hoffen, die Ware kommt pünktlich und in gutem Zustand bei Ihnen an.
We trust that the quality of our garments will meet your expectations.	Wir sind überzeugt, dass die Qualität unserer Bekleidungsartikel Ihren Erwartungen entspricht.
We feel sure that your customers will be pleased with our new range of …	Wir sind sicher, dass unser neues Sortiment von … Ihren Kunden gefallen wird.

Unit 13
Payment and reminders

WORD BANK

currency • commercial invoice • proforma invoice • IBAN • BIC • bank account • unit price • subtotal • total price • cash • credit card • debit card • cheque • bill of exchange • payment in advance • cash on delivery • open credit • open account • letter of credit • reminder • statement of account • amount due • settlement • to make out an invoice • to transfer • to delay • to collect • to take legal steps

CURRENCY QUIZ

Questions:
1. Which is the youngest of the currencies shown above?
2. Which is the oldest of these currencies?
3. Which of these currencies is the most widely used in international business transactions?
4. Which of these currencies do most individuals use for their daily purchases?

1. The Euro. Euro banknotes and coins replaced 12 former European currencies on 1 January 2002.
2. The Pound Sterling. It has been in use since the Middle Ages. The US Dollar was introduced in 1785, (the Swiss Frank in 1798 and the Yen in 1871).
3. The US Dollar. On a global scale the US-Dollar is still the most widely used currency in business transactions.
4. The Euro. The number of inhabitants in the Euro zone (EU without Denmark, Sweden and the United Kingdom) is estimated at 325,7 million, approx. 306 million people live in the USA.

Online-Link
808262-0013

A The invoice

The **commercial invoice** (Handelsrechnung) is sent by the seller to the buyer and provides full details on the transaction, such as names, dates, numbers, descriptions, quantities, prices, discounts, terms, taxes (VAT) etc. When making out an export invoice you should make sure that it includes your company's IBAN and your bank's BIC.

A **proforma invoice** (Proformarechnung) contains all the details of the eventual commercial invoice. It may serve as a quotation or be required to apply for an import licence.

1 **The above text contains three abbreviations. Study their German translations and find the words that have been left out in the full English expressions.**

R

VAT	Value-added **1** = Mehrwert**steuer**
IBAN	International Bank **2** Number = Internationale **Konto**nummer
BIC	Bank Identifier **3** = Internationaler Bank-**Code**.

2 Philipp Schäfer is processing the trial order for Turbostar Running shoes which his company, Herkules, has received from Sports Island, a major British chain of sports equipment retailers. (See Unit 11, A). The necessary arrangements for transportation having been made Philipp Schäfer now confirms the order by e-mail and sends the invoice as an attachment.

R

Study Philipp Schäfer's e-mail and decide which of the tenses in brackets is correct.

Dear Ms Brookfield

Thank you very much for your above-mentioned order.

We are pleased to inform you that the consignment **1** **is picked up / will be picked up** by Transeurope Hauliers for transportation to the UK in two days' time, that is to say on Wednesday, 10 October. The forwarders **2** **have given / had given** us the assurance that the running shoes **3** **will be delivered / will have been delivered** to your premises in London on the following Friday, 12 October, between 9 and 11 a.m. your time.

Since this is a first order we **4** **were sending / are sending** you our invoice No. GB113-14 as an attachment and would appreciate it if you **5** **instructed / have instructed** your bankers at your earliest convenience to remit the sum of € 30,375.00 to our account with Bayernbank. For particulars see the attached invoice.

We **6** **feel / felt** sure that your customers **7** **will be pleased / are pleased** with the Turbostar running shoes as they are not merely comfortable, serviceable and durable but stylish as well. We look forward to receiving further orders from you in the near future.

Herkules
the global sports brand

Ziegelberg 8–12
89331 Neustadt
Tel. +49 8358 888-0
Fax +49 8358 88820
www.Herkules.com

USt. ID No. DE 812 039 979

INVOICE No. GB113-14

Sports Island
41 Bryant Road
London W7 9QB
UK

VAT No. 186 4405 32

Customer No. UK 22267

Date: 8 Oct 201_
Your Order No. 5347 of 5 Oct 201_

Person in charge: Mike Kappler
Tel.: +49 8358 888 317
Fax: +49 8358 888 300
E-Mail: accounts@herkules.com

Quantity	Item	Sizes	Unit Price	Subtotal
25 pairs each	Turbostar Running Shoes	5, 5 ½ ,11, 12	€ 40.50	€ 4,050.00
50 pairs each		6, 6 ½, 7, 7 ½, 10	€ 40.50	€ 10,125.00
100 pairs each		8, 8 ½, 9, 9 ½	€ 40.50	€ 16,200.00

Total Price   € 30,375.00

tax-exempt intra-Community delivery

Terms of delivery: EXW Neustadt
Terms of payment: Cash on receipt of invoice

Please instruct your bank to forward the payment order through

Bank: Bayernbank AG
BIC: BABADET TS08
In favour of: Herkules AG
Bank account number: 214365987
IBAN: DE49 2006 0460 0214 3659 87

3
R Study the invoice and find words and expressions for the following German equivalents.

1. Gesamtpreis
2. Preis pro Einheit/Stückpreis
3. Zahlungsbedingungen
4. Artikel
5. Lieferbedingungen
6. Größen
7. Menge
8. Rechnung
9. Zwischensumme

✳ 4
P Study the invoice again and draw up the invoice Cornelia Klinkenberg sent James Leigh on 14 August. Use your imagination for the missing details and refer back to:

1. the enquiry James Leigh sent Cornelia Klinkenberg (Unit 10, A)
2. the dispatch advice Cornelia Klinkenberg sent James Leigh (Unit 12, C)
3. James Leigh's reply to Cornelia Klinkenberg's reminder (Unit 13, C).

B Means and terms of payment

1 Means of payment in trade

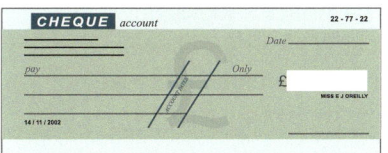

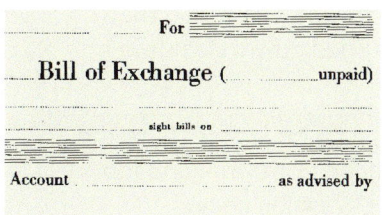

A **credit card** (Kreditkarte) issued by a major credit card company is widely accepted as a means of payment all over the world. The amount to be paid is advanced by the credit card company and debited to the cardholder's account at a later date.

A **debit (or bank) card** (Bankkarte) is issued by a bank. The account-holder may use it to pay for goods and services in shops without handling cash. It differs from credit cards in that the customer's account is immediately debited with the amount of the transaction. Bank cards can also be used to withdraw money from cash points (ATMs). The German EC card is a debit card.

A **cheque** (Scheck) is a written order to a bank to pay a sum of money to a named person or to the bearer (Überbringer) of the cheque. Crossed cheques (Verrechnungsschecks) require the sum to be paid into a bank account. In the UK cheques are still widely used in private and business transactions.

A **bill of exchange** (Wechsel) is a written order telling one person to pay a certain sum of money to a named person on demand or at a certain time in the future. Nowadays bills of exchange are used mainly in foreign trade. If the exporter wishes payment to be made immediately, he orders the importer to pay the invoice amount on demand, or "at sight", that means on presentation of the bill of exchange (B/E). Should the exporter be obliged to grant the importer credit, he will order him to pay the invoice amount at a certain time in the future, e.g. 60 days after the date of the B/E.

1 Match the following expressions with their German equivalents.

1. to accept a credit card	a. Geld abheben
2. to advance an amount	b. eine Kreditkarte annehmen
3. to debit an account	c. eine Bankkarte ausstellen
4. to grant credit	d. ein Konto belasten
5. to issue a bank card	e. Kredit gewähren
6. to withdraw money	f. einen Betrag vorschießen

∗ 2 Study the text on the bill of exchange on page 179 and translate the following
M text.

Mittels eines Wechsels kann der Verkäufer den Käufer auffordern, eine
bestimmte Summe zu einem bestimmten Zeitpunkt an eine bestimmte Person
zu zahlen. Der Verkäufer könnte auf dem Wechsel auch vorschreiben, dass der
Käufer den Betrag „auf Verlangen" zahlt. Die entsprechende Formulierung wäre
dann „zahlbar bei Sicht", d.h. bei Vorlage des Wechsels.

∗ 3 Übersetzen Sie nachstehenden Text zum Einsatz von Kreditkarten in
KMK Großbritannien ins Deutsche. Im Internet haben Sie Übersetzungen für folgende
Ausdrücke gefunden:

overindebted – überschuldet; to turn down an application – einen Antrag
ablehnen; debit card – Bankkarte; cashback – Auszahlung von Bargeld;
debt levels – Ausmaß der Verschuldung; check-out – Ladenkasse

Payment by plastic cards

In the UK payment by plastic cards overtook cash payments several years ago as
consumers use credit or debit cards more frequently. The vast majority of retail outlets
accept these cards as a matter of course and supermarkets offer cashback*. Adults now
have an average of 4 cards each and this is expected to rise to 5 cards by 2013. Last year
the number of credit cards issued rose by 13 per cent and the number of debit cards rose
by 6 per cent. Well over half of all debit card holders use their cards on a regular basis
when shopping.

Recently banks and other credit card providers have come in for criticism because of
fears that consumers are becoming over-indebted. A spokesman for the banks said that
between 40 and 50 per cent of all credit card applications were turned down. Debt levels
were a problem only for 4 per cent of households.

Plastic cards are essential for e-commerce. Four out of five adults who have access use the
internet for online shopping. A third of all online purchases are made from work and top
sites include major supermarkets and a well-known young people's fashion chain.

* If the customer wishes, they provide a sum in cash at the check-out, as stipulated by the customer.

4 Use the internet to find statistics on the preferred payment methods – cash, credit card, debit card, cheque, bank transfer – in Germany and the UK.

2 Terms of payment in foreign trade

The terms of payment chosen in an international transaction will depend on the size of the order, the creditworthiness of the customer and the banking system and political situation in the customer's country.

Payment in advance (Vorauszahlung) provides maximum security for the seller, e.g. when the goods have to be manufactured to the buyer's specifications. Payment in advance may also be part of staggered payment, e.g. ⅓ with order, ⅓ on delivery, ⅓ 30 days after delivery.

If **Cash on delivery (COD)** (Zahlung durch Nachnahme) has been agreed upon, the carrier (e.g. the postman) will hand over the goods to the buyer against payment or against written proof by the bank that payment has been effected.

Open credit (Zahlung gegen einfache Rechnung) terms are terms like "30 days net, 10 days 2%", which means that the buyer has to remit the invoice amount within 30 days. If he pays the amount within 10 days he will be entitled to deduct 2% cash discount from the invoice amount. Open credit terms provide little security for the seller but are widely used in transactions involving comparatively small sums and/or trusted customers.

In long-standing business relations it is customary to trade on **open account** terms (offenes Zahlungsziel). This means that the buyer does not pay individual invoices, but waits for the monthly statement of account.

A **letter of credit (L/C)** (Akkreditiv) is a promise made by the importer's bank to pay a certain sum to the exporter on presentation of specified documents, the most important of which is a clean bill of lading (see Unit 12). Nowadays L/Cs are irrevocable (unwiderruflich) that means they cannot be revoked without the consent of all parties concerned. As the L/C offers maximum security for both buyer and seller it has become one of the most widely used methods of payment in foreign trade. The exporter can be sure to receive payment as he can rely on the promise made by the importer's bank (the opening bank) – and in the case of a confirmed (bestätigtes) L/C – also on the promise of a bank in his own country (the confirming bank). The importer can be sure to receive the goods as the bank(s) will only advance the money against presentation of the shipping documents which prove that shipment has been effected.

1

R / M

Study the paragraph on the Letter of Credit on page 181. Choose the correct prepositions from the box for the following text. Then translate the text into German.

at • by • in • until

In a major export transaction the terms of payment may read as follows: **Terms of payment:** Payment **1** irrevocable and confirmed letter of credit, to be opened **2** our favour, payable **3** a German bank and valid **4** 31 July.

2

R

Complete the following business transactions by matching the terms of payment from the box with the numbers.

cash on delivery • letter of credit • open account terms • open credit • payment in advance

Wilson & Thatcher Ltd, a British retailer, also sells its high-quality shirts and blouses via the Internet. As a means of payment the firm accepts all major credit cards. For customers who refuse to disclose their credit card details on the internet, the retailer's terms of payment are **1** which means that the postman will collect the amount due.

International Snacks GmbH, a German food processing company, gets a phone call from its long-standing customer, Global Catering in Manchester, asking for another 500 tins of mini smoked sausages. These two business partners most likely trade on **2** .

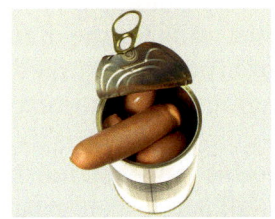

Powertools plc from Cardiff has received an enquiry from a new German customer who wishes to have 10,000 drill heads (Bohrköpfe) manufactured to the German firm's specifications. As Powertools would be unable to sell these drill heads to another customer if the deal broke down, Powertools will insist on **3** .

Norland Industries made an offer for colour printers to De Boer Office Equipment in Durban, South Africa. The terms of payment stipulated were: net cash within 30 days from receipt of invoice. Such terms of payment are referred to as **4** .

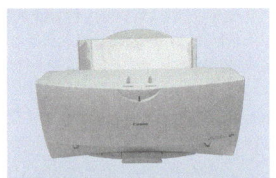

At Herkules, a German manufacturer of sports shoes and bags, the managers in charge of exports are discussing the terms of payment for a substantial order for sports bags from a firm in Bolivia they do not know. They decide to demand payment by **5** .

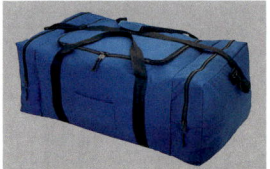

C Reminders

There are times when bills go unpaid and steps must be taken to collect the invoice amount. One or several reminders may have to be sent, with the requests for payment becoming increasingly insistent. At first a copy of the invoice or statement of account is sent suggesting that the invoice may have been overlooked. If further reminders by telephone, e-mail, fax, or letter have failed to produce the desired reaction, the seller will threaten to charge interest on arrears and to take legal steps unless payment is received by a certain deadline.

1 Reminders in writing

On 18 August the British department stores Hamilton's placed an urgent order for men's shirts with Superdress GmbH. Payment was to be effected 30 days after date of invoice. The goods were shipped by air and must have arrived at Manchester Airport on 22 August. It is now 10 October and no communication from Hamilton's has been received. Bastian Schneider, who is in charge of accounts at Superdress GmbH, decides to send a first polite reminder by fax.

1 **Complete Bastian Schneider's fax using the words from the box.**

R

above • aware • dated • due • grateful • immediate

Superdress GmbH

Fritz-Walter-Str. 28, 80469 München
Tel. +49 89 4677524, Fax +49 89 4677625
www.superdress.munich.de

Telefax Message

Date: 10 Oct 201_

Sender: Bastian Schneider, Accounts

To: Hamilton's Department Stores
Hamilton House
Beaumont Rd
Bolton
BL3 4TA

Attention: Richard Knight

Fax : +44 161 234 57799

Pages : 1 (including this)

Re: Our invoice no. OHGB / 42778 **1** 21 August

reference to invoice

Dear Mr. Knight

According to our records the **2** invoice, which was **3** on 21 September, has not been settled.

I wonder whether the invoice has been overlooked or if there has been a problem with this order of which we are not **4** ?

request for explanation

We should be **5** for an **6** settlement and look forward to serving you again.

request for settlement

Yours sincerely
Superdress GmbH

2

P

You are Richard Knight, purchasing manager at Hamilton's Department Stores, e-mail: richard.knight@hamiltons.co.uk. You have just received the fax on page 183 from Superdress GmbH.

Send Mr Schneider, whose e-mail address is b.schneider@superdress.munich.de, an e-mail:

- thanks for fax
- apologize for the delay in payment
- reason: new software in accounts department faulty
- operations now running smoothly at last
- bank instructed to remit invoice amount
- further orders probably next month

3

R

Restore the correct order of these jumbled elements of a final request for payment.

1 I still hope that you will make this action unnecessary by remitting the amount in full within the next seven days.

2 Dear Mr Clarke

3 This account has now remained unpaid for eight weeks and I cannot allow this state of affairs to continue. I regret that I will have to take legal steps unless payment is received in the course of one week.

4 Yours sincerely

Barbara Bruno
Legal Department

5 I am surprised to have received no reply to our previous e-mails and faxes asking for immediate settlement of the attached statement of account.

6 Re: Our statement of account number NZ / 7034 of 9 December 201_

4 Sie arbeiten bei Topelektronik in der Exportabteilung. Ihre Chefin hat gestern
KMK nachstehende E-Mail eines britischen Kunden erhalten.

**Bitte beantworten Sie die E-Mail und berücksichtigen Sie dabei die
handschriftlichen Anweisungen Ihrer Chefin.**

From:	james.leigh@leigh.co.uk
To:	cornelia.klinkenberg@topelektronik.de
Cc:	
Sent:	201_-09-27
Subject:	Your invoice No. 149 / 08 / 14

Attachments:

Dear Ms Klinkenberg

We have received your fax of 15 September concerning the above invoice and would like to
apologize for the delay in payment.

Today we have instructed our bank to transfer € 30,000 to your account. Much to our regret
we have to ask you to grant us a respite of eight weeks for the rest of the invoice amount.

Dank für Überweisung

You may have heard of the severe gale that devastated the South of England two weeks ago.
Unfortunately our warehouse was severely hit by the storm, parts of the roof were taken
off and much of our stock was soaked by the rain. As the insurance company will take some
time to assess the damage and compensate us, we are having to advance considerable sums
for the repairs to our warehouse and for the replacement of the damaged stock. This is why
we must ask you for the extension.

Bedauern über Sturmschäden, im Fernsehen Bilder gesehen

We hope you will understand our difficulties and grant us this concession.

Mit Aufschub grundsätzlich einverstanden

We are very sorry for the inconvenience caused and look forward to your comments.

Dennoch Bitte um Überweisung des Restbetrags sobald Leigh dazu in der Lage

Yours sincerely

*Grußformel: Best wishes
(Setzen Sie meinen Namen darunter)*

James Leigh
Leigh & Co. Ltd.
17 Camden Place   *Klinkenberg*
Bristol
BS6 6HR
Tel. 0117 4430030

✳ 5

KMK Sie (eigener Name) arbeiten im Rechnungswesen des Reisebüros Ferne Horizonte, Erfurt, Fax. +49 361 476903, Tel. +49 361 476900. Für den britischen Reiseveranstalter Sunshine Flights Ltd., Fax +44 1233 443006, hatten Sie für eine Gruppe eine Mountainbike-Tour im Thüringer Wald organisiert. Die Rechnung hierfür ist seit 6 Wochen überfällig. Eine erste Erinnerung war ohne Reaktion geblieben.

Schreiben Sie eine Mahnung unter Berücksichtigung folgender Punkte:

- Datum: 28. November
- Ansprechpartner: Margaret Allen
- Bezug auf Rechnung Nr. 009575 vom 04. Oktober
- Verweis auf Ihr Schreiben vom 14. November
- Rechnung inzwischen 6 Wochen überfällig
- Frage nach möglichen Gründen für Zahlungsverzug, da früher pünktlich gezahlt
- Bitte um sofortige Überweisung des Rechnungsbetrags, sonst Rücknahme der günstigen Zahlungsbedingungen
- Erwartung einer umgehenden Reaktion

2 Reminders and replies to reminders by telephone

1

R

◎ A1.27 Angela Schirmer from Digitaldruck GmbH in Wiesbaden rings their Spanish customer Imago S.A.

Listen to the dialogue and mark on your own sheet of paper whether the following statements are TRUE or FALSE.

1. Carmen Gonzales is the best person to talk to.
2. Olivia Rubio works in accounts.
3. The reference number is Z2P 7900.
4. Olivia Rubio transferred the amount of €13,723 five weeks ago.
5. This is the first time this year that there has been a delay in payment.
6. Olivia Rubio is going to transfer the amount immediately.

2

KMK

◎ A1.27 Sie sind Angela Schirmer und überwachen bei Digitaldruck GmbH den Rechnungseingang. Sie haben soeben einen spanischen Kunden wegen einer überfälligen Rechnung angerufen und das Gespräch aufgezeichnet.

Hören Sie sich das Gespräch noch einmal an und verfassen Sie darüber eine Aktennotiz für den Abteilungsleiter Dr. Klaus Werner.

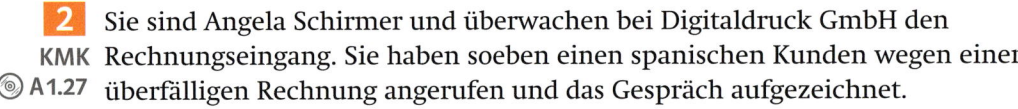

```
MEMO

Für:

Verfasser/in:                    Datum:

Gesprächspartner/in:

Betreff:
```

3 Work with a partner. Sit back to back and act out the telephone conversation using the prompts on the role cards on pages 251 and 252. Then change roles.

Language and grammar
Translate the following sentences.

1. Wir machen Sie darauf aufmerksam, dass die Zahlung per Kreditkarte erfolgen soll.
2. Das Unternehmen soll in 5 selbstständige Geschäftseinheiten aufgeteilt werden.
3. Sollen wir Ihnen die Preisliste per E-Mail zukommen lassen?
4. Soll die Rechnung Nr. ABC/1234 storniert werden?
5. Die neue Geschäftsleitung soll weiteren Stellenabbau planen.
6. Die neue Autobahn soll von einem privaten Unternehmen betrieben werden.
7. Der neue Exportleiter soll sehr tüchtig sein.

Language and grammar:
How to translate the German word "sollen"

Wendungen mit **sollen** werden von Deutschen häufig ungeschickt wiedergegeben.

Die direkte Entsprechung **shall** passt nur bei • Fragen • und juristischen Texten	Shall I help you? The parties to this contract shall notify the administrator within 24 hours.
should bedeutet **sollte (eigentlich)**:	You should put more emphasis on this point.
sollen kann im Geschäftskontext in Fragen mit **do you want me / us to ...?** übersetzt werden: Sollen wir diese Teile zurückschicken?	Do you want us to return these components?
to be to ... ist eine passende Übersetzung für **sollen** im Sinne einer Anordnung oder einer Absicht bzw. eines festen Planes: Die Bauarbeiter sollen sofort anfangen. Das Problem soll durch weitere Verhandlungen gelöst werden.	The builders are to start work immediately. The problem is to be solved by further negotiations.
Im Falle einer Absicht / eines Plans kann **to be to ...** durch **to be intended to / planned to ...** präzisiert werden: Die Erhöhung der Mehrwertsteuer soll den Haushalt ausgleichen. Die Ausstellung soll Anfang nächsten Jahres stattfinden.	The increase in VAT is intended to balance the budget. The exhibition is planned to take place early next year.
to be said to ... bedeutet **sollen** im Sinne von **es heißt, man sagt**: Die Firma soll sich in Schwierigkeiten befinden.	The company is said to be in trouble.

Industry expert

1 Documentary letter of credit (L/C)

✱ **KMK** **Clarissa ist Auszubildende in einem deutschen Industrieunternehmen. In ihrem Büro findet sie das folgende Fax vor. Lesen Sie den Text und beantworten Sie die Fragen dazu auf Deutsch.**

```
+ + + + + + + + + + + + + + + FAX + + + + + + + + + + + + + + + + + + + + + +

Ruhr Bank e.G., Karnaper Strasse 1904, 45329 Essen
Incoming message                                          Date: 1006201_
Issue of a documentary letter of credit

Sender address (applicant bank): India-Asia Bank of Commerce, Harrington Road,
Chetpet, Chennai 600031

Form of documentary letter of credit: irrevocable      Date of issue: 0806201_
Applicant: Ganesha Elecs private limited
Beneficiary: Hoffmann Maschinen GmbH, Lindenallee 4, 45894 Gelsenkirchen

Deferred payment details: 35 months from the date of shipment
Partial shipment: prohibited        Port of loading: Hamburg Seaport, Germany
Port of discharge: Chennai Seaport, India    Latest date of shipment: 2906201_

Description of goods: 250 fire detectors, series ABL

Documents required: 1. Manually signed commercial invoice in two originals
and two copies certifying that the goods are freely importable into India.
2. Certificate of origin issued by the chamber of commerce certifying that the
goods are of German origin. 3. Full set of three clean on board bill of lading
copies. 4. Signed packing list in duplicate stating net and gross weight.
5. Marine insurance policy certificate dated not later than the date of B/L
made to order and blank endorsed for 105 percent of invoice value from shipper's
warehouse to the warehouse of applicant.

Additional conditions: 1. All documents must be in English. 2. Shipping company
must certify that the vessel is registered with an approved classification
society and that the vessel is seaworthy and not more than 20 years old.

Period for presentation: within 15 days from the date of issue
```

1. In welcher Firma und in welcher Abteilung arbeitet Clarissa?
2. Beschreiben Sie die Situation, die diesem Fax zu entnehmen ist.
3. Wer ist der Antragsteller?
4. Wo ist der Bestimmungshafen?
5. Welche Art der Ware wird verschickt?
6. Wer stellt das Ursprungszeugnis aus?
7. Was bedeutet der Zusatz *clean on board* bei einem Konnossement?
8. Welche Angaben müssen auf der Packliste bestätigt werden?
9. Nennen Sie die Bedingungen für die Versicherungspolice.
10. Welche drei Voraussetzungen muss die Reederei erfüllen?
11. Innerhalb welcher Frist müssen die Dokumente der Ruhr Bank vorgelegt werden?

2 Documents against payment (D/P) and acceptance (D/A)

1 Match the expressions (a.–i.) with the correct numbers (1.–12.) in the diagramm
P below illustrating the process of D/P.

a. conclusion of contract of sales
b. credit to account
c. documents (B/L) (2x)
d. documents for collection (2x)
e. goods (2x)

f. money transfer
g. payment
h. presentation of documents
i. shipment of goods

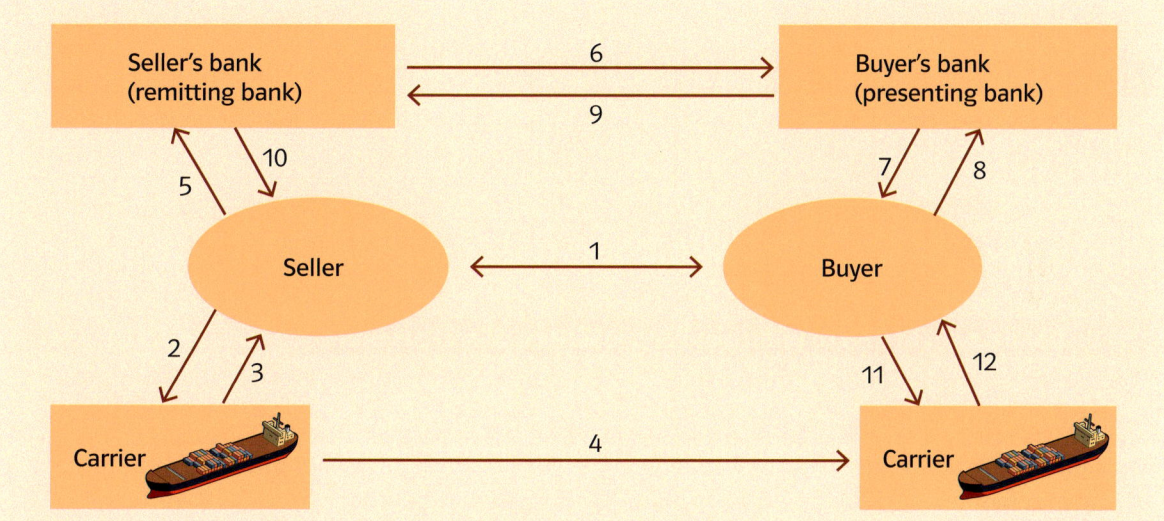

Advantage: Buyer cannot get the goods before payment.
Risks: If the buyer is not willing to pay or no longer able to pay the seller will
have a problem with the goods. He may sell them to someone else or he may
have to find a solution as to how to get the goods back at his own expense.

2 Give reasons why Clarissa's company has chosen L/C as term of payment.
P

Info: Documents against payment and acceptance

When a company chooses the payment method D/P it wants to make sure
that the buyer only gets the goods when he pays for the documents (e.g. B/L).
The seller hands over the documents to his bank and they pass them over to the
buyer's bank. The buyer's bank is only allowed to hand out the documents to the
buyer when he makes payment or, in the case of D/A, when he accepts the draft.

Phrases: Invoices and reminders

To refer to the invoice or statement of account

We are sending you our invoice No. 43-298 **amounting to** €304.75 as an attachment.	Als Anhang senden wir Ihnen unsere Rechnung Nr. 43-298 in Höhe von €304,75.
The enclosed statement of account shows a balance of €5,402.90 **in** our favour.	Der beiliegende Kontoauszug weist einen Saldo von €5.402,90 zu unseren Gunsten auf.
The invoice was due **on** 31 July.	Die Rechnung war am 31. Juli fällig.
The invoice amount is now four weeks overdue.	Der Rechnungsbetrag ist nun vier Wochen überfällig.

To suggest an oversight or demand an explanation

I wonder whether the invoice has been overlooked.	Ich frage mich, ob die Rechnung übersehen wurde.
You have not given us any explanation for the delay **in** payment.	Sie haben uns keinerlei Erklärung für den Zahlungsverzug gegeben.

To demand payment and to point out consequences of non-payment

Please remit the amount due immediately.	Bitte überweisen Sie den fälligen Betrag umgehend.
We should be grateful for an early settlement of our statement of account.	Für baldigen Ausgleich unseres Kontoauszugs wären wir dankbar.
We would ask you to clear the balance without further delay.	Wir möchten Sie bitten, den Saldo unverzüglich auszugleichen.
We must insist that you make payment **by** 5 May at the latest.	Wir müssen darauf bestehen, dass Sie die Zahlung bis spätestens 5. Mai vornehmen.
Should you fail to meet this deadline we shall have no option **but** to change our terms of payment.	Sollten Sie diese Frist nicht einhalten, bleibt uns keine andere Wahl als unsere Zahlungsbedingungen zu ändern.
If we do not receive payment **by** the end of the week, we will have to stop further deliveries.	Wenn Ihre Zahlung nicht bis Ende der Woche hier eingeht, müssen wir die Belieferung einstellen.
I will have to take legal steps if you do not settle the account within 7 days.	Ich werde juristische Schritte einleiten müssen, falls Sie die Rechnung nicht innerhalb von 7 Tagen begleichen.
Unless you remit the amount **in** time, we will hand the matter over to a collection agency.	Wenn Sie den Betrag nicht rechtzeitig überweisen, übergeben wir die Angelegenheit einem Inkassounternehmen.

To close the reminder

If payment has already been effected in the meantime, please disregard this letter.	Sollte die Zahlung inzwischen erfolgt sein, betrachten Sie diesen Brief bitte als gegenstandslos.
We should be sorry to lose a long-standing customer and would ask you to contact us immediately.	Wir würden einen langjährigen Kunden nur ungern verlieren, setzen Sie sich deshalb bitte sofort mit uns in Verbindung.
We are looking forward to an early settlement.	Wir erwarten Ihre baldige Zahlung.

To reply to a reminder

We have instructed our bank to transfer the sum of € 7,455 **to** your account **with** Sachsenbank.	Wir haben unsere Bank angewiesen, den Betrag von € 7.455 auf Ihr Konto bei der Sachsenbank zu überweisen.
We have received your letter **of** 2 July and thank you for your patience.	Wir haben Ihr Schreiben vom 2. Juli erhalten und danken Ihnen für Ihre Geduld.
We assure you that payment will be effected in full as soon as our computers are operational again.	Wir versichern Ihnen, dass die Zahlung in voller Höhe erfolgt, sobald unsere Rechner wieder funktionieren.
We are deeply sorry that the invoice has become overdue.	Es tut uns sehr leid, dass die Rechnung überfällig wurde.
We apologize for the delay **in** payment.	Wir entschuldigen uns für den Zahlungsverzug.
The delay was due to • an oversight. • a breakdown of our computer system. • an error **by** our bank.	Der Grund für den Zahlungsverzug war • ein Versehen. • eine Störung unserer EDV-Anlage. • ein Irrtum unserer Bank.
We are afraid we must ask you **for** an extension of 4 weeks.	Wir müssen Sie leider um einen Aufschub von 4 Wochen bitten.
We suggest that we pay **in** 3 instalments **of** $30,330.	Wir schlagen vor, dass wir in 3 Raten von $30.330 zahlen.
We are prepared to pay 7% interest on arrears.	Wir erklären uns bereit, Verzugszinsen in Höhe von 7% zu entrichten.
We hope you will understand our difficult situation and grant us this concession.	Wir hoffen, Sie haben Verständnis für unsere schwierige Lage und machen uns dieses Zugeständnis.

Unit 14
Complaints and adjustments

A   Making complaints

Even though in business transactions not "everything that can go
wrong, will" – as the saying goes – it will sometimes be necessary to
make a complaint. Goods or services may have been supplied too late,
goods may be faulty or damaged, services may prove unsatisfactory, the wrong goods
or the wrong quantities may have been delivered etc. In such cases the customer
must promptly notify the seller of the problem in writing, especially if a complaint by
telephone has not brought the desired result. A complaint should not be written to
express anger, but to get results. It should be calm and polite but also firm. In your
written complaint you should
- give all the necessary details of the transaction (order No., date of delivery, etc.)
- describe the problem clearly (327 mugs broken, hotel noisy, etc.)
- stress the inconvenience caused
- suggest a solution (replacement, discount, etc.)
- ask for immediate action

Online-Link
808262-0014

1 Übertragen Sie den Text auf Seite 192 ins Deutsche.

KMK

2 Match the causes for complaint on the left with the suggested solutions on the right. Sometimes several solutions may be appropriate.

1. delay in delivery	a. grant a price reduction
2. faulty goods	b. improve the service rendered
3. goods damaged	c. repair the goods
4. services unsatisfactory	d. replace the goods
5. the wrong goods	e. send the goods by air freight
6. wrong quantity	f. send the missing quantity
	g. take back the goods
	h. take back the surplus goods
	i. send a credit note

3 Describe to your class a recent experience when you had reason to complain or

P   actually made a complaint. If you can't think of any, use the prompts below.

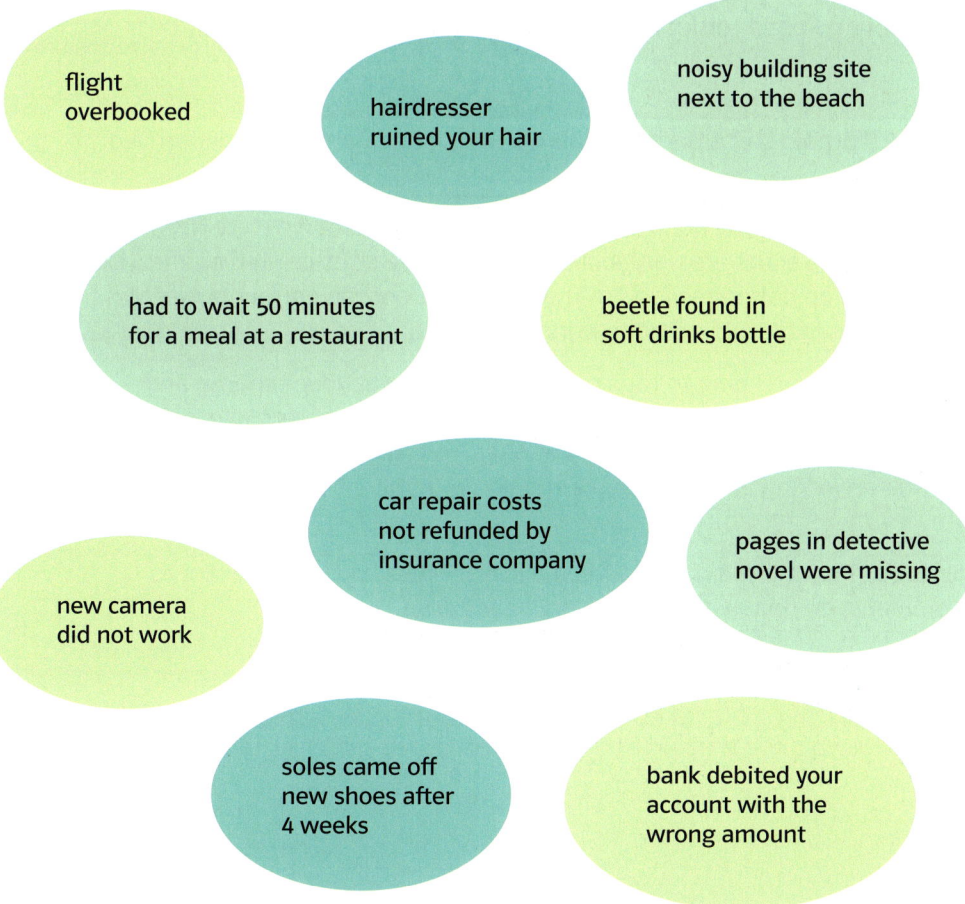

flight overbooked

hairdresser ruined your hair

noisy building site next to the beach

had to wait 50 minutes for a meal at a restaurant

beetle found in soft drinks bottle

car repair costs not refunded by insurance company

pages in detective novel were missing

new camera did not work

soles came off new shoes after 4 weeks

bank debited your account with the wrong amount

1 Complaints in writing

The British chain of sports equipment, SPORTS ISLAND, has just received a consignment of polo shirts from a new supplier in India. Unfortunately their Incoming Goods Control has found that most of the polo shirts are not correctly labelled. Sarah Brookfield, the purchasing manager, decides to complain by e-mail.

From:	sarah.brookfield@sportsisland.co.uk
To:	mahajan@indiasports.id
Cc:	
Sent:	201_-01-31
Subject:	Polo shirts, our purchase order No. PH / 346 / 06 of 18 Dec 201_

Attachments:

Dear Mr Mahajan

The consignment of 5,000 polo shirts under our above-mentioned purchase order arrived yesterday in due course.

> detailed reference to order

However, when our Incoming Goods Control checked the merchandise we were dismayed to find that most of the polo shirts are not labelled correctly. The sizes printed on the inside tags sewn onto the shirts do not correspond to the actual sizes of the garments. Needless to say, the polo shirts cannot be sold with these incorrect tags.

> description of problem

As it would be rather time-consuming to return the goods to you at your expense and wait for a replacement delivery, I would like to suggest that we commission a local firm to remove the tags and replace them with the right ones. You would, of course, have to bear the costs for the reworking and send us the required number of tags by air as soon as possible.

> solution suggested

We are disappointed at the way you have handled our first order and look forward to receiving your comments on this matter in the very near future.

> request for prompt adjustment

Best regards

Sarah Brookfield
Purchasing Manager

SPORTS ISLAND
41 Bryant Road
London W7 9QB
Tel. 020 74127333
Fax 020 74127334

1 Read Sarah Brookfield's e-mail several times. Then cover it up and complete these
R   sentences on your own sheet of paper.

1. The consignment of polo shirts arrived yesterday **1**.
2. We were dismayed to find that most of the polo shirts **2**.
3. **3** the polo shirts cannot be sold with these incorrect tags.
4. As it would be **4** to return the goods to you at your expense …
5. You would, of course, **5** for the reworking …
6. We are disappointed **6** our first order …

2 Restore the correct order of these jumbled elements of a complaint about a delay
R   in delivery.

1   This matter is causing us great inconvenience and we hope you will do your
       utmost to deliver the tool kits without any further delay.

2   On 31 July we placed the above mentioned order with you which you
       confirmed the next day assuring us of delivery within 3 weeks.

3   Subject: Delay in delivery of our order No. W-549 / 07 for 1000 household
       tool kits

4   We hope to receive your comments by return.

5   Dear Mr Vernon

6   Since then 5 weeks have passed and we have neither received the tool
       kits nor heard anything from you.

7   Yours sincerely
       Hammer Werkzeughandel

8   Tanja Kirchner
       Purchasing Department

9   As our own customers are getting impatient we must insist on immediate
       delivery. Should you fail to deliver by the end of next week we are afraid that
       we shall have no option but to cancel the order and seek another supplier.

3 You (Markus Reber) work in the personnel department of Otto Greiling GmbH
P (e-mail: personnel@ottogreiling.aol.com), a major supplier to the car industry. For several years your firm has been sending junior executives to a language school in Brighton, UK, for intensive coaching in business English. This year's two participants were, however, not completely satisfied with the language school's services when they attended the course from October 14 to 20.

Send the principal an e-mail. (E-mail: pam.robinson@businessspeak.co.uk)

- Point out the following shortcomings:
  - accommodation at private hotel inadequate – central heating system out of order
  - participants' needs (the language of export procedures) not properly taken into account
  - one morning teacher did not turn up, took school three hours to organise replacement
  - golf course closed for refurbishment.
- Ask for refund of part of the course fees.
- Ask the school to take up the matter with the hotel.
- Close on a friendly note considering your long business relationship.

✳ 4 Sie sind Christiane Sauer und sind bei Ihrer Firma, Zuckermann & Sacher,
KMK Farinweg 19, 73979 Suessen, für den Einkauf von Büromaterial zuständig. Seit 4 Jahren beziehen Sie jedes Quartal Drucker- und Kopierpapier sowie Umschläge aller Art von der britischen Firma East Anglia Stationery Ltd., 6 Malvern Business Park, Ely, CB6 4JR, UK. In der letzten Zeit hat Ihnen dieser Lieferant wiederholt Anlass zur Unzufriedenheit gegeben.

Schreiben Sie einen förmlichen Beschwerdebrief an den Geschäftsführer, Charles Bingley, und führen Sie dabei Folgendes an:

- Datum: 30 Juli
- In den ersten Jahren keine Beanstandungen
- Seit letztem Jahr allmähliche Verschlechterung des Service:
  - Ware häufig nicht vorrätig
  - Lieferzeiten immer länger
  - keine prompte Reaktion auf E-Mails und Faxe
  - stets wechselnde Ansprechpartner am Telefon
  - dieses Jahr schon einmal zu viel und einmal zu wenig geliefert
- Mängel bei der heutigen Lieferung:
  - 150 000 Umschläge DIN A3 nicht selbstklebend (self-adhesive), (Auftrag Nr. 200-5437 vom 23. Juni)
  - Muster der beanstandeten Umschläge beigefügt
  - Bitte um Abholung der beanstandeten Umschläge bei nächster Gelegenheit
  - sofortiger Ersatz erforderlich
- Drei Monate Frist für Verbesserung des Service
- Andernfalls keine Verlängerung des Liefervertrags
- Anlage

2 Complaints by telephone

1
R Maria Sanchez from Papier Gehrke in Schwerin has placed an order for multilingual wall calendars with the US firm Calendars 4 U. Two weeks after the date the calendars should have arrived in Germany she rings Joan Reid at Calendars 4 U, whom she knows very well from numerous previous transactions.

Restore the order of their jumbled dialogue. Match the numbers with the letters.

Joan	Maria
1. Calendars 4U. Joan speaking. How can I help you?	a. Certainly. It is 4900/312 dated 18 July.
2. Hi Maria. Can you give me the order number and date?	b. You're welcome. Good bye Joan.
3. Here it is on my monitor. Is there a problem?	c. Yes, there certainly is. The calendars have not arrived yet. They ought to have been here two weeks ago.
4. I see that they should arrive in Germany any day now. We dispatched them a week ago by air-mail.	d. You could have mailed me.
5. I am very sorry about this. I was going to call you but whenever I got around to it, it seemed to be the wrong time of day in Europe.	e. Hello Joan, this is Maria Sanchez from Papier Gehrke in Schwerin, Germany. I'm calling about our order for calendars.
6. That's true. I am so sorry. I promise it won't happen again.	f. Well, as long as the calendars arrive in the next few days, no harm will be done.
7. Thank you very much for your patience.	g. Why didn't you let us know that delivery would be made two weeks later?
8. Bye Maria.	

2013

English
French
German

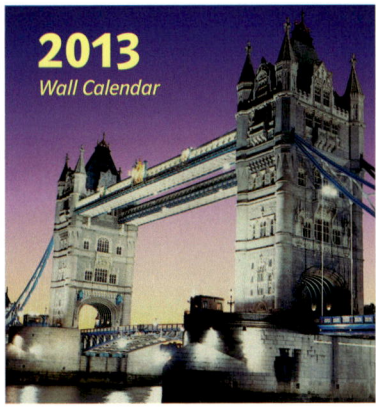

2013

Wall Calendar

2
I **Work with a partner. Draw up a similar dialogue about a delay in delivery. Then act it out with your partner.**

Phrases ▶

3

R

◎ A1.28

Kirsty Burnham of Global Catering in Manchester asks Kevin Sears to ring an Italian firm about their consignment of Italian speciality convenience foods.

Listen to the dialogue and answer the following questions.

1. Which firm does Kevin Sears work for?
2. What is Chiara Durini's position at Buongusto Italiano?
3. What is the problem with the sell-by date of the Parma ham and the mortadella antipasti?
4. Would it help if Chiara Durini gave Global Catering a discount?
5. By which means of transport is Chiara Durini going to send the replacement delivery?

4

R / P

◎ A1.28

You are Kevin Sears. First copy the form below. Then listen to the conversation again and write a memo in English for your boss, Kirsty Burnham.

```
TELEPHONE MEMO

For:      _____

From:     _____

Date:     _____

Caller:   _____

Subject:  _____
```

5

Nicole Sachse from Getränke König in Halle, Germany, had ordered 3000 sets of long drink glasses from Wexford Crystal in Sanditon, County Cork, Ireland. The consignment arrived punctually, but inspection has revealed that some glasses are broken und some are smaller than the others. Nicole rings Sean O'Sullivan at Wexford Crystal.

Act out their dialogue with your neighbour using the prompts below.

Nicole Sachse	Sean O'Sullivan
	Wexford Crystal/Exports/ Sean O'Sullivan
Nicole Sachse/Getränke König/Halle, Germany/ order of 10 September/3000 sets of long drink glasses	
	on monitor/colours red, blue and green/arrived?
arrived punctually/ inspection/disappointed/ one box damaged/50 sets of green glasses broken	
	sorry to hear/all sets checked before dispatch/ must have happened in transit/contact forwarders immediately
terms of delivery DAP Halle/Wexford Crystal deal with forwarder and/or insurance company/need replacements urgently	
	send replacements/by air/ this afternoon
transport free of charge/ confirmation by fax	
	certainly/once more apologies
afraid/must mention/ roughly ⅓ of the glasses/ slight differences in height/ about 1mm shorter	
	easy to explain/glasses pipe-blown by hand/differences inevitable/sign of hand-made glass/much more valuable/machine-made glasses always identical
sounds plausible/customers may not notice	
	pleased with the sets?
yes/colours brilliant/crystal glass clear/remind of replacements/good-bye	
	promise immediate dispatch/ again sorry thanks for call/bye

6 Work with a partner. Sit back to back and act out the telephone conversation using the prompts on the role cards. Then change roles.

Role card: Partner A (buyer)   Role card partner B ⇨ page 251

Sie haben über das Internet ein überaus preiswertes Skateboard gekauft und mit Kreditkarte bezahlt. In der Beschreibung des Skateboards auf der Webseite des Verkäufers war als zulässiges Höchstgewicht für den Benutzer 70 kg angegeben. Als das Skateboard wie versprochen nach 3 Tagen ankommt, müssen Sie feststellen, dass auf dem englisch beschrifteten Karton ein zulässiges Höchstgewicht von (nur) 90 lbs (= 40,8 kg) aufgedruckt ist. Sie rufen die Firma an und verlangen Rücknahme des Skateboards.

7 Communicating across cultures

Drücken Sie folgende Aussagen in (möglichst höflichem) Englisch aus:

1. Wir teilen Ihnen hiermit mit, dass wir mit Ihrem Kundendienst sehr unzufrieden sind.
2. Die Farbe entspricht nicht dem Muster.
3. Wir bestehen darauf, dass Sie uns den vollen Kaufpreis erstatten.

**Communicating across cultures:
Complaining about products or services**

In Germany correspondence in connection with complaints tends to be direct, stating the facts bluntly and requiring adjustment in no uncertain tones. This is the accepted usage here and nobody takes offence at the curt and no-nonsense style of German complaints. In the English-speaking world, on the other hand, complaints are formulated in a different way. The style is much more indirect, polite and conciliatory as nothing would be gained by antagonizing the other party; he / she would simply be less cooperative. So remember to express your complaint in a friendly and understanding manner.

Do not say:	**Say instead:**
I want to complain about …	I'm afraid I have to raise the matter of …
The glasses are broken.	Unfortunately, the glasses are broken.
You have made a mistake.	There must have been an error on your part / There seems to have been a mix-up somewhere.
You are wrong.	I'm afraid I cannot quite agree.
We expect you to send replacements.	We would be grateful if you would send replacements.
Therefore, we request a discount of 20%.	We think a discount of 20% would be appropriate.

 8 Use the Internet to find other examples of cultural differences or problems of intercultural communication. Make notes and compare your findings with the group.

B   Adjusting complaints

It is much easier to hold on to existing customers than to find new ones, so it is essential to manage customer complaints well. Remember, disgruntled customers are twice as likely as satisfied customers to tell others about their experience with your firm. When dealing with customer complaints you should

- thank the customer for making you aware of the problem
- treat the customer with courtesy and patience and tell him that you are sorry
- respond to the complaint quickly, telling the customer what will happen next
- if possible, give an explanation for what has happened
- involve the customer in the process of finding a solution
- suggest a compromise that meets the customer halfway if the complaint is not wholly justified
- ensure that all action promised is executed promptly
- explain the reasons before saying no, if the complaint is unjustified.

1 **Study the text above and translate the following recommendations**
M **taken from a textbook.**

                                                                21
_____

     Die Erledigung von Reklamationen muss mit großer
     Sorgfalt geschehen, um den Kunden nicht zu
     verlieren. Zunächst sollten Sie dem Kunden dafür
     danken, dass er Sie auf ein Problem aufmerksam
5   gemacht hat, und ihn dann in die Suche nach einer
     Lösung einbeziehen.
     Beschwerden müssen umgehend beantwortet und
     der Kunde über den Fortgang der Erledigung auf
     dem Laufenden gehalten werden. Wenn möglich,
10   sollten Sie dem Kunden erklären, wie es zu der für
     ihn unbefriedigenden Situation kommen konnte.
     Zudem müssen Sie den Kunden davon überzeugen,
     dass Sie Maßnahmen treffen werden oder schon
     eingeleitet haben, die sicherstellen, dass sich
15   solche Vorfälle nicht wiederholen.
     Falls die Reklamation nur teilweise begründet ist,
     sollten Sie versuchen, sich mit dem Kunden auf
     einen Kompromiss zu einigen. Sind Sie gezwungen,
     die Reklamation als völlig unbegründet
20   zurückzuweisen, empfiehlt es sich zuerst die
     Gründe zu erläutern, bevor die Absage erteilt wird.

2 Match the complaints on the left with the appropriate explanations on the right.

R

1. Although you promised delivery within a week, our order no. 7040 has not yet arrived. Could you please look into this matter?

2. On 18 January we ordered 700 jars of tomato relish by phone but you sent us only 400 jars. Would you please arrange for the missing 300 to be shipped to us immediately?

3. When we signed the contract for the building of the conservatory you promised that the work would be completed in four weeks. That was 2 months ago and the work is still only half finished.

4. The packaging of the DVDs appeared to be in perfect condition. On unpacking the DVDs, however, we discovered a number of scratches. A list of the damaged DVDs is enclosed.

a. 300 jars of tomato relish have already been handed over to our forwarders for transportation to Germany. We are very sorry for this oversight. It seems that the person processing your order must have mistaken the handwritten 7 on the telephone memo for a 4.

b. We are at a loss to understand how this could have happened. Nevertheless we will be sending you replacements for the damaged goods first thing tomorrow morning. A thorough investigation into our quality control procedures has already been initiated.

c. Please accept our apologies for the delay. Your order was dispatched the day before yesterday and should reach you in the next few days. We apologize once more for the delay that was due to the introduction of new software in our dispatch department.

d. I would like to apologize for the delay for which we are, however, not entirely to blame. When work was in progress you asked for a number of alterations that held up work. For example, there was an additional delivery time for the Italian tiles you insisted on instead of the British ones provided for in our offer.

3 Kunal Mahajan from India Sports replies to Sarah Brookfield's e-mail concerning
R the faulty labelling of the polo shirts SPORTS ISLAND had ordered from India
Sports.

Complete Kunal's e-mail using the expressions from the box.

prepared to • promise to improve • the inconvenience caused • the trouble you
have had • to our attention

From:	mahajan@indiasports.id	
To:	sarah.brookfield@sportsisland.co.uk	
Cc:		
Sent:	201_-02-01	Attachments:
Subject:	Polo shirts, your purchase order No. PH / 346 / 06 of 18 Dec 201_	

Dear Ms Brookfield

Thank you for your e-mail drawing a serious problem **1** .

> thanks for information

We are very sorry for **2** by the incorrect labelling of the polo shirts and thank you for
suggesting a solution. We perfectly agree with you that it would be best to ask a firm in
Britain to replace the tags. An ample quantity of new tags have already been dispatched to
your address by air.

> apologies and suggestion for adjustment

It goes without saying that we are **3** bear the costs for the re-labelling of the polo shirts.

Meanwhile we have started investigations into how this faulty labelling could have
happened and **4** our quality control procedures.

> promise of improvement

To make up for **5** , we would like to offer you a price reduction of 10% on your next order.

> goodwill ending

We look forward to hearing from you again.

Best regards

Kunal Mahajan
Export Manager
India Sports
112 Delhi Road, Meerut-250 001
Uttar Pradesh, India
Tel. +91 121 2512270
Fax +91 121 2512275

4 Restore the correct order of these jumbled elements of a reply to a complaint
R about a delay in delivery.

1 We are, therefore, prepared to release you from the contract.

2 Dear Ms Kirchner

3 We have not contacted you before because we were hoping to locate
another manufacturer willing to supply similar tool kits at short notice.
So far, however, we have not met with success.

4 Yours sincerely
James Vernon
Export Manager

5 Please accept our sincere apologies. We hope to be of service to you at
another time in the future.

6 Re: Your order no. W-549 / 07

7 I'm afraid we are after all unable to execute your order for 1000 household
tool kits for the time being as our own supplier, our parent company, has
become insolvent.

8 Thank you for your e-mail.

5 You are Pam Robinson, principal of BUSINESS SPEAK, the language school
P in Brighton which 2 junior executives from Otto Greiling GmbH, Germany, attended for a week's intensive coaching in business English. Markus Reber from their human resources department has sent you an e-mail complaining about some shortcomings concerning the course from October 14 to 20:

- accommodation at private hotel inadequate – central heating system out of order
- participants' needs (the language of export procedures) not properly taken into account
- one morning teacher did not turn up, took school three hours to organise replacement
- golf course closed for refurbishment

Reply by e-mail, bearing in mind that Markus Reber has been sending staff to your courses for several years.

- spoken with hotel manager, hotel prepared to reduce price by ⅓, cheque under way by post
- export procedures dealt with as always, never any complaint about this before
- apologies for teacher not turning up one morning, had a fall in the bathroom, had to be taken to hospital, you did your best to organise replacement
- participants informed in advance that the golf course would be out of use
- very sorry that participants should be dissatisfied
- sent them each a copy of "Doing Business in the UK" in compensation
- hope that cordial relations will not be affected

✶ 6 Sie sind Henry Crawford, der neue Geschäftsführer von East Anglia Stationery
KMK Ltd., 6 Malvern Business Park, Ely CB6 4JR, UK. Die deutsche Firma Zuckermann & Sacher, Farinweg 19, 73979 Suessen, bezieht von Ihnen seit Jahren Drucker- und Kopierpapier sowie Umschläge. Christiane Sauer, zuständig für den Einkauf von Büromaterial, ist inzwischen mit Ihrem Service unzufrieden und hat sich bei Ihnen in einem förmlichen Schreiben beschwert (siehe S. 196).

Beantworten Sie ihren Brief in Englisch unter Berücksichtigung folgender Punkte:

- Datum: 5. August
- Vorstellung Ihrer Person
- Ihr Vorgänger, Charles Bingley, nach längerer Krankheit im Ruhestand
- Beanstandete Unzulänglichkeiten verursacht durch Mr. Bingley's Abwesenheit
- Radikale Maßnahmen eingeleitet
- Service in Kürze wieder einwandfrei
- Entschuldigung
- Ersatzlieferung Umschläge bereits unterwegs
- 20 % Rabatt auf diesen Auftrag
- Beanstandete Umschläge werden kommenden Mittwoch abgeholt
- Hoffnung auf weitere gute Beziehungen

Language and grammar
Find the correct form of the verbs in brackets.

1. We will grant you 10% quantity discount if you (order) at least 500 units.
2. We would place a substantial order if you (can promise) delivery within one week.
3. We would not have dispatched the goods if they (not be) in perfect condition.
4. We (be glad) if you looked into the matter without delay.
5. Unless you instruct us to the contrary, shipment (be effected) on receipt of new supplies.
6. It (be) most helpful if the sets could reach us before the end of the month.
7. You would be taking a great risk if you (invest) your money in that project.
8. Should you be uncertain about any aspect of it, please (not hesitate) to give me a call.
9. If we (accept) their order we would have to recruit three additional workers.
10. If she had worked harder she (not fail) the exam.

Language and grammar: Conditional clauses

Bedingungssätze (conditional clauses) werden im Englischen nach einem relativ festen Schema gestaltet. Es gibt drei Grundtypen von Bedingungssätzen:

Hauptsatz	Nebensatz der Bedingung
We will take the goods back (FUTURE) (wir **werden** …)	if you return them at your expense. (PRESENT TENSE)
We would grant you a discount (CONDITIONAL) (wir **würden** …)	if you increased your order. (SIMPLE PAST)
He would have taken part in the meeting (CONDITIONAL PERFECT) (er **hätte** …)	if he had not been away on a business trip. (PAST PERFECT)

Das Schema gilt auch dann, wenn der Nebensatz der Bedingung vor dem Hauptsatz steht:

If it is fine on Friday	we will have the office party in the park.
If you applied	you would get the job.
If you had applied	you would have got the job.

Ferner gilt das Schema, wenn der Nebensatz durch eine andere Konjunktion eingeleitet wird: wie z. B. unless (wenn nicht, außer wenn), provided (that) (vorausgesetzt, dass), on condition (that) (unter der Bedingung, dass):

They will not place any further orders	unless you offer a satisfactory solution.
Employees may smoke	provided they go out into the courtyard.

Eine besondere Form stellt der Bedingungssatz ohne Konjunktion dar:

Should you have any further questions	please do not hesitate to ask.
But for John helping out (If John had not helped out …)	we would never have coped with the sudden demand.

Eine Ausnahme von diesem Schema bildet die höfliche Bitte in der Geschäftskorrespondenz:

We would be grateful	if you would grant us a respite of 4 weeks.

Industry expert

Complaints in the industrial sector

1 Read the following text and answer the questions below.

R

Too few, too many, defective, poor packaging, goods damaged or lost in transit – there are many possible reasons for a complaint. Whatever the reason might be, it is always an uncomfortable situation for the industrial company. It normally costs a lot of money because you need staff to deal with the complaints and you have to fulfil the customers' requirements and offer compensation as you do not want to lose them. The best way to minimise complaints is to avoid mistakes during production.

In a globalised world, competition is getting fierce and management is focused on short-term profits. David Kusnet, a former speechwriter for President Clinton and author of *Love the Work, Hate the Job*, draws the conclusion that workers love their work, their skills, the products they make and the services they provide, but they are beginning to hate their jobs. Instead of product improvements and dedication to quality, CEOs often choose the cost-cutting way to gain as much profit as possible and that leads to a reduction in product quality. But is this really the most efficient approach in the long run?

1. Name the most common reasons for complaints.
2. Why are complaints costly for companies?
3. Who is David Kusnet?
4. Why are workers beginning to hate their jobs?
5. What are cost-cutting measures? Think also about your company.

2 Lilith Stern arbeitet als Abteilungsleiterin für die Hoffmann Maschinen GmbH und hat von der Firma Ganesha Elecs einen Beschwerdebrief erhalten. Lesen Sie den Brief auf Seite 208 und schreiben Sie für Lilith Stern einen höflichen Antwortbrief unter Verwendung der folgender Angaben:

KMK

`Phrases` ▶

- Bezug auf den Beschwerdebrief mit Angabe der Auftragsnummer
- Bringen Sie Ihr Bedauern zum Ausdruck
- Bis heute keine Beschwerden über defekte Sensoren
- Verkratzte Feuermelder wegen unsachgemäßer Behandlung beim Transport
- Werden mit Spediteur Kontakt aufnehmen
- Vorschlag: Sie stimmen 25 % Preisreduktion auf zerkratzte Feuermelder zu
- Selbstverständlich Ersatz der defekten Sensoren innerhalb 1 Woche nach Erhalt der defekten Sensoren; Rücksendung der defekten Sensoren auf unsere Kosten
- Nochmalige Entschuldigung und Hoffnung, dass Geschäftsbeziehung nicht beeinträchtigt wird

GANESHA ELECS *private limited*
Peters Road
600031 Chennai
India

Hoffmann Maschinen GmbH
Lilith Stern
Lindenallee 4
45894 Gelsenkirchen
Germany

26 July 201_

Dear Ms Stern

Defective fire detectors

We are writing with reference to our order no 643.B. We regret to inform you that the consignment has not turned out to our satisfaction. On unpacking the cases we discovered that three units are seriously scratched. Furthermore we have received several complaints about your fire detectors from our heads of department, who found that some of the sensors are defective.

We would ask you to replace the eight defective fire detectors, which we will return to you at your expense. We would be willing to keep the scratched items if you grant us a price reduction of 25 %.

We expect you to settle the matter immediately and to our full satisfaction.

Yours sincerely

Amal Farhat

Amal Farhat
Purchasing Manager

---

3 Donna Peterson ruft bei der Firma Wattner AG, einem Hersteller von Telefonsystemen, in Kassel an und beschwert sich über eine nicht zufrieden stellend erbrachte Leistung. Beantworten Sie stichwortartig die folgenden Fragen auf Deutsch. Sie hören den Text zweimal.

KMK
◎ A 2.4

1. Aus welcher Stadt ruft Donna Peterson an?
2. Wie lautet die Auftragsnummer?
3. Was wurde installiert?
4. Welche zwei Sonderwünsche hatte das Cancer Research Centre?
5. Worüber beschwert sich Donna Peterson?
6. Auf welche Schadensregelung einigen sie sich?
7. Welche Gründe führt Herr Kuntz für die kulante Schadensregelung seitens seiner Firma an?
8. Wie lautet Donna Petersons E-Mail-Adresse?

✳ 4 Schreiben Sie im Namen der Wattner AG eine E-Mail an Donna Peterson, in der Sie die Vereinbarungen, die Matthias Kuntz mit Donna Peterson getroffen hat, bestätigen.

KMK

Phrases ▶

Phrases: Complaints and adjustments

To start a complaint

We are writing **with** reference to our order no …	Wir nehmen Bezug auf unseren Auftrag Nr. …
We regret to report that we have not yet received the goods ordered **on** 18 May.	Wir bedauern, Ihnen mitteilen zu müssen, dass wir die am 18. Mai bestellten Waren noch nicht erhalten haben.

To give reasons for your complaint

On unpacking the cases our Incoming Goods Control discovered that 15 items are missing.	Beim Auspacken der Kisten stellte unsere Warenannahme fest, dass 15 Positionen fehlen.
We are afraid that several units are – seriously damaged/defective. – broken/badly scratched/stained.	Leider sind mehrere Teile – schwer beschädigt/schadhaft. – zerbrochen/stark zerkratzt/verschmutzt.
The goods should have arrived a week **ago**.	Die Waren hätten schon vor einer Woche eintreffen sollen.
We are sorry to point out that the repair work has been poorly executed.	Wir müssen leider darauf hinweisen, dass die Reparatur schlecht ausgeführt wurde.

To mention likely reasons for the problem

We believe that the damage may be due to rough handling **in** transit.	Wir glauben, dass der Schaden auf unsachgemäße Behandlung beim Transport zurückzuführen ist.
Apparently, our order was **mixed up** with another customer's order.	Unser Auftrag wurde anscheinend mit einem anderen verwechselt.

To inform the seller what you expect him to do and what steps you are taking

Please arrange **for** the immediate dispatch of the missing items.	Bitte sorgen Sie dafür, dass die fehlenden Artikel sofort abgeschickt werden.
We would ask you to – replace the faulty goods **at** your expense. – have the defective articles collected **at** our warehouse. – grant us a price reduction **of** 20%. – cut the price **to** €780.	Wir möchten Sie bitten, – die mangelhafte Ware auf Ihre Kosten zu ersetzen. – die schadhaften Artikel von unserem Lager abholen zu lassen. – uns einen Preisnachlass von 20% zu gewähren. – den Preis auf €780 zu senken.

To demand prompt adjustment

We expect that you will settle this matter speedily and **to** our entire satisfaction.	Wir erwarten, dass Sie die Sache rasch und zu unserer vollen Zufriedenheit regeln.

To refer to a complaint received

Thank you for your e-mail drawing a serious problem **to** our attention.	Danke für Ihre E-Mail, mit der Sie uns auf ein ernstes Problem aufmerksam gemacht haben.

To apologize

We wish to apologize for this mistake.	Wir bitten für diesen Fehler um Entschuldigung.
We are extremely sorry **for** the poor service you have received.	Es tut uns außerordentlich leid, dass Sie so schlecht bedient wurden.

To explain the problem or promise to investigate it

The damage was caused **by** a software failure.	Der Schaden wurde durch fehlerhafte Software verursacht.
We will investigate the matter thoroughly and inform you of the steps taken.	Wir werden die Angelegenheit gründlich untersuchen und Sie über die Schritte informieren, die wir unternommen haben.

To suggest a solution and inform the buyer what you expect him to do

We are pleased to say that replacements are now **on** their way to you.	Wir freuen uns, Ihnen mitteilen zu können, dass Ersatz bereits unterwegs ist.
Please return the faulty items **at** our expense.	Bitte senden Sie die mangelhaften Artikel auf unsere Kosten zurück.
We are prepared to reduce the price **by** 15 % if you decide to keep the goods.	Wir sind bereit, den Preis um 15 % zu senken, wenn Sie sich entschließen, die Ware zu behalten.

To reject an unfounded claim

After careful examination of the case we must say that the order was carried out in accordance with the contract.	Nach gründlicher Untersuchung des Falles müssen wir festhalten, dass der Auftrag vertragsgemäß ausgeführt wurde.
As we are **in no way** to blame we have no alternative but to reject your claim.	Da uns keinerlei Schuld trifft, bleibt uns nichts anderes übrig, als Ihre Reklamation zurückzuweisen.

To close on a note designed to promote goodwill

We hope that this proposal will find your approval.	Wir hoffen, dieser Vorschlag findet Ihre Zustimmung.
We trust that the solution suggested will help to settle the matter **to** the satisfaction of all parties concerned.	Wir hoffen, dass die vorgeschlagene Lösung dazu beiträgt, die Angelegenheit zur Zufriedenheit aller Beteiligten zu erledigen.

Unit 15
Marketing products and services

Marketing includes a wide range of activities. Even when a product or service is still at the idea or design stage, companies set about finding out what sort of a market exists – for instance, what age group they should aim at and how likely people in this age group are to buy this product or service. When a company is planning a new product they need to decide on the "marketing mix" or 4Ps (product, price, place, promotion) – i.e. what kind of product to develop, what price to charge and what channels to sell it through – cheap chain or exclusive boutique, for instance. Finally, they will have to decide how and where to advertise.

1 Life cycle of a product

Products may be thought of as having a life cycle with five phases – introduction, growth, maturity, decline and phasing out. The focus of marketing changes, depending on the phase.

Online-Link
808262-0015

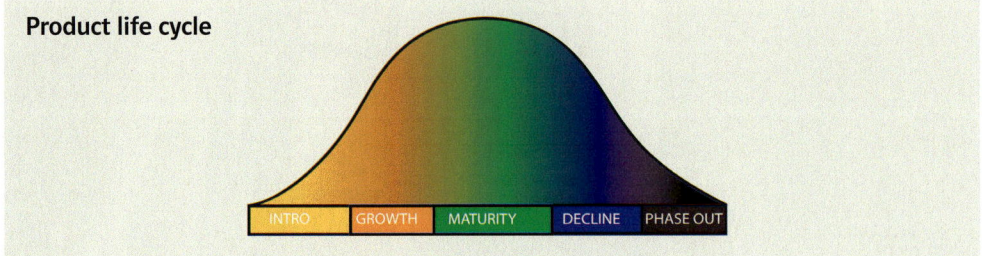

Product life cycle

INTRO   GROWTH   MATURITY   DECLINE   PHASE OUT

1 **Study the text on page 211 and the illustration above and decide whether the**
R   **following statements are TRUE or FALSE.**

1. Marketing is the same as advertising.
2. Marketing includes advertising.
3. Companies first design and produce a product and then see whether there's a
   market for it or not.
4. It is important for a company to have a clear idea of what group it is targeting.
5. Marketing is the same as selling.
6. It is always best to sell as cheaply as possible.
7. A product has a life cycle of six phases.
8. Sales reach a peak in the last phase.

2 **Use the internet to select what you consider to be the five leading brands in the**
UK. Make a few notes on what is associated with the brands and discuss your
results with the group.

2   Market research

Companies conduct market research to find out what people think about them and
their products. They also try to establish what needs or desires a particular target
group may have and how able or willing they will be to pay for a particular product
or service. This may involve "desk" research (e.g. statistics) or "field research".
The following is an example of field research.

Listen to the interview. The interviewer is ringing a random sample of people
R   **taken from the local telephone book. Complete the following sentences.**
◎ A1.29
1. Could you possibly spare a few minutes **1** ?
2. I am actually in a bit **2** .
3. We are doing a market survey **3** .
4. I tend to book flights and holidays **4** .
5. We are particularly interested in **5** .
6. Do you buy these articles regularly and how much do you **6** ?
7. I can do my shopping when I **7** .
8. Prices are often more **8** .
9. I often give up in **9** .
10. Would you visit the website more often if it were **10** ?

A Distribution channels

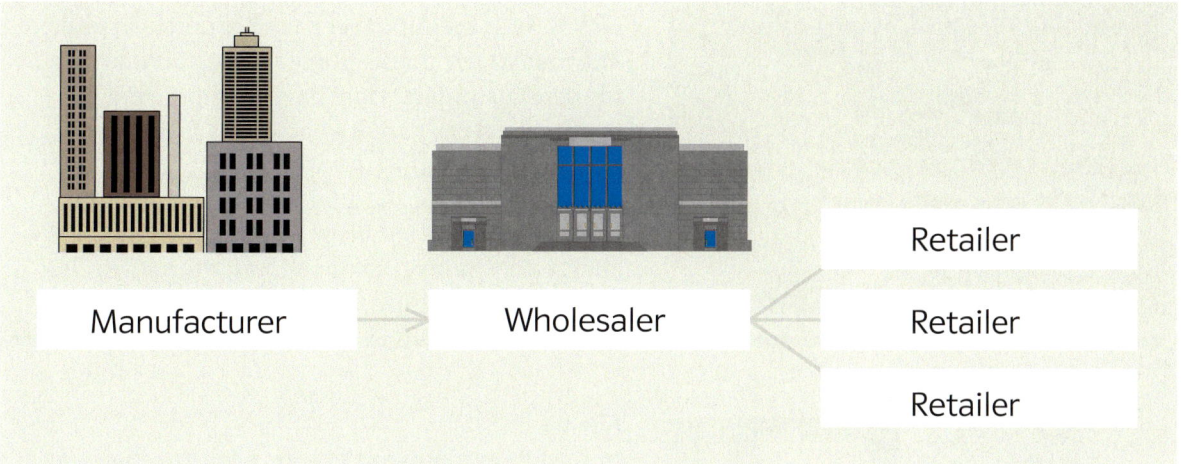

Distribution is also a part of marketing. Traditionally, wholesalers are the link between manufacturers and retailers. Manufacturers generally sell goods in large quantities to wholesalers who sell them on in smaller quantities to retailers (= "breaking bulk"). Retailers sell them to end users.

1 Retailers, wholesalers and agents

Retailers

Retailers ensure a supply of goods to the general public. There is a wide variety of retail outlets, starting with small specialist shops such as independent chemists, beauty consultants, opticians and exclusive fashion boutiques. Most High Street stores are, however, major chains with branches in a large number of towns and often in several countries. Supermarkets generally belong to one of a small number of major chains. Department stores sell many different kinds of goods under one roof. Large retailers, who buy in bulk, may order directly from manufacturers without involving a wholesaler.
Recently, online retailing has become the fastest growing segment.

Wholesalers

Wholesalers provide a range of services from which both manufacturers and retailers benefit. They may have a sales force to keep contact to their customers, they have warehousing facilities, offer a range of products from a number of manufacturers, and may offer credit facilities to their customers. Finally, they provide advisory services. However, wholesalers charge for their services and are, therefore, also a cost factor (putting up the price).

Agents

In foreign trade manufacturers often appoint an agent in the foreign country. This has a number of advantages. The agent speaks the language, he is familiar with the foreign market and will have the necessary contacts. He has an office and possibly warehousing facilities. He is usually paid on a commission basis which means he receives a percentage (say 3%) on sales. He is thus only paid when he succeeds in selling something. His principal has therefore few overheads.

1 Übertragen Sie folgende Sätze ins Deutsche.

KMK

1. Wholesalers are the link between manufacturers and retailers.
2. They may offer credit facilities to their customers.
3. Supermarkets belong to a small number of major chains.
4. Wholesalers charge for their services and are therefore a cost factor.
5. Wholesalers generally have warehousing facilities.

2 Answer the following questions.

1. In what way do wholesalers make life easier for manufacturers?
2. Why does a small retailer (e.g. a 24-hour mini-market or a small fashion boutique) need wholesalers?
3. Why may large retailers try to cut out the wholesaler?
4. Give examples of independent retailers (not part of chains).
5. What is the characteristic feature of a department store?

✳ **3** Übertragen Sie den obigen Text über „Agents" ins Deutsche.

KMK

4 Decide whether the following statements are TRUE or FALSE.

R

1. Agents are paid a commission whether they sell anything or not.
2. Wholesalers generally have warehousing facilities.
3. Retailers sell to end users.
4. Retailers buy in bulk and sell to wholesalers.
5. Wholesalers perform a useful service both for manufacturers and retailers.

5 Describe briefly the activities of retailers, wholesalers and agents.

P

6 Listen to the following statements in which young people taking part in a
R training seminar describe their place of employment. Take notes.

A 1.30

7 Now listen to the statements again, use your notes and answer the following
R / P questions in writing.

A 1.30

1. Does speaker 1 work for a wholesaler?
2. Does speaker 2 work for a retailer?
3. What does speaker 3 mean by "retail customers"?
4. Does speaker 4 work for a retailer or a wholesaler?
5. What sort of a company does speaker 5 work for?
6. What kind of customers help the shop of speaker 6 to survive?
7. Who does the company of speaker 7 sell its products through?
8. What kind of an organisation does speaker 8 work for?

2 E-commerce

1 Complete the following text using words from the box.

R

> outlets • major • credit cards • retail • via • online • charges • customers •
> facilities • wholesalers

An important development at the present time is the rapid growth of
e-commerce. This is revolutionising some **1** sectors. Internet retailing operations
are growing faster than traditional retail **2** . Shopping and booking flights,
hotels and holidays **3** the internet is becoming more and more popular. Some **4**
supermarkets have large internet operations. You can do your shopping **5** and
have the goods delivered.

Airlines offer online booking **6** , which makes it easy to compare prices and
avoid paying travel agents' **7** .

Wholesalers may also offer their **8** internet facilities (Business to Business –
B2B – services) to enable them to do their ordering at any time of the day or
night. However, internet exchanges are making **9** superfluous in some fields.

E-commerce is at present the fastest growing retail segment paralleled by a rapid
increase in the number of **10** .

2
KMK Beantworten Sie die Fragen zum folgenden Zeitungstext schriftlich in deutscher Sprache.

1. Warum mussten Online-Einzelhändler ihren Service stark verbessern?
2. Welche Vorteile bietet das Internet beim Preisvergleich?
3. Welche Möglichkeiten gibt es im Internet, sich über Produkte zu informieren?
4. Warum mussten Firmen neue Strategien in der Werbung und im Marketing entwickeln?
5. Welche Altersgruppe soll besonders durch die Internet-Werbung angesprochen werden?

E-Commerce takes off

Consumers love to shop on the internet. After initial problems leading websites now offer an excellent service. Competition on
5 the web is fierce and many sites have had little choice but to raise service levels, often far above those of off-line retailers. Price transparency is the great advantage for the
10 consumer. It is possible to check the price offered by hundreds of merchants with a couple of mouse clicks. Consumers also have access to an unprecedented amount of information, not just from manufacturers' 15 websites but also from online reviews written by other customers.

To reach online customers companies have had to look at new and different advertising and 20 marketing strategies. This is why firms pay for sponsored links to appear on search sites like *Google* and *Yahoo!*. It has become one of the most effective marketing tools, especially 25 for people who spend as much time on the internet as watching television, such as teenagers.

© V 7 Video lounge Retailing

BBC Motion Gallery

You are about to see a video on retail marketing.
Watch it carefully and then answer the following questions:

1. Describe the marketing expert.
2. The video speaks of "sales consultants" and "professional friends". How is this different from the traditional sales assistant?
3. What method is used to show them how NOT to approach the customer?
4. What is meant by "linked selling"?
5. What are the rewards of successful customer care for the "consultants"?
6. Would you like to be served by this kind of assistant?

B Advertising

There are many different ways of promoting sales and attracting potential clients or customers depending on the product and target group.

1 Advertising consumer goods

Mail shots: One form of advertising we are all confronted with is mail shots. Since a large proportion go straight into the wastepaper basket, companies will try to obtain up to date and selective lists of people who are likely to be really interested. This may be the cheapest and most effective way for local companies to make potential clients aware of their goods and services.

TV advertising is suitable for consumer goods with a very wide appeal. Like **cinema** advertising it can suggest a whole lifestyle associated with the product. TV advertising is very expensive.

Consumer goods can also be advertised on the **radio**, in **newspapers** and **magazines**. In the case of magazines, the manufacturer will be able to appeal to a specific target group (affluent men between the ages of 20 and 30, keen gardeners with sufficient money to buy a glossy magazine, health-conscious young women, retired people with money and time on their hands (grey power!)).

Posters, **hoardings/billboards** are an effective means of out of home advertising as they reach a large number of people who cannot help noticing them as they pass or drive through the streets.

Internet advertising is also a rapidly growing segment. A website itself is an important part of the way in which a company presents itself. How well-designed and efficient is the website? Does it allow you to do what you want to do with a minimum of complication? We have all experienced frustrating websites which provide a lot of information that one is not interested in, or that do not seem to have a "BACK" button.

1 Match the expressions on the left with the translations on the right.

1. affluent	a. Anziehungskraft
2. appeal	b. ausgewählt
3. glossy	c. hier: auf Hochglanzpapier gedruckt
4. hoardings	d. im Ruhestand/in Rente
5. mail shots	e. Plakatwände
6. retired	f. Postwurfsendungen
7. selective	g. wohlhabend
8. target group	h. Zielgruppe

2 Work in groups. Discuss recent advertisements on TV, in magazines, in the cinema and on posters. Tell your group what you liked or disliked about them. What kind of advertisements are you most influenced by? The following expressions may help to start you off.

I think it's effective because …

I don't like this kind of advertisement because …

It doesn't really appeal to …

Have you seen the most recent ad for … ?

In my opinion the message is …

I'm afraid I don't agree with you because …

I think it is …

I think this commercial is very convincing as …

Internet advertising boom helps Ad.Slot.com to double sales

Ad.Slot.com, one of Europe's biggest independent media buying agencies, says that it will double turnover from placing advertisements on the internet this year as its clients continue to seek alternatives to traditional media.

5 The company said yesterday that it expects to achieve total sales of more than $450 million this year, up from about $350 million last year. The proportion of sales contributed by the new media rose rapidly to 17 per cent.

In the first few months of
10 the year more money was spent on advertising on the internet and mobile phones and less on advertising in conventional media, like the
15 radio, TV and print media.

A spokesman for the company said that the trend towards advertising in the new media was the result
20 of changing technology and habits. People still watch television and read newspapers, but they use the internet and their mobile
25 phones to socialise and search for information. They have DVD recorders that allow them to skip TV commercials.

3 Beantworten Sie folgende Fragen zu diesem Zeitungsartikel auf Deutsch.

KMK

1. Wodurch erwartet Ad.Slot.com dieses Jahr seinen Umsatz zu verdoppeln?
2. Welchen Beitrag werden die neuen Medien dabei leisten?
3. Welche Veränderung hat sich in den ersten Monaten dieses Jahres ergeben?
4. Warum nimmt das Interesse an den alternativen Medien zu?
5. In welchen Medien sucht man zunehmend nach Informationen?
6. Warum wird TV-Werbung häufig nicht wahrgenommen?

2 Advertising industrial goods

Where do you advertise if your product is not a consumer good but, say, a specialised machine or precision instrument?

A company can place an advertisement in a trade journal, a specialist periodical devoted to a particular sector.

For these companies the relevant **trade fairs** at which companies in the given sector present their latest products are important. They are attended by many people from the trade, some of them buyers who intend to place orders and competitors who use the trade fair as a means of seeing what the competition is up to. Trade fairs are, therefore, a way of advertising industrial goods.

Companies may write directly to potential customers (direct mail) informing them of their range of products and enclosing sales literature.

Übertragen Sie den obigen Text ins Deutsche.

M

3 Public relations (PR)

This is usually distinguished from advertising as the focus is the company rather than specific products. Some companies sponsor sports events, others donate money to universities, schools and cultural events. It may be important for a company to emphasise the amount of money it invests in research, its respect for the environment or multi-ethnic society. They may emphasise their commitment to the local community and try to get positive coverage in the local press. Large companies have PR departments, while in smaller companies there is at least one person responsible for PR. Companies large and small take outside advice from specialist agencies.

Study the above text and say whether the following statements are TRUE or FALSE.

R

1. PR is the same as advertising.
2. Companies sponsor sports events to project a particular image.
3. Small companies are less interested in PR than large companies.
4. All companies use the services of specialist agencies.
5. Some companies are more interested in donating money to universities and schools than sponsoring sports events.

Language and grammar

Choose the correct form of the adjective or adverb in brackets.

1. Our elegant sofas are the (good) value ever.
2. We are the market leaders because we have reacted (swiftly) to changing markets.
3. This company has expanded (dramatic) than its competitors over the past year.
4. Last year the winter was (severe) than this year.
5. These are the (late) designer furnishings from Milan.
6. This is the (expensive) holiday I have booked so far.

Language and grammar:
Comparatives and superlatives

Adjektive, meist in Form von Komparativen oder Superlativen, spielen in der Werbung eine große Rolle.

Einsilbig gesprochene Adjektive bilden Komparativ und Superlativ durch Anhängen von -er, -est an das Adjektiv.

bright – brighter – brightest
This car has **smoother** handling than any other car in its class.

Drei- oder mehrsilbige Adjektive bilden Komparativ und Superlativ durch Voranstellen von *more* und *most* vor das Adjektiv.

interesting – more interesting – most interesting
This is the **most sophisticated** MP3 player available today.

Zweisilbige Adjektive werden entweder wie einsilbige oder wie mehrsilbige gesteigert: Adjektive, die auf -er, -ow, -y oder -le enden, hängen -er, -est an. Vor Adjektive, die auf -ful oder -re enden, wird *more* oder *most* gesetzt.

clever – cleverer – cleverest   narrow – narrower – narrowest
pretty – prettier – prettiest   noble – nobler – noblest
careful – more careful – most careful   obscure – more obscure – most obscure
This is a **most restful** way of spending a weekend abroad.

Einige englische Adjektive besitzen die Wirkung von Superlativen.
Cutting-edge* technology goes into this stereo system.
Get this **state of the art** handset at all authorised dealers.
Get the coolest, **up to the minute**, **must-have** accessories at all our boutiques.
This car has **superb** handling.

Auch Adverbien können gesteigert werden. Komparativ und Superlativ von Adverbien wird durch Voranstellen von *more* und *most* gebildet.
quickly – more quickly – most quickly
They dealt with our order **more efficiently** than we had expected.
Technology is changing **more and more rapidly** (= immer schneller).

---

* Diese Wendungen können sowohl mit als auch ohne Bindestriche geschrieben werden.

Industry expert

1 The instruments of marketing

1 The following organigram shows the position of marketing in an industrial company in Germany. Find the English equivalents of the marketing terms and draw a new organigram in English with the help of the words in the box.

> advertising • areas of decision • areas of market research • development •
> direct distribution • distribution policy • indirect distribution • market research •
> use • communication policy • design • main tasks • market analysis • market
> observation • market forecast • pricing • price policy • pricing strategies •
> primary research • product elimination • product innovation • product policy •
> product variation • public relations • sales promotion • secondary research •
> survey methods • target group • terms / service

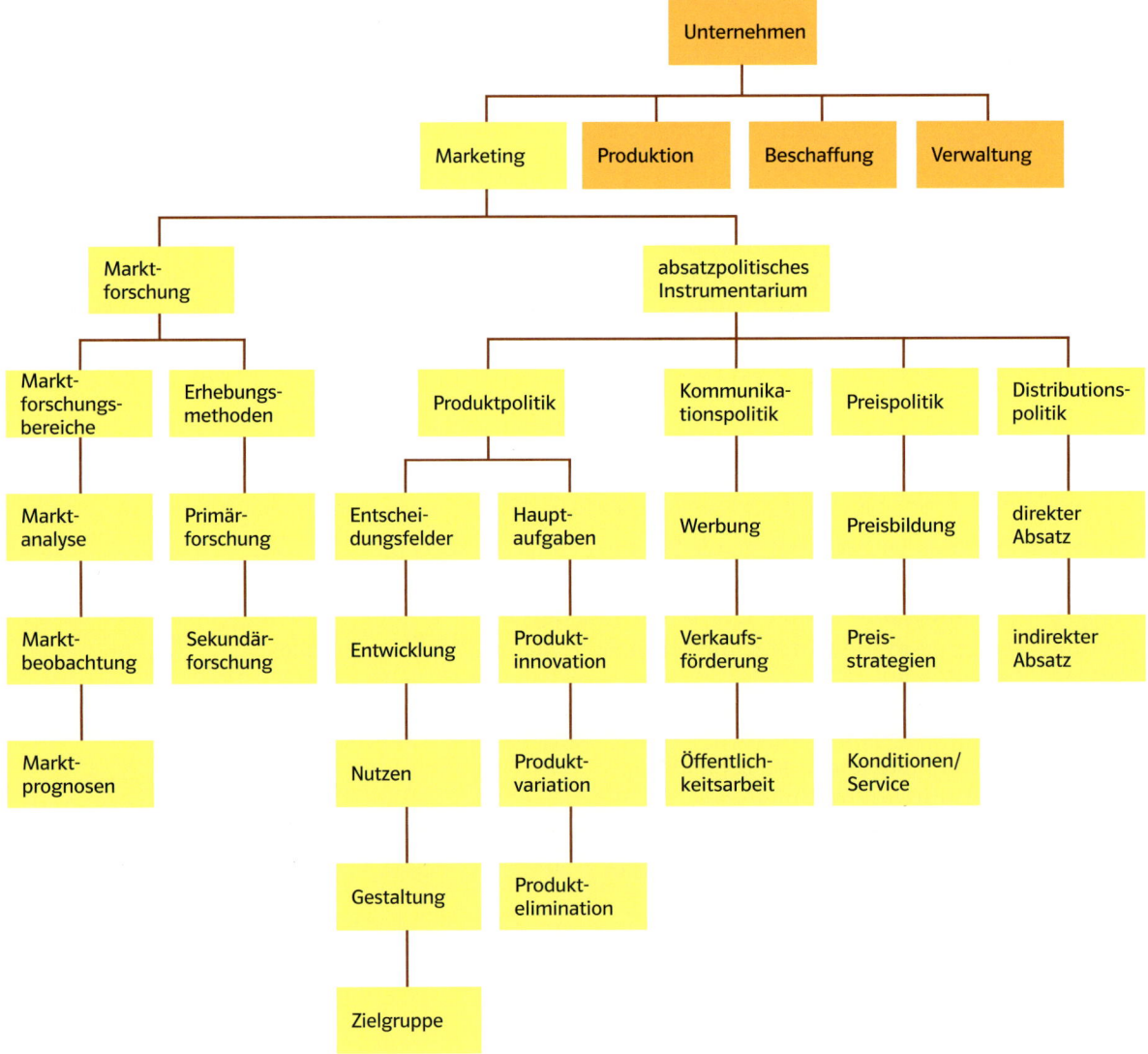

2 **Explain which marketing instrument is described or shown.**

P

1. The current cash discount is changed from 2 % to 3 %.
2. In Germany the product is sold for a lower price than in the USA.
3. A new fragrance of a shampoo is launched on the market.
4. On TV, a commercial for an environmentally friendly product is shown.
5. A company donates money for new computers to a school.
6. Sales representatives of wholesalers are trained on the manufacturer's premises.

7

The bicycles are only available at a specialist shop.

8

Advertisement for a product.

9

This radio is not produced anymore.

10

This plastic bottle is given an imprint.

2 Market research and distribution policy

1 **Answer the following questions on market research. Search for information in your business studies books or on the internet.**

P

1. Explain the differences between primary (field) and secondary (desk) research and think about the advantages and disadvantages. Give an example of a situation in which you think that either primary or secondary research would be appropriate.
2. Name three internal and three external sources for secondary research.
3. There are four methods of field research: a. survey, b. observation, c. experiment, d. test market. Explain the methods.
4. In a survey you can interview people personally or send them a questionnaire by e-mail or mail. What are the advantages and disadvantages?

✳ **2**
KMK Ihr Unternehmen hat auf dem deutschen Markt erfolgreich eine Energie-
sparlampe eingeführt und möchte nun auch den britischen Markt erobern.
Dafür hat Ihre Firma in britischen Tageszeitungen eine Anzeige aufgegeben, in
der sie Handelsvertreter sucht. Morgen fliegen Sie und Ihr Chef nach London,
um den Bewerbern Ihr Vertriebssystem zu erläutern.

Phrases ▶

Ihr Chef bittet Sie, seinen Vortrag ins Englische zu übertragen.

- Unser Unternehmen, ein Hersteller von Energiesparlampen, sucht geeignete Handelsvertreter für Südengland.
- In Deutschland hat das Unternehmen ein großes Vertriebs-
  netz zu dem Groß- und Einzelhändler gehören.
- Das Unternehmen bevorzugt den indirekten Absatzweg,
  da so mehr Kunden erreicht werden können.
- Da wir uns auf die Produktion von Energiesparlampen
  spezialisiert haben, ist das Sortiment zu klein für eigene
  Verkaufsfilialen (direkter Absatz nicht möglich).
- Weil unser Produkt in Massenfertigung hergestellt wird,
  ist eine direkte Lieferung an Endkunden unwirtschaftlich.
- Wir versuchen nun unser Produkt auf dem englischen
  Markt über Handelsvertreter einzuführen, da wir keine
  Erfahrung und bisher keine Kontakte aufgebaut haben.
- Mit den Marktkenntnissen der Handelsvertreter soll das
  neue Absatzgebiet erschlossen werden.
- Wir erwarten engagierte, gut qualifizierte Handels-
  vertreter, die auf Kommissionsbasis arbeiten.
- Das Werbematerial wird kostenlos gestellt und die Waren
  werden direkt von unserem Warenlager in Hamburg nach
  Großbritannien geliefert.
- Das Zahlungsziel für englische Kunden beträgt 30 Tage
  netto, Lieferung erfolgt 5 Tage nach Auftragseingang.
  Wir liefern kostenfrei bei Erstaufträgen.

3 Communication and price policy

1
P **Explain the process of planning an advertising campaign with the help of the
following diagram. Give examples for each stage.**

The process of planning an advertising campaign

| 1. Define the target group | → | 2. Advertising message | → | 3. Advertising method | → | 4. Advertising period | → | 5. Advertising region | → | 6. Advertising budget |

2 **Read the following text and answer the questions.**

PRICING

There are two basic situations when a company has to set a price: (1) When it launches a totally new product or introduces an already existing product on a new market. (2) When it has to fix a new price for a product from the current range because the costs or demand for the product has changed, or the competitors have changed their strategies, and this has influenced their prices.

PRICING STRATEGIES

Companies can decide between the high-price strategy and the low-price strategy. Normally the invention and development of new products costs a lot of money. As competitors succeed in imitating successful products quickly, companies can try to set a high price during the introduction phase to cover the costs immediately. Nevertheless, psychology plays an important role as well. Normally customers associate expensive products with high quality. If a company is able to convince the prospective customers of the high quality, for example, by an advertising campaign, there will be a high demand from the beginning (price skimming).

When a low price is set, even more sceptical customers will place trial orders. This leads to an increase in demand and the market share of the product will grow fast. If the customers like your product and they buy it regularly you can raise the price slightly to make more profit (penetration pricing).

1. When do companies have to set a price?
2. Which three factors influence the price?
3. Explain **price skimming** and **penetration pricing** in your own words.
4. Give two examples for **price skimming** and **penetration pricing**.
5. What is **psychological pricing**? Give an example.

4 Marketing mix

KMK Sie arbeiten in der Marketing Abteilung eines deutsch-amerikanischen Unternehmens, das alkoholfreie Getränke herstellt. Die Marktforschung hat ergeben, dass eine große Nachfrage für gesunde, mit natürlichen Zutaten hergestellte Energiegetränke besteht und die Konkurrenz Energiegetränke mit chemischen Zusätzen für ca. €2,00 pro 0,33l Flasche anbietet.

Sie werden beauftragt, einen Absatzplan auszuarbeiten und der Firmenleitung diesen auf Englisch vorzutragen. Gehen Sie in Ihrer Präsentation auf alle Punkte des Marketing Mix ein und wählen Sie vorher eine Zielgruppe aus. Verwenden Sie das folgende Mind Map zur Unterstützung.

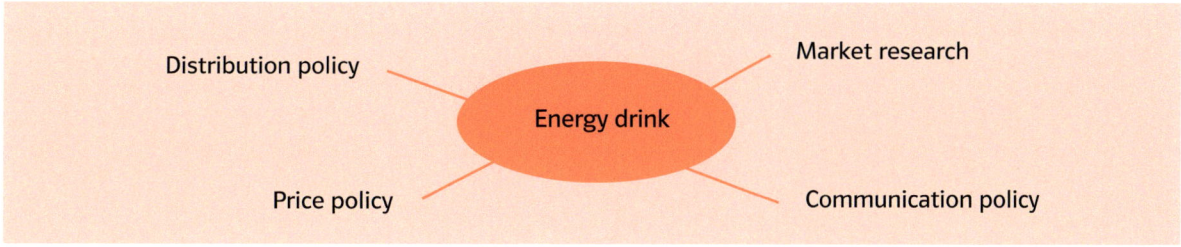

Phrases: Advertising

This state-of-the-art mobile phone is easy to operate with its simple slide-out keyboard.	Dieses Handy, das auf dem neuesten technischen Stand ist, hat eine leicht zu bedienende ausziehbare Tastatur.
It has an easy to use touch screen.	Es hat einen leicht zu bedienenden Touch-Screen.
This must-have versatile gizmo includes all the latest features.	Dieses vielseitige Hi-Tech-Spielzeug, das man unbedingt haben muss, hat all die neuesten Funktionen.
You'll love its slim compact shape.	Die schlanke, kompakte Form wird Sie begeistern.
You'll be bewitched by the dazzling designs of our new collection.	Lassen Sie sich verführen von den bestechenden Designs unserer neuen Kollektion.
The ultimate **in** costume jewellery.	Der ultimative Modeschmuck.
We use a minimum of packaging to minimise the environmental impact.	Wir verwenden ein Minimum an Verpackung, um die Auswirkungen auf die Umwelt so gering wie möglich zu halten.
Your finger-nails will look flawless and perfectly cared **for**.	Ihre Fingernägel sehen makellos und perfekt gepflegt aus.
… subdued autumnal colours …	… dezente Herbstfarben …
This is a portable stereo-system **of** truly diminutive dimensions.	Es handelt sich um eine tragbare Super-Mini-Stereoanlage.
This hand-crafted leather bag combines perfect chic with amazing capacity.	Diese handgearbeitete Ledertasche ist superschick und dabei unglaublich geräumig.
We rely **on** tried and tested craftsmanship.	Wir verlassen uns auf unser erprobtes handwerkliches Können.
Weekends feel simply wonderful in our silky soft-touch tops.	Erleben Sie romantische Wochenenden mit unseren flauschig-kuscheligen Tops.
This downy soft luxury scarf will go with all your winter garments.	Dieser daunenweiche Luxusschal passt zu Ihrer gesamten Wintergarderobe.
… ideal for sensitive skins …	… ideal für die empfindliche Haut …

Unit 16
Job applications in Germany and the EU

WORD BANK

job application • vacancy • opening • job exchange • job centre • research facilities • recruitment agencies • letter of application • CV • education • training • experience • skills • hobbies • interview • strengths • references • to advertise • to recruit • to apply • to paraphrase • to invite • to shortlist • to employ • European Union • free movement • member countries • European Commission • president • commissioners • Council of Ministers • European Parliament

The first thing is to find a vacancy. Companies advertise openings in newspapers on certain days which differ from place to place and country to country and also from sector to sector. Job exchanges on the Internet have become an important source of information. Often, it is possible to type in your job specification and receive notification by e-mail when anything suitable turns up. Job centres may be able to assist in the search for a suitable position and provide research facilities such as directories and internet access. Finally, there are private sector recruitment agencies which specialise in a particular sector. People often send unsolicited applications to major organisations on the off-chance that they are looking to recruit people.

1 Tell the class how you found your job / apprenticeship. Discuss which of the above are the most effective ways of looking for a job. Give reasons to support your answers.

Online-Link
808262-0016

THE CARING COMPANY
NATURAL BEAUTY
first-rate natural products for hair and skin care

We are seeking young persons from the Continent to

assist our Birmingham-based sales team

REF.: NB 605

We offer employment in a challenging, fast-paced environment where enthusiasm is the norm.

Successful applicants will have
- sales experience
- good English language skills
- native speaker competence in Italian, French or German

Successful applicants will be
- PC literate, including Excel
- able to meet deadlines
- self-motivated and hard-working

We offer an attractive salary and will help you with finding accommodation.

If you are interested please send your CV with a covering letter to

Catherine Bennet ▪ Recruitment Officer ▪ NATURAL BEAUTY ▪ 17 Laura Place ▪ Birmingham ▪ BI2 1AC

Automotive Services Ltd

Wholesaler and Importer of Automotive Parts

REF.: JR 673

In view of our rapidly growing business with Continental Europe
we are looking to recruit bilingual assistants (German-English or French-English)
to work in our import department.

Applicants should be fluent in German or French and have a good command of English. Office skills and familiarity with import procedures are essential. Must enjoy working in a team.

Send application enclosing CV and certificates in English to:

Jennifer O'Rourke (Mrs) | Automotive Services Ltd | 103 Selsdown Drive | London E14 9LA

Small Tour Operator

Requires well-organised full-time travel consultant with admin and accounts background and fluent German and/or French. Hotel or travel experience desirable, but not essential. Must be team worker and have MS Office and typing skills.

Send CV and letter of application by e-mail to jobs@dreamworldholidays.com or by post to:

 Dreamworld Holidays

28 Percival St
London
WIT 1DW

Quote ref.: DH 15 Pw

2
R
Read the advertisement on page 228 (Natural Beauty) and formulate the questions to which the following statements are the answers. The elements suggesting the question word are in bold type.

Example:

Answer: 1. Natural Beauty is based **in Birmingham**.
Question: 1. **Where** is Natural Beauty based?

Answers

1. Natural Beauty is based **in Birmingham**.
2. Natural Beauty is seeking **young persons**.
3. Successful applicants will have **good English language skills**.
4. Successful applicants' mother tongue will be **Italian, French or German**.
5. **The following qualifications** are essential: PC-literacy, ability to work hard and meet deadlines.
6. **Natural Beauty** will help you with finding accommodation.
7. Your CV should be sent **to Catherine Bennet**.

3
I
Discuss with a partner what German qualifications would equip you for the jobs advertised in the three advertisements on page 228.

4
P
Describe your (future) qualifications (school leaving certificate, e.g. Abitur, apprenticeship, traineeship etc, language certificates) and state briefly what kind of job you would like. For job titles refer back to UNIT 1.

Example:

"I have just completed my training as a publisher's assistant and would like to work in a publishing house in or around Cologne. I spent a year in the United States and attended High School there, so I'd welcome the opportunity to use my English in my job."

5
KMK
Stellen Sie einem Freund / einer Freundin die Stellenanzeigen auf der Seite 228 auf Deutsch vor. Beachten Sie dabei folgende Punkte:

• Firma bzw. Branche
• Anforderungen an Bewerber
• Gehalt
• Sonstige Leistungen der Firma
• Standort des Arbeitsplatzes
• Gewünschte Art der Kontaktaufnahme

A Letter of application

Your letter of application should be set out clearly and include the points below:

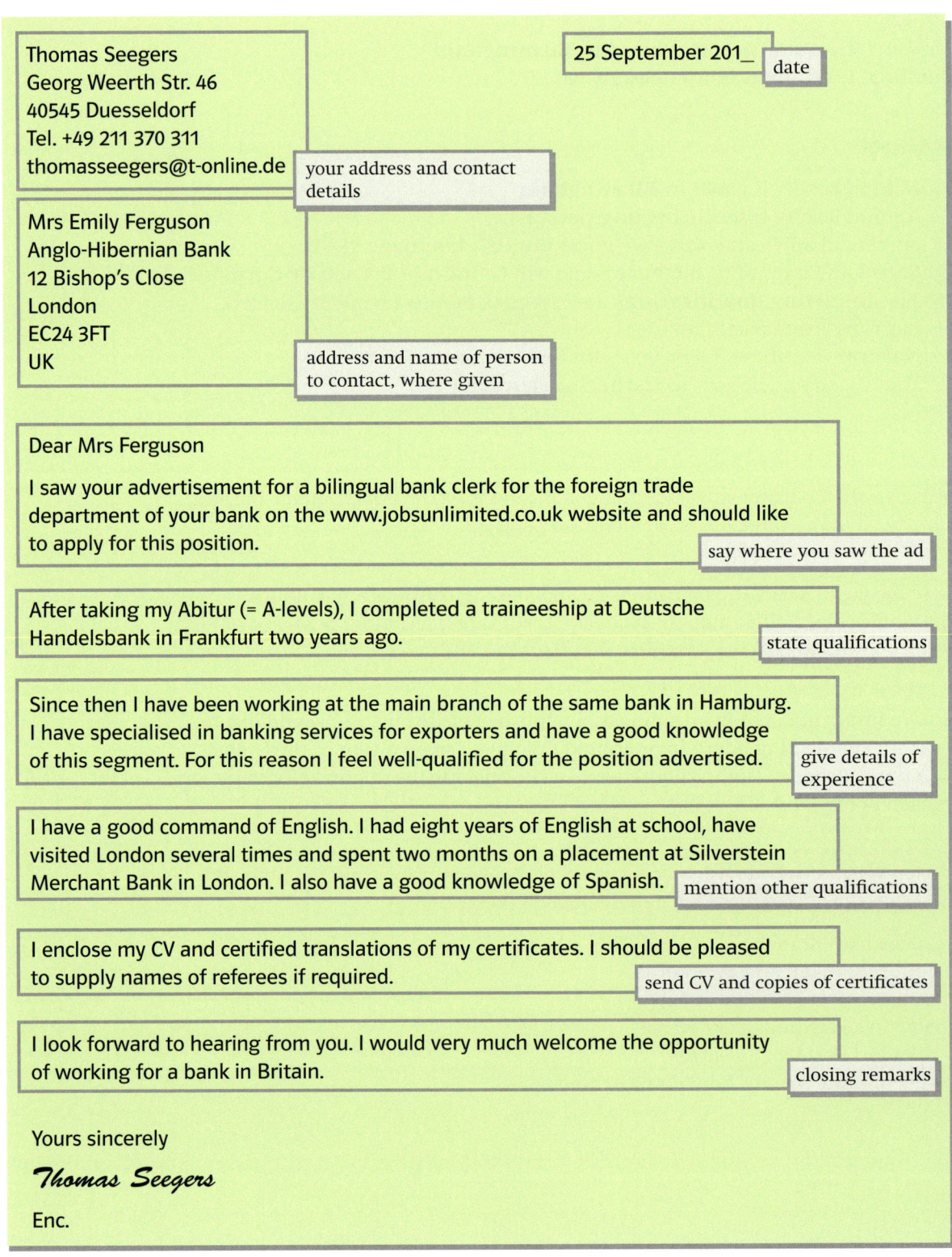

Thomas Seegers
Georg Weerth Str. 46
40545 Duesseldorf
Tel. +49 211 370 311
thomasseegers@t-online.de

> your address and contact details

25 September 201_

> date

Mrs Emily Ferguson
Anglo-Hibernian Bank
12 Bishop's Close
London
EC24 3FT
UK

> address and name of person to contact, where given

Dear Mrs Ferguson

I saw your advertisement for a bilingual bank clerk for the foreign trade department of your bank on the www.jobsunlimited.co.uk website and should like to apply for this position.

> say where you saw the ad

After taking my Abitur (= A-levels), I completed a traineeship at Deutsche Handelsbank in Frankfurt two years ago.

> state qualifications

Since then I have been working at the main branch of the same bank in Hamburg. I have specialised in banking services for exporters and have a good knowledge of this segment. For this reason I feel well-qualified for the position advertised.

> give details of experience

I have a good command of English. I had eight years of English at school, have visited London several times and spent two months on a placement at Silverstein Merchant Bank in London. I also have a good knowledge of Spanish.

> mention other qualifications

I enclose my CV and certified translations of my certificates. I should be pleased to supply names of referees if required.

> send CV and copies of certificates

I look forward to hearing from you. I would very much welcome the opportunity of working for a bank in Britain.

> closing remarks

Yours sincerely

Thomas Seegers

Enc.

1 Übertragen Sie die folgenden Sätze ins Deutsche.

KMK
1. I have decided to apply on the off-chance.
2. I am interested in applying for this vacancy.
3. I know you are recruiting staff at present.
4. I feel I am suitably qualified for this position.
5. I have completed a traineeship as an export clerk.

2 Complete the following letter of application as the applicant using one of the

P advertisements on page 228.

> (Your address etc)

(Company address)

Reference no. (given in advertisement)

Dear Sir/Madam

I saw your **1** in the **2** yesterday and am interested in **3** this position.
I have now completed a **4** as an export clerk. My experience is limited to the **5**
of my present firm.
I have a good **6** of English and Spanish and am keen **7** these languages.
I **8** my curriculum vitae and copies of certificates. Please let me know if you **9** the
names and addresses of referees.

I look forward to **10** you soon.

With best regards*
(Your name and signature)

Enclosures: CV, certificates

* "Yours sincerely" is also possible. "Yours faithfully" is very formal and is hardly
  used nowadays.

B Curriculum Vitae (CV)

A neatly arranged CV is an essential part of any application. The following are two German CVs with paraphrases in English. As indicated in UNIT 1 German job titles often have no direct equivalent in English. It is important that you paraphrase your job title (e.g. Industriekaufmann, Hotelfachfrau etc.) in such a way that a potential employer has a clear and realistic impression of your training and experience. When applying for a job in English – and there is an increasing number of companies in continental Europe whose company language is English – it is important to be aware of differences. In an English CV do not give details of your parents' profession, your religious denomination, or the number of your brothers and sisters. International CVs do not include a photograph. Modern CVs often reverse the chronological order and start with the most recent developments in your career.

1 **Study the following CVs of Fatma Gülsuyu and Daniel Paulat with a suggested paraphrase in English.**

German CV I

Tabellarischer Lebenslauf

Persönliche Angaben

Name	Fatma Gülsuyu
Adresse	Dülkener Str. 5, 40235 Düsseldorf
	Tel.: 0211 571364, E-Mail: fatmaguelsuyu@t-online.de
Staatsangehörigkeit	türkisch
Geburtstag	23.01.89
Geburtsort	Düsseldorf
Familienstand	ledig

Schulbildung

1995–1999	Grundschule Niederkassel
1999–2007	Schiller-Gymnasium, Düsseldorf
2007	Abitur (Leistungskurse: Englisch, Mathematik, Grundkurse: Sozialwissenschaften, Türkisch, Gesamtnote: 2,2)

Tätigkeiten

August 2005–Juli 2006	Hausaufgabenhilfe im „Lernzentrum", Düsseldorf
August 2006–Juni 2007	Aushilfstätigkeit im Reisebüro „Evren", Düsseldorf
seit September 2007	Ausbildung als Kauffrau für Bürokommunikation im Reisebüro „Evren"

Sprachkenntnisse

Deutsch: wie Muttersprache
Türkisch: Muttersprache
Englisch: gut in Wort und Schrift
Italienisch: Grundkenntnisse

PC-Kenntnisse Windows, Excel, Powerpoint

Interessen Musik (Saz spielen, im Chor singen), Volleyball

English paraphrase CV I

Curriculum Vitae

Personal details

Name and address	Fatma Gülsuyu Dülkener Str 5 40235 Düsseldorf, Germany Tel. + 49 (0)211 571364 E-mail: fatmaguelsuyu@t-online.de
Nationality	Turkish
Date of birth	23 January, 1989
Place of birth	Düsseldorf, Germany
Marital status	single

Education

1995–1999	Primary School Niederkassel
1999–2007	Schiller Gymnasium Düsseldorf (grammar school)
2007	Abitur (= A-Levels) Major subjects: English, Mathematics Basic courses: Social Sciences, Turkish Overall grade: 2.2 (= good = B)

Job experience and other activities

August 2005 to July 2006	Assisting pupils with homework at the Lernzentrum (Learning Centre) in Düsseldorf
August 2006–June 2007	Temporary employment at the "Evren" travel agency in Düsseldorf
from September 2007	Traineeship as office communications clerk/office management assistant at the "Evren" travel agency

Languages

	German: native command Turkish: mother tongue English: good command of both spoken and written English Italian: basic knowledge

Computer skills

Windows, Excel, Powerpoint

Hobbies

Music (playing saz, singing in a choir), volleyball

German CV II

Tabellarischer Lebenslauf

Persönliche Angaben

Name	Daniel Paulat
Adresse	44369 Dortmund
	Servatiusstr. 37
	Tel. 0231 4669834
	E-Mail: danielpaulat@aol.com
Staatsangehörigkeit	deutsch
Geburtstag	17. 1. 1990
Geburtsort	Hagen
Familienstand	ledig

Schulbildung

1996–2000	Grundschule Haspe, Hagen
2000–2004	Albert-Einstein-Realschule, Hagen
2004–2006	Gesamtschule am Teich, Dortmund
	Abschluss: Fachoberschulreife
2006–2008	Höhere Handelsschule, Kaufmännische Schule II, Dortmund
	Abschluss: Fachhochschulreife

Ausbildung

2009–2012	Ausbildung zum Industriekaufmann bei Kabel AG, Leverkusen
	Schwerpunkte: Rechnungswesen, Einkauf
2011	Zertifikatsprüfung Englisch für kaufmännische und verwaltende Berufe, Niveau I
voraussichtlich Mai 2012	Abschlussprüfung

Tätigkeiten

2006–2008	Aushilfstätigkeit als Fahrradkurier
2008–2009	Zivildienst in einer Behindertenwerkstatt

Sonstige Kenntnisse

MS Office, Linux
Englisch fließend, Spanisch ausbaufähig

Interessen

Fitness, Fußball, Fantasy-Literatur

English paraphrase CV II

Curriculum Vitae

Personal details

Name	Daniel Paulat
Address	44369 Dortmund, Germany
	Servatiusstr. 37
	Tel.: +49 (0)231 4669834
	E-mail: danielpaulat@aol.com
Nationality	German
Date of birth	17 January, 1990
Place of birth	Hagen (North Rhine-Westphalia)
Marital status	single

Education/Training

1996–2000	Primary school Haspe, Hagen
2000–2004	Albert Einstein Realschule (= higher secondary school), Hagen
2004–2006	Gesamtschule am Teich (comprehensive), Dortmund
	School-leaving certificate: Fachoberschulreife
	(= certificate enabling student to continue education at higher vocational school)
2006–2008	Höhere Handelschule, Kaufmännische Schule II (higher commercial college), Dortmund
	Final examination: Fachhochschulreife (examination enabling student to enrol at a polytechnic university)
2009–2012	Traineeship as an industrial clerk/industrial business management assistant at Kabel AG, Leverkusen
2011	Special subjects: accounting, purchasing
	Zertifikatsprüfung (state examination)
probably May, 2012	English for clerical and administrative professions, Level I
	Final examination traineeship

Job activities

2006–2008	Temporary employment as cycle courier
2008–2009	Social service (in lieu of military service) in a workshop for handicapped people

Other skills MS Office, Linux/Fluent English, basic Spanish

Personal interests Working out, football, fantasy literature

✳ **2**
P

Now write your own CV in English using the examples above and referring back to UNIT 1 for job titles. Use a dictionary if necessary.

Phrases ▶

3

You have applied for a job with GlaxoSmithKline (UK). You feel you have a good chance of being invited to an interview. Research the company and its products and make brief notes in English.

4
I

Daniela Zeischegg sent off an application three weeks ago to the British company Tolaron plc in reply to an advertisement in which the company was looking for a German mother-tongue export clerk. Since she has not received a reply she decides to ring the company. Roleplay the dialogue below.

Daniela Zeischegg	David Stedman
put through/human resources department	help?
application/three weeks ago/no reply yet/lost in post?	spell name/reference
name/reference T027 68P	computer/application found/process/send invitation/interview in the next few days
when? how much notice?/book flight	1 week/ring immediately/if date inconvenient
look forward/receive reply/thank you	

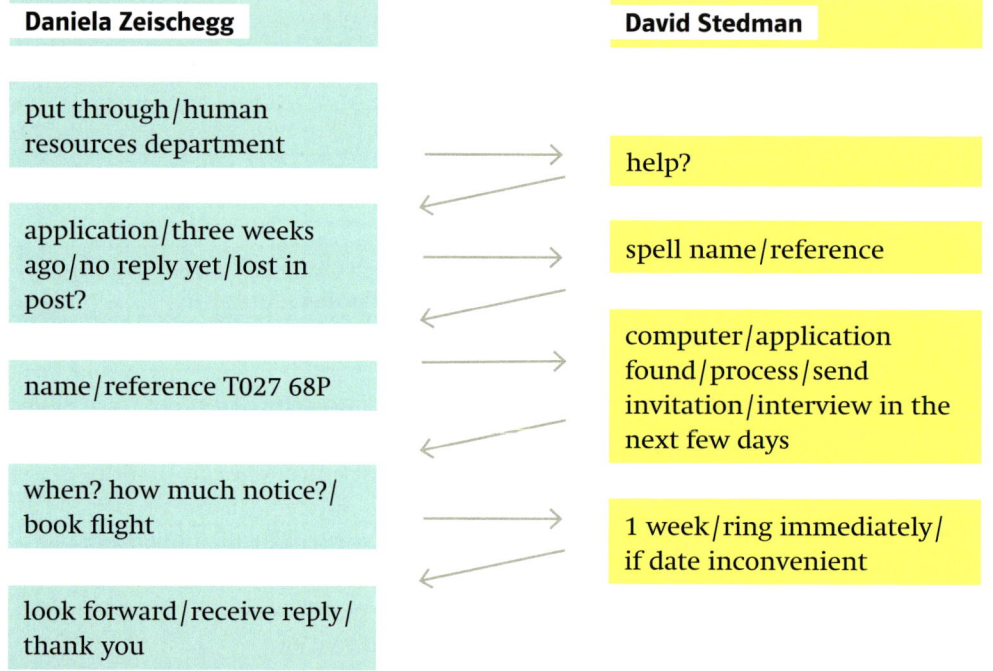

◎ V8 **Video lounge** Travel and Tourism

B B C Motion Gallery

You are about to see a video on the travel and tourist industry. Read through the questions below and listen for the answers as you watch the video:

1. What kind of tour operator does the young man work for?
2. Try and list as many of the qualifications and characteristics that are mentioned as desirable in a tour leader.
3. What kind of person is likely to apply for a job as a tour leader?
4. How did he prepare for his job in Egypt?
5. What sort of disadvantages does life as a tour leader have?

C Interviews

If your application meets with the approval of the company or its personnel department, your name will be put on a shortlist and you will be invited to an interview.

How can you prepare for the interview?

It is important to find out as much as you can about the company, its products and the image it projects so that you make an informed impression and demonstrate that you are interested in the company.

Think beforehand of any questions you would like to ask if they are not covered by the interviewer, e.g. location, type of work, starting salary, opportunities for further training, opportunities to use your language skills, catering arrangements, company pension scheme, how big is the office you will be working in? Will you have contact with customers or is it a back office?

What are your other interests? Think carefully about this. If you say "cinema" expect to be asked about the last film you saw. If you mention an interest in your CV, e.g. working out at a gym, you should think in advance what you would say if asked about it.

Finally, do not underestimate the importance of so-called "soft skills" – a neat, clean appearance, shirt tucked neatly into trousers, polished shoes with laces tied, hair neatly cut and combed, etc. Women should go for a suit or skirt or trousers and jacket. Don't risk wearing jeans and a T-shirt.

1 **Answer the following questions on the text above.**

R

1. What may happen if the company has a lot of applications and you are one of the fortunate ones?
2. Why is it a good idea to know something about the company?
3. What questions might you want to ask if the interviewer doesn't cover them?
4. What interests or hobbies would you mention?
5. What is meant by the term "soft skills"?

2 **Choose what you regard as appropriate from this list of do's and don'ts.**

R

1. Your first question should be about annual holidays.
2. You should dress smartly.
3. You should take some gum with you to chew to help you relax.
4. The interviewer can't expect you to know much about the firm before you even work there.
5. You should feel free to tell the interviewer that you are bored with your present job.
6. You should be prepared (and able) to talk about any interests you mention.
7. You should make eye contact with the interviewer, smile and nod to express agreement or ethusiasm.
8. You should tell the interviewer straight away that you are applying for other jobs at the moment.
9. You should refuse to describe your strengths and weaknesses.

3 **Send an encouraging e-mail to an anxious friend who has an interview in a couple of days. Make sentences by matching the bubbles with suitable parts from the list below.**

P

... go to bed early the night before.
... go to the hairdresser's beforehand.
... put on a clean set of clothes.
... a sweatshirt or fleece (boy)/see-through top or mini-skirt (girl).
... a smart costume (girl)/jacket (boy).
... wear sneakers.
... have a look at the firm's website before the interview.
... get there on time.
... yourself and act naturally.
... answer "yes" or "no". Take the initiative and volunteer information.
... that there are other fish in the sea.

4 Daniela Zeischegg has been invited to an interview at Tolaron plc's head office
R in Croydon, South London. She takes an early flight from Cologne-Bonn airport
◎ A1.31 to London Gatwick. She takes the train from Gatwick to South Croydon and
presents herself at Tolaron at 11 am. She wears a neatly tailored suit in navy blue
and a white blouse.

Listen to the interview and write down the job details mentioned.

5 Listen to the interview again and translate the following sentences into English.

R/M
A1.31
1. Sie haben eine Ausbildung bei einem großen Kölner Unternehmen der verarbeitenden Industrie gemacht.
2. Wir benötigen jemanden, der Deutsch spricht, weil wir eine große Anzahl von Kunden in Deutschland und Österreich haben.
3. Leider können wir Ihnen bei der Suche nach einer Unterkunft nicht behilflich sein.
4. Müsste ich am 1. August anfangen, wie in der Anzeige angegeben?
5. Ich habe mich gefreut, Sie kennen zu lernen. Sie werden von mir hören.

6 Match these 10 questions with the answers given below.

R
1. Why do you wish to leave your present position?
2. What would you say are your strengths and weaknesses?
3. Why would you like to work for this company?
4. Which animal do you most readily identify with?
5. What are your professional aims?
6. What are your expectations as far as salary is concerned?
7. What would you say was your advantage compared with other applicants?
8. What did you find most satisfying in your previous jobs?
9. What three positive things would your previous boss say about you?
10. What reasons would you give why we should employ you?

A. I particularly like lions/monkeys/elephants.
B. I don't know the other applicants. All I know is that I am highly motivated and keen to do this job.
C. Eventually I would like to be an export manager/head of department/set up in business on my own.
D. I am very enthusiastic and have all the necessary qualifications plus good references.
E. I have always enjoyed dealing with people. I liked being in the front office. I had a good rapport with customers.
F. I like my present job and the people I work with but it doesn't give me any opportunity to use my languages/I have no contact with clients.
G. My previous boss would probably say I had a good sense of humour, was good at working to deadlines and that I had a good manner with customers.
H. My strengths are that I'm good at working with clients, deadlines don't faze me. My weaknesses – I need praise and to feel that I'm needed. My motivation level drops if I feel unloved or unappreciated.
I. The company has a very good reputation for well-designed products and a positive approach to the environment. I also know that you have a good reputation as an equal opportunities employer.
J. From advertisements for similar positions I know that the usual starting salary is about Euro 2000. I would be happy with this salary but would hope that the career structure makes promotion possible.

✳ **7** Work with a partner. Prepare and act out the following interview as a role play in
| English using the prompts on the role cards.

Phrases ▶

Role card: Partner A (interviewer)   **Role card partner B ⇨ page 252**

Sie sind Jennifer O'Rourke von Automotive Services Ltd., London, oder
deren Kollege John Middleton. Mittels einer Stellenanzeige haben Sie eine/n
zweisprachige/n Mitarbeiter/in für die Importabteilung gesucht.
Ein/e Bewerber/in kommt zum Vorstellungsgespräch.

Beginnen Sie das Gespräch mit allgemeinen Fragen z. B. nach:
- Flug
- Heimatstadt des Bewerbers
- Wetter

Fassen Sie die Anforderungen kurz zusammen:
- zweisprachig
- teamfähig
- vertraut mit Einfuhrformalitäten

Fragen Sie nach Berufserfahrung:
- Dauer
- Arbeitsgebiete
- Software-Kenntnisse

Erkundigen Sie sich nach den Gründen für den Wunsch in GB zu arbeiten.

Fragen Sie nach den Gehaltsvorstellungen.

Gehen Sie auf das im CV genannte Interesse an Tennis ein:
- Sie spielen selbst.
- Ihre Firma besorgt für die Mitarbeiter Karten für Wimbledon.

Versprechen Sie in einer Woche Bescheid zu geben.

Verabschieden Sie den Bewerber freundlich.

D   Employment in the EU

One of the central principles of the EU is the free movement of labour. This means that in principle any EU citizen can look for a job in any EU member country without having to apply for permits etc. An EU citizen also has the right to take up residence in any EU country.

1
R
A1.32

Jonathan Oxfurt, a 23-year-old German from Quedlinburg who has recently completed an apprenticeship as an export clerk, is thinking of looking for a job in another European country. He is talking on the telephone to an English friend, Daniel Peterson, whom he met while on a work placement in England and who is working in Bracknell at the logistics and warehousing operation of a major supermarket.

Listen to the conversation and decide whether the following statements are TRUE or FALSE.

1. Jonathan has sent off lots of applications.
2. He would need a green card to work in Britain.
3. A lot of companies have their head offices in Bracknell.
4. Jonathan's certificates do not need to be translated into English.
5. Jonathan could stay for a while with Daniel.
6. Daniel suggests he should apply to the export department.

2
R
A1.33

Marcel Krenz has seen that Global Catering are looking for an assistant to the export manager who speaks French and German. Kirsty Burnham has been promoted and the new export manager is Zoe Lovegrove. Marcel is excited about the job and would love to work in Manchester. He decides to ring Kirsty Burnham.

Listen to the dialogue and complete the following sentences.

Would you **1** for a moment, please?
As you know, **2** are now the big thing.
I have seen that your company is advertising for **3** who can speak German.
Of course, it will have to go through **4** .
Tell Herr Diepholz this is **5** for you.
I'll get **6** off right away.

3 **Listen to the dialogue again and translate the following sentences into German.**

R / M
 A1.33

1. Kirsty Burnham has been promoted.
2. Global Catering are looking for an assistant to the export manager.
3. We are in the process of acquiring a US chain of organic snack outlets.
4. I would be able to involve you in the US projects.
5. I am dreading telling Herr Diepholz.
6. Keep your fingers crossed!

Communicating across cultures: Job applications

You should NOT include references from previous employers in your application when applying in Britain. You will usually be asked to give the names and addresses of possible referees so that the company can approach them direct. In your covering letter you may indicate that you are prepared to provide names of referees on request.

It is obviously a good idea to ask possible referees beforehand whether they are happy to provide a reference.

You should NOT include a photo in your application when applying in the USA or Britain nor make any reference to your religion or race, unless specifically asked to do so.

Info: EU-Facts and figures

EU member countries (27 at present):

Austria, Belgium, Bulgaria, Cyprus, Czech Republic, Denmark, Estonia, Finland, France, Germany, Greece, Hungary, Ireland, Italy, Latvia, Lithuania, Luxemburg, Malta, The Netherlands, Poland, Portugal, Romania, Slovakia, Slovenia, Spain, Sweden, United Kingdom

Total area: 4,324,782 sq. km.

Total population: c. 501.26 million

Total GDP: between $14 and $16 trillion

Languages: There are over 20 official languages. English is spoken by 34% of European citizens – the most widely spoken foreign language.

Industry expert

Applying for a job in industry

1 **Read the following text and summarize the differences between having a job**
R/P **decades ago and nowadays. Think about your parents' or grandparents' working**
lives and your own. Do you agree with the text?

Applying for a job is becoming more and more important for young people today.
People used to worked for only one company. After graduating from school they
started an apprenticeship at a company and 30 or 40 years later they retired.
They worked for the same company for the whole of their lives and they were not
forced to apply for any other job.
But times have changed. Nowadays hardly anyone begins and ends his or her
professional career at the same company. Increased mobility and structural
economic changes mean that everybody has to be flexible. Applying for jobs and
life-long learning will therefore be an important part of everyone's life.

2 **Project work: Work in teams of 4–5 people and do the following application project.** `Phrases ▶`
P/I
Step 1:
- Choose one of your company presentations from Unit 7 or create a "fantasy
  company" which is a mixture of your companies.
- Write down basic information about the company you have chosen in a
  handout. Address 4–6 different aspects and write one page per person plus
  a cover sheet. The handout will provide the background information for the
  prospective job applicants to prepare for the job interview.
- Two students from each group will be applicants at the other companies and
  the rest of the group will be the employer for their own company.

Step 2:
Use the checklist below and write a job advertisement for your company. `Phrases ▶`

✓ Your company: name, sector of industry, location
✓ The job: job title, tasks and responsibilities
✓ The applicant: qualifications, skills, experience, personal qualities
✓ Payment: salary, benefits
✓ Application: contact address, documents required, deadline

Info: Benefits

In the USA it is not obligatory for companies to pay for the insurance of their
employees. So it is important to know whether or not the company pays, for
example, for health insurance. American companies are flexible concerning this
issue and may grant benefits like health insurance, life insurance, increased
pension, more paid holidays, childcare vouchers or school/college tuition.

Step 3:

Publish the job advertisements (e.g. on the board). The applicants read all the advertisements and choose an appropriate one to apply for. Make sure that only a limited number of students choose the same advert. Each student writes an application (letter of application, CV, certificates) for their advert.

Phrases ▶

Step 4:

Evaluate the job applications with the help of the following table and prepare a ranking of the applicants.

Name:	
Job requirements:	Fulfilled:
Positive aspects:	Negative aspects:
Comments:	

Then write invitations for job interviews. When planning your schedule for the interviews, bear in mind that each interview will take about 10 minutes. After the interview you need a few minutes to make some notes. Together with the invitations, hand out the company description (step 1) to the applicants, so that they can use the information to prepare themselves for the interview.

Step 5:

Conduct the job interviews. During the job interview, you won't have a lot of time to make detailed notes, so use the following evaluation sheet instead.

Phrases ▶

	Applicant's name:					Applicant's	
Contents	+ +	+	0	–	– –	+ +	+
	+ +	+	0	–	– –	+ +	+
	+ +	+	0	–	– –	+ +	+
	+ +	+	0	–	– –	+ +	+
Personality	+ +	+	0	–	– –	+ +	
	+ +	+	0	–	– –	+ +	
	+ +	+	0	–	– –	+ +	
Language	+ +	+	0	–	– –	+	
	+ +	+	0	–	– –		
Special remarks							
Result							

Step 6:

The final step is to discuss who is the best applicant for the job. Make a ranking and give feedback to the applicants. Tell them individually about the strengths and weaknesses you observed during the interview. The applicants should also get the chance to say how they perceived the interview situation.

Phrases: Applications

To refer to the source of address

I saw your advertisement **in** …	Ich habe Ihre Anzeige in … gesehen.
I saw this vacancy advertised **on** the … website.	Ich habe diese Stellenanzeige auf der … Webseite gefunden.
I should like to apply for the position advertised in the …	Ich möchte mich für den in der … ausgeschriebenen Posten bewerben.
I have been given your address **by** … who told me that you have a vacancy **for** …	Ich habe Ihre Anschrift von … bekommen, der mich darauf aufmerksam machte, dass bei Ihnen die Stelle eines … frei geworden ist.
I am applying on the off-chance that you may have a vacancy.	Ich erlaube mir, Ihnen eine Initiativbewerbung zu schicken, für den Fall, dass bei Ihnen eine Stelle frei ist.

To give reasons for applying

I am particularly attracted **to** this position as …	Ich bin an dieser Stelle besonders interessiert, weil …
I have just completed a traineeship **at** …	Ich habe gerade meine Ausbildung bei … abgeschlossen.
I completed an apprenticeship two years ago.	Vor zwei Jahren haben ich meine Ausbildung abgeschlossen.
I have some experience in the export trade.	Ich habe Erfahrungen im Außenhandel.
I am familiar **with** this kind of work.	Mit dieser Tätigkeit bin ich vertraut.
I am used to working with people.	Ich bin es gewohnt mit Menschen zu arbeiten.
I enjoy working with people.	Ich arbeite gern mit anderen Menschen zusammen.
I enjoy working in a team.	Ich arbeite gern im Team.
I would welcome the opportunity to …	Ich würde mich über die Möglichkeit freuen …
I am keen to use my knowledge **of** English and French.	Ich möchte sehr gerne meine Englisch- und Französischkenntnisse anwenden.

To refer to your German school career

From … to … I attended … comparable **to** • primary (UK)/elementary (USA) school • grammar school (UK) • higher secondary school • secondary modern school	Von … bis … besuchte ich • die Grundschule • das Gymnasium • die Realschule • die Hauptschule

• comprehensive (school) • high school (USA) • vocational school • commercial school • business college • polytechnic university, university of applied sciences	• Gesamtschule (Einheitsschule für die Sekundarstufe) • die Berufsschule • die Höhere Handelsschule • das Berufskolleg • die Fachhochschule
In … I obtained the • certificate enabling a student to continue education at higher vocational school • German higher education entrance qualification • German university entrance qualification	Im Jahre … erwarb ich das Zeugnis der • Fachoberschulreife • Fachhochschulreife • allgemeine Hochschulreife (Abitur)

In … I passed the
 • state examination in English for clerical and administrative professions
 	
 • Chamber of Commerce examination
  – "Certified Foreign Language Correspondent"
  – "English for Commercial Trainees"
	Im Jahre … legte ich die …
	 • Zertifikatsprüfung Englisch für kaufmännische und verwaltende Berufe (KMK-Zertifikat)
	 • IHK-Prüfung
	  – „Geprüfte/r Fremdsprachen- korrespondent/in"
	  – „Zusatzqualifikation Englisch für kaufmännische Auszubildende"
	 ab.

To refer to qualifications

I **took** my Abitur two years ago.	Vor zwei Jahren machte ich das Abitur.
My main subjects included English and Maths.	Meine Leistungskurse waren Englisch und Mathematik.
I have trained **as a** …	Ich bin gelernte/r …
I have completed an apprenticeship **in** …	Ich habe eine Ausbildung als … abgeschlossen.
I did my apprenticeship **with** the … company.	Ich habe eine Ausbildung bei der Firma … gemacht.
I spent two months in St. Albans **on** a placement.	Ich war zwei Monate zu einem Praktikum in St. Albans.
I have done a practical **with** a small travel operator.	Ich habe ein Praktikum bei einem kleinen Reiseveranstalter gemacht.
I have good admin and bookkeeping skills.	Ich verfüge über gute Kenntnisse und Fertigkeiten, was Organisation und Buchhaltung angeht.

To refer to certificates and references

I enclose certified copies of my certificates.	Als Anlage übersende ich Ihnen beglaubigte Zeugniskopien.
I enclose certified translations of …	Ich füge beglaubigte Übersetzungen von … bei.
I should be happy to provide the names of referees.	Ich würde Ihnen gerne Referenzen angeben.

To refer to starting date and relocation

I would be able to start **at** short notice.	Ich kann kurzfristig anfangen.
I would have to give the usual notice **at** my present firm.	Ich müsste die übliche Kündungsfrist einhalten.
I could start **on** 1 August.	Ich könnte am 1. August anfangen.
I would be prepared to move **to** …	Ich wäre bereit nach … umzuziehen.

To close the letter

I look forward to hearing from you.	Ich sehe Ihrer Antwort mit Interesse entgegen.
I should be grateful if you would consider my application.	Ich würde mich freuen, wenn Sie meine Bewerbung berücksichtigen.
I hope that you will consider my application suitable and give me the opportunity to present myself **at** an interview.	Ich hoffe, dass Sie meine Bewerbung in Betracht ziehen und mir die Möglichkeit geben, mich Ihnen persönlich vorzustellen.

Role cards Partner B

Unit 5 C `5`

Role card: Partner B   **Role card partner A ⇨ page 69**

1. 0033 (0) 4 92 04 89 20
2. 12 Gansevoort Street New York, NY 10014 USA Tel.: 001-212-2422455
   info@usatech.com,
3. www.visitengland.com
4. e-mail: info@shanghai-cd.com, phone: 86-21-5365-8941
5. address: 12J-1 Golden Bell Plaza 18 Huaihai Zhong Lu Shanghai 200021
   China

Unit 5 C `8`

Role card: Partner A / B

Persons for whom the message is intended:	Possible contents of message:
Mr. Collins	Mr. Campbell ill with the flu / can't take part in the conference
Sales Manager	Meeting on Wednesday scheduled from 1:00 pm to 3:30 pm / 15 participants
Miss Otway in Purchasing	Proposal accepted / further details tomorrow
Dr. Temme	New deadline for application 16 October, must be kept whatever happens
Frau Sabine Johänntges	Flight delayed by one hour / arrival now at 10:15 London Heathrow

Unit 6 A 8

Role card: Partner B   **Role card partner A** ⇨ **page 84**

Sie sind James Critchley von der Firma SmartMart Ltd. und wollen für eine Geschäftsreise in den USA ein Auto mieten. Jennifer Ainsworth von Saskatchewan Airlines hat Ihnen die Mietwagenfirma Excelsior Limos Inc. in Chicago empfohlen. **Rufen Sie dort an.**

- Auto vom 25. bis 30. Juni benötigt
- Abholung und Rückgabe am Flughafen O'Hare in Chicago
- Kleinwagen genügt / Preis für fünf Tage? / Versicherung inbegriffen?
- Zusatzversicherung für Selbstbeteiligung (excess coverage) erwünscht
- Rabatt für Kunden der Saskatchewan Airlines?
- Gesamtpreis für eine Woche?
- Zahlung per Kreditkarte?
- Visa Nr. 4731 5026 7100 5314, gültig bis 07/14
- Adresse: Brunswick Avenue, Brighton BN3 1NA, UK

Unit 6 B1 1

Role card: Partner B   **Role card partner A** ⇨ **page 85**

Kirsty Burnham's appointment diary

Monday   **13 June**
9–11 am: meeting to discuss Madrid; 1 pm working lunch with John Markham from PolisMedia; 2.30 pm meeting at office with Barbara Lonsdale from Cosmopolitan Gourmet

Tuesday   **14 June**

Wednesday   **15 June**
From 10 am: visiting suppliers in Birmingham

Thursday   **16 June**
5 pm: work-out at Royal Gym with Laurie

Friday   **17 June**
10 am: Leeds / Amanda Rees from Snack Attack / introduction of trial range
4 pm: hairdresser

Unit 6 Industry expert 2 `1`

Role card: Partner B   **Role card partner A** ⇨ **page 92**

Sie (Shawn McNeil) arbeiten für das Caledonian Royal Hotel in Edinburgh/UK.
Sie werden wegen einer Zimmerreservierung angerufen.

- Melden Sie sich am Telefon.
- Fragen Sie nach dem Datum für die Buchung.
- Ein Einzelzimmer mit Bad ist frei.
- Preis: £130,00 mit Frühstück, £150,00 mit Halbpension. (Verhandeln Sie mit dem Kunden.)
- Das Frühstück wird von 7.30 Uhr bis 10.30 Uhr serviert.
- Die Rezeption ist 24h geöffnet.
- Alle Hotelzimmer sind kostenlos mit WLAN ausgestattet.
- Ein Konferenzzimmer ist noch frei. Preis: £100,00 pro Tag.
- Ein erstklassiger Cateringservice wird für £200,00 am Tag jederzeit angeboten. (Überlegen Sie, was Sie konkret anbieten würden.)
- Das Hotel verfügt über: Sauna, Swimmingpool, Restaurant und Bar.
- Lassen Sie sich den Namen buchstabieren und notieren Sie ihn. Für die feste Buchung benötigen Sie eine Kreditkartennummer und Gültigkeitsdatum.
- Sie senden eine Bestätigung per E-Mail. Fragen Sie nach der E-Mail Adresse.
- Bedanken und verabschieden Sie sich.

Unit 6 Industry expert 3 `1`

Role card: Partner B   **Role card partner A** ⇨ **page 94**

Sie (Nick/Nicola Wain) arbeiten für das Buchungsbüros (booking office) der
Chicago Fair plc/USA. Sie werden wegen einer Standbuchung für die Pack
Exhibition International in Chicago angerufen.

- Melden Sie sich am Telefon.
- Die Pack Exhibition International findet vom 9.–13. November statt. Welche Standgröße wird benötigt?
- Sie messen in Fuß (feet). Der kleinste Stand misst 25' × 20' Fuß. Halle A ist komplett ausgebucht, aber in Halle B sind noch Plätze frei.
- Der kleinste Stand kostet $23,50 per square feet.
- Jeder Stand verfügt über eine komplett eingerichtete Kücheneinheit, Teppich, Regale für die Ausstellungsstücke sowie vier Steckdosen.
- Extra Einrichtungen müssen auf dem Anmeldeformular vermerkt werden.
- Die Messeorganisation übernimmt den Aufbau (installation) und den Abbau.
- Die Aussteller können ab 7. November 9.00 Uhr ihre Ausstellung vorbereiten.
- Öffnungszeiten: täglich 9.00 Uhr bis 17.00 Uhr, am letzten Tag bis 14.00 Uhr.
- Es werden etwa 5.000 Aussteller und 100.000 Besucher erwartet. Sie senden das Anmeldeformular und weitere Informationen per Fax. Fragen Sie nach dem Firmennamen und der Faxnummer.
- Sie benötigen die Bestätigung bis zum 30.06.201_.
- 10 % Anzahlung sind erforderlich (für die Bankdaten, siehe Anmeldeformular).
- Bedanken Sie sich für die Buchung und verabschieden Sie sich.

Unit 9 B 4

Role card: Partner B Role card partner A ⇨ page 131

Jane/James Vernon from Powertools plc, Cardiff, gets a call.
He/she offers to send brochures, price lists and detailed technical descriptions by e-mail and asks for Hammer Werkzeughandel's e-mail address.
Details about delivery times, quantity discounts etc. are dealt with in the brochure.
Jane/James thanks the caller for his/her interest in Powertool's products.

Unit 13 C2 3

Role card: Student B (buyer) Role card partner A ⇨ page 252

Sie (eigener Name) bearbeiten die Rechnungen der Firma Zuckermann & Sacher in Suessen. Ende vorletzten Monats hatten Sie von der Firma Topsweets Ltd aus Edinburgh, Schottland, 1500 kg Pfefferminzriegel bezogen. Die Rechnung war vor 14 Tagen fällig. Nun ruft Sie Jane/John Thorpe deswegen an.

Fragen Sie nach Rechnungsnummer, -datum und -betrag.
Kein Versehen, kein Grund zur Beanstandung
Entschuldigung für Zahlungsverzug
Grund: Insolvenz eines wichtigen Kunden, einer Kette von Süßwarengeschäften
Bitte um 3 Monate Zahlungsaufschub
Falls abgelehnt: Ihr Verhandlungsspielraum für Anzahlung: € 7,000–10,000
Ihr Verhandlungsspielraum für Restzahlung:
• in 3 Raten im Abstand von 6 Wochen oder
• gesamter Rest in 10 Wochen.
Bei Entgegenkommen weitere Aufträge

Unit 14 A2 6

Role card: Partner B (seller) Role card partner A ⇨ page 200

You receive a call from a customer who had expected to be supplied with a skateboard for a maximum weight of 70 kg. On checking the package the customer has found that the maximum admissible weight is only 90 lbs. The price the customer paid is the price for this smaller model. However, on your website you had quoted this lower price for the bigger model by mistake. Apologize. Try to persuade the customer to keep the smaller skateboard – as a present for a kid? – and promise to let him have the bigger one half price. Should the customer refuse this generous offer you will have to agree to take back the small skateboard at your expense and refund the purchase price.

Unit 13 C2 `3`

Role card: Student A (seller)   **Role card partner B** ⇨ **page 251**

You are the chief-accountant Jane/John Thorpe at Topsweets Ltd. in Edinburgh. At the end of last month but one (use the appropriate month) you supplied 1,500 kgs mint bars to Zuckermann & Sacher in Suessen, Germany, a regular customer of yours.

Ring Zuckermann & Sacher and remind them of your invoice
- invoice No. 34500-2; invoice amount: € 20,450.50
- due date: 14 days ago

Up to now punctual settlements
- invoice overlooked?
- reason for complaint?

Be helpful and polite but insist on payment by the end of next week.
Impossible to grant 3 months' respite for the entire sum.
Insist on down payment of at least half the sum.
Accept one of the solutions offered and close on a friendly note.

Unit 16 C `7`

Role card: Partner B (interviewee)   **Role card partner A** ⇨ **page 240**

Sie haben sich bei Automotive Services Ltd., London, als zweisprachige/r Importsachbearbeiter/in beworben und sind zu einem Vorstellungsgespräch eingeladen worden. Sie sind 23 Jahre alt und haben vor einem Jahr ihre Ausbildung als Kaufmann/-frau im Groß- und Außenhandel beendet.

Beantworten Sie die allgemeinen Fragen zu Beginn ganz nach Wunsch
- Flug angenehm/unruhig
- Wetter heiter/wolkig
- einige Sätze zu ihrer Heimatstadt

Sie kennen die Anforderungen und glauben sie vollständig zu erfüllen
- Deutsch Muttersprache, Englisch gut: 9 Jahre in der Schule, 1 Jahr in USA
- arbeiten gern im Team
- mit allen Export- und Importverfahren vertraut

Berufserfahrung
- Ausbildung in verschiedenen Abteilungen eines Stuttgarter Automobilherstellers (Verkauf, Einkauf, Lagerhaltung, Rechnungs- und Personalwesen)
- nach Abschluss der Lehre ein volles Jahr bis jetzt in einer Importabteilung für elektronische Bauelemente
- vertraut mit SAP Office

Begründen Sie Ihre Absicht in GB zu arbeiten ganz nach Ihrer Wahl
Gehaltsvorstellung noch nicht konkret, in Deutschland ca. € 2000 pro Monat

Tennis
- Sie spielen für Ihren Klub in der Regionalliga
- Sie versuchen möglichst viel von Wimbledon im Fernsehen zu sehen

Bitten Sie um baldige Nachricht, weil Sie rechtzeitig kündigen müssen.

Videotraining: Englische Aussprache

Perfekte englische Aussprache leicht gemacht: Mit dem Lernprogramm zur englischen Lautschrift können Sie alle Laute einüben. Wählen Sie einfach in der Navigation rechts den entsprechenden Reiter (*Vowels* oder *Consonants*) aus und dann klicken Sie auf das gewünschte phonetische Symbol. Sprechen Sie die Wörter laut nach.
Unter www.klett.de geben Sie einfach den Online-Link 808201-1000 ein. Von dort aus können Sie die Webanwendung online starten.

Hinweis: Unitbegleitendes Vokabular zum Herunterladen über Online-Link 808262-0000.

(AE) = American English
(BE) = British English

A

abbreviation [ə,briːvɪˈeɪʃn] Abkürzung 113

ability [əˈbɪlətɪ] Fähigkeit 98

able to work in a team [ˌeɪbl tʊ ˌwɜːk ɪn ə ˈtiːm] teamfähig 240

abroad [əˈbrɔːd] im/ins/aus dem Ausland 39

to absorb [əbˈzɔːb] aufnehmen 99

access [ˈækses] Zugang 49

accident [ˈæksɪdənt] Unfall 84

to accommodate [əˈkɒmədeɪt] aufnehmen, unterbringen, entgegenkommen 163

accommodation [ə,kɒməˈdeɪʃn] Unterkunft, Wohnung 228

to accompany [əˈkʌmpənɪ] begleiten 167

according to [əˈkɔːdɪŋ tʊ] entsprechend, gemäß 99

account [əˈkaʊnt] Konto 177

accountant [əˈkaʊntənt] Bilanzprüfer/in, Buchprüfer/in, Buchhalter/in 54

account-holder [əˈkaʊntˌhəʊldə] Kontoinhaber/in 179

accounting [əˈkaʊntɪŋ] Rechnungswesen 235

accounts [əˈkaʊnts] Buchhaltung, Rechnungswesen 63

to accumulate [əˈkjuːmjʊleɪt] *(hier:)* kumulieren 57

accurate(ly) [ˈækjərət(lɪ)] genau, präzise, akkurat 67

to ache [eɪk] schmerzen, wehtun 63

to achieve [əˈtʃiːv] erreichen, erzielen 219

a couple of [ə ˈkʌpl əv] ein paar 216

to acquire [əˈkwaɪə] sich aneignen 98

actually [ˈæktʃʊəlɪ] eigentlich 212

additions [əˈdɪʃnz] Hinzufügungen 86

additional [əˈdɪʃənl] zusätzlich 72

additional / supplementary insurance [əˌdɪʃənl / ˌsʌplɪmentərɪˌɪnˈʃɔːrəns] Zusatzversicherung 84

addressee [ˌædresˈiː] Adressat, Empfänger 114

to adjust [əˈdʒʌst] anpassen, sich anpassen 142

adjustment [əˈdʒʌstmənt] Ausgleich, Bereinigung, Erledigung 192

admin and accounts [ˈædmɪn ənˌ əˈkaʊnts] Verwaltung und Rechnungswesen 228

administration [ədˌmɪnɪˈstreɪʃn] Verwaltung 54

administrator [ədˈmɪnɪstreɪtə] Vergleichs-, Vermögensverwalter 187

adult [ˈædʌlt] Erwachsene/r 180

to advance [ədˈvɑːns] vorschießen, auslegen 179

advantage [ədˈvɑːntɪdʒ] Vorteil 216

advent [ˈædvent] Ankunft 61

advertisement [ədˈvɜːtɪsmənt, ˈædvətaɪzmənt] Anzeige 128

advertising [ˈædvətaɪzɪŋ] Werbung 159

advertising agency [ˈædvətaɪzɪŋ ˌeɪdʒənsɪ] Werbeagentur 8

advertising assistant [ˈædvətaɪzɪŋ əˌsɪstənt] Kaufmann/-frau für Marketingkommunikation 8

advertising campaign [ˈædvətaɪzɪŋ kæmˌpeɪn] Werbekampagne, -feldzug 126

to advise [ədˈvaɪz] (be)raten; benachrichtigen 116

advisory services [ədˈvaɪzərɪ ˌsɜːvɪsɪz] Beratungsdienst 214

to affect [əˈfekt] betreffen, beeinflussen 198

affluent [ˈæflʊənt] wohlhabend 217

age group [ˈeɪdʒ ˌgruːp] Altersgruppe 211

agenda [əˈdʒendə] Tagesordnung; Termine 81

agent [ˈeɪdʒənt] (Handels-)Vertreter/in 126

a good command of English [ə ˌgʊd kəˌmɑːnd əv ˈɪŋglɪʃ] gute Englischkenntnisse 228

air-conditioning [ˈeəkənˌdɪʃənɪŋ] Klimaanlage 24

air freight [ˈeəfreɪt] Luftfracht 122

airline [ˈeəlaɪn] Fluggesellschaft 215

airy [ˈeərɪ] luftig 24

aisle [aɪl] Gang (Flugzeug/Kirche/Supermarkt) 83

alteration [ˌɒltəˈreɪʃn, ˌɔːltəˈreɪʃn] Änderung 24

amateur chef [ˌæmətʊə ˈʃef] Hobbykoch 27

amazing [əˈmeɪzɪŋ] erstaunlich 39

ambitious [æmˈbɪʃəs] ehrgeizig, anspruchsvoll 102

among [əˈmʌŋ] unter 18

amount [əˈmaʊnt] Betrag, Summe 169

ample [ˈæmpl] reichlich, üppig 203

ancient [ˈeɪnʃnt] (ur)alt 23

anger [ˈæŋgə] Zorn 192

to announce [əˈnaʊns] bekanntgeben, ankündigen 173

annual(ly) [ˈænjʊəl(lɪ)] jährlich 57

annual holidays [ˌænjʊəl ˈhɒlɪdeɪz] Jahresurlaub 238

annual statement [ˌænjʊəl ˈsteɪtmənt] Jahresabschluss 13

answering machine (BE), voice mail (AE) [ˈɑːnsərɪŋ məˌʃiːn, ˈvɔɪs ˌmeɪl] Anrufbeantworter 62

to antagonize [ænˈtægənaɪz] vor den Kopf stoßen 200

apart from [əˈpɑːt frəm] abgesehen von 38

apology [əˈpɒlədʒɪ] Entschuldigung 88

appeal [əˈpiːl] Anziehung(skraft) 217

to appeal to [əˈpiːl tuː] ansprechen, gefallen; appellieren 121

appetising [ˈæpətaɪzɪŋ] schmackhaft 53

apple juice [ˈæpl ˌdʒuːs] Apfelsaft 19

appliances [əˈplaɪənsɪz] Geräte 62

applicant [ˈæplɪkənt] Bewerber/in 228

application [æplɪˈkeɪʃn] Bewerbung 227

applications [æplɪˈkeɪʃnz] Anwendungen, Funktionen 62

to appoint [əˈpɔɪnt] ernennen, bestellen 214

appointment [əˈpɔɪntmənt] Termin 84

approach [əˈprəʊtʃ] Haltung, Herangehensweise, Ansatz 239

to approach [əˈprəʊtʃ] sich nähern, herangehen an, ansprechen 216

appropriate [əˈprəʊprɪət] geeignet, passend, angebracht 114

approval [əˈpruːvl] Billigung, Zustimmung, Beifall 154

approved [əˈpruːvd] anerkannt 188

area of decision [ˌeərɪə ˌəv dɪˈsɪʒn] Entscheidungsfeld 222

to arouse [əˈraʊz] wecken (Interesse, Gefühle) 99

artificial [ˌɑːtɪˈfɪʃl] künstlich 160

as a result of [əz ə rɪˈzʌlt əv] auf Grund 18

as a rule [əz ə ˈruːl] in der Regel 85

as a whole [əz ə ˈhəʊl] insgesamt 98

a set break [ə ˌset ˈbreɪk] eine Pause zu festgesetzter Zeit 53

as long as stocks last [əz ˌlɒŋ əz ˌstɒks ˈlɑːst] solange Vorrat reicht 136

asparagus [əˈspærəgəs] Spargel 26

to assess [əˈses] (hier:) bewerten, einschätzen 102

assessment point [əˈsesmənt ˌpɔɪnt] Bewertungspunkt 150

to assign [əˈsaɪn] anweisen, beauftragen; benennen 57

to assist [əˈsɪst] helfen 227

assistance [əˈsɪstəns] Hilfe 87

to associate with [əˈsəʊʃɪeɪt wɪð] in Verbindung bringen mit 217

association [əˌsəʊʃɪˈeɪʃn] Vereinigung, Verband 138

assortment [əˈsɔːtmənt] Sortiment, Auswahl 17

to assume [əˈsjuːm] annehmen, von etwas ausgehen 115

assurance [əˈʃɔːrəns] Zusicherung, Versicherung 167

athlete [ˈæθliːt] Sportler/in, Athlet/in 37

athletics [æθˈletɪks] (Leicht-)Athletik 41

ATM (automated teller machine) [ˌeɪtiːˈem, ˌɔːtəmeɪtɪdˈtelə məˌʃiːn] Geldautomat 179

at short notice [ət ˌʃɔːt ˈnəʊtɪs] kurzfristig 65

at sight [ət ˈsaɪt] bei Sicht/Vorlage 179

to attach [əˈtætʃ] anhängen (Datei), befestigen, anbringen 113

attached [əˈtætʃt] angeschlossen 53

attachment [əˈtætʃmənt] Anhang (E-Mail) 90

to attempt [əˈtempt] versuchen, sich bemühen 36

to attend a course [əˌtend ə ˈkɔːs] an einem Kurs teilnehmen 196

to attend a fair [əˌtend ə ˈfeə] an einer Messe teilnehmen 81

at the latest (nachgestellt) [ət ðə ˈleɪtɪst] spätestens 160

at your disposal [ət ˌjɔː dɪˈspəʊzl] zu Ihrer Verfügung 99

at your earliest convenience [ət ˌjɔːrˌ ˈɜːlɪəst kənˈviːnɪəns] so bald wie möglich 177

at your expense [ət ˌjɔːrˌɪkˈspens] auf Ihre Kosten 189

audience [ˈɔːdɪəns] Publikum 98

author [ˈɔːθə] (hier:) Urheber/in; Verfasser/in, Autor/in 74

automated production [ˌɔːtəmeɪtɪd prəˈdʌkʃn] automatisierte Fertigung 47

automobile sales management assistant [ˌɔːtəməʊbiːl ˌseɪlz ˈmænɪdʒmənt əˌsɪstənt] Automobilkaufmann/-frau 11

availability [əˌveɪləˈbɪləti] Verfügbarkeit 108

available [əˈveɪləbl] erhältlich, zur Verfügung stehend 157

average [ˈævrɪdʒ] Durchschnitt 180

average consumer [ˌævrɪdʒ kənˈsjuːmə] Durchschnittsverbraucher 163

average price [ˌævrɪdʒ ˈpraɪs] Durchschnittspreis 104

to avoid [əˈvɔɪd] vermeiden 215

to award points [əˌwɔːd ˈpɔɪnts] Punkte vergeben (z. B. Wettbewerb) 102

aware [əˈweə] bewusst 232

awful [ˈɔːfəl] schrecklich, scheußlich 19

B

background [ˈbækgraʊnd] (hier:) Ausbildung/Erfahrung 228

backlit [ˈbæklɪt] von hinten/innen beleuchtet 140

back office [ˌbæk ˈɒfɪs] Büro ohne Publikumsverkehr 49

to bake [beɪk] backen, im Ofen braten 26

balance [ˈbæləns] (hier:) Rest(betrag) 71

to balance [ˈbæləns] ausgleichen, ins Gleichgewicht bringen 187

balanced [ˈbælənst] ausgewogen 24

bale [beɪl] Ballen 166

ballet [ˈbæleɪ] (klassisches) Ballett 8

bank business management assistant [ˌbæŋk ˌbɪznɪs ˈmænɪdʒmənt əˌsɪstənt] Bankkaufmann/-frau 9

bank clerk [ˈbæŋk ˌklɑːk] Bankkaufmann/-frau 8

banknote [ˈbæŋknəʊt] Geldschein 176

bank transfer [ˈbæŋk ˌtrænsfɜː] Banküberweisung 156

bar chart [ˈbɑː ˌtʃɑːt] Balkendiagramm 103

barman/barmaid [ˈbɑːmən/ˈbɑːmeɪd] Bedienung hinter der Theke 85

based in [ˈbeɪst ɪn] mit Sitz in 229

basically [ˈbeɪsɪkli] im Grunde 159

batch production [ˌbætʃ prəˈdʌkʃn] Chargenfertigung 46

battery [ˈbætəri] Batterie 140

Bavarian cuisine [bəˌveərɪən kwɪˈziːn] bayerische Küche 81

to be able [bɪˈeɪbl] in der Lage sein 212

bean [biːn] Bohne 26

bearer [ˈbeərə] (hier:) Überbringer/in 179

to bear in mind, bore, born [ˌbeərˌɪn ˈmaɪnd, bɔː, bɔːn] berücksichtigen 244

to bear with someone [beə ˈwɪð ˌsʌmwʌn] (hier:) etwas Geduld haben; so lange warten (am Telefon) 63

beauty consultant [ˈbjuːti kənˌsʌltənt] Kosmetiker/in 213

to be aware of a problem [bɪ ˌəˌweər ˌəv ə ˈprɒbləm] sich eines Problems bewusst sein 183

to become aware of [bɪˌkʌm əˈweə ˌəv] bewusst werden 101

to be cooperative [bɪ kəʊˈɒprətɪv] zur Zusammenarbeit bereit sein 200

beef broth [ˌbiːf ˈbrɒθ] Fleischbrühe 26

to be entitled [bɪ ɪnˈtaɪtld] berechtigt sein, Anspruch haben 181

beetle [ˈbiːtl] Käfer 193

beforehand [bɪˈfɔːhænd] vorher 237

to be in a hurry [bɪˌɪn ə ˈhʌri] es eilig haben 212

to be inclined [bɪ ɪnˈklaɪnd] dazu neigen, geneigt sein 123

to be in demand [bɪ ɪn dɪˈmɑːnd] gefragt sein, nachgefragt werden 159

to be in line with [bɪ ɪn ˈlaɪn wɪð] übereinstimmen, im Einklang stehen mit 120

to be in progress [bɪ ɪn ˈprəʊgres] im Gang sein, in Bearbeitung sein 202

to be likely [bɪ ˈlaɪkli] wahrscheinlich sein/geschehen 111

bend [bend] Kurve 22

beneficiary [ˌbenəˈfɪʃəri] Begünstigte/r 188

to benefit [ˈbenəfɪt] profitieren 214

benefits [ˈbenəfɪts] Arbeitgeberzuschüsse 243

to be on a familiar footing [bɪ ˌɒn ə fəˌmɪlɪə ˈfʊtɪŋ] auf vertrautem Fuße stehen 115

to be on hand [bɪ ˌɒn ˈhænd] zugegen sein, da sein 87

to be put on a shortlist [bɪ ˌpʊt ɒn ə ˈʃɔːtlɪst] in die engere Auswahl kommen 237

berry ['berɪ] Beere 27

to be subject to [bɪ 'sʌbdʒɪkt‿tuː] unterliegen, abhängen von, unterworfen sein 136

to be to blame [bɪ tʊ 'bleɪm] schuld sein 202

to be up to [bɪ‿ʌp tuː] im Schilde führen, anstellen; in der Lage sein 220

beverage wholesaler [ˌbevərɪdʒ 'həʊlˌseɪlə] Getränkegroßhandlung 129

BIC (bank identifier code) [ˌbiːaɪˈsiː (ˌbæŋk aɪˈdentɪfaɪə ˌkəʊd)] internationaler Bank-Code 177

bilingual [baɪˈlɪŋwəl] zweisprachig 228

bill [bɪl] Rechnung 86

billboards *(AE)* ['bɪlbɔːdz] Plakatwände 217

bill of exchange [ˌbɪl‿əv ɪksˈtʃeɪndʒ] Wechsel 179

bill of lading (B / L) [ˌbɪl‿əv ˈleɪdɪŋ] Konnossement, Seefrachtbrief 170

biomass ['baɪəʊˌmæs] Biomasse 50

biro ['baɪrəʊ] Kugelschreiber 50

blank [blæŋk] blanko 188

blunt(ly) [blʌnt(lɪ)] *(hier:)* unverblümt 200

board meetings ['bɔːd ˌmiːtɪŋz] Vorstandssitzungen 100

body language ['bɒdɪ ˌlæŋgwɪdʒ] Körpersprache 101

to boil [bɔɪl] kochen, sieden 26

bold type [ˌbəʊld ˈtaɪp] Fettdruck 120

booked (up) [bʊkt ('ʌp)] ausgebucht 91

booking charge ['bʊkɪŋ ˌtʃɑːdʒ] Buchungsgebühr 71

booking reference ['bʊkɪŋ ˌrefrəns] Buchungsnummer 83

bookkeeping ['bʊkˌkiːpɪŋ] Buchhaltung 13

to bore [bɔː] langweilen 100

bored [bɔːd] gelangweilt 238

both ... and ... [bəʊθ ... ənd ...] sowohl ... als auch ... 117

brackets ['brækɪts] Klammern 113

branch [brɑːntʃ] Filiale 17

brand [brænd] Marke, Markenartikel 215

breadcrumbs ['bredkrʌmz] Brotkrümel, Paniermehl 25

to break bulk [ˌbreɪk 'bʌlk] große Gebinde aufbrechen 213

brewery ['bruːərɪ] Brauerei 23

brief(ly) [briːf(lɪ)] kurz 7

briefcase ['briːfkeɪs] Aktentasche 100

bright [braɪt] hell, glänzend; klug 157

bright yellow [ˌbraɪt ˈjeləʊ] leuchtend gelb 23

to bring forward [brɪŋ ˈfɔːwəd] vorziehen, vorverlegen 117

brochure ['brəʊʃə] Broschüre, Prospekt 37

Brussels sprouts [ˌbrʌslz ˈspraʊts] Rosenkohl 26

bubble ['bʌbl] Blase, Bläschen 17

budget ['bʌdʒɪt] (Staats-)Haushalt, Etat 187

building site ['bɪldɪŋ ˌsaɪt] Baustelle 193

bulb [bʌlb] Glühbirne 47

bulk goods [ˌbʌlk ˈgʊdz] Massen-, Schüttgüter 164

bulky ['bʌlkɪ] sperrig, unhandlich, übergroß 164

bumpy ['bʌmpɪ] unruhig, holprig 18

bundle with steel strapping [ˌbʌndl wɪð ˌstiːl ˈstræpɪŋ] Bündel mit Stahlbandumreifung 166

business relations ['bɪznɪs rɪˌleɪʃnz] Geschäftsbeziehungen 138

business section ['bɪznɪsˌsekʃn] Gewerbeteil 62

business studies [ˌbɪznɪs ˈstʌdɪz] Betriebswirtschaft 12

business terms ['bɪznɪs ˌtɜːmz] Geschäftsbedingungen 126

business unit, division ['bɪznɪs ˌjuːnɪt, dɪˈvɪʒn] Geschäftseinheit, Unternehmensbereich 187

business venture ['bɪznɪs ˌventʃə] geschäftliches Unternehmen 25

buyer ['baɪə] Einkäufer/in 220

by means of [ˌbaɪ 'miːnz‿əv] mittels 180

by return [baɪ rɪˈtɜːn] umgehend 116

C

cabbage ['kæbɪdʒ] Kohl 25

to calculate ['kælkjəleɪt] berechnen 149

calculator ['kælkjəleɪtə] Taschenrechner 50

calm [kɑːm] ruhig, gelassen 192

calorie count ['kælərɪ ˌkaʊnt] Kalorienangabe 53

to cancel an invoice [ˌkænsl ən ˈɪnvɔɪs] Rechnung stornieren 187

to cancel an order [ˌkænsl ən ˈɔːdə] einen Auftrag annullieren 195

cancellation [ˌkænsəˈleɪʃn] Stornierung 91

canteen [kænˈtiːn] Kantine 21

capable of ['keɪpəbl‿əv] in der Lage zu; fähig, tüchtig 39

to capitalize ['kæpɪtəlaɪz] in Großbuchstaben schreiben 115

to capture ['kæptʃə] (ein)fangen 157

carbon dioxide [ˌkɑːbn daɪˈɒksaɪd] Kohlenstoffdioxid 105

carbon footprint [ˌkɑːbn ˈfʊtprɪnt] CO_2-Fußabdruck, persönliche CO_2 Bilanz 105

carbon paper ['kɑːbn ˌpeɪpə] Kohlepapier 113

car carrier ['kɑː ˌkærɪə] Autotransporter, -transportschiff 163

cardholder ['kɑːdˌhəʊldə] Karteninhaber/in 179

care [keə] Sorgfalt 201

cargo ['kɑːgəʊ] (See-)Fracht, Ladung 163

car hire / rental company ['kɑːˌhaɪə /ˌrentl ˌkʌmpənɪ] Mietwagenfirma 84

carnivorous [kɑːˈnɪvərəs] fleischfressend 25

carriage ['kærɪdʒ] Transport(kosten), Fracht(kosten) 144

carriage by sea [ˌkærɪdʒ baɪ 'siː] Seetransport 164

carrier ['kærɪə] Frachtführer 163

carrots ['kærəts] Möhren, Karotten 26

to carry out work [ˌkærɪ aʊt ˈwɜːk] Arbeit ausführen 137

cartage ['kɑːtɪdʒ] Rollgeld, Fuhrgeld 150

case [keɪs] Kiste, Schachtel 208

cash discount [ˌkæʃ ˈdɪskaʊnt] Skonto, Barzahlungsrabatt 181

cash on delivery [ˌkæʃ ɒn dɪˈlɪvərɪ] Zahlung durch Nachnahme/bei Lieferung 181

cash payment [ˌkæʃ ˈpeɪmənt] Barzahlung 180

cash point ['kæʃpɔɪnt] Geldautomat 179

cash with order [ˌkæʃ wɪð ˈɔːdə] Bezahlung bei Auftragserteilung, Vorkasse 138

casual ['kæʒjʊəl] zwanglos, leger 6

to catch, caught, caught [kætʃ, kɔːt, kɔːt] *(hier:)* mitbekommen 65

to cater for ['keɪtə fɔː] *(hier:)* etwas bieten für 81

cauliflower ['kɒlɪˌflaʊə] Blumenkohl 26

certificate of origin [səˌtɪfɪkət‿əv ˈɒrɪdʒɪn] Ursprungszeugnis 170

certified ['sɜːtɪfaɪd] beglaubigt; zertifiziert 230

chair, chairperson [tʃeə, ˈtʃeəˌpɜːsn] Vorsitzende/r 88

chairman of the board [ˌtʃeəmən əv‿ðə ˈbɔːd] Vorstandsvorsitzender 54

challenging ['tʃælɪndʒɪŋ] herausfordernd 228

change(s) [tʃeɪndʒ, 'tʃeɪndʒɪz] Veränderung 219

change [tʃeɪndʒ] Wechselgeld 86

changeable ['tʃeɪndʒəbl] wechselhaft 19

channel ['tʃænl] *(hier:)* Vertriebsweg 211

characters ['kærəktəz] *(hier:)* Buchstaben, Zeichen 113

characteristic feature [ˌkærəktərɪstɪk ˈfiːtʃə] typisches Merkmal 214

charge [tʃɑːdʒ] Kosten, Gebühr 72

to charge [tʃɑːdʒ] *(hier:)* berechnen 211

to charge for ['tʃɑːdʒ fɔː] bezahlen lassen 214

cheap chain [ˌtʃiːp ˌtʃeɪn] Billigladenkette 211

to check [tʃek] (über)prüfen 57

check-out ['tʃekaʊt] (Supermarkt-)Kasse 180

chemist ['kemɪst] Apotheker/in 213

cheque (BE), check (AE) [tʃek] Scheck 179

chicken ['tʃɪkɪn] Hähnchen, Hühnerfleisch 26

chief accountant [,tʃiːf ə'kaʊntənt] Leiter/in des Rechnungswesens 21

chief executive officer (CEO) [,tʃiːf ɪg,zekjətɪv 'ɒfɪsə] Firmenchef/in, Vorstandsvorsitzende/r 54

childcare ['tʃaɪldkeə] Kinderbetreuung 243

chilled [tʃɪld] eisgekühlt 25

to choose, chose, chosen [tʃuːz, tʃəʊz, 'tʃəʊzn] wählen 83

to chop [tʃɒp] klein schneiden, hacken 26

clean bill of lading ['kliːn ,bɪl əv 'leɪdɪŋ] reines Konnossement 181

cleaning agent ['kliːnɪŋ ,eɪdʒənt] Reinigungsmittel 29

clerical staff ['klerɪkl ,stɑːf] Büropersonal, Sachbearbeiter 80

club [klʌb] Disko; Verein 18

coaching ['kəʊtʃɪŋ] Training 196

coffee break ['kɒfɪ ,breɪk] Kaffeepause 53

coffee table ['kɒfɪ ,teɪbl] Couchtisch 169

coil on euro-pallet [,kɔɪl ɒn 'juːrəʊ,pælɪt] Rolle, Coil auf Europalette 166

coin [kɔɪn] Münze, Geldstück 176

to collect [kə'lekt] abholen, (ein)sammeln 154

to collect the invoice amount [kə,lekt ðɪ 'ɪnvɔɪs ə,maʊnt] den Rechnungsbetrag eintreiben 183

colour printer ['kʌlə ,prɪntə] Farbdrucker 142

column ['kɒləm] (Text-)Spalte 46

to comb [kəʊm] kämmen 237

to come across [,kʌm ə'krɒs] (hier:) wirken 71

comeback ['kʌmbæk] (hier:) Reaktion 63

comfort ['kʌmfət] Behaglichkeit, Komfort; Trost 138

comfortable ['kʌmftəbl] bequem 177

command [kə'mɑːnd] (hier:) Beherrschung 233

commercial invoice [kə,mɜːʃl 'ɪnvɔɪs] Handelsrechnung 167

commercial management [kə,mɜːʃl 'mænɪdʒmənt] Steuerung 12

to commission [kə'mɪʃn] beauftragen 194

commission [kə'mɪʃn] Provision 39

commitment [kə'mɪtmənt] Engagement 105

communication [kə,mjuːnɪ'keɪʃn] Nachricht, Mitteilung, Information 183

community [kə'mjuːnətɪ] Gemeinschaft 220

comparative(ly) [kəm'pærətɪv(lɪ)] verhältnismäßig 181

to compare [kəm'peə] vergleichen 215

comparing prices [kəm,peərɪŋ 'praɪsɪz] Preisvergleich 216

to compensate ['kɒmpənseɪt] entschädigen 185

to compete [kəm'piːt] an einem Wettkampf teilnehmen, konkurrieren 37

competition [,kɒmpə'tɪʃn] Konkurrenz, Wettbewerb 142

competitive prices [kəm,petətɪv 'praɪsɪz] günstige, konkurrenzfähige Preise 212

competitor [kəm'petɪtə] Wettbewerber/in, Mitbewerber/in 90

complaint [kəm'pleɪnt] Beschwerde, Beanstandung, Reklamation, Mängelrüge 192

to complete [kəm'pliːt] abschließen 229

complimentary close [,kɒmplɪmentərɪ 'kləʊz] Grußformel 112

to comply with regulations [kəm,plaɪ wɪð ,regjə'leɪʃnz] Vorschriften einhalten 198

components [kəm'pəʊnənts] Bestandteile 112

compressed gas [kəm,prest 'gæs] Gasflasche 31

to comprise [kəm'praɪz] umfassen 13

computer projector [kəm,pjuːtə prə'dʒektə] Beamer 101

concept ['kɒnsept] Konzept, Begriff, Auffassung 153

concerns [kən'sɜːnz] (hier:) Sorgen, Fragen 86

conciliatory [kən'sɪlɪətrɪ] versöhnlich 200

conclusion [kən'kluːʒn] Schluss 99

conclusion of contract [kən'kluːʒn əv 'kɒntrækt] Vertragsabschluss 189

to conduct a test [kən,dʌkt ə 'test] einen Test durchführen 154

confectionery [kən'fekʃənrɪ] Süßwaren 128

confident ['kɒnfɪdənt] selbstbewusst 101

to confirm [kən'fɜːm] bestätigen 177

confirmation [,kɒnfə'meɪʃn] Bestätigung 83

consent [kən'sent] Zustimmung, Einwilligung 181

conservatory [kən'sɜːvətrɪ] Wintergarten 202

to consider [kən'sɪdə] erwägen, überlegen; ansehen als 123

consideration [kən,sɪdə'reɪʃn] Erwägung, Überlegung 24

consignee [,kɒnsaɪ'niː] Empfänger/in (einer Warensendung) 171

consignment [kən'saɪnmənt] (Waren-)Sendung, Lieferung 164

consignment note [kən'saɪnmənt ,nəʊt] Frachtbrief 167

conspicuous [kən'spɪkjʊəs] auffällig 23

construction work [kən'strʌkʃn ,wɜːk] Bauarbeiten 102

consumer [kən'sjuːmə] Verbraucher/in 216

consumer goods [kən'sjuːmə ,gʊdz] Konsumgüter 217

contact person ['kɒntækt ,pɜːsn] Ansprechpartner/in 196

to contain [kən'teɪn] enthalten 160

content ['kɒntent] Inhalt 98

context ['kɒntekst] Zusammenhang, Kontext 111

contract ['kɒntrækt] Vertrag 111

to contribute [kən'trɪbjuːt] beitragen 219

contribution [,kɒntrɪ'bjuːʃn] Beitrag 219

control [kən'trəʊl] Kontrolle 12

convenience food [kən'viːnɪəns ,fuːd] Fertiggerichte 53

convenient [kən'viːnɪənt] bequem, praktisch 126

conventional [kən'venʃənl] herkömmlich, traditionell 212

converted [kən'vɜːtɪd] umgebaut 49

to convince [kən'vɪns] überzeugen 139

convincing [kən'vɪnsɪŋ] überzeugend 42

cooking ['kʊkɪŋ] Art zu kochen, Küche 7

co-operation [kəʊ,ɒpə'reɪʃn] (hier:) Hilfe; Mit-, Zusammenarbeit 117

to cope with something ['kəʊp wɪð ,sʌmθɪŋ] fertig werden mit etwas, etwas schaffen 206

copper ['kɒpə] Kupfer 102

cordial ['kɔːdɪəl] herzlich, freundlich 205

corner stand ['kɔːnə ,stænd] Eckstand 89

corn starch ['kɔːn ,stɑːtʃ] Stärkemehl 27

corporate (e.g. culture) ['kɔːpərət] Unternehmens- (z.B. -kultur), bezogen auf Firmen/Unternehmen 100

corridor ['kɒrɪdɔː] Gang 16

corrosive [kə'rəʊsɪv] ätzend 31

cost-cutting [,kɒst'kʌtɪŋ] kostensparend 207

cost estimate ['kɒst ,estɪmət] Kostenvoranschlag 136

cost-performance analysis [,kɒstpə'fɔːməns ə,næləsɪs] Kosten- und Leistungsanalyse 13

cost price ['kɒst ,praɪs] Selbstkostenpreis 24

cottage ['kɒtɪdʒ] (hier:) Ferienhäuschen 71

Could you tell me the way to . . . ? [kʊd ,jʊ ,tel mɪ ðə 'weɪ tʊ] Können Sie mir sagen, wie ich zu/nach … komme? 22

countryside ['kʌntrɪsaɪd] Landschaft, Gegend; ländliche Gegend 24

court [kɔːt] Gericht(shof), Hof 111

courtesy ['kɜːtəsɪ] Höflichkeit 201

courtyard ['kɔ:tjɑ:d] Hof 206

to cover ['kʌvə] decken, abdecken 99

covering letter ['kʌvərɪŋ ˌletə] Begleitschreiben 228

covering page ['kʌvərɪŋ ˌpeɪdʒ] Deckblatt 116

cover sheet ['kʌvə ˌʃi:t] Deckblatt 243

crash course ['kræʃ ˌkɔ:s] Kompaktkurs 131

crate [kreɪt] Lattenkiste 166

to create [krɪ'eɪt] (er)schaffen, erzeugen, erstellen 36

to credit ['kredɪt] gutschreiben 189

credit note ['kredɪt ˌnəʊt] Gutschrift 193

creditworthiness ['kredɪtˌwɜ:ðɪnəs] Kreditwürdigkeit 181

crossed cheque [ˌkrɒst 'tʃek] Verrechnungsscheck 179

crowded ['kraʊdɪd] überfüllt 85

crude oil [ˌkru:d 'ɔɪl] Rohöl 164

crystal glass [ˌkrɪstl 'glɑ:s] Kristallglas 129

cucumber ['kju:kʌmbə] Gurke 26

cues [kju:z] Stichworte 99

currency ['kʌrənsɪ] Währung 176

current ['kʌrənt] laufend, gegenwärtig, derzeitig, aktuell, gültig 55

curt [kɜ:t] knapp, schroff 200

customary ['kʌstəmərɪ] üblich 181

customer service / relations [ˌkʌstəmə 'sɜ:vɪs / rɪ'leɪʃnz] Kundendienst 54

customs formalities ['kʌstəmz fɔ:ˌmælɪtɪz] Zollformalitäten 144

to cut off [kʌt 'ɒf] (hier:) unterbrechen 65

to cut out [kʌt 'aʊt] (hier:) umgehen; ausschneiden 214

cutting-edge [ˌkʌtɪŋ 'edʒ] auf dem neuesten Stand 221

CV (curriculum vitae) [ˌsi:'vi: (kəˌrɪkjələm 'vi:taɪ)] tabellarischer Lebenslauf 228

cycling ['saɪklɪŋ] Radfahren 9

D

damage ['dæmɪdʒ] Beschädigung, Schaden 170

data processing, EDP ['deɪtə ˌprəʊsesɪŋ, ˌi:di:'pi:] Datenverarbeitung, EDV 21

day light lamp [ˌdeɪlaɪt 'læmp] Tageslichtlampe 47

deadline ['dedlaɪn] letzte Frist, letzter Termin 133

debit card ['debɪt ˌkɑ:d] Bankkarte 179

to debit to an account [ˌdebɪt ˌtʊ ˌən ə'kaʊnt] von einem Konto abbuchen 179

to debit to someone's account [ˌdebɪt ˌtʊ ˌsʌmwʌnz ə'kaʊnt] das Konto von jemandem belasten 169

debt collection ['det kəˌlekʃn] Inkasso(verfahren) 173

debt level ['det ˌlevl] Schuldenstand 180

decade ['dekeɪd] Jahrzehnt 163

decline [dɪ'klaɪn] Rückgang 104

to decline [dɪ'klaɪn] ablehnen 173

dedication [ˌdedɪ'keɪʃn] Engagement, Hingabe 207

to deduct [dɪ'dʌkt] abziehen 181

to deepen ['di:pn] vertiefen, tiefer machen 163

deer [dɪə] Rotwild 25

defective [dɪ'fektɪv] schadhaft, beschädigt, unzulänglich 198

deferred payment [dɪˌfɜ:d 'peɪmənt] verschobene Auszahlung 188

definitely ['defɪnətlɪ] auf jeden Fall 18

degree [dɪ'gri:] Grad, Ausmaß; akademischer Grad 110

degree of automation [dɪˌgri: ˌəv ˌɔ:tə'meɪʃn] Automatisierungsgrad 47

delay [dɪ'leɪ] Verzögerung 122

delay in payment [dɪˌleɪ ˌɪn 'peɪmənt] Zahlungsverzug 186

to delete [dɪ'li:t] löschen, tilgen, streichen 113

delicatessens [ˌdelɪkə'tesənz] Feinkostgeschäfte 159

delighted [dɪ'laɪtɪd] entzückt, begeistert 139

delivery [dɪ'lɪvərɪ] Lieferung; das Halten (eines Vortrags) 91

delivery date [dɪ'lɪvərɪ ˌdeɪt] Lieferdatum 58

delivery on demand [dɪˌlɪvərɪ ˌɒn dɪ'mɑ:nd] Lieferung auf Abruf 58

demand [dɪ'mɑ:nd] Nachfrage 225

denomination [dɪˌnɒmɪ'neɪʃn] Konfession (Religion) 232

department store [dɪ'pɑ:tmənt ˌstɔ:] Warenhaus, Kaufhaus 213

depending on [dɪ'pendɪŋ ˌɒn] je nach, abhängig von 211

to depend on [dɪ'pend ˌɒn] abhängen von; sich verlassen auf 139

deposit [dɪ'pɒzɪt] Anzahlung 91

description [dɪ'skrɪpʃn] Beschreibung 155

to design [dɪ'zaɪn] entwerfen, erstellen 7

desirable [dɪ'zaɪərəbl] wünschenswert 228

desires [dɪ'zaɪəz] Wünsche 212

desk [desk] Schreibtisch 50

desk lamp ['desk ˌlæmp] Schreibtischlampe 50

desk research ['desk ˌri:sɜ:tʃ] (Markt-) Forschung am Schreibtisch, Sekundärforschung 212

desk tidy ['desk ˌtaɪdɪ] Stifteköcher 50

despair [dɪ'speə] Verzweiflung 63

to despatch, dispatch [dɪ'spætʃ] (ab-/ver-)senden, (ab-/ver-)schicken 138

dessert [dɪ'zɜ:t] Nachspeise 25

destination [ˌdestɪ'neɪʃn] Ziel, Bestimmung(sort) 22

to destroy [dɪ'strɔɪ] vernichten, zerstören 198

details ['di:teɪlz] Einzelheiten 230

detailed ['di:teɪld] ausführlich 122

detective novel [dɪ'tektɪv ˌnɒvl] Kriminalroman 193

determination of material requirements [dɪˌtɜ:mɪ'neɪʃn ˌəv məˌtɪərɪəl rɪ'kwaɪəmənts] Bedarfsermittlung 58

to devastate ['devəsteɪt] verwüsten 185

devastating ['devəsteɪtɪŋ] zerstörerisch, verheerend 105

to develop [dɪ'veləp] entwickeln 216

development [dɪ'veləpmənt] Entwicklung 215

development stage [dɪ'veləpmənt ˌsteɪdʒ] Entwicklungsphase 47

devoted [dɪ'vəʊtɪd] gewidmet 220

dialling tone ['daɪəlɪŋ ˌtəʊn] Freizeichen 62

diameter [daɪ'æmɪtə] Durchmesser 47

diary ['daɪərɪ] Terminkalender, Tagebuch 84

to differ ['dɪfə] unterschiedlich sein 227

dimmable ['dɪməbl] dimmbar 47

directory [daɪ'rektərɪ, dɪ'rektərɪ] Nachschlagewerk, Verzeichnis 227

directory enquiries [daɪˌrektərɪ ɪn'kwaɪərɪz, dɪˌrektərɪ ɪn'kwaɪərɪz] Telefonauskunft 62

to direct someone [daɪ'rekt ˌsʌmwʌn, dɪ'rekt ˌsʌmwʌn] jemandem den Weg sagen/zeigen 21

discerning [dɪ'sɜ:nɪŋ] anspruchsvoll, guten Geschmack besitzend 139

disclaimer [dɪ'skleɪmə] Haftungsausschluss, Widerruf 41

to disclose [dɪ'skləʊz] offenlegen, preisgeben 182

discount ['dɪskaʊnt] Rabatt, Nachlass 127

disgruntled [dɪs'grʌntld] verärgert, verstimmt 201

disgusting [dɪs'gʌstɪŋ] abscheulich 25

dish [dɪʃ] (hier:) Speise, Gericht 100

to dislike [dɪs'laɪk] nicht mögen 218

dismayed [dɪs'meɪd] entsetzt 194

dispatch [dɪ'spætʃ] (hier:) Versand 29

dispatch advice [dɪ'spætʃ ədˌvaɪs] Versandanzeige 167

distribution [ˌdɪstrɪ'bju:ʃn] Vertrieb 222

distribution channels [dɪstrɪ'bju:ʃn ˌtʃænlz] Vertriebskanäle/wege 213

to divide up [dɪˌvaɪd 'ʌp] einteilen, aufteilen 99

diving ['daɪvɪŋ] Tauchen, Tauchsport 8

to do a traineeship / an apprenticeship [ˌdu: ə ˌtreɪ'ni:ʃɪp / ˌən ə'prentɪʃɪp] eine Ausbildung machen 7

dock [dɒk] Dock, Kai, Hafenbecken 145

document of title [ˌdɒkjəmənt əv ˈtaɪtl] Eigentumsurkunde 170

documents against acceptance (D/A) [ˌdɒkjʊmənts əˌɡenst ækˈseptəns] Dokumente gegen Akzept 189

documents against payment (D/P) [ˌdɒkjʊmənts əˌɡenst ˈpeɪmənt] Dokumente gegen Bezahlung, Dokumenteninkasso 189

domestic market [dəˌmestɪk ˈmɑːkɪt] Inlandsmarkt 101

dominant [ˈdɒmɪnənt] beherrschend, dominierend 38

dominated [ˈdɒmɪneɪtɪd] beherrscht, dominiert 23

to donate [dəʊˈneɪt] spenden 220

to double [ˈdʌbl] (hier:) eine doppelte Funktion erfüllen 99

draft [drɑːft] (hier:) Tratte 189

to draw up, drew, drawn [drɔːˈˌʌp, druː, drɔːn] zusammenstellen, verfassen 143

dreadful [ˈdredfəl] schrecklich 63

to dread something [dred ˌsʌmθɪŋ] Angst vor etwas haben 242

dressing [ˈdresɪŋ] Salatsoße 27

drill head [ˈdrɪl ˌhed] Bohrkopf 182

drizzle [ˈdrɪzl] Nieselregen 19

to drop [drɒp] fallen 104

drum [drʌm] Fass, Barrel 166

to dry [draɪ] abtrocknen 28

due [djuː] fällig 182

dumpling [ˈdʌmplɪŋ] Kloß, Knödel 25

duplicate [ˈdjuːplɪkət] Duplikat 188

durability [ˌdjʊərəˈbɪlətɪ] Haltbarkeit 154

durable [ˈdjʊərəbl] haltbar 177

duties [ˈdjuːtɪz] (hier:) Aufgaben 54

duty [ˈdjuːtɪ] (hier:) Zoll(gebühr) 144

E

early order discount [ˌɜːlɪˌɔːdə ˈdɪskaʊnt] Frühbuchungsrabatt 121

to earn one's living [ˌɜːn wʌnz ˈlɪvɪŋ] seinen Lebensunterhalt verdienen 40

e-commerce [ˈiːˌkɒmɜːs] Internethandel 180

economic growth [ˌiːkənɒmɪkˈɡrəʊθ] Wirtschaftswachstum 163

economics [ˌiːkəˈnɒmɪks] Gesamtwirtschaft 12

to effect [ɪˈfekt] vornehmen, durchführen 149

effective [ɪˈfektɪv] wirksam 216

efficient [ɪˈfɪʃnt] leistungsfähig, wirksam, tüchtig 39

effort [ˈefət] Anstrengung, Bemühung 41

elderly person [ˌeldəlɪ ˈpɜːsn] ältere Person 54

electrical equipment [ɪˌlektrɪkl ɪˈkwɪpmənt] Elektrogeräte 51

electrical goods industry [ɪˌlektrɪkl ˈɡʊdz ˌɪndəstrɪ] Elektroartikelbranche 10

electronic components [elekˌtrɒnɪkˌkəmˈpəʊnənts] elektronische Bauelemente 238

embarrassed [ɪmˈbærəst] peinlich, verlegen 86

embarrassment [ɪmˈbærəsmənt] Verlegenheit 63

embassy [ˈembəsɪ] Botschaft(sgebäude) 128

emission [ɪˈmɪʃn] Ausstoß 105

emphasis [ˈemfəsɪs] Nachdruck 187

to emphasise [ˈemfəsaɪz] betonen, hervorheben 36

to employ [ɪmˈplɔɪ] beschäftigen, einstellen 37

employment [ɪmˈplɔɪmənt] Beschäftigung 228

empty [ˈemptɪ] leer 198

to enable [ɪˈneɪbl] in die Lage versetzen 215

to enclose [ɪnˈkləʊz] beifügen 228

enclosure [ɪnˈkləʊʒə] Anlage (Brief) 111

endorsed [enˈdɔːst] indossiert 188

to end up [end ˈʌp] (hier:) landen 23

end user [ˈend ˌjuːzə] Endverbraucher/in 213

energy content [ˈenədʒɪ ˌkɒntent] Brennwert (Energiegehalt) 53

energy efficiency class [ˌenədʒɪ ɪˈfɪʃənsɪ ˌklɑːs] Energieeffizienzklasse 47

engaged [ɪnˈɡeɪdʒd] besetzt 62

engine [ˈendʒɪn] Motor 166

enquiry (BE), inquiry (AE) [ɪnˈkwaɪərɪ] Anfrage, Nachfrage 126

to enrol [ɪnˈrəʊl] sich einschreiben 235

ensuite bathroom [ˌɒnswiːtˌˈbɑːθruːm] eigenes Bad (Hotelzimmer) 82

to ensure [ɪnˈʃɔː] sichern, gewährleisten 213

to enter [ˈentə] eintreten, eintragen, eingeben 113

enterprise [ˈentəpraɪz] Unternehmen 61

to entertain [ˌentəˈteɪn] sich um jemanden kümmern, unterhalten 16

enthusiasm [ɪnˈθjuːzɪæzm] Begeisterung 228

to entrust [ɪnˈtrʌst] anvertrauen 122

envelope [ˈenvələʊp] (Brief-)Umschlag 196

environment [ɪnˈvaɪərənmənt] Umwelt, Umfeld 164

environmentally friendly [ɪnˌvaɪərənˌmentəlɪ ˈfrendlɪ] umweltfreundlich 101

environmental policy [ɪnˌvaɪərəmentl ˈpɒləsɪ] Umweltpolitik 105

equal opportunities employer [ˌiːkwəl ɒpəˈtjuːnətɪz ɪmˌplɔɪə] Firma, der Chancengleichheit ein Anliegen ist 239

to equip [ɪˈkwɪp] (hier:) befähigen; ausstatten, ausrüsten 229

equipment [ɪˈkwɪpmənt] Geräte 50

equivalent [ɪˈkwɪvələnt] Entsprechung 232

error [ˈerə] Irrtum, Fehler 200

escape route [ɪˈskeɪp ˌruːt] Rettungsweg 31

essential [ɪˈsenʃl] wichtig, wesentlich 229

to establish [ɪˈstæblɪʃ] (hier:) feststellen 212

established [ɪˈstæblɪʃt] eingeführt, feststehend 116

to evaluate [ɪˈvæljʊeɪt] bewerten 244

evaluation scheme [ɪˌvæljʊˈeɪʃn ˌskiːm] Bewertungsschema 102

even though [ˌiːvn ˈðəʊ] obgleich 192

event management assistant [ɪˌvent ˈmænɪdʒmənt əˌsɪstənt] Veranstaltungskaufmann/-frau 10

eventual(ly) [ɪˈventʃʊəl(ɪ)] mit der Zeit, letztendlich, schließlich 177

evidence [ˈevɪdəns] Beweis, Nachweis 111

to exceed [ɪkˈsiːd] übersteigen, überschreiten 138

excitement [ɪkˈsaɪtmənt] (hier:) Interesse 102

exclamation mark [ˌekskləˈmeɪʃn ˌmɑːk] Ausrufezeichen 115

to execute [ˈeksɪkjuːt] aus-, durchführen 133

executives [ɪɡˈzekjətɪvz] leitende Angestellte 81

exhibition [ˌeksɪˈbɪʃn] Ausstellung 126

exhibition booth [ˌeksɪˈbɪʃn ˌbuːð] Messestand 91

exhibition grounds [ˌeksɪˈbɪʃn ˌɡraʊndz] Ausstellungsgelände 82

expenditure [ɪkˈspendɪtʃə] Ausgaben, Auslagen 39

experience [ɪkˈspɪərɪəns] Erfahrung 228

to experience [ɪkˈspɪərɪəns] erleben 218

expiry date [ɪkˈspaɪərɪ ˌdeɪt] Gültigkeitsdatum 91

exploration [ˌekspləˈreɪʃn] Erkundung neuer Lagerstätten, Probegrabungen/-bohrungen 102

export clerk [ˈekspɔːt ˌklɑːk] Exportkaufmann/-frau 7

to express [ɪkˈspres] ausdrücken 63

expressly [ɪkˈspreslɪ] ausdrücklich 136

extension [ɪkˈstenʃn] Durchwahl, Nebenstelle 63

F

fabulous [ˈfæbjələs] fabelhaft, sagenhaft, toll 121

to face [feɪs] sich gegenübersehen, konfrontiert sein mit 142

to facilitate [fəˈsɪlɪteɪt] ermöglichen, erleichtern 163

facilities [fəˈsɪlətɪz] Einrichtungen, Anlagen 163

factual ['fæktʃʊəl] sachlich, den Tatsachen entsprechend 123

fair [feə] Messe 39

familiarity [fə,mɪlɪ'ærətɪ] Vertrautheit 228

familiar with [fə'mɪlɪə wɪð] vertraut mit 214

family-owned [,fæməlɪ 'əʊnd] in Familienbesitz 57

fare [feə] Fahrpreis 86

fashion ['fæʃn] Mode 41

fashion chain ['fæʃn ,tʃeɪn] Kette von Modegeschäften 180

fast-paced [,fɑ:st'peɪst] tempogeladen, hektisch 228

faultless, perfect, unobjectionable ['fɔ:ltləs/'fɜ:fɪkt, ʌnəb'dʒekʃənəbl] einwandfrei 205

faulty ['fɒltɪ, 'fɔ:ltɪ] fehlerhaft, mangelhaft 192

favourite (dish) [,feɪvərɪt ('dɪʃ)] Lieblings(-gericht) 27

to faze [feɪz] aus der Fassung bringen 239

feasibility study [,fi:zə'bɪlətɪ ,stʌdɪ] Machbarkeitsstudie 39

feature ['fi:tʃə] Eigenschaft, Merkmal 46

to feature ['fi:tʃə] eine Rolle spielen, sich auszeichnen, kennzeichnen 37

feedback ['fi:dbæk] Rückmeldungen, Feedback 101

fermented white cabbage [fə,mentɪd ,waɪt 'kæbɪdʒ] Sauerkraut 27

ferry ['ferɪ] Fähre 163

field (of work) [fi:ld (əv,wɜ:k)] Arbeitsgebiet 240

field research ['fi:ld ,ri:sɜ:tʃ] Feldforschung, Primärforschung 212

fierce [fɪəs] *(hier:)* scharf 216

figures ['fɪgəz] Zahlen 88

file [faɪl] Akte, Datei 13

filing cabinet ['faɪlɪŋ ,kæbɪnət] Aktenschrank, Ablage 50

filled rolls [,fɪld 'rəʊlz] belegte Brötchen 53

filling quantity ['fɪlɪŋ ,kwɒntətɪ] Füllmenge 46

to finalise ['faɪnəlaɪz] abschließen 24

fire extinguisher ['faɪər ɪk,stɪŋgwɪʃə] Feuerlöscher 31

fire protection ['faɪə prə,tekʃn] Brandschutz 31

first aid [,fɜ:st'eɪd] erste Hilfe 31

first floor [,fɜ:st 'flɔ:] erste Etage *(BE)*, Erdgeschoss *(AE)* 21

first name [,fɜ:st 'neɪm] Vorname 7

first-rate [,fɜ:st'reɪt] erstklassig 228

to fit in with [,fɪt 'ɪn wɪð] sich richten nach; übereinstimmen mit 84

fixed line set [,fɪkstlaɪn 'set] Festnetzanlage 62

flat [flæt] flach 104

flavouring ['fleɪvərɪŋ] Geschmackszusatz, Aroma 160

floor plan ['flɔ: ,plæn] Grundriss 21

flowchart ['fləʊ,tʃɑ:ts] Flussdiagramm 99

to fluctuate ['flʌktʃʊeɪt] schwanken 104

fluent ['flu:ənt] fließend 228

focus ['fəʊkəs] Schwerpunkt 211

to focus ['fəʊkəs] (sich) konzentrieren, in den Mittelpunkt stellen 115

fog [fɒg] Nebel 20

foil-wrapped cardboard box [,fɔɪlræpt ,kɑ:dbɔ:d 'bɒks] folienumwickelter Karton 166

folder ['fəʊldə] Falt-, Prospektblatt 139

follow-up order [,fɒləʊ,ʌp 'ɔ:də] Folgeauftrag 159

font type ['fɒnt ,taɪp] Schriftart 107

food processing ['fu:d ,prəʊsesɪŋ] Verarbeitung von Lebensmitteln 118

food processing company ['fu:d ,prəʊsesɪŋ ,kʌmpənɪ] Lebensmittel verarbeitendes Unternehmen 17

for approval [fər ə'pru:vl] zur Genehmigung 88

to forecast ['fɔ:kɑ:st] vorhersagen 163

foreign language correspondent / secretary with modern languages [,fɒrən 'læŋwɪdʒ kɒrɪ,spɒndənt /,sekrətrɪ wɪð ,fɒrən 'læŋwɪdʒɪz] Fremdsprachenkorrespondent / in 10

foreign trade [,fɒrən 'treɪd] Außenhandel 214

for instance [fər 'ɪnstəns] zum Beispiel 6

form [fɔ:m] Formular; Form 67

formal ['fɔ:ml] förmlich, formell 110

formal park [,fɔ:ml 'pɑ:k] Parkanlage 23

for the time being [fə ðə ,taɪm 'bi:ɪŋ] zurzeit, vorläufig 204

to forward ['fɔ:wəd] weiterleiten, befördern, transportieren 113

forwarder ['fɔ:wədə] Spedition 199

forwarding agent ['fɔ:wədɪŋ ,eɪdʒənt] Spediteur / in 150

fossil fuels [,fɒsl 'fjʊəlz] fossile Brennstoffe 105

to found [faʊnd] gründen 38

free movement of labour [,fri: ,mu:vmənt əv 'leɪbə] Freizügigkeit der Arbeitnehmer, freie Wahl des Arbeitsplatzes 241

freight forwarding and logistics services clerk [,freɪt 'fɔ:wədɪŋ ənd lə,dʒɪstɪks,'sɜ:vɪsɪz ,klɑ:k] Kaufmann/-frau für Spedition und Logistikdienstleistung 9

freight forwarding company [,freɪt 'fɔ:wədɪŋ ,kʌmpənɪ] Spedition, Transportunternehmen 164

French fries [,frentʃ 'fraɪz] Pommes frites 26

frequent(ly) ['fri:kwənt(lɪ)] häufig, oft 41

fridge [frɪdʒ] Kühlschrank 53

fried potatoes [,fraɪd pə'teɪtəʊz] Bratkartoffeln 26

front office [,frʌnt 'ɒfɪs] Büro mit Publikumsverkehr 49

full board [,fʊl'bɔ:d] Vollpension 91

furnishings ['fɜ:nɪʃɪŋz] Einrichtungsgegenstände 221

further training [,fɜ:ðə 'treɪnɪŋ] Weiterbildung 237

to fuse [fju:z] verschmelzen 41

G

gale [geɪl] Orkan, Sturm 185

gale-force winds [,geɪlfɔ:s 'wɪndz] stürmische Winde 20

game [geɪm] Wild 26

garlic ['gɑ:lɪk] Knoblauch 25

garment ['gɑ:mənt] Kleidungsstück 194

gatekeeper ['geɪt,ki:pə] Pförtner / in 29

gathering ['gæðərɪŋ] Versammlung 104

generally ['dʒenrəlɪ] im Allgemeinen 213

general manager [,dʒenərəl 'mænɪdʒə] Hauptgeschäftsführer / in 55

general terms and conditions [,dʒenərəl 'tɜ:mz ənd kən'dɪʃnz] allgemeine Geschäftsbedingungen 158

to generate ['dʒenəreɪt] erzeugen 105

generous ['dʒenərəs] großzügig 142

Gents / Ladies [dʒents/'leɪdɪz] Herren-/ Damen-WC 21

germ [dʒɜ:m] Bazillus, Keim 114

gestures ['dʒestʃəz] Gesten, Gestik 63

get [get] *(hier:)* mitbekommen, hören 65

to get around to it [get ə'raʊnd ,tʊ,ɪt] dazu kommen, Zeit dazu haben 197

to get on well [get ,ɒn 'wel] gut miteinander auskommen 52

to get something over [,get ,sʌmθɪŋ 'əʊvə] etwas hinter sich bringen 101

ghastly ['gɑ:stlɪ] entsetzlich 19

gift box ['gɪft ,bɒks] Geschenkkarton 158

gig [gɪg] Musikevent 18

ginger cookies [,dʒɪndʒə 'kʊkɪz] Ingwerkekse 146

to give a refusal, to refuse a request [,gɪv ə rɪ'fju:zl, rɪ,fju:z ə rɪ'kwest] Absage erteilen 201

to give notice [,gɪv 'nəʊtɪs] *(hier:)* im Voraus Bescheid sagen 236

to give someone a lift [gɪv ,sʌmwʌn ə 'lɪft] jemanden mitnehmen (im Wagen) 28

to give someone a ring [gɪv ,sʌmwʌn ə 'rɪŋ] jemanden anrufen 28

global economy [,gləʊbl ɪ'kɒnəmɪ] Weltwirtschaft 163

glossy ['glɒsɪ] Hochglanz- 217

to go clubbing [ˌgəʊ ˈklʌbɪŋ] in die Disko gehen 9

to go for [ˈgəʊ fə] wählen 237

good value [ˌgʊd ˈvæljuː] preisgünstig 221

to go public [ˌgəʊ ˈpʌblɪk] sich in eine Aktiengesellschaft umwandeln, an die Börse gehen 39

to go through the usual channels [ˌgəʊ θruː ðə juːʒʊəl ˈtʃænlz] die üblichen Instanzen durchlaufen 242

to go window-shopping [ˌgəʊ ˈwɪndəʊ ˌʃɒpɪŋ] einen Schaufensterbummel machen 8

to go without saying [ˌgəʊ wɪðˌaʊt ˈseɪɪŋ] selbstverständlich sein 203

gradual(ly) [ˈgrædʒʊəl(ɪ)] allmählich 104

to grant [grɑːnt] gewähren 131

to grant a concession [ˌgrɑːnt ə kənˈseʃn] ein Zugeständnis machen 185

to grant a discount [ˌgrɑːnt ə ˈdɪskaʊnt] Rabatt einräumen 140

to grant a respite [ˌgrɑːnt ə ˈrespaɪt] einen Zahlungsaufschub gewähren 185

to grant credit [ˌgrɑːntˈkredɪt] Kredit gewähren 179

graph [grɑːf] Grafik 99

green card [ˌgriːnˈkɑːd] Arbeitserlaubnis für die USA 241

greenhouse gases [ˌgriːnhaʊs ˈgæsɪz] Treibhausgase 105

grid [grɪd] (hier:) Stromnetz; Raster 106

gross [grəʊs] brutto 188

gross weight [ˌgrəʊs ˈweɪt] Bruttogewicht 171

ground [graʊnd] gemahlen 26

ground beef [ˌgraʊndˈbiːf] Rindergehacktes 26

ground floor [ˌgraʊnd ˈflɔː] Parterre, Erdgeschoss 21

groupage [ˈgruːpɪdʒ] Sammelladung 150

growth [grəʊθ] Wachstum 211

to guarantee [ˌgærənˈtiː] garantieren 24

gym [dʒɪm] Turnhalle, Fitnessraum 7

H

habits [ˈhæbɪts] Gewohnheiten 219

haddock [ˈhædək] Schellfisch 26

half board [ˌhɑːfˈbɔːd] Halbpension 91

ham [hæm] Schinken 198

handicapped [ˈhændɪkæpt] behindert 235

to handle [ˈhændl] handhaben, erledigen, bearbeiten 164

handling [ˈhændlɪŋ] (hier:) Fahreigenschaften 221

hand protection [ˈhænd prəˌtekʃn] Handschutz 31

hard hat [ˈhɑːˌhæt] Schutzhelm 31

harmful [ˈhɑːmfəl] schädlich 173

harvesting [ˈhɑːvɪstɪŋ] Ernte 148

to have access to [ˌhæv ˈækses tuː] Zugang haben zu 216

to have little choice but [ˌhæv ˌlɪtl ˈtʃɔɪs bət] keine andere Wahl haben als 216

to have the goods delivered [ˌhæv ðə ˌgʊdz dɪˈlɪvəd] sich die Ware liefern lassen 215

heading [ˈhedɪŋ] Rubrik 102

head of department [ˌhed əv dɪˈpɑːtmənt] Abteilungsleiter/in 54

headquarters [ˌhedˈkwɔːtəz] Hauptsitz, -verwaltung 57

health [helθ] Gesundheit 86

health-conscious [ˌhelθˈkɒnʃəs] gesundheitsbewusst 217

health insurance [ˈhelθ ɪnˌʃɔːrəns] Krankenversicherung 243

height [haɪt] Höhe 199

helpful [ˈhelpfəl] hilfsbereit 16

high street bank [ˌhaɪstriːtˈbæŋk] Bank mit zahlreichen Zweigstellen 10

high street stores [ˌhaɪstriːt ˈstɔːz] Geschäfte in der Innenstadt 213

highway robbery [ˌhaɪweɪ ˈrɒbəri] Raubüberfälle auf Fernstraßen 164

hint [hɪnt] Hinweis, Andeutung 8

hit [hɪt] (hier:) Zugriff; Schlag, Stoß, Treffer 39

hoardings (BE) [ˈhɔːdɪŋz] Plakatwände 217

to hold, held, held [həʊld, held, held] (hier:) warten 63

horseradish [ˈhɔːsˌrædɪʃ] Meerrettich 159

hot [hɒt] heiß, scharf 26

to house [haʊz] beherbergen 23

household tool kit [ˌhaʊshəʊldˈtuːl ˌkɪt] Haushaltswerkzeugsatz 131

however [haʊˈevə] jedoch 110

how you come across [ˌhaʊ jʊ ˌkʌm əˈkrɒs] welchen Eindruck man macht 101

to hug [hʌg] umarmen 174

human resources (department) [ˌhjuːmən ˈriːsɔːsɪz (dɪˌpɑːtmənt)] Personalabteilung 205

humorous [ˈhjuːmərəs] humorvoll 102

hydropower [ˈhaɪdrəʊpaʊə] Wasserkraft 105

I

IBAN (international bank account number) [ˈaɪbæn, ˌaɪbiːeɪˈen (ˌɪntənæʃənl ˈbæŋk əˌkaʊnt ˌnʌmbə)] internationale Kontonummer 177

icing [ˈaɪsɪŋ] Glasur 57

illegible [ɪˈledʒəbl] unleserlich 198

I'm afraid ... [aɪm əˈfreɪd] Leider ... 71

image [ˈɪmɪdʒ] Bild, Vorstellung 36

imagination [ɪˌmædʒɪˈneɪʃn] Phantasie, Vorstellungskraft 128

imaginative [ɪˈmædʒɪnətɪv] phantasievoll 100

immediate [ɪˈmiːdɪət] sofortig 63

I'm on a diet [aɪm ˌɒn ə ˈdaɪət] ich mache eine Diät 19

impact [ˈɪmpækt] Belastung, Auswirkung 107

impatient [ɪmˈpeɪʃnt] ungeduldig 195

impolite [ˌɪmpəˈlaɪt] unhöflich 71

import licence [ˈɪmpɔːt ˌlaɪsəns] Importlizenz, Einfuhrgenehmigung 74

to impress [ɪmˈpres] beeindrucken 154

impression [ɪmˈpreʃn] Eindruck 16

imprint [ˈɪmprɪnt] Aufdruck 223

to improve [ɪmˈpruːv] verbessern 216

inadequate [ɪˈnædɪkwət] unzureichend 163

in advance [ɪn ədˈvɑːns] im Voraus 237

in bulk [ɪn ˈbʌlk] in großen Mengen 213

incentive [ɪnˈsentɪv] Anreiz 108

in charge of [ɪn ˈtʃɑːdʒ əv] verantwortlich für 17

incident [ˈɪnsɪdənt] Zwischenfall, Ereignis 122

to include [ɪnˈkluːd] einschließen, beinhalten, umfassen 6

included in the price [ɪnˌkluːdɪd ɪn ðə ˈpraɪs] im Preis enthalten 84

incoming goods control [ˌɪnkʌmɪŋ ˈgʊdz kənˌtrəʊl] Wareneingangskontrolle 194

in conclusion [ɪn kənˈkluːʒn] zum Abschluss, abschließend 127

in confidence [ɪn ˈkɒnfɪdəns] vertraulich 133

inconvenience [ˌɪnkənˈviːnɪəns] Unannehmlichkeiten 122

inconvenient [ˌɪnkənˈviːnɪənt] unbequem 105

to increase [ɪnˈkriːs] zunehmen, steigern 104

increasing(ly) [ɪnˈkriːsɪŋ(lɪ)] zunehmend 110

to incur [ɪnˈkɜː] übernehmen, hinnehmen müssen 173

independent [ˌɪndɪˈpendənt] unabhängig 74

to indicate [ˈɪndɪkeɪt] angeben, nennen; andeuten 140

indicator [ˈɪndɪkeɪtə] Anzeiger, Anzeigetafel 85

individual production [ɪndɪˌvɪdjʊəl prəˈdʌkʃn] Einzelfertigung 46

in due course [ɪn ˌdjuː ˈkɔːs] fristgemäß 194

industrial business management assistant [ɪnˌdʌstrɪəl ˌbɪznɪs ˈmænɪdʒmənt əˌsɪstənt] Industriekaufmann/-frau 7

industrial clerk [ɪnˈdʌstrɪəl ˌklɑːk] Industriekaufmann/-frau 7

industrial goods [ɪnˌdʌstrɪəl ˈgʊdz] Industrieerzeugnisse 220

industry analyst [ˈɪndəstrɪ ˌænəlɪst] Branchenexperte/-expertin 163

I need to freshen up a bit [aɪ ˌniːd tə ˌfreʃn ˈʌp ə ˌbɪt] ich muss mich ein bisschen frisch machen 22

to Influence [ˈɪnflʊəns] beeinflussen 218

information technology [ˌɪnfəˈmeɪʃn tekˌnɒlədʒɪ] Informationsverarbeitung/-technologie 12

in full [ɪn ˈfʊl] in voller Höhe 184

inhabitant [ɪnˈhæbɪtənt] Einwohner/in 176

initials [ɪˈnɪʃlz] Initialen, Anfangsbuchstaben des Namens 119

initial(ly) [ɪˈnɪʃə(lɪ)] anfänglich, zunächst 173

initial order [ɪˌnɪʃl ˈɔːdə] Erstauftrag 153

to initiate [ɪˈnɪʃɪeɪt] in die Wege leiten, einleiten 202

to initiate measures [ɪˌnɪʃɪeɪt ˈmeʒəz] Maßnahmen einleiten 205

in law [ɪn ˈlɔː] rechtlich, vor Gericht 88

in lieu of [ɪn ˈljuː əv] an Stelle von 235

in line with [ɪn ˈlaɪn wɪð] in Übereinstimmung mit, parallel zu 39

in our favour [ɪn ˌaʊə ˈfeɪvə] zu unseren Gunsten 182

in principle [ɪn ˈprɪnsɪpl] im Prinzip 86

to insert [ɪnˈsɜːt] einfügen 113

to insist on [ɪnˈsɪst ɒn] bestehen auf 182

insistent [ɪnˈsɪstənt] nachdrücklich 183

insolvent [ɪnˈsɒlvənt] zahlungsunfähig 204

in stock [ɪn ˈstɒk] vorrätig, auf Lager 70

to instruct [ɪnˈstrʌkt] anweisen, unterweisen 177

to instruct to the contrary [ɪnˌstrʌkt tʊ ðə ˈkɒntrərɪ] gegenteilige Anweisungen erteilen 206

insurance [ɪnˈʃɔːrəns] Versicherung 144

insurance business management assistant [ɪnˌʃɔːrəns ˌbɪznɪs ˈmænɪdʒmənt əˌsɪstənt] Versicherungskaufmann/-frau, Kaufmann/-frau für Versicherungen und Finanzen 9

insurance certificate [ɪnˈʃɔːrəns səˌtɪfɪkət] Versicherungsschein, -zertifikat 170

insurance clerk [ɪnˈʃɔːrəns ˌklɑːk] Versicherungskaufmann/-frau, Kaufmann/-frau für Versicherungen und Finanzen 9

insurance policy [ɪnˈʃɔːrəns ˌpɒləsɪ] Versicherungspolice 170

insured [ɪnˈʃɔːd] (hier:) Versicherungsnehmer/in, Versicherte/r 171

integration [ˌɪntɪˈgreɪʃn] Eingliederung, Integration 84

to intend [ɪnˈtend] beabsichtigen 220

interest [ˈɪntrəst] Zinsen 183

interest in [ˈɪntrəst ɪn] Interesse an 219

interest on arrears [ˌɪntrəst ɒn əˈrɪəz] Verzugszinsen 183

in terms of [ɪn ˈtɜːmz əv] in Bezug auf, was … betrifft 163

internet exchanges [ˈɪntənet ɪksˌtʃeɪndʒɪz] Online-Börsen 215

to interpret [ɪnˈtɜːprɪt] dolmetschen 87

interpreter [ɪnˈtɜːprɪtə] Dolmetscher/in 89

to interrupt [ˌɪntəˈrʌpt] unterbrechen, stören 117

interval [ˈɪntəvl] Abstand 153

interview [ˈɪntəvjuː] Vorstellungsgespräch, Interview 37

in the course of [ɪn ðə ˈkɔːs əv] im Laufe von 86

in the foreseeable future [ɪn ðə fɔːˌsiːəbl ˈfjuːtʃə] in absehbarer Zukunft 102

in transit [ɪn ˈtrænzɪt] beim Transport 199

introduction [ˌɪntrəˈdʌkʃn] Einführung; Vorstellung 211

introductory discount [ˌɪntrəˈdʌktərɪ ˈdɪskaʊnt] Einführungsrabatt 131

investigation [ɪnˌvestɪˈgeɪʃn] Untersuchung 203

investment portfolio [ɪnˈvestmənt pɔːtˌfəʊlɪəʊ] Bestand an Wertpapieren 102

invoice [ˈɪnvɔɪs] Rechnung 154

to invoice [ˈɪnvɔɪs] in Rechnung stellen 13

to involve [ɪnˈvɒlv] (hier:) beinhalten 212

in working order [ɪn ˌwɜːkɪŋ ˈɔːdə] funktionstüchtig 87

iron ore [ˈaɪən ˌɔː] Eisenerz 164

irrevocable [ɪrɪˈvəʊkəbl] unwiderruflich 181

irritation [ˌɪrɪˈteɪʃn] Verärgerung 163

is paralleled by [ɪz ˈpærəleld ˌbaɪ] geht einher mit 215

issue [ˈɪʃuː] (hier:) Ausgabe, Heft; Ausstellung 128

to issue [ˈɪʃuː] ausstellen, (her)ausgeben 179

it doesn't appeal to me [ɪt ˌdʌznt əˌpiːl tʊ ˈmiː] es gefällt mir nicht 218

IT specialist [ˌaɪtiː ˌspeʃəlɪst] Fachinformatiker/in 9

it tastes like … [ɪt ˌteɪsts laɪk ˈ…] es schmeckt wie … 26

J

jar [dʒɑː] Glas (z.B. Marmelade), Topf (z.B. Senf) 202

jelly [ˈdʒelɪ] Götterspeise, Gelee, Aspik 27

job exchanges [ˈdʒɒb ɪksˌtʃeɪndʒɪz] Job-, Stellenbörsen 227

job specification [ˌdʒɒb ˌspesɪfɪˈkeɪʃn] Stellenbeschreibung 227

to join [dʒɔɪn] (hier:) sich jemandem anschließen, mitkommen 25

joint [dʒɔɪnt] gemeinsam 25

joint venture [ˌdʒɔɪnt ˈventʃə] Joint Venture (Gemeinschaftsunternehmen) 69

to jumble [ˈdʒʌmbl] durcheinander werfen/bringen 114

jumbled [ˈdʒʌmbld] durcheinander geworfen 19

to jump [dʒʌmp] springen, sprunghaft ansteigen 102

to jump by … from … to … [ˈdʒʌmp ˌbaɪ … frəm … tʊ …] sprunghaft ansteigen um … von … auf … 104

junction [ˈdʒʌŋkʃn] Kreuzung 22

junior executive [ˌdʒuːnɪə ɪgˈzekjətɪv] Nachwuchsführungskraft 196

justified [ˈdʒʌstɪfaɪd] gerechtfertigt, berechtigt 201

justified complaint [ˌdʒʌstɪfaɪd kəmˈpleɪnt] begründete Reklamation 201

K

keen [kiːn] sehr interessiert, eifrig 217

to keep an eye on [ˌkiːp ən ˈaɪ ɒn] aufpassen auf 28

to keep a record [ˌkiːp ə ˈrekɔːd] aufzeichnen 80

to keep informed [ˌkiːp ɪnˈfɔːmd] auf dem Laufenden halten 201

to keep one's fingers crossed [ˌkiːp wʌnz ˈfɪŋgəz ˌkrɒst] den Daumen halten 242

key [kiː] Schlüssel 98

keyboard [ˈkiːbɔːd] Tastatur 50

kitchenette [ˌkɪtʃɪˈnet] Kochgelegenheit; Teeküche 89

kitchen facilities [ˈkɪtʃɪn fəˌsɪlətɪz] Küchenanlagen 24

kitten [ˈkɪtn] Kätzchen 157

L

label [ˈleɪbl] Etikett, Aufkleber 24

to label, to provide with an inscription [ˈleɪbl, prəˌvaɪd wɪð ən ɪnˈskrɪpʃn] beschriften, etikettieren, kennzeichnen 194

laces [ˈleɪsɪz] Schnürsenkel 237

ladies' room (AE) [ˈleɪdɪz ˌruːm] Damentoilette 21

lamb [læm] Lamm 26

lamp holder [ˈlæmp ˌhəʊldə] Lampenfassung 47

landlady [ˈlændˌleɪdɪ] Vermieterin 241

landline [ˈlændlaɪn] Festnetz(leitung) 62

landslide [ˈlændslaɪd] Erdrutsch 105

largely [ˈlɑːdʒlɪ] weitgehend 88

lately [ˈleɪtlɪ] in letzter Zeit 18

to launch [lɔːntʃ] einführen, starten, in die Wege leiten 132

lawful holder [ˌlɔːfəl ˈhəʊldə] rechtmäßige(r) Inhaber(in)/Besitzer(in) 170

Law on Safety and Health at Work ['lɔː ˌɒn ˌseɪftɪ ˌənd ˌhelθ ət 'wɜːk] Arbeitsschutzgesetz 32

Law on Safety at Work ['lɔː ˌɒn ˌseɪftɪ ət 'wɜːk] Arbeitssicherheitsgesetz 32

layout ['leɪaʊt] Anordnung, Gestaltung 112

lbs (pounds) [paʊndz] *(englisches Gewichts-)*Pfund *(453,59 g)* 200

leading ['liːdɪŋ] führend 129

to leave much to be desired [liːv ˌmʌtʃ tʊ bɪ dɪ'zaɪəd] viel zu wünschen übrig lassen 87

leeks [liːks] Lauch 25

legal ['liːgl] rechtlich, juristisch, gesetzlich 54

to legalize ['liːgəlaɪz] beglaubigen, legalisieren 170

legal steps [ˌliːgl 'steps] juristische Schritte 183

leisure ['leʒə] Freizeit, freie Zeit 100

lentils ['lentəlz] Linsen 27

less [les] abzüglich 141

to let someone know [let ˌsʌmwʌn 'nəʊ] Bescheid sagen 28

letterhead ['letəhed] Briefkopf 119

letter of credit (L/C) [ˌletər ˌəv 'kredɪt] Akkreditiv 181

letting agent ['letɪŋ ˌeɪdʒənt] Makler/in für Mietimmobilien, -wohnungen 238

lettuce ['letɪs] Kopfsalat 27

life [laɪf] Lebensdauer 140

life insurance ['laɪf ɪnˌʃɔːrəns] Lebensversicherung 243

lift [lɪft] Aufzug 21

likewise ['laɪkwaɪz] ebenfalls 84

limit ['lɪmɪt] Beschränkung 84

line [laɪn] Verbindung 65

line graph ['laɪn ˌgrɑːf] Liniendiagramm 103

liner ['laɪnə] Linienschiff 171

lingua franca [ˌlɪŋgwə 'fræŋkə] Verkehrssprache 16

link [lɪŋk] Verbindung, Bindeglied 213

to link [lɪŋk] verbinden, verknüpfen 216

list purchase price [ˌlɪst 'pɜːtʃɪs ˌpraɪs] Listeneinkaufspreis 149

to load [ləʊd] beladen, einladen 163

loading charges ['ləʊdɪŋ ˌtʃɑːdʒɪz] Verladekosten 150

local ['ləʊkl] örtlich, ortsansässig, hiesig 37

to locate [ləʊ'keɪt] ausfindig machen, lokalisieren 126

location [ləʊ'keɪʃn] Standort 101

logistics and warehousing operation [ləˌdʒɪstɪks ənd 'weəhaʊzɪŋ ˌɒpəˌreɪʃn] Logistik- und Lagerungsunternehmen 241

long-distance running [ˌlɒŋdɪstəns 'rʌnɪŋ] Langstreckenlauf 8

to lose one's way, lost, lost [ˌluːz wʌnz 'weɪ, lɒst, lɒst] sich verirren, sich verlaufen 21

low [ləʊ] Tief(punkt) 104

lump sum [ˌlʌmp 'sʌm] Pauschalsumme 171

M

machinery [mə'ʃiːnərɪ] Maschinen 37

magnificent [mæg'nɪfɪsənt] großartig, prächtig 23

mail shots ['meɪl ˌʃɒts] Postwurfsendungen 217

main branch [ˌmeɪn 'brɑːntʃ] Hauptfiliale 230

main course [ˌmeɪn 'kɔːs] Hauptgericht, -gang 25

main entrance [ˌmeɪn 'entrəns] Haupteingang 21

main road [ˌmeɪn 'rəʊd] Hauptstraße 22

major ['meɪdʒə] groß, wichtig, Haupt- 49

to make an offer [ˌmeɪk ən 'ɒfə] ein Angebot abgeben 137

to make someone aware of [ˌmeɪk ˌsʌmwʌn ə'weər ˌəv] jemanden aufmerksam machen auf 217

to make someone feel welcome [ˌmeɪk ˌsʌmwʌn fiːl 'welkəm] dafür sorgen, dass sich jemand wohl fühlt 16

to make sure [meɪk 'ʃɔː] sich vergewissern 101

to make up [meɪk 'ʌp] *(hier:)* erfinden 67

to manage complaints [ˌmænɪdʒ kəm'pleɪnts] Beschwerden bearbeiten 201

management ['mænɪdʒmənt] Geschäftsleitung 122

management assistant for tourism and leisure ['mænɪdʒmənt əˌsɪstənt fə ˌtʊərɪzm ən 'leʒə] Kaufmann/-frau für Tourismus und Freizeit 11

management assistant in advertising ['mænɪdʒmənt əˌsɪstənt ɪn 'ædvətaɪzɪŋ] Werbekaufmann/-frau 11

management assistant in event organisation ['mænɪdʒmənt əˌsɪstənt ɪn ɪˌvent ˌɔːgənaɪ'zeɪʃn] Veranstaltungskaufmann/-frau 11

management assistant in freight forwarding ['mænɪdʒmənt əˌsɪstənt ɪn ˌfreɪt 'fɔːwədɪŋ] Speditionskaufmann/-frau 9

management assistant in informatics ['mænɪdʒmənt əˌsɪstənt ɪn ˌɪnfə'mætɪks] Informatikkaufmann/-frau 11

management assistant in office communication ['mænɪdʒmənt əˌsɪstənt ɪn ˌɒfɪs kəˌmjuːnɪ'keɪʃn] Kaufmann/-frau für Bürokommunikation 11

management assistant in publishing ['mænɪdʒmənt əˌsɪstənt ɪn 'pʌblɪʃɪŋ] Verlagskaufmann/-frau 9

management assistant in retail business ['mænɪdʒmənt əˌsɪstənt ɪn ˌriːteɪl 'bɪznɪs] Kaufmann/-frau im Einzelhandel 9

management assistant in wholesale and foreign trade ['mænɪdʒmənt əˌsɪstənt ɪn ˌhəʊlseɪl ənd ˌfɒrən 'treɪd] Kaufmann/-frau im Groß- und Außenhandel 9

managing director [ˌmænɪdʒɪŋ daɪ'rektə] Geschäftsführer/in 54

mandatory ['mændətrɪ] Gebots- 31

manner ['mænə] Umgangsstil 239

manually ['mænjʊəlɪ] *(hier:)* handschriftlich 188

manual production [ˌmænjʊəl prə'dʌkʃn] manuelle Fertigung 47

manufacturer [ˌmænjə'fæktʃərə] Hersteller/in, Produzent/in 213

to manufacture to specification [ˌmænjə'fæktʃə tʊ ˌspesɪfɪ'keɪʃn] als Sonderanfertigung herstellen 181

manufacturing [ˌmænjə'fæktʃərɪŋ] Fertigung, Fabrikation 37

manufacturing (industry) [ˌmænjə'fæktʃərɪŋ (ˌɪndəstrɪ)] verarbeitende Industrie 239

to marinate ['mærɪneɪt] marinieren, einlegen 25

marital status [ˌmærɪtl 'steɪtəs] Familienstand 119

market analysis [ˌmɑːkɪt ə'næləsɪs] Marktanalyse 222

market forecast [ˌmɑːkɪt 'fɔːkɑːst] Marktprognose 222

marketing tools [ˌmɑːkɪtɪŋ ˌtuːlz] Marketinginstrumente 216

market leader [ˌmɑːkɪt 'liːdə] Marktführer 37

market observation [ˌmɑːkɪt ˌɒbsə'veɪʃn] Marktbeobachtung 222

market research [ˌmɑːkɪt 'riːsɜːtʃ] Marktforschung 212

market share [ˌmɑːkɪt 'ʃeə] Marktanteil 225

market survey [ˌmɑːkɪt 'sɜːveɪ] Marktstudie, -untersuchung 212

markings ['mɑːkɪŋz] Markierung 168

mart [mɑːt] Markt 39

mashed potatoes [ˌmæʃt pə'teɪtəʊz] Kartoffelpüree 26

mass production [ˌmæs prə'dʌkʃn] Massenproduktion 46

maturity [mə'tjʊərətɪ] Reife 211

maximum admissible weight [ˌmæksɪməm əd'mɪsəbl 'weɪt] zulässiges Höchstgewicht 200

means of payment ['miːnz ˌəv 'peɪmənt] Zahlungsmittel 179

measure ['meʒə] Maßnahme 207

measurement [ˈmeʒəmənt] *(hier:)* Abmessungen 171

meat [miːt] Fleisch 26

meatball [ˈmiːtbɔːl] Frikadelle 26

mechanical production [məˌkænɪkl prəˈdʌkʃn] mechanisierte (maschinelle) Fertigung 47

medical supplies [ˌmedɪkl səˈplaɪz] Artikel zur medizinischen Versorgung 165

Mediterranean countries [medɪtərˌeɪniən ˈkʌntrɪz] Länder am Mittelmeer 8

to meet deadlines [miːtˌˈdedlaɪnz] Termine/Fristen einhalten 228

to meet halfway [miːtˌhɑːˈfweɪ] auf halbem Weg entgegenkommen 201

to meet someone [ˈmiːtˌsʌmwʌn] jemanden kennenlernen, treffen 16

to meet with approval [ˌmiːt wɪð əˈpruːvl] auf Zustimmung stoßen 237

member [ˈmembə] Mitglied 161

memo [ˈmeməʊ] Aktennotiz 24

memory stick [ˈmemrɪ ˌstɪk] USB-Speicher 50

menu [ˈmenjuː] Speisekarte; Menü *(Computer)* 27

merchandise [ˈmɜːtʃəndaɪs] Ware, Gut, Handelsartikel 153

merchant [ˈmɜːtʃənt] Händler 216

message [ˈmesɪdʒ] Nachricht, Botschaft 113

Middle Ages [ˌmɪdl ˈeɪdʒɪz] Mittelalter 176

mince(d) meat [ˈmɪns(t) ˌmiːt] Gehacktes 26

minor [ˈmaɪnə] gering(fügig) 133

mint bar [ˈmɪnt ˌbɑː] Pfefferminzriegel 139

minute [maɪˈnjuːt] peinlich genau; winzig 41

minutes [ˈmɪnɪts] Protokoll 86

misunderstanding [ˌmɪsʌndəˈstændɪŋ] Missverständnis 110

mixed [mɪkst] gemischt 27

mix-up [ˈmɪksʌp] Verwechslung 200

mode of transport [ˌməʊd əv ˈtrænspɔːt] Transportart 164

moderate(ly) [ˈmɒdərət(lɪ)] mäßig, maßvoll 104

modification [ˌmɒdɪfɪˈkeɪʃn] Änderung 81

to modify [ˈmɒdɪfaɪ] ab-, verändern 24

monitor [ˈmɒnɪtə] PC-Bildschirm 83

monotonous(ly) [məˈnɒtənəs(lɪ)] eintönig 101

mood [muːd] Stimmung 173

mother tongue [ˌmʌðə ˈtʌŋ] Muttersprache 229

motor-car mechanic [ˌməʊtəkɑː məˈkænɪk] Kfz-Mechaniker/in 54

move [muːv] *(hier:)* Umzug 28

mug [mʌg] Becher 192

multilingual [ˌmʌltɪˈlɪŋgwəl] mehr-, vielsprachig 197

mushrooms [ˈmʌʃruːmz] Champignons, Pilze 25

mustard [ˈmʌstəd] Senf 159

N

named [neɪmd] namentlich genannt 179

navy (blue) [ˌneɪvɪ (ˈbluː)] marine-, dunkelblau 116

neat(ly) [niːt(lɪ)] ordentlich, adrett 232

needs [niːdz] Bedarf, Bedürfnisse 212

to need, to require [niːd, rɪˈkwaɪə] benötigen 239

negotiation [nɪˌgəʊʃɪˈeɪʃn] Verhandlung 13

neighbouring [ˈneɪbərɪŋ] benachbart 37

net [net] netto 139

newsagent [ˈnjuːzˌeɪdʒənt] Zeitungshändler/in 19

nobility [nəʊˈbɪlətɪ] Adel, Vornehmheit 157

noisy [ˈnɔɪzɪ] laut 20

non-attendance [ˌnɒnəˈtendəns] Fehlen, Abwesenheit 88

non-bulk cargo [ˌnɒnbʌlk ˈkɑːgəʊ] Stückgutfracht 163

note pad [ˈnəʊtpæd] Notizblock 50

notification [ˌnəʊtɪfɪˈkeɪʃn] Benachrichtigung 227

to notify [ˈnəʊtɪfaɪ] benachrichtigen 187

novel [ˈnɒvl] Roman 9

nowadays [ˈnaʊədeɪz] heutzutage 179

nutritionally conscious [njuːˌtrɪʃənlɪ ˈkɒnʃəs] ernährungsbewusst 24

nutritional science [njuːˌtrɪʃənl ˈsaɪəns] Ernährungswissenschaft 24

O

obesity [əʊˈbiːsətɪ] Fettleibigkeit, klinisches Übergewicht 86

objective [əbˈdʒektɪv] Ziel 99

obligation [ˌɒblɪˈgeɪʃn] Verpflichtung, Verbindlichkeit 143

obligatory [əˈblɪgətrɪ] verpflichtend 243

obscure [əbˈskjʊə] unbekannt 221

to observe [əbˈzɜːv] beachten 85

to observe the delivery period [əbˌzɜːv ðə dɪˈlɪvərɪ ˌpɪərɪəd] Lieferfrist einhalten 158

to obtain [əbˈteɪn] erhalten 217

obvious(ly) [ˈɒbvɪəs(lɪ)] offensichtlich 159

occasion [əˈkeɪʒn] Anlass, Gelegenheit 118

to occur, to result [əˈkɜː, rɪˈzʌlt] sich ergeben 46

offer [ˈɒfə] Angebot 136

to offer credit facilities [ˈɒfə ˈkredɪt fəˌsɪlətɪz] Kredite anbieten 214

office administration clerk [ˌɒfɪs ədˌmɪnɪˈstreɪʃn ˌklɑːk] Bürokaufmann/-frau 7

office management assistant [ˌɒfɪs ˈmænɪdʒmənt əˌsɪstənt] Bürokaufmann/-frau 9

old-established [ˌəʊldɪˈstæblɪʃt] alteingesessen 36

old-fashioned [ˌəʊldˈfæʃnd] altmodisch 62

to omit [əʊˈmɪt] aus-, weglassen 119

on a large scale [ɒn ə ˌlɑːdʒ ˈskeɪl] in großem Stil/Umfang 38

on behalf of [ɒn bɪˈhɑːf əv] im Auftrag von, für 80

on delivery [ɒn dɪˈlɪvərɪ] bei Lieferung 181

on demand [ɒn dɪˈmɑːnd] auf Verlangen/Abruf 179

one-off [ˌwʌnˈɒf] Einmal- 142

onion [ˈʌnjən] Zwiebel 25

on presentation [ɒn ˌprezənˈteɪʃn] bei Vorlage 179

on request [ɒn rɪˈkwest] *(hier:)* wenn gewünscht; auf Anfrage 242

on the left/left-hand side [ɒn ðə ˈleft/ˌlefthænd ˈsaɪd] links 21

on the off-chance [ɒn ðɪ ˈɒftʃɑːns] auf Verdacht 227

on/to the right [ɒn/tʊ ðə ˈraɪt] rechts 21

open account (terms) [ˌəʊpn əˌkaʊnt (ˈtɜːmz)] offenes Zahlungsziel 138

open credit [ˌəʊpn ˈkredɪt] Zahlung gegen einfache Rechnung 181

openings [ˈəʊpnɪŋz] offene Stellen 227

opening bank [ˌəʊpnɪŋ ˈbæŋk] ausstellende Bank 181

open-plan office [ˌəʊpnplæn ˈɒfɪs] Großraumbüro 21

to operate [ˈɒpəreɪt] bedienen 101

operations [ˌɒpəˈreɪʃnz] *(hier:)* Betrieb 184

opposite [ˈɒpəzɪt] gegenüber 22

opposite number [ˌɒpəzɪt ˈnʌmbə] Gegenüber, Kollege/Kollegin 81

optician [ɒpˈtɪʃn] Optiker/in 213

oral [ˈɔːrəl] mündlich 98

order [ˈɔːdə] Auftrag, Bestellung 153

to order [ˈɔːdə] bestellen; anordnen 37

order confirmation [ˈɔːdə kɒnfəˌmeɪʃn] Auftragsbestätigung 157

order on call [ˈɔːdər ɒn ˈkɔːl] Abrufauftrag 153

order processing [ˈɔːdə ˌprəʊsesɪŋ] Bestellverfahren 58

Ordinance on Hazardous Material [ˈɔːdɪnəns ɒn ˌhæzədəs məˈtɪərɪəl] Gefahrstoffverordnung 32

or else [ɔːrˈels] andernfalls, sonst 113

organic [ɔːˈgænɪk] biologisch, Bio- 24

organic foods [ɔːˈgænɪk ˌfuːdz] Bio-Lebensmittel 86

organisation [ˌɔːɡənaɪˈzeɪʃn] Firma, Unternehmen, Organisation 215

original(ly) [əˈrɪdʒənl(ɪ)] ursprünglich 7

other business [ˌʌðə ˈbɪznɪs] Verschiedenes 86

outcome [ˈaʊtkʌm] Ergebnis 122

outlet [ˈaʊtlet] Verkaufsstelle, Vertriebsmöglichkeit 127

out of order [ˌaʊt əv ˈɔːdə] kaputt, außer Betrieb 196

outside advice [ˌaʊtsaɪd ədˈvaɪs] Beratung von außen 220

overcast [ˈəʊvəkɑːst] bedeckt, bezogen (Himmel) 18

overdue [ˌəʊvəˈdjuː] überfällig 186

overheads [ˈəʊvəhedz] fixe Kosten 214

overindebted [ˌəʊvərɪnˈdetɪd] überschuldet 180

to overlook [ˌəʊvəˈlʊk] übersehen 183

overseas [ˌəʊvəˈsiːz] aus dem/ins Ausland, ausländisch 142

to oversee, oversaw, overseen [ˌəʊvəˈsiː, ˌəʊvəˈsɔː, ˌəʊvəˈsiːn] beaufsichtigen, leiten 81

oversight [ˈəʊvəsaɪt] Versehen 122

to overtake, overtook, overtaken [ˌəʊvəˈteɪk, ˌəʊvəˈtʊk, ˌəʊvəˈteɪkn] überholen 180

overview [ˈəʊvəvjuː] Überblick 99

overwhelmed [ˌəʊvəˈwelmd] überwältigt 39

owner [ˈəʊnə] Eigentümer/in 54

ozone layer [ˈəʊzəʊn ˌleɪə] Ozonschicht 105

P

package tour [ˈpækɪdʒ ˌtʊə] Pauschalreise 112

packaging material [ˈpækɪdʒɪŋ məˌtɪəriəl] Verpackungsmaterial 71

packing unit [ˈpækɪdʒɪŋ ˌjuːnɪt] Verpackungseinheit 47

packing list [ˈpækɪŋ ˌlɪst] Packliste 167

pair of scissors [ˌpeər əv ˈsɪzəz] Schere 50

pallet [ˈpælɪt] Palette 166

paper [ˈpeɪpə] (hier:) Vortrag 69

paramount [ˈpærəmaʊnt] vorrangig 24

to paraphrase [ˈpærəfreɪz] umschreiben 232

parcel post [ˈpɑːsl ˌpəʊst] Paketpost 146

parent company [ˌpeərənt ˈkʌmpənɪ] Muttergesellschaft 204

parsley [ˈpɑːslɪ] Petersilie 27

partial [ˌpɑːʃl] Teil- 188

participant [pɑːˈtɪsɪpənt] Teilnehmer/in 196

particular [pəˈtɪkjələ] besonders, speziell 36

partnership [ˈpɑːtnəʃɪp] Personengesellschaft 119

to pass a message on [ˌpɑːs ə ˈmesɪdʒ ɒn] eine Nachricht weitergeben 28

passing of risk [ˌpɑːsɪŋ əv ˈrɪsk] Gefahrenübergang 144

to pass on [ˌpɑːs ˈɒn] weiterreichen, -geben 114

patience [ˈpeɪʃəns] Geduld 65

patron saint [ˌpeɪtrən ˈseɪnt] Schutzheilige/r 23

payable at [ˈpeɪəbl ət] zahlbar bei 182

payable to [ˈpeɪəbl tuː] zahlbar an 71

to pay into a bank account [peɪ ˌɪntʊ ə ˈbæŋk əˌkaʊnt] auf ein Konto einzahlen 179

payment in advance [ˌpeɪmənt ɪn ədˈvɑːns] Vorauszahlung 181

payment, money transfer, remittance [ˈpeɪmənt, ˌmʌnɪ ˈtrænsfɜː, rɪˈmɪtəns] Überweisung 90

payroll [ˈpeɪrəʊl] Gehaltsabrechnung 13

PC-literacy [ˌpiːsiːˈlɪtrəsɪ] PC-Kenntnisse 229

PC literate [ˌpiːsiːˈlɪtrət] PC-erfahren 228

peak [piːk] Gipfel, Höchststand 104

peak season [ˌpiːk ˈsiːzn] Hochsaison 71

pea soup [ˌpiː ˈsuːp] Erbsensuppe 26

penetration pricing [ˌpenəˈtreɪʃn ˌpraɪsɪŋ] Marktdurchdringungspolitik, Penetrationspolitik 225

pension [ˈpenʃn] Rente 243

peppers [ˈpepəz] Paprikaschoten 26

to perceive [pəˈsiːv] wahrnehmen 244

percentage of [pəˈsentɪdʒ əv] prozentualer Anteil, Prozentsatz 57

periodical [ˌpɪərɪˈɒdɪkl] Zeitschrift 220

perishable [ˈperɪʃəbl] (leicht) verderblich 164

permit [ˈpɜːmɪt] Genehmigung, Erlaubnis 241

personal assistant [ˌpɜːsənl əˈsɪstent] Sekretär/in 54

personnel [ˌpɜːsənˈel] Personal 54

personnel department [ˌpɜːsənˈel dɪˌpɑːtmənt] Personalabteilung 196

person to contact [ˌpɜːsn tə ˈkɒntækt] Kontaktperson 230

to persuade [pəˈsweɪd] überreden 56

pesticide [ˈpestɪsaɪd] Schädlingsbekämpfungsmittel 148

to phase out [feɪz ˈaʊt] allmählich vom Markt zurückziehen 211

to pick someone up [pɪk ˌsʌmwʌn ˈʌp] jemanden abholen 28

picnic hamper [ˈpɪknɪk ˌhæmpə] Picknickkorb 114

pie chart [ˈpaɪ ˌtʃɑːt] Tortendiagramm 102

pipe-blown by hand [ˌpaɪpbləʊn baɪ ˈhænd] mundgeblasen 199

to place an order [ˌpleɪs ən ˈɔːdə] einen Auftrag erteilen 127

placement [ˈpleɪsmənt] Praktikum 230

place of destination [ˌpleɪs əv ˌdestɪˈneɪʃn] Bestimmungsort 144

place of employment [ˌpleɪs əv ɪmˈplɔɪmənt] Arbeitsstätte 215

plaice [pleɪs] Scholle 26

plain [pleɪn] (hier:) ungemustert, einfarbig; schlicht, unscheinbar 116

plant [plɑːnt] Werk, Fabrik 108

plastic box with mouldings [ˌplæstɪk ˈbɒks wɪð ˈməʊldɪŋz] Kunststoffbox mit Formeinlagen 166

platter [ˈplætə] Servierplatte, (Holz-)Teller 159

plausible [ˈplɔːzɪbl] plausibel, einleuchtend, glaubhaft 199

to point out [pɔɪnt ˈaʊt] hinweisen auf 156

polished [ˈpɒlɪʃt] mit Schuhcreme geputzt, poliert 237

polite [pəˈlaɪt] höflich 71

pollution [pəˈluːʃn] (Umwelt-)Verschmutzung 164

to pop into [ˌpɒp ˈɪntʊ] eben schnell hineintun 100

pork escalope [ˌpɔːk ˈeskələp] Schweineschnitzel 27

port [pɔːt] Hafen 163

port dues [ˌpɔːt ˈdjuːz] Hafengebühren 150

port of destination [ˌpɔːt əv ˌdestɪˈneɪʃn] Bestimmungshafen 144

port of discharge [ˌpɔːt əv ˈdɪstʃɑːdʒ] Entladehafen 171

port of loading [ˌpɔːt əv ˈləʊdɪŋ] Verladehafen 188

port of shipment [ˌpɔːt əv ˈʃɪpmənt] Verschiffungshafen 144

postcode (BE), postal code (BE), zip code (AE) [ˈpəʊstkəʊd, ˈpəʊstl ˌkəʊd, ˈzɪpkəʊd] Postleitzahl 67

poster [ˈpəʊstə] Plakat 217

to postpone [pəsˈpəʊn] verschieben 69

potential customer [pəˌtenʃl ˈkʌstəmə] Interessent/in, möglicher Kunde 137

pot plant [ˈpɒt ˌplɑːnt] Topfpflanze 50

poultry [ˈpəʊltrɪ] Geflügel 26

power station [ˈpaʊə ˌsteɪʃn] Kraftwerk 106

praise [preɪz] Lob 239

to precede [priːˈsiːd] vor(an)gehen, -stehen 120

precise(ly) [prɪˈsaɪs(lɪ)] (hier:) genau, exakt, präzise 67

precisely then [prɪˌsaɪslɪ ˈðen] gerade dann 65

precision instruments [prɪˌsɪʒn ˈɪnstrəmənts] Präzisionsinstrumente 220

preferably [ˈprefrəblɪ] vorzugsweise 101

preliminary [prɪˈlɪmɪnərɪ] vorläufig 112

premises [ˈpremɪsɪz] Geschäftsräume, Firmengebäude, -gelände 139

premium [ˈpriːmɪəm] Prämie 171

prerequisite [ˌpriːˈrekwɪzɪt] Voraussetzung, Bedingung 101

to present [prɪˈzent] vorstellen 218

preservation [ˌprezəˈveɪʃn] Erhaltung, Bewahrung 174

press coverage [ˈpres ˌkʌvərɪdʒ] Berichterstattung in der Presse 220

prestigious [presˈtɪdʒəs] repräsentativ 49

pretzel [ˈpretsl] Brezel 23

to prevent [prɪˈvent] hindern, verhindern, vermeiden 113

previous [ˈpriːvɪəs] früher, vorhergehend 239

price policy [ˈpraɪs ˌpɒləsɪ] Preispolitik 222

price reduction [ˈpraɪs rɪˌdʌkʃn] Preisnachlass 193

prices are subject to change without notice [ˈpraɪsɪz ə ˌsʌbdʒɪkt tʊ ˌtʃeɪndʒ wɪðˌaʊt ˈnəʊtɪs] Preisänderungen vorbehalten 136

price skimming [ˈpraɪs ˌskɪmɪŋ] Marktabschöpfungspolitik 225

pricing [ˈpraɪsɪŋ] Preisbildung 222

pricing strategy [ˈpraɪsɪŋ ˌstrætədʒɪ] Preistrategie 222

primary research [ˌpraɪmərɪ ˈriːsɜːtʃ] Primärforschung, Feldforschung 222

principal [ˈprɪnsɪpl] (hier:) Schulleiter/in; Auftraggeber/in 196

printing press [ˈprɪntɪŋ ˌpres] Druckerpresse 165

privacy [ˈpraɪvəsɪ] private Atmosphäre 52

private individual [ˌpraɪvət ˌɪndɪˈvɪdʒʊəl] Privatperson 39

procedures [prəˈsiːdʒəz] Verfahren 228

proceedings [prəˈsiːdɪŋz] (hier:) Ablauf der Konferenz 80

to process [ˈprəʊses] bearbeiten, verarbeiten 137

produce [ˈprɒdjuːs] (landwirtschaftliche) Erzeugnisse 24

product elimination [ˌprɒdʌkt ɪˌlɪmɪˈneɪʃn] Produktelimination 222

production facility [prəˈdʌkʃn fəˌsɪlətɪ] Produktionsanlage 57

production line [prəˈdʌkʃn ˌlaɪn] Fertigungsstraße 46

production site [prəˈdʌkʃn ˌsaɪt] Fertigungsstätte, Produktionsbetrieb 37

product range [ˈprɒdʌkt ˌreɪndʒ] Produktpalette 84

product variation [ˌprɒdʌkt ˌveərɪˈeɪʃn] Produktvariation 222

professional [prəˈfeʃənl] beruflich, professionell 6

proforma invoice [prəʊˌfɔːmər ˈɪnvɔɪs] Proformarechnung 177

progress [ˈprəʊgres] Fortgang 201

prohibited [prəˈhɪbɪtɪd] verboten 188

prohibitory [prəˈhɪbɪtrɪ] Verbots- 31

to project an image [prəˌdʒekt ən ˈɪmɪdʒ] ein Image pflegen 220

to promote [prəˈməʊt] befördern 241

to promote sales [prəˌməʊt ˈseɪlz] den Absatz fördern 217

promotion [prəˈməʊʃn] Beförderung 239

prompt [prɒmpt] Hinweis, Stichwort 20

prompt cards [ˈprɒmpt ˌkɑːdz] Stichwortkarten 99

pronounced [prəˈnaʊnst] ausgeprägt 56

proof [pruːf] Beweis, Nachweis 181

proportion [prəˈpɔːʃn] Anteil 217

proposal [prəˈpəʊzl] Vorschlag 161

prospective [presˈpektɪv] zukünftig, voraussichtlich, potentiell 137

to prosper [ˈprɒspə] gedeihen, florieren 37

protectionism [prəˈtekʃənɪzm] Protektionismus 173

protective footwear [prəˌtektɪv ˈfʊtweə] Fußschutz 31

protective software [prəˌtektɪv ˈsɒftweə] Software zum Schutz 111

proud(ly) [praʊd(lɪ)] stolz 157

to prove [pruːv] beweisen, nachweisen 181

to provide [prəˈvaɪd] (be)liefern, beschaffen, versorgen, zur Verfügung stellen, bieten 13

provider [prəˈvaɪdə] Versorger, Anbieter, Lieferant 180

public [ˈpʌblɪk] Öffentlichkeit 61

public relations [ˌpʌblɪk rɪˈleɪʃnz] Öffentlichkeitsarbeit 220

publisher's assistant [ˈpʌblɪʃəz əˌsɪstənt] Verlagskaufmann/-frau 229

publishing house [ˈpʌblɪʃɪŋ ˌhaʊs] Verlag 229

punch [pʌntʃ] Locher 50

punctual [ˈpʌŋktʃʊəl] pünktlich 19

puppy [ˈpʌpɪ] Hündchen, Welpe 157

purchase order [ˈpɜːtʃɪs ˌɔːdə] Bestellung, Lieferungsauftrag 194

purchasing (department) [ˈpɜːtʃəsɪŋ (dɪˌpɑːtmənt)] Einkauf(sabteilung) 54

purchasing manager [ˈpɜːtʃəsɪŋ ˌmænɪdʒə] Einkaufsleiter/in 127

pure new wool [ˌpjʊə njuː ˈwʊl] reine Schurwolle 166

purpose-built [ˌpɜːpəsˈbɪlt] für bestimmten Zweck gebaut 49

to put someone through [pʊt ˌsʌmwʌn ˈθruː] durchstellen, verbinden 63

Q

to qualify for [ˈkwɒlɪfaɪ fɔː] Voraussetzungen erfüllen für, Anspruch haben auf 156

quality comparison [ˌkwɒlətɪ kəmˈpærɪsn] qualitativer Angebotsvergleich 150

quantity comparison [ˌkwɒntətɪ kəmˈpærɪsn] quantitativer Angebotsvergleich 149

quantity discount [ˌkwɒntətɪ ˈdɪskaʊnt] Mengenrabatt 138

quarter finals [ˌkwɔːtə ˈfaɪnlz] Viertelfinale 18

quarterly [ˈkwɔːtəlɪ] vierteljährlich 138

quay [kiː] Kai, Dock, Anlegestelle 143

query [ˈkwɪərɪ] Anfrage 81

quota [ˈkwəʊtə] Quote, Rate, Kontingent, Anteil 161

quotation [kwəʊˈteɪʃn] Angebot mit Preisangabe 126

to quote [kwəʊt] Preis angeben; zitieren 138

R

rabbit [ˈræbɪt] Kaninchen 26

Radiation Protection Ordinance [reɪdɪˌeɪʃn prəˈtekʃn ˌɔːdɪnəns] Strahlenschutzverordnung 32

rail siding [ˈreɪl ˌsaɪdɪŋ] Gleisanschluss 164

rail transport [ˈreɪl ˌtrænspɔːt] Schienentransport 164

rainwater harvesting [ˈreɪnwɔːtə ˈhɑːvəstɪŋ] Regenwasseraufbereitung 107

to raise [reɪz] erhöhen 216

to raise a matter [ˌreɪz ə ˈmætə] eine Sache ansprechen 200

random sample [ˌrændəm ˈsɑːmpl] Zufallsprobe 212

range [reɪndʒ] Sortiment, Kollektion, Auswahl 157

to range from ... to [ˈreɪndʒ frəm ... tʊ] reichen von ... bis 98

range of products [ˌreɪndʒ əv ˈprɒdʌkts] Produktpalette 37

rapid [ˈræpɪd] schnell 102

rapport [ræˈpɔː, rəˈpɔː] Verhältnis 239

raw materials [ˌrɔː məˈtɪərɪəlz] Rohstoffe 13

re [riː] bezüglich, wegen 204

reasonable [ˈriːznəbl] vernünftig 173

receipt of order [rɪˌsiːt əv ˈɔːdə] Auftragseingang 139

to receive [rɪˈsiːv] erhalten, empfangen 62

receiver [rɪˈsiːvə] Hörer 62

recent [ˈriːsənt] nicht lange zurückliegend, vor kurzem geschehen 110

reception [rɪˈsepʃn] Empfang 128

receptionist [rɪˈsepʃənɪst] Rezeptionist/in, Mitarbeiter/in am Empfang 21

recipient [rɪˈsɪpɪənt] Empfänger/in 113

to recognize [ˈrekəgnaɪz] erkennen, anerkennen 111

to recommend [ˌrekəˈmend] empfehlen 89

record [ˈrekɔːd] Aufzeichnung 88

records [ˈrekɔːdz] Unterlagen, Verzeichnisse 183

to record [rɪˈkɔːd] aufzeichnen, eintragen 117

to recruit [rɪˈkruːt] einstellen 227

recruitment agencies [rɪˈkruːtmənt ˌeɪdʒənsɪz] Stellenvermittlungsagenturen 227

to redesign [ˌriːdɪˈzaɪn] neu-, umgestalten 24

to redirect [ˌriːdaɪˈrekt, ˌriːdɪˈrekt] umleiten 63

referee [ˌrefəˈriː] (hier:) jemand, der eine Empfehlung/ein Zeugnis schreibt 230

reference [ˈrefrəns] Bezug 141

references [ˈrefrənsɪz] Referenzen, Empfehlungsschreiben 149

to refer to [rɪˈfɜː tuː] sich beziehen auf 74

refreshments [rɪˈfreʃmənts] Erfrischung(en) 17

refund [ˈriːfʌnd] Erstattung 196

to refund [ˌriːˈfʌnd] erstatten 193

refurbishment [ˌriːˈfɜːbɪʃmənt] Renovierung 196

regardless of [rɪˈɡɑːdləs əv] ungeachtet, trotz 166

to register [ˈredʒɪstə] eintragen, registrieren 132

regularly [ˈreɡjələlɪ] regelmäßig 212

regulations [ˌreɡjəˈleɪʃnz] Vorschriften, Verordnungen 118

to rehearse [rɪˈhɜːs] proben, einüben 101

to reinforce [ˌriːɪnˈfɔːs] verstärken 99

to reject [rɪˈdʒekt] zurückweisen 201

to release from a contract [rɪˌliːs frəm ə ˈkɒntrækt] von einem Vertrag entbinden 204

relevant [ˈreləvənt] wichtig, sachdienlich 67

reliable [rɪˈlaɪəbl] zuverlässig 36

relieved [rɪˈliːvd] erleichtert 69

remainder, balance [rɪˈmeɪndə, ˈbæləns] Restbetrag 185

to remain unchanged [rɪˌmeɪn ʌnˈtʃeɪndʒd] unverändert bleiben 104

to remind [rɪˈmaɪnd] erinnern 101

reminder [rɪˈmaɪndə] (Zahlungs-)Erinnerung, Mahnung 176

to remit [rɪˈmɪt] überweisen 177

remittance [rɪˈmɪtəns] Überweisung 185

to remove [rɪˈmuːv] entfernen 194

to render a service [ˌrendər ə ˈsɜːvɪs] einen Dienst leisten, eine Dienstleistung erbringen 193

renewable energies [rɪˌnjuːəbl ˈenədʒɪz] erneuerbare Energien 105

to renew a contract [rɪˌnjuː ə ˈkɒntrækt] einen Vertrag verlängern 196

rent [rent] Miete 71

to rent [rent] mieten 37

repairs [rɪˈpeəz] Reparatur 41

repeat order [rɪˌpiːt ˈɔːdə] Folgeauftrag 153

to replace [rɪˈpleɪs] ersetzen 47

replacement [rɪˈpleɪsmənt] Ersatz(lieferung) 192

replacement Mp3 player [rɪˌpleɪsmənt ˌempiːˈθriː ˌpleɪə] Ersatz-MP3-Spieler 166

to report to [rɪˈpɔːt tuː] unterstehen 54

representative [ˌreprɪˈzentətɪv] Vertreter/in 133

reputation [ˌrepjəˈteɪʃn] Ruf 239

request [rɪˈkwest] Bitte 71

to request [rɪˈkwest] bitten um 86

to require [rɪˈkwaɪə] (hier:) verlangen, auffordern 98

rescue [ˈreskjuː] Rettung 31

research [rɪˈsɜːtʃ] Forschung 21

residence permit [ˈrezɪdəns ˌpɜːmɪt] Aufenthaltsgenehmigung 241

resilient [rɪˈzɪlɪənt] unverwüstlich, zäh 173

respiratory protection [rɪˌspɪrətrɪ prəˈtekʃn] Atemschutz 31

respite [ˈrespaɪt] Zahlungsaufschub 206

to respond [rɪˈspɒnd] antworten, reagieren 201

responsible for [rɪˈspɒnsəbl fɔː] verantwortlich für 55

to restore [rɪˈstɔː] wiederherstellen, restaurieren 114

restricted [rɪˈstrɪktɪd] beschränkt 88

restroom (AE) [ˈrestˌruːm] Toilette 21

retail customer [ˌriːteɪl ˈkʌstəmə] Privatkunde (bei einer Bank) 215

retailer [ˈriːteɪlə] Einzelhändler/in 127

retailing operations [ˈriːteɪlɪŋ ˌɒpəˌreɪʃnz] Einzelhandelsgeschäftstätigkeit 215

retail outlet [ˌriːteɪl ˈaʊtlet] Einzelhandelsgeschäft, -verkaufsstelle 180

retail trade [ˈriːteɪl ˌtreɪd] Einzelhandel 159

to retain [rɪˈteɪn] halten, beibehalten 131

retired [rɪˈtaɪəd] im Ruhestand, pensioniert 217

retirement [rɪˈtaɪəmənt] Ruhestand 205

to retrofit [ˈretrəʊfɪt] umrüsten 46

to return [rɪˈtɜːn] (hier:) zurückschicken 89

to reveal [rɪˈviːl] enthüllen, aufzeigen 199

revenue [ˈrevnjuː] Erlös, Einkünfte 174

to reverse [rɪˈvɜːs] umkehren 232

reviews [rɪˈvjuːz] Berichte, Besprechungen 216

to revoke [rɪˈvəʊk] widerrufen, annullieren, stornieren 181

reworking [ˌriːˈwɜːkɪŋ] Um-, Nacharbeitung 194

rice [raɪs] Reis 26

right away [ˌraɪtəˈweɪ] sofort 241

to rise, rose, risen [raɪz, rəʊz, rɪzn] steigen 104

rising demand for [ˌraɪzɪŋ dɪˈmɑːnd fə] steigende Nachfrage nach 102

roast pork [ˌrəʊstˈpɔːk] Schweinebraten 26

to romp [rɒmp] herumtollen 157

roof [ruːf] Dach 213

roughly one third [ˌrʌflɪ ˌwʌn ˈθɜːd] rund/etwa ein Drittel 199

roundabout [ˈraʊndəbaʊt] Kreisverkehr 22

to round up [raʊnd ˈʌp] aufrunden 86

rubber (BE), **eraser** (AE) [ˈrʌbə, ɪˈreɪzə] Radiergummi 50

rude [ruːd] grob, ungehobelt, unverschämt 123

to rule [ruːl] entscheiden, verfügen, anordnen 161

rules [ruːlz] Regeln, Vorschriften 118

ruler [ˈruːlə] Lineal 50

to run out of something [rʌn ˈaʊt əv ˌsʌmθɪŋ] ausgehen, zur Neige gehen 142

rush [rʌʃ] Ansturm 82

S

salary [ˈsælərɪ] Gehalt 228

sales (department) [ˈseɪlz (dɪˌpɑːtmənt)] Verkauf(sabteilung) 54

sales assistant [ˈseɪlz əˌsɪstənt] Verkäufer/in 216

sales consultant [ˈseɪlz kənˌsʌltənt] Verkaufsberater/in 216

sales force [ˈseɪlz ˌfɔːs] Vertreterstab 214

sales literature [ˈseɪlz ˌlɪtrətʃə] Prospektmaterial 36

sales promotion [ˈseɪlz prəˌməʊʃn] Verkaufsförderung 222

sales representative [ˈseɪlz reprɪˌzentətɪv] Handelsvertreter/in, Außendienstmitarbeiter/in 112

sales volume [ˈseɪlz ˌvɒljuːm] Absatzmenge 57

salmon [ˈsæmən] Lachs 26

salutation [ˌsæljəˈteɪʃn] (hier:) Anrede; Begrüßung 112

sample [ˈsɑːmpl] Muster, Probestück 127

satisfaction [ˌsætɪsˈfækʃn] Zufriedenheit 198

to satisfy [ˈsætɪsfaɪ] zufrieden stellen 196

sausage [ˈsɒsɪdʒ] Wurst 26

savoury [ˈseɪvərɪ] herzhaft, pikant 26

scale [skeɪl] Maß, Maßstab 176

scarce(ly) [ˈskeəs(lɪ)] knapp; kaum 146

scared [skeəd] ängstlich 98

schedule [ˈʃedjuːl; ˈskedjuːl] (Zeit-/Termin-/Fahr-)Plan; Schema, Aufstellung 244

school / college tuition *(AE)* [ˌskuːl / ˌkɒlɪdʒ tjuːˈɪʃn] Schulgeld, Collegegebühr 243

school-leaving certificate [ˌskuːl ˈliːvɪŋ səˈtɪfɪkət] Schulabschlusszeugnis 229

Sci-Fi film [ˈsaɪfaɪ ˌfɪlm] Science-Fiction-Film 9

scope [skəʊp] Umfang, Bereich 54

scotch tape [ˌskɒtʃ ˈteɪp] Klebeband 50

scratch [skrætʃ] Kratzer 202

scratched [skrætʃt] zerkratzt 208

search engine [ˈsɜːtʃ ˌendʒɪn] Suchmaschine 126

seaworthy packing [ˌsiːwɜːði ˈpækɪŋ] seetaugliche Verpackung 164

secondary research, desk research [ˌsekəndrɪ ˈriːsɜːtʃ, ˌdesk ˈriːsɜːtʃ] Sekundärforschung, Schreibtischforschung 222

second floor [ˌsekənd ˈflɔː] zweite Etage *(BE)*, erste Etage *(AE)* 21

sector [ˈsektə] Branche 215

secure [sɪˈkjʊə, sɪˈkjɔː] sicher 39

to seek, sought, sought [siːk, sɔːt, sɔːt] suchen 228

segment [ˈsegmənt] Marktsegment 213

selection [səˈlekʃn] Auswahl 101

selective [səˈlektɪv] ausgewählt 217

sell-by date [ˈselbaɪˌdeɪt] Verfallsdatum *(Lebensmittel)* 198

to sell on [ˌsel ˈɒn] weiterverkaufen 213

to sell well [ˌsel ˈwel] sich gut verkaufen, gut gehen 157

semi-finished [ˌsemɪˈfɪnɪʃt] halbfertig 13

semi-skilled [ˌsemɪˈskɪld] angelernt 108

senior [ˈsiːnjə] höherrangig 24

series production [ˌsɪəriːz prəˈdʌkʃn] Serienfertigung 46

serious [ˈsɪəriəs] ernst, schwerwiegend 203

serviceable [ˈsɜːvɪsəbl] zweckdienlich, praktisch, strapazierfähig 177

service centre *(BE)* **/ center** *(AE)* [ˈsɜːvɪsˌsentə] Kundendienst(zentrum) 200

service life [ˈsɜːvɪs ˌlaɪf] Lebensdauer 47

to set [set] festsetzen, ansetzen, einrichten 161

to set about [set əˈbaʊt] sich daran machen 211

to set a price [set ə ˈpraɪs] einen Preis bestimmen 225

to settle an invoice [ˌsetl ən ˈɪnvɔɪs] eine Rechnung begleichen 183

settlement [ˈsetlmənt] Abrechnung, Bezahlung, Ausgleich, Erledigung 138

to settle the matter [ˈsetl ðə ˌmætə] die Angelegenheit erledigen 198

to set up in business on one's own [set ʌp ɪn ˈbɪznɪs ɒn wʌnzˌəʊn] eine eigene Firma gründen 239

severe(ly) [səˈvɪə(lɪ)] hart, streng, strikt, scharf 185

to sew, sewed, sewn [səʊ, səʊd, səʊn] nähen 194

to share the costs [ˌʃeə ðə ˈkɒsts] sich die Kosten teilen 159

sharp [ʃɑːp] scharf 22

to ship [ʃɪp] versenden, verschiffen 70

shipper [ˈʃɪpə] *(hier:)* Versender/in, Verfrachter/in 171

shipping [ˈʃɪpɪŋ] Seetransport, Verschiffung, Versand 163

shirt [ʃɜːt] (Herren-)Hemd 156

shoemaker [ˈʃuːˌmeɪkə] Schuhmacher/in, Schuster/in 37

shopping cart [ˈʃɒpɪŋˌkɑːt] Einkaufswagen 41

shortcomings [ˈʃɔːtˌkʌmɪŋz] Unzulänglichkeiten 196

shortly [ˈʃɔːtlɪ] in Kürze, bald 154

short-term [ˌʃɔːtˈtɜːm] kurzfristig 207

shuttle service [ˈʃʌtl ˌsɜːvɪs] Pendelbus 82

sights [saɪts] Sehenswürdigkeiten 22

sign [saɪn] Zeichen 31

signatory [ˈsɪgnətərɪ] Unterzeichner/in 119

signature [ˈsɪgnətʃə] Unterschrift 111

signature footer [ˈsɪgnətʃə ˌfʊtə] Unterschriftsfußzeilen 112

significant(ly) [sɪgˈnɪfɪkənt(lɪ)] bedeutend 104

to simplify [ˈsɪmplɪfaɪ] vereinfachen 212

single [ˈsɪŋgl] ledig 233

single room [ˌsɪŋgl ˈruːm] Einzelzimmer 81

sister-in-law [ˈsɪstərɪnlɔː] Schwägerin 54

site [saɪt] Standort, Abbaustelle 102

size [saɪz] Größe 72

skill [skɪl] Fertigkeit 98

skilled [skɪld] qualifiziert, ausgebildet 108

skin care [ˈskɪn ˌkeə] Hautpflege 228

to skip [skɪp] überspringen 219

to sleep [sliːp] *(hier:)* Schlafmöglichkeit bieten 71

slice [slaɪs] Scheibe, Anteil 102

slide [slaɪd] Folie 99

slight(ly) [slaɪt(lɪ)] gering(fügig), leicht, kaum merklich 104

slight drizzle [ˌslaɪt ˈdrɪzl] leichter Nieselregen 20

to slim down [ˌslɪm ˈdaʊn] schlanker werden, abbauen 173

to slump [slʌmp] stark fallen 104

smart [smɑːt] ordentlich, gepflegt, schick 238

smitten [ˈsmɪtn] hingerissen 157

smoked [sməʊkt] geräuchert 26

smoked salmon [ˌsməʊkt ˈsæmən] Räucherlachs 132

smudged [smʌdʒd] verwischt, verschmiert 198

to soak [səʊk] durchnässen, einweichen 185

to soar [sɔː] sprunghaft steigen, in die Höhe schnellen 142

sociable [ˈsəʊʃəbl] gesellig, umgänglich 24

social service [ˌsəʊʃl ˈsɜːvɪs] Ersatzdienst 235

social studies [ˌsəʊʃl ˈstʌdɪz] Gemeinschaftskunde 12

soft drinks [ˌsɒft ˈdrɪŋks] alkoholfreie Getränke 87

solar panel [ˌsəʊlə ˈpænl] Solarkollektor 106

sole [səʊl] Sohle 193

solicited offer [səˌlɪsɪtɪd ˈɒfə] verlangtes Angebot 136

to some extent [tə ˌsʌm ɪkˈstent] in gewissem Maße 63

sophisticated [səˈfɪstɪkeɪtɪd] hoch entwickelt, technisch ausgefeilt 221

sour [saʊə] sauer 26

source [sɔːs] Quelle 227

spacing [ˈspeɪsɪŋ] Abstände, Abstandseinteilung 117

spacious [ˈspeɪʃəs] geräumig 49

to spare [speə] übrig haben 212

spare parts [ˌspeə ˈpɑːts] Ersatzteile 164

sparing(ly) [ˈspeərɪŋ(lɪ)] sparsam, mäßig 115

sparkling mineral water [ˌspɑːklɪŋ ˈmɪnərəl ˌwɔːtə] Mineralwasser mit Kohlensäure 87

special features [ˌspeʃl ˈfiːtʃəz] besondere Eigenschaften 82

specialist agency [ˌspeʃəlɪst ˈeɪdʒənsɪ] Fachagentur 220

specialist shops [ˌspeʃəlɪst ˈʃɒps] Fachgeschäfte 213

speechwriter [ˈspiːtʃˌraɪtə] Redenschreiber/in 207

to spend, spent, spent [spend, spent, spent] ausgeben 212

spicy [ˈspaɪsɪ] würzig 25

spirits [ˈspɪrɪts] Spirituosen 215

spokesman [ˈspəʊksmən] Sprecher 219

square [skweə] Platz 23

squeezed [skwiːzd] eingezwängt 173

to stack [stæk] aufstapeln, aufschichten 163

staff [stɑːf] Belegschaft, Personal 37

staff member [ˈstɑːf ˌmembə] Mitarbeiter/in 172

stage [steɪdʒ] *(hier:)* Stadium 211

to stage [steɪdʒ] veranstalten 159

staggered payment [ˌstægəd ˈpeɪmənt] gestaffelte Zahlungsweise 181

stagnation [stægˈneɪʃn] Stillstand 163

standard lamp [ˈstændəd ˌlæmp] Stehlampe 169

to stand in for someone [stænd ˈɪn fə ˌsʌmwʌn] jemanden vertreten 28

standing order [ˌstændɪŋ 'ɔːdə] Dauer-auftrag 153

stapling machine / stapler ['steɪplɪŋ məˌʃiːn / 'steɪplə] Tacker 50

starter ['stɑːtə] Vorspeise 25

start-up (business) ['stɑːtʌp (ˌbɪznɪs)] Neugründung, junges Unternehmen 39

statement ['steɪtmənt] Aussage, Äußerung 8

statement of account [ˌsteɪtmənt əv ə'kaʊnt] Kontoauszug 181

state of affairs [ˌsteɪt əv ə'feəz] Zustand, Stand der Dinge 184

state-of-the-art [ˌsteɪtəvðɪ'ɑːt] auf dem neuesten Stand (der Technik) 36

state rooms ['steɪt ˌruːmz] Empfangs-säle 23

stationery ['steɪʃənrɪ] Büromaterial 196

steady, steadily ['stedɪ(lɪ)] stetig 104

steel [stiːl] Stahl 142

steel rods [ˌstiːl 'rɒdz] Stahlstäbe 166

stew, soup [stjuː, suːp] Eintopf 27

to stew [stjuː] kochen, dünsten, schmoren 26

to stipulate, to specify ['stɪpjəleɪt, 'spesɪfaɪ] vorschreiben 180

stock [stɒk] Vorrat, Lager(bestand) 136

stock level ['stɒk ˌlevl] Lagerbestand 58

to stock up on [stɒk 'ʌp ɒn] Lager(bestand) auffüllen 142

storage ['stɔːrɪdʒ] Abstellraum; Lagerung 21

storage costs ['stɔːrɪdʒ ˌkɒsts] Lager-kosten 57

straight [streɪt] (hier:) geradewegs, direkt 217

straight away [ˌstreɪtə'weɪ] sofort, un-verzüglich 159

straightforward [ˌstreɪt'fɔːwəd] einfach, unkompliziert 18

strengths [streŋkθs] Stärken 238

to stress [stres] betonen 156

striking ['straɪkɪŋ] auffallend 23

study group ['stʌdɪ ˌgruːp] Arbeits-gruppe 74

stuffed [stʌft] gefüllt 26

stylish ['staɪlɪʃ] schick, modisch 177

subject ['sʌbdʒɪkt] (hier:) Betreff; Gegen-stand 112

subject matter ['sʌbdʒɪkt ˌmætə] Gegen-stand, Thema 113

to submit [səb'mɪt] vorlegen 149

subsidiary [səb'sɪdɪərɪ] Tochtergesell-schaft 161

subsidy ['sʌbsədɪ] Zuschuss, Subventi-on 108

substantial [səb'stænʃl] erheblich, beträchtlich 182

substitute ['sʌbstɪtjuːt] Ersatz (durch Ähnliches) 140

suburb ['sʌbɜːb] Vorort, Stadtteil im Außenbezirk 69

to succeed in [sək'siːd ɪn] gelingen 214

sufficient(ly) [sə'fɪʃənt(lɪ)] genügend, ausreichend 39

to suggest [sə'dʒest] (hier:) hinweisen auf, suggerieren 217

suggestion [sə'dʒestʃn] Vorschlag 159

suit [suːt] Kostüm (Damen), Anzug 237

suitable ['suːtəbl] geeignet 227

sunset ['sʌnset] Sonnenuntergang 160

superb [suː'pɜːb] hervorragend 19

superfluous [suː'pɜːfluəs] überflüssig 215

superior [suː'pɪərɪə] Vorgesetzte / r 54

to supervise ['suːpəvaɪz] beaufsichtigen 87

supplementary charge [ˌsʌplɪmentərɪ 'tʃɑːdʒ] Zuschlag 85

supplier [sə'plaɪə] Lieferant, Anbieter 126

supply [sə'plaɪ] Angebot 213

supply / demand ratio [səˌplaɪ dɪ'mɑːnd ˌreɪʃəʊ] Verhältnis zwischen Angebot und Nachfrage 163

to support [sə'pɔːt] unterstützen, helfen 7

to suppose [sə'pəʊz] vermuten 212

surname ['sɜːneɪm] Familienname 8

surplus ['sɜːpləs] überschüssig 193

surprisingly [sə'praɪzɪŋlɪ] überra-schenderweise 18

to surround [sə'raʊnd] umgeben 24

survey method ['sɜːveɪ ˌmeθəd] Erhe-bungsmethode 222

to survive [sə'vaɪv] überleben 215

suspicious [sə'spɪʃəs] verdächtig 114

sustainability [səˌsteɪnə'bɪlətɪ] Nach-haltigkeit 106

sweets [swiːts] Süßwaren, Süßigkeiten 128

swift(ly) ['swɪft(lɪ)] schnell 221

swivel chair [ˌswɪvl 'tʃeə] Drehstuhl 50

T

tag [tæg] Etikett, Anhängeschildchen 194

tailback ['teɪlbæk] Stau 20

tailored suit [ˌteɪləd 'suːt] Kostüm 238

to take [teɪk] (hier:) in Anspruch neh-men, dauern 18

to take a call [ˌteɪk ə 'kɔːl] einen Anruf entgegennehmen 84

to take advantage of [ˌteɪk əd'vɑːntɪdʒ ɒv] sich zunutze machen, ausnutzen 36

to take a message [ˌteɪk ə 'mesɪdʒ] eine Nachricht entgegennehmen 67

to take down [teɪk'daʊn] notieren 67

to take into account [teɪk ˌɪntʊ ə'kaʊnt] berücksichtigen 196

to take offence at something [teɪk ə'fens ət ˌsʌmθɪŋ] etwas übel nehmen 200

to take off the roof [ˌteɪk ɒf ðə 'ruːf] das Dach abdecken 185

to take over [ˌteɪk 'əʊvə] (eine Firma) übernehmen 37

to take part in [ˌteɪk 'pɑːt ɪn] teilneh-men an 215

to take the minutes [ˌteɪk ðə 'mɪnɪts] Protokoll führen 88

to take up [teɪk 'ʌp] aufnehmen, sich verlegen auf; hochheben 37

to take up residence [ˌteɪk ʌp 'rezɪdəns] wohnhaft werden 241

to target ['tɑːgɪt] ansprechen, anpeilen 212

target purchase price [ˌtɑːgɪt 'pɜːtʃɪs ˌpraɪs] Zieleinkaufspreis 149

tart [tɑːt] herb, säuerlich 26

to taste [teɪst] schmecken 26

tax [tæks] Steuer 108

tax-exempt intra-Community delivery [ˌtæksɪg'zempt ˌɪntrəkə'mjuːnətɪ dɪ'lɪvərɪ] steuerfreie Innergemeinschafts-lieferung (innerhalb der EU) 178

tax relief ['tæks rɪˌliːf] Steuererleichte-rung 108

tedious ['tiːdɪəs] langweilig, lästig 20

telephone directory ['telɪfəʊn daɪˌrektərɪ, 'telɪfəʊn dɪˌrektərɪ] Telefon-buch 62

telephony [tə'lefənɪ] Telefonverkehr 61

temporary ['tempərərɪ] vorübergehend, befristet 233

to tempt [tempt] in Versuchung führen 25

to tend to be ['tend ˌtʊ biː] dazu neigen 123

to tend to book flights [ˌtend ˌtʊ ˌbʊk 'flaɪts] Flüge häufig buchen 212

terminal operator ['tɜːmɪnl ˌɒpəreɪtə] Betreiber eines Terminals 163

terms of delivery [ˌtɜːmz ˌəv dɪ'lɪvərɪ] Lieferbedingungen 58

terms of payment and delivery [ˌtɜːmz ˌəv ˌpeɪmənt ənd ˌdɪ'lɪvərɪ] Zahlungs- und Lieferbedingungen 127

terrible ['terɪbl] furchtbar 19

theft [θeft] Diebstahl 164

to thicken ['θɪkn] eindicken 27

those involved [ˌðəʊz ɪn'vɒlvd] die Beteiligten 88

those present [ˌðəʊz 'preznt] die Anwe-senden 88

to threaten ['θretn] drohen 183

threshold value [ˌθreʃhəʊld 'væljuː] Schrankenwert 57

thus [ðʌs] daher 214

to tie [taɪ] binden 237

tiles [taɪlz] Fliesen, Kacheln 202

time-consuming ['taɪmkənˌsjuːmɪŋ] zeitraubend 39

to have time on their hands [hæv ˌtaɪm ɒn ðeə 'hændz] Zeit (übrig) haben 217

timetable ['taɪmˌteɪbl] Fahrplan 85

tip [tɪp] *(hier:)* Trinkgeld 86
tomato relish [təˌmɑːtəʊ ˈrelɪʃ] Tomatenrelish 202
tool [tuːl] Werkzeug 61
tool kit [ˈtuːl ˌkɪt] Werkzeugsatz 195
topics [ˈtɒpɪks] *(hier:)* Punkte, Themen 88
topic of conversation [ˌtɒpɪk əv ˌkɒnvəˈseɪʃn] Gesprächsthema 19
total value [ˌtəʊtl ˈvæljuː] Gesamtwert 57
tournament [ˈtɔːnəmənt] Turnier 20
tour operator [ˈtʊərˌɒpəreɪtə] Reiseveranstalter 228
towering [ˈtaʊərɪŋ] turmhoch, überragend 23
town hall [ˌtaʊn ˈhɔːl] Rathaus 22
toxic [ˈtɒksɪk] giftig 31
to track [træk] verfolgen 41
trade association [ˈtreɪd əsəʊʃiˌeɪʃn] Branchenverband 126
trade discount [ˈtreɪd ˌdɪskaʊnt] Händler-, Wiederverkaufsrabatt 131
trade fair [ˈtreɪd ˌfeə] (Fach-)Messe 126
trade flows [ˈtreɪd ˌfləʊz] Handelsströme 163
trade journal [ˈtreɪd ˌdʒɜːnl] Fachzeitschrift 220
trainee [ˌtreɪˈniː] Auszubildende/r 10
train ride [ˈtreɪn ˌraɪd] Zugfahrt 19
to transfer [trænsˈfɜː] überweisen, übertragen 154
transparencies [trænˈspærənsɪz] Folien 99
travel agency / agent [ˈtrævl ˌeɪdʒənsɪ / ˌeɪdʒənt] Reisebüro 8
travel consultant [ˈtrævl kənˌsʌltənt] Reiseverkehrskaufmann/-frau 8
tray [treɪ] Ablagekorb 50
trial order [ˌtraɪəl ˈɔːdə] Probeauftrag 153
to trim [trɪm] kürzen, senken 173
triple-walled cardboard box [ˌtrɪplwɔːldˌkɑːdbɔːdˈbɒks] 3-wandiger Karton 167
trousers [ˈtraʊzəz] Hose 237
trout [traʊt] Forelle 26
to trust [trʌst] vertrauen 181
to tuck into [ˌtʌk ˈɪntuː] hineinstecken in 237
turkey [ˈtɜːkɪ] Pute, Truthahn 26
to turn down [tɜːn ˈdaʊn] ablehnen 180
turnover, sales [ˈtɜːnˌəʊvə, seɪlz] Umsatz 219
turn-taking [ˈtɜːnˌteɪkɪŋ] sich anstellen, warten bis man dran ist 85
to turn up [tɜːn ˈʌp] auftauchen 227
TV advertising, TV commercials [ˌtiːviː ˈædvətaɪzɪŋ, ˌtiːviː kəˈmɜːʃlz] TV-Werbung 217
types of production processes [ˈtaɪps əv prəˈdʌkʃn ˌprəʊsesɪz] Fertigungstypen 46

U

unappreciated [ˌʌnəˈpriːʃieɪtɪd] nicht genügend geschätzt 239
unauthorised [ʌnˈɔːθəraɪzd] unbefugt 111
unavoidable [ˌʌnəˈvɔɪdəbl] unvermeidlich 63
to undercut, undercut, undercut [ˌʌndəˈkʌt, ˌʌndəˈkʌt, ˌʌndəˈkʌt] unterbieten 90
to underestimate [ˌʌndərˈestɪmeɪt] unterschätzen 100
underscore [ˌʌndəˈskɔː] Unterstreichung 91
understanding [ˌʌndəˈstændɪŋ] verständnisvoll 200
unemployment [ˌʌnɪmˈplɔɪmənt] Arbeitslosigkeit 241
unique [juːˈniːk] einzigartig 23
unit costs [ˈjuːnɪt ˈkɒsts] Stückkosten 57
to unload [ʌnˈləʊd] entladen, löschen 163
unprecedented [ʌnˈpresɪdəntɪd] noch nie dagewesen 216
unreliable [ˌʌnrɪˈlaɪəbl] unzuverlässig 111
unsatisfactory [ʌnˌsætɪsˈfæktərɪ] unbefriedigend, ungenügend, unzureichend 111
unsolicited offer [ˌʌnsəlɪsɪtɪd ˈɒfə] unverlangtes Angebot 136
to update [ʌpˈdeɪt] aktualisieren 143
uplighter [ˈʌplaɪtə] Deckenfluter 169
upmarket [ʌpˈmɑːkɪt] im oberen Marktsegment 53
upper and lower case letters [ˌʌpərˌən ˌləʊə keɪs ˈletəz] Groß- und Kleinbuchstaben 99
up the hill [ʌp ðə ˈhɪl] den Berg hinauf 22
up to date [ˌʌptəˈdeɪt] aktuell 217
urgent [ˈɜːdʒənt] dringend, eilig 159
usage [ˈjuːsɪdʒ] übliche Praxis, Gepflogenheit, Gewohnheit 119

V

vacancy [ˈveɪkənsɪ] offene Stelle 227
valid (until) [ˈvælɪd (ʌnˌtɪl)] gültig (bis); bindend, rechtskräftig 136
valuable [ˈvæljʊbl] wertvoll 199
van [væn] Kleintransporter 164
variety [vəˈraɪətɪ] Vielfalt 213
VAT (value-added tax) [ˌviːeɪˈtiː (ˌvæljuːˌædɪdˈtæks)] Mehrwertsteuer 177
veal [viːl] Kalbfleisch 26
vegan [ˈviːgən] Veganer/in 25
vegetable(s) [ˈvedʒtəbl(z)] Gemüse 26
veggieburger [ˈvedʒɪˌbɜːgə] Gemüsebratling 25
vehicle [ˈviːəkl] Fahrzeug 163
venison [ˈvenɪsən] Hirsch, Rotwild *(als Fleisch)* 25

venue [ˈvenjuː] Veranstaltungsort, Gerichtsstand 101
vessel [ˈvesl] Schiff 171
via [vaɪə, ˈviːə] über 100
vibrant [ˈvaɪbrənt] lebendig 18
view [vjuː] *(hier:)* Ausblick 52
vinegar [ˈvɪnɪgə] Essig 27
virtually [ˈvɜːtʃʊəlɪ] nahezu, so gut wie, praktisch 164
visible [ˈvɪzəbl] sichtbar 85
visual aids [ˌvɪʒʊəl ˈeɪdz] visuelle Hilfsmittel 99
vocational college [vəʊˈkeɪʃənl ˌkɒlɪdʒ] Berufskolleg, Berufsfachschule 10
vocational school [vəʊˈkeɪʃənl ˌskuːl] Berufsschule 7
volume order [ˌvɒljuːm ˈɔːdə] Großauftrag 130
voucher [ˈvaʊtʃə] Gutschein 243

W

waiter service [ˈweɪtə ˌsɜːvɪs] Bedienung 85
to wait one's turn [ˌweɪt wʌnz ˈtɜːn] warten bis man an die Reihe kommt 25
wall calendar [ˈwɔːl ˌkæləndə] Wandkalender 197
warehouse [ˈweəhaʊs] Lagerhaus / halle 148
waste disposal [ˌweɪst dɪˈspəʊzl] Abfallentsorgung 107
wastepaper bin / basket [weɪstˈpeɪpə ˌbɪn / ˌbɑːskɪt] Papierkorb 50
to watch [wɒtʃ] aufpassen auf 53
watt [wɒt] Watt 47
to wave your arms around [ˌweɪv jɔːr ˈɑːmz əˌraʊnd] mit den Armen herumfuchteln 101
waybill [ˈweɪbɪl] Frachtbrief 170
weather forecast [ˈweðə ˌfɔːkɑːst] Wettervorhersage 19
weighting [ˈweɪtɪŋ] Gewichtung 150
well-substantiated [ˌwelsʌbˈstænʃieɪtɪd] gut belegt 102
we've already met [wiːv ɔːlˈredɪ ˈmet] wir kennen uns schon 17
whatever the price [wɒtˌevə ðə ˈpraɪs] ganz unabhängig vom Preis 198
What is the weather like …? [ˌwɒt ɪz ðə ˈweðə ˌlaɪk] Wie ist das Wetter …? 19
whenever [wenˈevə] immer dann, wenn 111
whereas [weəˈræz] wohingegen, dagegen 119
wholesale and export clerk [ˌhəʊlseɪl ənd ˈekspɔːt ˌklɑːk] Kaufmann/-frau im Groß- und Außenhandel 8
wholesaler [ˈhəʊlˌseɪlə] Großhändler 213
wide range [ˌwaɪd ˈreɪndʒ] breite Palette 211

willing ['wɪlɪŋ] bereit 212

to withdraw money from an account, withdrew, withdrawn [wɪð'drɔː ˌmʌnɪ frəm ən ə'kaʊnt, wɪð'druː, wɪð'drɔːn] Geld von einem Konto abheben 179

with order [wɪð 'ɔːdə] bei Auftragserteilung 181

without engagement [wɪˌðaʊt ɪn'geɪdʒmənt] freibleibend 136

to wonder ['wʌndə] sich fragen 63

wooden case [ˌwʊdn 'keɪs] Holzkiste 166

wording ['wɜːdɪŋ] Formulierung 180

work contract ['wɜːkˌkɒntrækt] Arbeitsvertrag 13

workforce ['wɜːkfɔːs] Belegschaft, Gesamtheit der Mitarbeiter 37

Working Reliability Regulation [ˌwɜːkɪŋ rɪlaɪə'bɪləti regjəˌleɪʃn] Betriebssicherheitsverordnung 32

work-out ['wɜːkaʊt] Fitnesstraining 8

to work out [wɜːk 'aʊt] sich körperlich fit halten, trainieren 7

work placement ['wɜːk ˌpleɪsmənt] Praktikum 241

Workplace Ordinance [ˌwɜːkpleɪs 'ɔːdɪnəns] Arbeitsstättenverordnung 32

world championship [ˌwɜːldˌ 'tʃæmpɪənʃɪp] Weltmeisterschaft 37

written order [ˌrɪtn 'ɔːdə] schriftliche Anweisung 179

Communication

Written communication
Spoken communication
Collocations relating to communication
On the phone
Information and communications technology (ICT)

Company organisation

Types of company and structure
Departments and functions
Jobs and responsibilities
Places at work

Products, brands and marketing

Describing products
Marketing and promotion

Sales and distribution

Distribution channels
Transport and shipping

Human resources

Hiring and firing
Issues
Wages and salaries
Training and assessment

Quality

Expressions with the word 'quality'
Standards
Measures and approaches

Business and the economy

Business sectors
Cycles and trends

International trade

Issues and policy
Documentation
Payment and delivery

Hinweis: Glossar zum Herunterladen über Online-Link 808262-0000.

Communication

Written communication
agenda Tagesordnung
application Bewerbung, Antrag
amount Summe
attach, to anhängen
attachment Anhang *(E-Mail)*
brochure Broschüre, Prospekt
catalogue *(BE)*, **catalog** *(AE)* Katalog
complaint Beschwerde, Reklamation
contract Vertrag
documents Unterlagen
draft Entwurf
enclosure Anlage *(Brief)*
enquiry *(BE)*, **inquiry** *(AE)* Anfrage
leaflet Flugblatt, Infoblatt
memo *(short for:* **memorandum)** interne Notiz, Vermerk
message Nachricht
minutes Protokoll
notice Aushang
offer Angebot
order Auftrag, Bestellung
paragraph Absatz, Paragraph
paperwork Verwaltungsarbeit, Schreibarbeit
post-it note Haftnotiz, Klebezettel
reminder (Zahlungs-)Erinnerung, Mahnung
report Bericht
sales literature Verkaufsliteratur

schedule *(≈ itinerary, timetable)* Zeitplan, Fahrplan, Stundenplan
subject *(in a letter / e-mail)* Betreff

Spoken communication
advise, to beraten
advice Rat, Ratschlag
announce, to ankündigen, bekannt geben, ansagen
announcement (to make an announcement) Ankündigung, Bekanntgabe, Durchsage
apologise for something, to sich für etwas entschuldigen
apology Entschuldigung
available erhältlich, erreichbar, verfügbar
chat, to plaudern, schwätzen
controversy Kontroverse, Auseinandersetzung
debriefing Nachbesprechung
demonstration (to give / do a demonstration) Vorführung, Demonstration
dispute Streit
gossip Klatsch, Gerede
interview (to hold / give an interview) Interview, Vorstellungsgespräch
lecture (to hold / give a lecture) Vortrag, Vorlesung
negotiate, to verhandeln
negotiation Verhandlung
speech (to hold / give a speech) Rede
thank somebody for something sich bei jemandem für etwas bedanken

271

Collocations relating to communication

circulate the agenda, to die Tagesordnung verteilen
clarify a matter, to eine Angelegenheit klären
co-ordinate an event, to eine Veranstaltung koordinieren/
   organisieren
confirm an agreement, to eine Vereinbarung bestätigen
courtesy Höflichkeit
directory Nachschlagewerk
evaluation scheme Bewertungsschema
**have an objection to something, to (= to object to
   something)** Einwand gegen etwas erheben, etwas
   beanstanden
make a complaint about something, to (= to complain)
   etwas reklamieren, sich über etwas beschweren
make an appointment, to einen Termin vereinbaren
notify somebody of something, to jemanden über etwas
   informieren, jemandem Bescheid geben
postpone an appointment, to einen Termin verschieben
solve a problem, to ein Problem lösen
take the minutes, to das Protokoll führen
update information, to Daten/Informationen
   aktualisieren
write up the minutes, to das Protokoll schreiben

On the phone

   "I'll put you through." „Ich stelle Sie durch."
   "Speaking." „Am Apparat."
   "The line is busy."/"The line is engaged." „Die Leitung
   ist besetzt."
**answerphone *(BE)*, answering machine *(BE)*, voice mail
   *(AE)*** Anrufbeantworter
bad line schlechte Verbindung
dial the wrong number, to sich verwählen
extension Durchwahl
hang up, to auflegen
hold the line, to am Apparat bleiben
landline phone Festnetztelefon
leave a message, to eine Nachricht hinterlassen
mobile phone *(BE)*, cell(ular) phone *(AE)* Mobiltelefon,
   Handy
put through, to durchstellen, verbinden
receiver Hörer
return a call, to zurückrufen

Information and communications technology (ICT)

cursor Cursor, Positionsmarke
click on something, to anklicken auf etwas
data processing, EDP Datenverarbeitung, EDV
digital / compluter projector Beamer
keyboard Tastatur
landline phone Festnetztelefon
screen Bildschirm
text message SMS

Company organisation

Types of company and structure

agency Agentur, Vertretung
board of directors Geschäftsleitung, Vorstand und
   Aufsichtsrat
branch Filiale, Niederlassung, Zweigstelle
childcare Kinderbetreuung
construction work Bauarbeiten
consultancy Beratungsfirma
cooperative Genossenschaft
core business Hauptgeschäft, Kerngeschäft
executive board Vorstand
firm Firma
franchise Franchise
franchisee Franchisenehmer
franchisor Franchisegeber
go public, to an die Börse gehen
group Konzern
headquarters Hauptsitz, Firmenzentrale, Hauptgeschäfts-
   stelle
holding company Holdinggesellschaft, Dachgesellschaft
Inc. (= incorporated) Abkürzung für amerikanische
   Kapitalgesellschaft
limited liability beschränkte Haftung
limited partnership Kommanditgesellschaft
Ltd. (= limited company) *(etwa:)* GmbH
mail order business Versandhandel
multinational company (MNC) multinationales
   Unternehmen
offshoring das Auslagern ganzer Geschäftsprozesse ins
   Ausland
outsourcing Produktionsverlagerung *(ins Ausland)*
parent company Muttergesellschaft
partnership Personengesellschaft, *(etwa:)* OHG
PLC (= public limited company) (UK) britische Aktiengesellschaft
private limited company britische Gesellschaft mit
   beschränkter Haftung
retail outlet Verkaufsstelle
retailer Einzelhändler
self-employed selbständig
service provider Dienstleister
sleeping partner stiller Teilhaber
sole trader *(BE)*, sole proprietorship *(AE)* Einzelunter-
   nehmer/in
stakeholder Interessenvertreter, Mitglied einer
   Interessengruppe
subcontractor Sub-Unternehmer
subsidiary Tochtergesellschaft, Tochterfirma
supervisory board Aufsichtsrat
supplier Lieferant, Zulieferer
wholesaler Großhändler

Departments and functions

accounts, accountancy Finanzbuchhaltung,
   Finanzabteilung
advertising Werbung
advertising agency Werbeagentur
after-sales service Kundendienst
board of directors Direktion, Geschäftsleitung
customer service Kundendienst, Kundenbetreuung
department (dept.) Abteilung

distribution Vertrieb
executive board Vorstand
resources / personnel Personal
legal department Rechtsabteilung
logistics Logistik
maintenance Wartung
marketing Marketing
organisation chart Organigramm
payroll Lohn- und Gehaltsabrechnung
PR (= public relations) Öffentlichkeitsarbeit
production Produktion
purchasing (≈ procurement) Einkauf, Beschaffung
quality assurance Qualitätssicherung
recruitment Personalbeschaffung
research and development (R&D) Forschung und
  Entwicklung
sales Verkauf
security Sicherheit
supervisory board Aufsichtsrat

Jobs and responsibilities
accountant Bilanzbuchhalter/in
administration Verwaltung
agent Vertreter/in *(auf Provisionsbasis)*
apprentice Lehrling, Auszubildende/r, Praktikant/in
automated teller machine (ATM) Geldautomat
blue-collar workers Arbeiter *(in der Produktion)*
board (of directors) Geschäftsleitung, Vorstand
boss Chef/in
caretaker *(BE)*, janitor *(AE)* Hausmeister/in
Chief Executive Officer (CEO) Vorstandsvorsitzende/r,
  Hauptgeschäftsführer/in
Chief Financial Officer Leiter/in der Finanzabteilung
co-worker *(AE)* Mitarbeiter/in
colleague Kollege/Kollegin
consultant Berater/in
determination of material requirements Bedarfsermittlung
director Mitglied des Vorstands/des Aufsichtsrats
employee Arbeitnehmer/in, Mitarbeiter/in
employer Arbeitgeber/in
equal opportunities employer Firma, der Chancengleichheit ein Anliegen ist
executive leitende/r Angestellte/r
executive board Vorstand
factory workers Fabrikarbeiter
foreman Vorarbeiter
founder Gründer/in
freelancer Freiberufler/in, freie/r Mitarbeiter/in
head of department, department head Abteilungs-
  leiter/in
health and safety officer Arbeitsschutzbeauftragte/r
internee Praktikant/in
machine operator Maschinist/in
maintenance engineer Wartungstechniker/in
maintenance Wartung und Instandhaltung
management Geschäftsleitung
management assistant (industrial business)
  (etwa:) Industriekaufmann/frau
managing director (MD) Geschäftsführer/in
owner Eigentümer/in, Besitzer/in
predecessor Vorgänger/in

sales representative Außendienstmitarbeiter/in,
  Vertriebsmitarbeiter/in
semi-skilled angelernt
skilled worker Facharbeiter/in
staff (= personnel) Personal
subordinate Untergebene/r
successor Nachfolger/in
supervisor Vorgesetzte/r, Betreuer/in, Aufseher/in,
  Kontrolleur/in
supervisory board Aufsichtsrat
technical support Technischer Dienst
temp (= temporary staff) Aushilfe, Zeitarbeiter/in
trainee Praktikant/in
trainer Ausbilder/in, Trainer/in
unskilled ungelernt
welder Schweißer/in
white-collar staff Büroangestellte
workforce Arbeiterschaft, Belegschaft

Places at work
assembly line (= production line) Fließband
body shop Karosseriewerkstatt, Autolackiererei
building site Baustelle
canteen Kantine, Mensa
clean-room Reinraum
conference room Konferenzraum, Sitzungszimmer
conference venue Konferenzort, Tagungsort
desk Schreibtisch
environment Umwelt
factory Fabrik
hard hat Schutzhelm
infrastructure Infrastruktur
lift *(BE)*, elevator *(AE)* Aufzug
located, to be (≈ situated) sich befinden
location Ort
locker room Umkleideraum
mill Mühle, Walzwerk, Walzanlage
open-plan office Großraumbüro
paint shop Abteilung für Mal- und Spritzarbeit,
  Lackiererei
plant Anlage
premises Räumlichkeiten, Firmengelände,
  Geschäftsräume
reception Empfang
shop floor (= production area) Produktionsbereich,
  Fertigungsbereich
stockroom Lager, Lagerraum
venue Veranstaltungsort
warehouse Lager, Lagerhalle
work station Arbeitsplatz, Arbeitsstation
workshop Werkstatt

Products, brands and marketing

Describing products
additives Zusatzstoffe
affordable bezahlbar, erschwinglich
appliances Geräte
artificial künstlich
batch production Chargenfertigung
brand image Markenimage

brand loyalty Markentreue
brand name Markenname
commodity Handelsware, Handelsgut, Gebrauchsgut
convenient praktisch, gelegen, bequem
convert (conversion), to umrechnen, konvertieren (Umrechnung)
crude oil Rohöl
degree of automation Automatisierungsgrad
device Gerät, Mittel
drill head Bohrkopf
economical sparsam, effizient, wirtschaftlich
electrical equipment Elektrogeräte
electronic components elektronische Bauelemente
energy efficiency class Energieeffizienzklasse
environmentally friendly umweltfreundlich
equipment Gerät, Ausrüstung, Ausstattung
expiry date Gültigkeitsdatum
fabric Stoff
faulty defekt, fehlerhaft
feature Eigenschaft, Merkmal
fossil fuels fossile Brennstoffe
fuel capacity Benzinverbrauch
gadget Gerät, Apparat
handy praktisch, nützlich
have a good reputation for something, to einen guten Ruf in Bezug auf etwas haben
high (height) hoch (Höhe)
hydropower Wasserkraft
impractical (impracticality) unpraktisch (Unbrauchbarkeit)
inconvenient (inconvenience) unpraktisch, ungelegen (Unannehmlichkeit)
individual production Einzelfertigung
industrial goods Industriegüter, Investitionsgüter, Produktionsgüter
ingredient Zutat
in working order funktionstüchtig
label Label, Marke
long (length) lang (Länge)
manufacturer's brand Herstellermarke
mass production Massenproduktion
measure (measurement), to messen (Maß)
merchandise Ware, Handelsware, Handelsgüter
obsolete überholt, veraltet
on average im Durchschnitt
option (Auswahl-)Möglichkeit
optional extras Extras auf Wunsch
own brand Eigenmarke, Hausmarke
practical (practicality) praktisch (Nutzbarkeit)
product line Produktlinie
product range Produkpalette, Produktsortiment
prototype Prototyp
range Sortiment, Auswahl
recognisable erkennbar
reliability
reliable (reliability) zuverlässig, Zuverlässigkeit
sell well, to sich gut verkaufen (lassen)
semi-finished halbfertig
series production Serienfertigung
sophisticated anspruchsvoll, hoch entwickelt
speed Geschwindigkeit
standard version Standardausführung
state-of-the-art auf dem neuesten Stand (der Technik)

sturdy robust
stylish (to have style) stilvoll (Stil haben)
synthetic künstlich, aus Kunststoff
tool Werkzeug
trademark Markenzeichen, Schutzmarke, Warenzeichen
unreliable (unreliability) unzuverlässig (Unzuverlässigkeit)
up-to-date modern, aktuell
user-friendly benutzerfreundlich, anwenderfreundlich
versatile (versatility) vielseitig (Vielseitigkeit)
weigh (weight), to wiegen (Gewicht)
well-designed gut gestaltet, gut konzipiert
wide (width) breit, weit (Breite)

Marketing and promotion

advertising agency Werbeagentur
advertising strategy Werbestrategie
after-sales Kundendienst
age group Altersgruppe
appeal to somebody, to (put somebody off, to) jemanden ansprechen, auf jemanden wirken
benchmarking test Vergleichstest
benefit Nutzen, Vorteil
bias Voreingenommenheit, Einseitigkeit
booth, stand Messestand
catchphrase Schlagwort, Werbespruch
compete with, to konkurrieren mit
competition Konkurrenz, Wettbewerb, Preisausschreiben
competitive konkurrenzfähig, wettbewerbsfähig
demand (for) Nachfrage (nach)
disposable income (≈ purchasing power) verfügbares Einkommen (Kaufkraft)
diversification Diversifikation, Ausweitung des Produktprogramms
end user Endverbraucher/in
exhibition Ausstellung
exhibition grounds Ausstellungsgelände
feature (≈ characteristic) Eigenschaft, Merkmal
giveaway (= freebie) Werbegeschenk
margin Gewinnmarge, Handelsspanne
market research Markforschung
market forecast Marktprognose
market observation Markbeobachtung
pricing Preisbildung
primary research Primärforschung (Feldforschung)
secondary research Sekundärforschung (Schreibtischforschung)
product elimination Produktelimination
purchasing power Kaufkraft
saturated (a saturated market) gesättigt
segment (≠ sector) Segment
segment, to segmentieren
subject to availability (= while stocks last) solange der Vorrat reicht
target group Zielgruppe

Sales and distribution

Distribution channels

agency contract Händlervertrag
agent Handelsvertreter/in *(auf Provisionsbasis)*
break bulk, to größere Mengen teilen und weiterkaufen; große Gebinde aufbrechen
broker Makler/in
bulk delivery Großlieferung
buy in bulk, to in großen Mengen einkaufen
chain Kette, Ladenkette
commission Provision
corner shop *(BE)*, mom'n pop store *(AE)* Tante-Emma-Laden
mail order Versandhaus
retail outlet Einzelhandelsgeschäft,
sales rep (representative) Vertreter/in, Außendienstmitarbeiter/in
sole distributer Alleinvertrieb
specialty shop *(BE)*, specialty store *(AE)* Fachgeschäft
vending machine Warenautomat

Transport and shipping

aircraft Flugzeug *(Sammelbegriff)*
barge Kahn
batch Bündel, Stapel, Charge, Los
bonded warehouse Zolllager, Freilager
bulk goods Massen-, Schüttgüter
bulky goods sperrige Waren
carbon footprint CO_2-Fußabdruck, persönliche CO_2-Bilanz
cargo Fracht, Ladung
carrier Frachtführer
commodities Handelswaren, Rohstoffe
consignee Empfänger (einer Warensendung)
consignment Warensendung, Lieferung
consignor Versender (einer Warensendung)
country of destination Bestimmungsland
country of origin Ursprungsland, Herkunftsland
customs clearance Zollabfertigung
depot Lager, Warendepot
embassy Botschaft
EU single market EU-Binnenmarkt
freight train Güterzug
haulier, haulage company Lkw-Unternehmer, Lkw-Spediteur
goods inwards / goods outwards Wareneingang/Warenausgang
in stock, to have am Lager führen, vorrätig haben
inland waterway Binnengewässer, Wasserstraße
loading charges Verladekosten
merchandise Waren
port of destination Bestimmungshafen
port of shipment Verschiffungshafen
road train (langer) Sattelzug, Lastwagenzug
sea transport Seetransport
ship goods, to Waren versenden
shipment Warensendung, Lieferung
shipper Versender

Human resources

Hiring and firing

annual holidays Jahresurlaub
application form Bewerbungsformular
apply for a job / a post, to sich bewerben
aptitude test Eignungstest
to assess *(hier:)* bewerten, einschätzen
covering letter *(BE)*, cover letter *(AE)* Begleitbrief
CV (= curriculum vitae) *(BE)*, résumé *(AE)* Lebenslauf
degree Hochschulabschluss
dismiss, to entlassen
draw up a short-list, to eine Liste der aussichtsreichsten Bewerber/innen anfertigen
early retirement Frührente
entry requirments Zugangsvoraussetzungen
equal opportunities Chancengleichheit
fire (someone), to (jemanden) feuern, entlassen
give (someone) notice, to (jemandem) kündigen
hand in one's notice, to die Kündigung einreichen, kündigen
hire (someone), to einstellen
hiring freeze Einstellungssperre
job vacancy offene Stelle
lay (someone) off, to (jemanden) entlassen
make (someone) redundant, to (jemanden) entlassen, freisetzen, überflüssig machen
period of notice Kündigungsfrist
recruit, to einstellen, anwerben, rekrutieren
recruitment Personalbeschaffung
reference *(BE)*, testimonial *(AE)* Referenzschreiben, Zeugnis
rejection letter Absagebrief
replacement Vertretung, Nachfolger/in
take (someone) on, to (jemanden) einstellen
vacancy offene (Arbeits-)Stelle
without notice fristlos

Issues

be off sick, to krankgeschrieben sein
bully, to mobben
collective bargaining Tarifverhandlungen mit Gewerkschaften
compulsory vepflichtend, Pflicht
discriminate (against somebody), to (jemanden) diskriminieren
employment law Arbeitsrecht
employment tribunal Arbeitsgericht
equal opportunities Chancengleichheit
flexitime Gleitzeit
full-time job Vollzeitstelle
go on strike, to streiken
harass, to belästigen
Human Resources (HR) Personalwesen
industrial relations Arbeitgeber-Arbeitnehmer Beziehungen
industrial dispute Streit zwischen Arbeitern und Geschäftsleitung
maternity leave Mutterschaftsurlaub
occupational accident Betriebsunfall
overtime Überstunden

parental leave Erziehungsurlaub
part-time job Teilzeitjob
paternity leave Vaterschaftsurlaub
pay negotiations Tarifverhandlungen
probationary period Probezeit
promotion Beförderung
qualifications Qualifikationen
retire, to in den Ruhestand gehen
shop steward Gewerkschaftsvertreter im Betrieb
staff Personal, Arbeitnehmer, Mitarbeiter
take a day off, to einen Tag frei nehmen
trade union Gewerkschaft
work permit Arbeitserlaubnis
workforce Arbeitskraft
working conditions Arbeitsbedingungen
works council Betriebsrat

Wages and salaries

annual salary Jahresgehalt
benefits Zusatzleistungen, Sozialleistungen
commission Provision
expenditure Ausgaben, Auslagen
expenses Auslagen
expenses claim form Reisekostenabrechnungsformular
fee (for a service) Honorar
holiday pay Urlaubsgeld
hourly rate Stundensatz
incentive Anreiz
lump sum payment Pauschalbetrag
minimum wage Mindestlohn
payment by seniority Zahlung nach Betriebszugehörigkeit
pay rise *(BE)*, **raise** *(AE)* Gehaltserhöhung
pension Rente, Pension
performance-related pay leistungsorientierte Bezahlung
redundancy pay *(BE)*, **severance pay** *(AE)* Abfindung
salary Gehalt
unemployment benefit Arbeitslosengeld
wage Lohn
weekly wage Wochenlohn

Training and assessment

appraisal Bewertung
apprentice Auszubildende/r
apprenticeship, traineeship Ausbildung, Lehre
assess, to bewerten, evaluieren
assessment Bewertung, Evaluierung
evaluate, to bewerten, evaluieren
job satisfaction Zufriedenheit am Arbeitsplatz
peer pressure Gruppendruck
promote, to befördern
promotion Beförderung
skills Fertigkeiten, Fähigkeiten, Kompetenzen
track record Erfolgsbilanz, (gute) Leistungen am Arbeitsplatz
trainee Auszubildende/r, Praktikant/in, Lehrling
vocational training berufliche Aus-/Weiterbildung, Berufsausbildung

Quality

Expressions with the word 'quality'

We provide quality at reasonable prices. Wir bieten Qualität zu einem vernünftigen Preis.
We have a reputation for quality. Wir sind bekannt für Qualität.
… is of (a) good / high / top quality ist von hervorragender Qualität
… is of (a) low / poor / varying quality ist von niedriger/ minderwertiger Qualität
a lack of quality mangelnde Qualität
Quality has declined. Die Qualität hat abgenommen.
Quality has improved. Die Qualität hat sich verbessert.
Quality is suffering. Die Qualität leidet.
She has leadership qualities. Sie hat Führungsqualitäten.
We specialise in quality products. Wir haben uns auf Qualitätsprodukte (Güteprodukte) spezialisiert.
quality assurance Qualitätssicherung, QM-Darlegung
quality control Qualitätskontrolle, Qualitätssteuerung
quality circle Qualitätssicherungsgruppe, Qualitäszirkel
Total Quality Management (TQM) umfassendes Qualitätsmanagement

Standards

below standard, to be unter dem Standard sein
compliance (with) Einhaltung, Übereinstimmung (mit)
comply with, to einhalten
conforming to specifications / requirements genau nach den technischen Vorgaben/Vorschriften entsprechend
conformity Übereinstimmung
contaminated verseucht
cracked gesprungen, rissig
customer satisfaction Kundenzufriedenheit
decline in quality, to in der Qualität sinken
defect Defekt
defective defekt
detect flaws, to Mängel entdecken
durable haltbar, robust
ensure compliance, to Gewährleistung erfüllen
error Irrtum, Fehler
exacting / tight specifications genaue/strenge Vorgaben
exceed expectations, to die Erwartungen übertreffen
excellent exzellent
failure Versagen, Misserfolg
fall short of expectations, to hinter den Erwartungen zurückliegen
fit for purpose, to be für eine besondere Verwendung geeignet sein
flawed defekt
flawless makellos
flimsy schwach, dünn, nicht sehr stabil
fragile zerbrechlich
fulfil a requirement, to (= to meet a need) eine Voraussetzung/Bedingung erfüllen
immaculate perfekt, makellos, vollkommen
imperfection Fehlerstelle, Mangel, Unvollkommenheit
improve (in quality), to (sich) verbessern
in compliance with entsprechend, gemäß, in Übereinstimmung mit
International Standards Organisation (ISO) ISO (Internationale Organisation für Normung)
latent defect verdeckter Mangel, verborgener Fehler

maintain standards, to Standards einhalten
non-compliance Nichteinhaltung
of (a) high / good / top quality, to be von hervorragender
  Güte (Spitzenqualität) sein
of (a) low / poor / varying quality, to be von
  minderwertiger Güte/Qualität sein
of a high standard, to be hohen Standard erfüllen
of a low standard, to be von niedrigem Standard sein
out of service außer Betrieb
pass inspection, to eine Kontrollprüfung überstehen
perfect einwandfrei
poorly-designed schlecht konstruiert sein
satisfy customers, to Kunden zufrieden stellen
scratched zerkratzt
set high standards, to hohe Anforderungen stellen
show a lack of quality, to zeigt Qualitätsmängel
substandard unzulänglich, minderwertig, unter der
  Norm liegend
tough, rigorous, exacting streng
up to standard, to be den Anforderungen entsprechen
value for money Preis-Leistungs-Verhältnis
waste Verschwendung

Measures and approaches

benchmarking Benchmarking, Vergleichstest
best practice optimaler Geschäftsablauf, bestes Verfahren
carry out checks, to Kontrollmaßnahmen durchführen,
  kontrollieren
certification Zertifizierung, Abnahme
corrective and preventive action Korrektur- und
  Vorbeugemaßnahme
customer feedback Kundenbewertung
investigate, to untersuchen, ermitteln
inspection Besichtigung, Prüfung, Kontrolle
external audit außerbetriebliche Revision/Prüfung
internal audit betriebseigene Revision/Prüfung
just-in-time (JIT) bedarfsorientierte Produktion
measurable objective messbares Ziel
peer review Begutachtung, geregelte Kollegenkontrolle
performance appraisal Leistungsbeurteilung
procedure Verfahren
quality audit Qualitätsaudit, Qualitätsmanagement
quality control Qualitätskontrolle
questionnaire Umfrage
random sample Stichprobe, Zufallsauswahl
verify, to auf Richtigkeit prüfen, kontrolliern
validation Gültigkeitsprüfung, Bewertung, Bestätigung
verification Nachweis, Nachprüfung, Feststellung der
  Richtigkeit

Business and the economy

Business sectors

aerospace Luft- und Raumfahrt
agriculture Landwirtschaft
automotive Automobil
biotechnology Biotechnologie, Biotechnik
chemicals Chemikalien
fashion Mode
civil engineering Hoch- und Tiefbau
construction Bauwesen, Konstruktion

consumer electronics Unterhaltungselektronik
cosmetics Kosmetik
electrical goods industry Elektroartikelbranche
energy Energie, Strom
engineering Maschinenbau, Technik
financial services Finanzdienstleistungen
fisheries Fischereien
food and beverages Lebensmittel
food processing company Lebensmittel verarbeitendes
  Unternehmen
furniture and furnishings Möbel und Ausstattung
healthcare Gesundheitsversorgung
household goods Haushaltswaren
insurance Versicherung
manufacturing Herstellung, Produktion, Fertigung
media and publishing Medien- und Verlagsbuchhandel
mining Förderung, Bergbau
pharmaceuticals Pharmaindustrie, Arzneimittelindustrie
restaurant and catering Gastronomie
retail Einzelhandel
telecommunications Telekommunikationsbranche
textiles Textilien
tobacco Tabak
tourism and leisure Touristik
transport and logistics Transport und Logistik
utilities Versorgungsunternehmen
waste and recycling Wiederverwertung
wholesale Großhandel

Cycles and trends

accelerate, to beschleunigen
appreciate (in value), to im Wert steigern, aufwerten
appreciation Wertzuwachs, Aufwertung
average, to durchschnittlich betragen
boom Hochkonjunktur
boom, to florieren, boomen
business cycle Konjunktur, Konjunkturzyklus
bust Abschwung
climb, to steigern, klettern
decline, to sinken, fallen
decrease, to sinken, fallen
depreciate (in value), to im Wert fallen
depreciation Wertverlust, Wertfall, Abschreibung
depression langanhaltende Rezession
deteriorate, to verschlechtern
dip, to (sich) senken, abfallen
downturn Abschwung
downward spiral Abwärtstrend
fluctuate, to (fluctuation) schwanken
economic cycle Konjunkturzyklus
economic situation Wirtschaftslage
go up, to steigern
growth (= expansion) Wachstum
hit a low / a high einen Tiefpunkt/einen Höhepunkt
  erreichen
improve, to (sich) verbessern
improvement Verbesserung
increase, to steigern
on average im Durchschnitt
plunge, to abstürzen, drastisch sinken
reach a peak, to einen Höchststand erreichen
recession Rezession, Tiefkonjunktur
recover, to sich erholen

recovery Wirtschaftsaufschwung
rise Anstieg
rise, to ansteigen
shoot up, to hochschießen
shrink, to schrumpfen
slowdown (in the economy) Abschwung, Konjunkturrückgang
slump Absturz
slump, to plötzlich fallen,
soar, to hochschießen, schnell aufsteigen
stand at, to stehen bei, liegen bei
steady gleichbleibend, stabil
volatile stark schwankend
weaken, to abschwächen

International trade

Issues and policy

apply for a licence, to eine Lizenz beantragen
arrange insurance, to eine Versicherung abschließen
balance of trade (= trade balance) Handelsbilanz
bilateral trade bilateraler Handel
conclusion of contract Vertrag abschließen
customs clearance Zollabfertigung
deal with customs formalities, to Zollformalitäten bearbeiten
domestic market Inlandsmarkt
domestic trade Binnenhandel, inländischer Handel
dumping unter Preis anbieten
environmental policy Umweltpolitik
export ban, embargo Ausfuhrsperre, Embargo
fair trade fairer Handel
free movement of labour Freizügigkeit der Arbeitnehmer, freie Wahl des Arbeitsplatzes
foreign trade Außenhandel
free trade Freihandel
free-trade agreement Freihandelsabkommen
import restriction Einfuhrbeschränkung
international trade Welthandel, Außenhandel, internationaler Handel
Law on Safety and Health at Work Arbeitsschutzgesetz
Law on Safety at Work Arbeitssicherheitsgesetz
notify the exporter that the goods have arrived, to den Lieferanten über den Empfang der Waren informieren
open an L/C in favour of the supplier, to ein Akkreditiv eröffnen zugunsten des Lieferanten
protectionism Protektionismus, Schutzzollpolitik
quota Kontingent, Quote
sign the sales contract, to den Kaufvertrag unterschreiben
subsidy Subvention
transfer the invoice amount, to den Rechnungsbetrag überweisen
translate documents, to Unterlagen übersetzen

Documentation

air waybill Luftfrachtbrief
bill of lading (B/L) Konossement, Frachtbrief, Ladeschein
certificate of origin Ursprungszeugnis
commercial invoice Handelsrechnung
consignment note Frachtbrief, Ladeschein

consular invoice Konsulatsfaktura
customs declaration Zollerklärung
customs invoice Zollfaktura, Zollrechnung
dispatch advice Versandanzeige
document of title Eigentumsurkunde
endorsed indossiert
export declaration Ausfuhrerklärung/-anmeldung
export/import licence (BE), export/import license (AE) Export-/Importlizenz
in duplicate / in triplicate In zweifacher/ dreifacher Ausfertigung
insurance policy/certificate Versicherungspolice/-schein
marine insurance Seeversicherung
packing list Packliste, Versandliste
pro-forma invoice Proforma Rechnung
shipping documents Versanddokumente

Payment and delivery

advance payment Vorauszahlung, Vorkasse, Vorschusszahlung, Anzahlung
bank guarantee Bankbürgschaft
bill of exchange (B/E) Wechsel
carriage paid to (CPT) frachtfrei, fracht bezahlt
cash against documents (Bar-)Zahlung gegen Dokumente
cash on delivery (COD) Lieferung gegen Nachnahme
cash with order (CWO) Zahlung bei Auftragserteilung
cost estimate Kostenvoranschlag
credit note Gutschrift
creditworthiness Kreditwürdigkeit
crossed cheque Verrechnungsscheck
currency Währung
customs duty Zoll
to debit to someone's account das Konto von jemandem belasten
debt collection Inkasso(verfahren)
deferred payment verschobene Auszahlung
deposit Anzahlung
documentary letter of credit (L/C) (Dokumenten-) Akkreditiv
documents against acceptance (D/A) Dokumente gegen Akzept
documents against payment (D/P) Dokumente gegen Zahlung
exchange rate Wechselkurs
IBAN (international bank account number) internationale Kontonummer
list purchase price Listeneinkaufspreis
open account terms offenes Zahlungsziel
open credit Zahlung gegen einfache Rechnung
staggered payment gestaffelte Zahlungsweise

Acronyms and abbreviations

Abbreviation: shortened form of a word.
Acronym: abbreviation formed from the first letters of
each word in a term.

Short form Full form German
a.m. / am ante meridian morgens / vormittags
(24 Uhr – 12 Uhr)
approx. approximately ungefähr
asap as soon as possible so schnell wie möglich
ATM automated teller machine Geldautomat
Attn. for the attention of zu Händen (von)
B / E bill of exchange Wechsel
B / L bill of lading Konnossement, Frachtbrief
B2B business to business Business-to-Business
BIC bank identifier code internationaler Bank-Code
BOP balance of payments Zahlungsbilanz
BOT balance of trade Handelsbilanz
BRIC Brazil, Russia, India, China Brasilien, Russland,
Indien, China
cc carbon copy, copy circulated, cubic centimeters (Kohle-
papier-)Durchschlag, Verteiler, Kubikzentimeter
CEO Chief Executive Officer *(etwa:)* (Haupt-)Geschäfts-
führer / in, Firmenchef / in, Vorstandsvorsitzende / r
CFO Chief Financial Officer Finanzleiter / in
CFR cost and freight (Incoterm) Kosten und Fracht
CIF cost, insurance and freight (Incoterm) Kosten,
Versicherung und Fracht; frachtfrei versichert
COD cash on delivery Lieferung per Nachnahme
CPT carriage paid to (Incoterm) frachtfrei, Fracht bezahlt
CRM customer relationship management Kundendienst,
Kundenbetreuung
CV curriculum vitae Lebenslauf
CWO cash with order Zahlung bei Auftragserteilung
D / A documents against acceptance Dokumente gegen
Akzept
D / P documents against payment Dokumente gegen
Zahlung
DAP delivery at place (Incoterm) geliefert benannter Ort
DAT delivery at terminal (Incoterm) geliefert Terminal
DDP delivered, duty paid (Incoterm) frei Haus, verzollt
geliefert
dept. department Abteilung
e.g. exempli gratia = for example zum Beispiel (z.B.)
encl. enclosed beiliegend, in der Anlage
etc. etcetera und so weiter (usw.)
EU European Union Europäische Union (EU)
EXW ex works (Incoterm) ab Werk
FAO for the attention of zu Händen von
FAQ frequently asked question häufig gestellte Frage
FAS free alongside ship (Incoterm) frei Längsseite Schiff
FCA free carrier (Incoterm) frei Frachtführer
FOB free on board (Incoterm) frei an Bord
GDP gross domestic product Bruttoinlandsprodukt (BIP)
GNP gross national product Bruttosozialprodukt (BSP)
HQ headquarters Hauptsitz, Zentrale
HR human resources Personalabteilung, -wesen
i.e. id est (Latin) = that is das heißt (d.h.)
IBAN International Bank Account Number Internationale
Kontonummer
ICC International Chamber of Commerce Internationale
Industrie- und Handelskammer (ICC)

IMF International Monetary Fund Internationaler
Währungsfond
Inc.; inc incorporated *(AE)* Aktiengesellschaft
ISO International Standards Organisation ISO (Norm)
JIT just-in-time bedarfsorientierte Produktion (gerade
rechtzeitig)
L / C letter of credit Akkreditiv
lbs pounds Pfunde *(Gewicht)*
Ltd. limited mit beschränkter Haftung
MD managing director Geschäftsführer / in
MNC multinational company multinationales
Unternehmen
mph miles per hour Meilen pro Stunde *(Geschwindigkeit)*
NGO non-governmental organisation Nichtregierungs-
organisation
no. number Nummer (Nr.)
OPEC Organisation of the Petroleum Exporting Countries
Organisation erdölexportierender Länder (OPEC)
P&L Profit and Loss Gewinn und Verlust
p.a. per annum jährlich, pro Jahr
p.m. / pm post meridian nachmittags / abends
(12 Uhr – 24 Uhr)
PIN Personal Identification Number PIN
(Erkennungsnummer)
plc; PLC public limited company *(etwa:)* AG
pp paginae = pages Seiten
pp / ppa per procurationem = on behalf of im Auftrag von
PR public relations Öffentlichkeitsarbeit
R&D research and development Forschung und
Entwicklung
Re. regarding bezüglich
Re. reply (e-mail) Antwort
Ref. reference Aktenzeichen
ROI return on investment Rentabilität, Kapitalertrag
SME small and medium(-sized) enterprise *(BE)*; **small to
mid-sized enterprise** *(AE)* Mittelstand; kleines und mit-
telständisches Unternehmen (KMU)
sq. square Quadrat *(Maß)*, Platz *(Ort)*
SWOT Strengths, Weaknesses, Opportunities, Threats
Stärken, Schwächen, Möglichkeiten, Gefahren / Risiken
WTO World Trade Organisation Welthandelsorganisation

False friends

False friends (= falsche Freunde) sind Wörter, die in Deutsch und Englisch identisch oder ähnlich aussehen, die aber nicht dieselbe Bedeutung haben. Im besten Fall kann das zu bloß lustigen, im schlimmsten Fall aber zu peinlichen oder gefährlichen Missverständnissen führen. Die wichtigsten falschen Freunde sollte man also gut kennen.

Deutsch	Englische Bedeutung	Nicht zu verwechseln mit	Deutsch
aktuell	topical, current(ly)	actual	wirklich, tatsächlich
also	therefore, then	also	auch
bald	soon	bald	kahl, glatzköpfig
bekommen	to receive, to get	to become	werden
Billion	1,000,000,000,000.00	billion	Milliarde
blamieren	to embarrass	to blame	jemanden beschuldigen
Brief	letter	brief	kurz
Chef	boss	chef chief *(adjective)*	Chefkoch haupt-, Haupt-
dezent	discreet, modest	decent	anständig; nett, großzügig
Direktion	management, administration	direction	Richtung
Distanz	detachment, coolness	distance	Entfernung
Dose	can, tin	dose	Dosis
engagiert	involved	engaged	verlobt; besetzt *(Telefon)*
eventuell	possibly, maybe	eventually	endlich, schließlich
Fabrik	factory, works	fabric	Gewebe, Stoff
familiär	family-related	familiar	bekannt
fast	almost	fast	schnell
Fotograf	photographer	photograph	Foto
Gift	poison	gift	Geschenk
Gymnasium	secondary school, high school *(AE)*, grammar school *(BE)*	gym(nasium)	Turnhalle
Handy	mobile phone *(BE)*, cell(ular) phone *(AE)*	handy *(adjective)*	praktisch
Hochschule	college, university	high school	Gymnasium, Oberschule
irritieren	confuse, distract	irritate	ärgern, auf die Nerven gehen
Kaution	deposit	caution	Vorsicht
Klosett	toilet	closet	Verschlag, Wandschrank
Konkurrenz	competition	concurrence	Übereinstimmung
konsequent	consistent	consequently	infolgedessen
kontrollieren	check, monitor	control	steuern, regulieren
Kritik	criticism	critic	Kritiker / in
Mappe	briefcase, folder	map	Landkarte
Meinung	opinion	meaning	Bedeutung

Deutsch	Englische Bedeutung	Nicht zu verwechseln mit	Deutsch
Menü	set meal	menu	Speisekarte; Menü *(Computer)*
Messe	trade fair, show	mess	Unordnung
Note	mark *(school)*	note	Notiz
ordinär	vulgar, cheap	ordinary	üblich, normal
Pension	small hotel	pension	Rente
plump	tactless, awkward, clumsy	plump	mollig
prinzipiell	on principle	principally	hauptsächlich
Promotion	doctor's exam	promotion	Beförderung, Förderung
Prospekt	brochure, leaflet	prospect	Aussicht
Provision	commission, percentage of price	provision	Vorsorge
prüfen	check	prove	beweisen
rentabel	profitable	rentable	(ver)mietbar
Rente	pension	rent	Miete
Rezept	recipe *(cooking)* prescription *(medical)*	receipt	Quittung
Rückseite	back, rear	backside	Hinterteil
selbstbewusst	self-confident	self-conscious	schüchtern, gehemmt
sensibel	sensitive	sensible	vernünftig
seriös	reliable	serious	ernsthaft
spenden	donate	to spend	ausgeben
Sympathie	a liking, a feeling of solidarity	sympathy	Mitleid
sympathisch	likable, nice	sympathetic	mitfühlend
übersehen	overlook, miss something	oversee	überwachen
Unternehmer/in	businessman, businesswoman, employer	undertaker	Leichenbestatter
Warenhaus	department store	warehouse	Lagerhalle

Countries, nationalities, languages

Land	Bürger	Eigenschaftswort / Sprache (wenn abweichend vom Eigenschaftswort oder bei mehreren Sprachen)
Algeria	an Algerian	Algerian / Arabic, French
Argentina	an Argentinian	Argentinian / Spanish
Australia	an Australian	Australian / English
Austria	an Austrian	Austrian / German
Belgium	a Belgian	Belgian / Dutch (Flemish), French, German
Bolivia	a Bolivian	Bolivian / Spanish, Quéchua
Brazil	a Brazilian	Brazilian / Portuguese
Bulgaria	a Bulgarian	Bulgarian / Bulgarian, Turkish
Canada	a Canadian	Canadian / English, French
Chile	a Chilean	Chilean / Spanish
China	a Chinese	Chinese
Colombia	a Colombian	Colombian / Spanish
Costa Rica	a Costa Rican	Costa Rican / Spanish
Croatia	a Croatian	Croatian
Cuba	a Cuban	Cuban / Spanish
Cyprus	a Cypriot	Cypriot / Greek, Turkish, English
Czech Republic	a Czech	Czech
Denmark	a Dane	Danish
Dominican Republic	a Dominican	Dominican / Spanish
Ecuador	an Ecuadorian	Ecuadorian / Spanish, Quéchua
Egypt	an Egyptian	Egyptian / Arabic, English
El Salvador	an El Salvadoran	El Salvadoran / Spanish
England	an Englishman an Englishwoman the English	English
Estonia	an Estonian	Estonian / Estonian, Russian
Finland	a Finn	Finnish / Finnish, Swedish
France	a Frenchman a Frenchwoman the French	French
Germany	a German	German
Great Britain	a Britishman a Britishwoman the British	British / English
Greece	a Greek	Greek
Hungary	a Hungarian	Hungarian
Iceland	an Icelander	Icelandic
India	an Indian	Indian / Hindi, English, Bengali, and many others

Land	Bürger	Eigenschaftswort / Sprache *(wenn abweichend vom Eigenschaftswort oder bei mehreren Sprachen)*
Indonesia	an Indonesian	Indonesian / Bahasa Indonesia *(official)*, English, Dutch, Javanese and others
Iran	an Irani	Iranian / Farsi, Turkic, Kurdish
Iraq	an Iraqi	Iraqi / Arabic, Kurdish
Ireland	an Irishman an Irishwoman the Irish	Irish / English, Gaelic
Israel	an Israeli	Israeli / Hebrew, Arabic, English
Italy	an Italian	Italian
Jamaica	a Jamaican	Jamaican / English, Jamaican Creole
Japan	a Japanese	Japanese
Jordan	a Jordanian	Jordanian / Arabic, English
Kenya	a Kenyan	Kenyan / English, Swahili
Korea, North	a (North) Korean	Korean
Korea, South	a (South) Korean	Korean / Korean, English
Kuwait	a Kuwaiti	Kuwaiti / Arabic, English
Latvia	a Latvian	Latvian / Latvian, Russian, Lithuanian
Lebanon	a Lebanese	Lebanese / Arabic, French, English
Libya	a Libyan	Libyan / Arabic, Italian, English
Liechtenstein	a Liechtensteiner	Liechtensteiner / German
Lithuania	a Lithuanian	Lithuanian / Lithuanian, Russian, Polish
Luxembourg	a Luxembourger	Luxembourger / Luxembourgish, French, German
Malaysia	a Malaysian	Malaysian / Malay, English, Chinese dialects
Malta	a Maltese	Maltese / Maltese, English
Mexico	a Mexican	Mexican / Spanish
Morocco	a Moroccan	Moroccan / Arabic, Berber dialects, French
Namibia	a Namibian	Namibian / English, Afrikaans, German
The Netherlands	a Dutchman a Dutchwoman the Dutch	Dutch / Dutch, Frisian
New Zealand	a New Zealander	New Zealand / English, Maori
Nicaragua	a Nicaraguan	Nicaraguan / Spanish, English
Nigeria	a Nigerian	Nigerian / English, Hausa, Yoruba
Norway	a Norwegian	Norwegian / Norwegian, Sami, Finnish
Northern Ireland	a Britishman a Britishwoman the British	British / English
Pakistan	a Pakistani	Pakistani / Urdu, English, Punjabi
Panama	a Panamanian	Panamanian / Spanish, English
Paraguay	a Paraguayan	Paraguayan / Spanish, Guarani
Peru	a Peruvian	Peruvian / Spanish, Quéchua

Land	Bürger	Eigenschaftswort / Sprache *(wenn abweichend vom Eigenschaftswort oder bei mehreren Sprachen)*
The Philippines	a Philippine	Philippine / Filipino (Tagalog), English
Poland	a Pole	Polish
Portugal	a Portuguese	Portuguese
Romania	a Romanian	Romanian / Romanian, Hungarian
Russia	a Russian	Russian
Saudi Arabia	a Saudi	Saudi Arabian / Arabic
Scotland	a Scotsman a Scotswoman the Scots	Scottish / English, Scots Gaelic
Serbia	a Serb	Serbian / Serbian *(official)*, Romanian, Hungarian, Slovak, Croatian
Singapore	a Singaporean	Singaporean / Mandarin, English, Malay
Slovakia	a Slovak	Slovakian / Slovak, Hungarian
Slovenia	a Slovene	Slovenian / Slovenian, Serbo-Croatian
South Africa	a South African	South African / IsiZulu, IsiXhosa, Afrikaans, Sepedi, English
Spain	a Spaniard	Spanish / Castilian Spanish, Catalan, Galician, Basque
Sri Lanka	a Singhalese	Sri Lankan / Singhalese, Tamil, English
Sweden	a Swede	Swedish / Swedish, Sami, Finnish
Switzerland	a Swiss	Swiss / German, French, Italian
Syria	a Syrian	Syrian / Arabic, Kurdish, Armenian, French
Taiwan	a Taiwanese	Taiwanese / Mandarin Chinese, Taiwanese
Tanzania	a Tanzanian	Tanzanian / Swahili, English, Arabic
Thailand	a Thai	Thai / Thai (Siamese), English
Tunisia	a Tunisian	Tunisian / Arabic, French
Turkey	a Turk	Turkish / Turkish, Kurdish
Uganda	a Ugandan	Ugandan / English, Swahili, Arabic
Ukraine	a Ukrainian	Ukrainian / Ukrainian, Russian, Romanian, Polish, Hungarian
United Arab Emirates	a citizen of the UAE	UAE / Arabic *(official)*, Persian, English, Hindi, Urdu
United Kingdom	a Britishman a Britishwoman the British	British / English, Welsh, Scots Gaelic
United States of America	an American	American / English, Spanish
Uruguay	a Uruguayan	Uruguayan / Spanish, Portuñol, Brazilero
Venezuela	a Venezuelan	Venezuelan / Spanish
Vietnam	a Vietnamese	Vietnamese / Vietnamese, English, French, Chinese, Khmer
Wales	a Welshman a Welshwoman the Welsh	Welsh / English, Welsh

Weights and measures

Auch wenn das metrische System am logischten und am einfachsten ist, gibt es keine große Hoffnung, dass die Menschen in GB oder in den USA ihre traditionellen Systeme in absehbarer Zukunft aufgeben werden. Hier folgt zur Orientierung ein Überblick der GB und US Einheiten für Gewicht, Länge und Fläche als die relevantesten Bereiche für Geschäftskorrespondenz sowie ein Überblick über mathematische Begriffe und Symbole.

Im Deutschen	Im Englischen/Amerikanischen	
Mathematische Begriffe und Symbole		
Grundrechen-arten	**Addition:** 2 + 3 = 5 (Two **plus** 3 equals five.) **Subtraction:** 8 – 4 = 4 (Eight **minus** 4 equals four.) **Multiplication:** 9 x 4 = 36 (Nine **multiplied** by four equals thirty-six; or nine **times** four …) **Division:** 55 ÷ 11 = 5 (Fifty-five **divided** by eleven equals five.)	
Bruchrechnen	**Fractions** (Brüche) ½ – one half, a half ⅓ – one third, a third ¼ – one quarter, a quarter ¾ – three quarters ⅕ – one fifth, a fifth ⅝ – five eighths	$\sqrt{2}$ – square root: $\sqrt{9}$ the square root of 9 equals three $\sqrt[3]{}$ – cube root: $\sqrt[3]{8}$ the cube root of 8 is 2 3^2 – three squared equals 9 4^3 – four cubed equals 64 2^4 – two to the power of 4 equals 16
Prozentrechnen	% per cent ‰ per thousand	≠ does not equal, is not equal to > is more than / greater than < is less than ° degree
Gewichte		
	1 ounce (oz) x 16 = 1 pound (lb) x 112 (GB) bzw. 100 (US) = 1 hundredweight (cwt) x 20 = 1 ton Bei *hundredweight* und *ton* unterscheiden sich die GB und US Systeme! *(alle Angaben sind gerundet)*	
Gramm und Kilogramm	**GB / US Gewichte**	**metrisches System**
	1 ounce (oz) = 28,35 g	1 g = 0.0353 oz
	1 pound (lb) = 16 oz = 453,59 g	1 Pfund = 500 g = 17.65 oz
	1 hundredweight (cwt) (GB) = 112 lb = 50,802 kg 1 hundredweight (cwt) (US) = 100 lb = 45,359 kg	1 kg = 1000 g = 2.205 lb
	1 Brit. ton (long ton) = 20 cwt (GB) = 1.016,05 kg 1 US ton (short ton) = 20 cwt (US) = 907.185 kg	1 Tonne = 1000 kg = 0.984 Brit. tons 1 Tonne = 1000 kg = 1.1023 US tons

Im Deutschen	Im Englischen/Amerikanischen
Längen	

1 inch (in) (auch 1″) x 12 = 1 foot (ft) (auch 1′) x 3 = 1 yard (yd) x 1760 = 1 mile

(alle Angaben sind gerundet)

Zentimeter und Meter

in	cm	cm	in	ft	m	m	ft
1	2,54	3	1.18	1	0,3048	1	3.28
2	5,08	4	1.57	2	0,6096	2	6.56
3	7,62	5	1.97	3	0,9144	3	9.84
4	10,16	10	3.94	4	1,2192	4	13.12
5	12,70	15	5.91	5	1,5240	5	16.40
6	15,24	20	7.87	6	1,8288	6	19.68
7	17,78	25	9.84	7	2,1336	7	22.96
8	20,32	30	11.81	8	2,4384	8	26.24
9	22,86	35	13.78	9	2,7432	9	29.52
10	25,40	40	15.75	10	3,0480	10	32.80
11	27,94	45	17.72	11	3,3528	11	36.08
12	30,48	50	19.69	12	3,6576	12	39.36

Meter und Kilometer

yd	m	m	yd	mile	km	km	mile
1	0,914	1	1.09	1	1,609	1	0.62
2	1,829	2	2.19	2	3,218	2	1.24
3	2,743	3	3.28	3	4,827	3	1.86
4	3,658	4	4.37	4	6,436	4	2.49
5	4,572	5	5.47	5	8,045	5	3.11
6	5,486	6	6.56	6	9,654	6	3.73
7	6,401	7	7.66	7	11,263	7	4.35
8	7,315	8	8.75	8	12,872	8	4.97
9	8,230	9	9.84	9	14,481	9	5.59
10	9,144	10	10.94	10	16,090	10	6.22

Flächen	

Die GB und US Standardeinheiten für Fläche sind *square inches (sq in)*, *square feet (sq ft)*, *square yards (sq yd)*, *acres* und *square miles (sq mi)*.

(alle Angaben sind gerundet)

Quadratzentimeter und Quadratmeter

Hektare und Quadratkilometer

GB / US Flächeneinheiten	metrisches System
1 square inch (sq in) = 6,451 cm²	1 cm² = 0.155 sq in
1 square foot (sq ft) = 929,03 cm² / 0,929 m²	1 m² = 10.764 sq ft
1 square yard (sq yd) = 0,836 m²	1 m² = 1.196 sq yd
1 acre (international) = 4840,856 m² 1 acre (international) = 0,485 hectare	1 ha = 11,959.9 sq yd 1 ha = 2.471 acres
1 square mile = 2,589 km²	1 km² = 0.386 sq mi

Bildquellennachweis

4 Thinkstock (Digital Vision), München; **5** shutterstock (Yuri Arcurs), New York, NY; **6** Corbis RF (Royalty-Free), Düsseldorf; **6** Getty Images RF (Digital Vision), München; **6** Getty Images (PhotoDisc), München; **6** Fotosearch Stock Photography, Waukesha, WI; **7** JupiterImages photos.com (Photos.com), Tucson, AZ; **8** plainpicture GmbH & Co. KG (Maria Simon), Hamburg; **8** Alamy Images (Janine Wiedel Photolibrary), Abingdon, Oxon; **8** iStockphoto (RF/ Locke), Calgary, Alberta; **10** Photothek.net Gbr (Ute Grabowsky), Radevormwald; **11** Robert Bosch GmbH, Stuttgart; **11** Imageshop (Imageshop), Düsseldorf; **11** Mauritius Images (Gilsdorf), Mittenwald; **12** Thinkstock (iStockphoto), München; **16** www.bilderbox.com, Thening; **16** Corbis (Eric K. K. Yu), Düsseldorf; **16** Joker (Marcus Gloger), Bonn; **16** JupiterImages photos.com (RF/Photos.com), Tucson, AZ; **17** Klett-Archiv (Meyle + Müller/Harter), Stuttgart; **18** Klett-Archiv (Meyle + Müller/Harter), Stuttgart; **19** iStockphoto (RF/artydanmark), Calgary, Alberta; **23** Kartographie Huber, München; **23** images.de digital photo GmbH (Giribas), Berlin; **23** MEV Verlag GmbH, Augsburg; **23** Jahns, Rainer, Siegsdorf; **25** Klett-Archiv (Meyle + Müller/ Harter), Stuttgart; **26** Fotolia LLC (Ralf Beier), New York; **26** StockFood GmbH (Newedel), München; **26** StockFood GmbH (Joff Lee Studios), München; **26** obs (ABCEuroRSCG), Hamburg; **26** Getty Images RF (PhotoDisc), München; **29** Fotolia LLC (pressmaster), New York; **30** Thinkstock (iStockphoto), München; **31** Fotolia LLC (Tortenboxer), New York; **31** URW, Hamburg; **31** Klett-Archiv (Fabian H. Silberzahn), Stuttgart; **31** Fotolia LLC (LaCatrina), New York; **31** Fotolia LLC (Dark Vectorangel), New York; **31** shutterstock (Miguel Angel Salinas Salinas), New York, NY; **31** Fotolia LLC (marog-pixcells), New York; **31** MEV Verlag GmbH, Augsburg; **31** Thinkstock (Hemera), München; **31** Thinkstock (iStockphoto), München; **31** Fotolia LLC (Matthias Krüttgen), New York; **31** shutterstock (Bakelyt), New York, NY; **36** Avenue Images GmbH (Corbis RF/Tom Grill), Hamburg; **36** MEV Verlag GmbH, Augsburg; **37** Picture-Alliance (akg), Frankfurt; **37** Picture-Alliance (epa), Frankfurt; **37** Picture-Alliance (Imaginechina), Frankfurt; **37** Klett-Archiv (Meyle + Müller/ Harter), Stuttgart; **39** Dreamstime LLC (Maksim Shmeljov), Brentwood, TN; **41** Klett-Archiv (Meyle + Müller/Harter), Stuttgart; **41** Mauritius Images (Pöhlmann), Mittenwald; **41** MEV Verlag GmbH, Augsburg; **41** Avenue Images GmbH (Ingram Publishing), Hamburg; **41** Ingram Publishing, Tattenhall Chester; **42** Fotosearch Stock Photography, Waukesha, WI; **42** Avenue Images GmbH (Image Source), Hamburg; **42** Avenue Images GmbH (Image Source RF), Hamburg; **42** Bananastock, Watlington/Oxon; **42** Imageshop, Düsseldorf; **42** BBC Information and archives, London; **46** Thinkstock (Digital Vision), München; **47** iStockphoto (Curt Pickens), Calgary, Alberta; **47** Thinkstock (Hemera), München; **47** iStockphoto (Felix Alim), Calgary, Alberta; **47** iStockphoto (Lise Gagne), Calgary, Alberta; **47** shutterstock (Kochergin), New York, NY; **49** shutterstock (Monkey Business Images), New York, NY; **49** Thinkstock (Erik Snyder), München; **49** iStockphoto (Dmitry Kutlayev), Calgary, Alberta; **49** Corbis RF (Image Source), Düsseldorf; **50** Klett-Archiv (Meyle + Müller/Harter), Stuttgart; **51** shutterstock (ArtmannWitte), New York, NY; **52** iStockphoto (Jason Stitt), Calgary, Alberta; **52** iStockphoto (RF/ Chen), Calgary, Alberta; **52** iStockphoto (RF/Anna Bryukhanova), Calgary, Alberta; **53** iStockphoto (Anna Bryukhanova), Calgary, Alberta; **53** iStockphoto (Jason Stitt), Calgary, Alberta; **53** iStockphoto (RF/Chen), Calgary, Alberta; **58** shutterstock (Beata Becla), New York, NY; **61** Thinkstock (Jupiterimages), München; **61** Avenue Images GmbH (Corbis RF/Jack Hollingsworth), Hamburg; **61** PhotoAlto, Paris; **61** Getty Images RF (Eyewire), München; **63** Klett-Archiv (Meyle + Müller/Harter), Stuttgart; **63** Fotosearch Stock Photography (Banana Stock), Waukesha, WI; **63** Avenue Images GmbH (Image Source), Hamburg; **65** Klett-Archiv (Meyle + Müller/Harter), Stuttgart; **68** iStockphoto (RF/peter chen), Calgary, Alberta; **68** Fotosearch Stock Photography (Banana Stock), Waukesha, WI; **72** BigStockPhoto.com (RF), Davis, CA; **72** Dreamstime LLC (Ronfromyork), Brentwood, TN; **72** iStockphoto (RF), Calgary, Alberta; **80** Thinkstock (Ryan McVay), München; **81** Klett-Archiv (Meyle + Müller/Harter), Stuttgart; **81** Fotosearch Stock Photography (Banana Stock), Waukesha, WI; **82** iStockphoto (RF/Thompson), Calgary, Alberta; **82** Klett-Archiv (Meyle + Müller/Harter), Stuttgart; **84** Klett-Archiv (Meyle + Müller/Harter), Stuttgart; **87** Klett-Archiv (Meyle + Müller/Harter), Stuttgart; **87** BBC Information and archives, London; **88** Klett-Archiv (Meyle + Müller/Harter), Stuttgart; **91** Thinkstock (Comstock), München; **98** Thinkstock (IT Stock), München; **103** LinguaTV GmbH, Berlin; **105** www. cartoonstock.com (Peter Welleman), Bath; **106** Avenue Images GmbH (stock disc), Hamburg; **110** iStockphoto (Jill Fromer), Calgary, Alberta; **110** Mauritius Images (B. Lehner), Mittenwald; **110** Thinkstock (Hemera/Keith Bell), München; **111** iStockphoto (RF/Hudson), Calgary, Alberta; **115** Thinkstock (Hemera), München; **136** Corbis (Talaie), Düsseldorf; **141** MEV Verlag GmbH, Augsburg; **142** Thinkstock (Jupiterimages), München; **143** shutterstock (Ralf Beier), New York, NY; **143** iStockphoto (Bogdan Lazar), Calgary, Alberta; **143** iStockphoto (William Bacon), Calgary, Alberta; **143** Avenue Images GmbH (Corbis RF/Jose Luis Pelaez, Inc./Blend Images), Hamburg; **143** Fotosearch Stock Photography (Corbis RF), Waukesha, WI; **147** iStockphoto (Stepan Popov), Calgary, Alberta; **147** BigStockPhoto.com (vladikpod), Davis, CA; **149** shutterstock (J. Henning Buchholz), New York, NY; **153** BLG Logistics Group AG, Bremen; **157** MEV Verlag GmbH, Augsburg; **157** Fotosearch Stock Photography (Digital Vision), Waukesha, WI; **157** Corel Corporation Deutschland, Unterschleissheim; **158** MEV Verlag GmbH, Augsburg; **159** Thomas Gremmelspacher, Stuttgart; **161** BBC Information and archives, London; **163** Corbis (Saloutos), Düsseldorf; **164** Fotosearch Stock Photography (PhotoDisc), Waukesha, WI; **164** Flughafen Frankfurt-Hahn, Hahn-Flughafen; **165** iStockphoto (bluenemo), Calgary, Alberta; **165** iStockphoto (RF/Prikhodho), Calgary, Alberta; **165** creativ collection Verlag GmbH, Freiburg; **166** iStockphoto (RF/David Meharey), Calgary, Alberta; **166** iStockphoto (RF/Paul Senyszyn), Calgary, Alberta; **166** iStockphoto (RF/Joe Gough), Calgary, Alberta; **166** iStockphoto (RF/Tschakert), Calgary, Alberta; **166** Thinkstock (Hemera Technologies, Getty Images), München; **166** Klett-Archiv (Ruth Feiertag), Stuttgart; **166** Thinkstock (iStockphoto), München; **168** iStockphoto (Rohde), Calgary, Alberta; **168** Getty Images RF (Annie Reynolds/ PhotoLink), München; **169** Klett-Archiv (Meyle + Müller/Harter), Stuttgart; **171** MEV Verlag GmbH, Augsburg; **172** BBC Information and archives, London; **173** iStockphoto (kastock), Calgary, Alberta; **176** iStockphoto (RF/Paul Cowan), Calgary, Alberta; **179** iStockphoto (RF/Hudson), Calgary, Alberta; **179** iStockphoto (RF), Calgary, Alberta; **179** MEV Verlag GmbH, Augsburg; **181** iStockphoto (fazon1), Calgary, Alberta; **182** Fotolia LLC (ExQuisine), New York; **182** iStockphoto (RF/Maureen Perez), Calgary, Alberta; **182** iStockphoto (RF/Caspel), Calgary, Alberta; **182** Mauritius Images (Pöhlmann), Mittenwald; **182** creativ collection Verlag GmbH, Freiburg; **186** Thinkstock (iStockphoto), München; **189** iStockphoto (exi5), Calgary, Alberta; **192** Thinkstock (Polka Dot Images), München; **194** Fotolia LLC (Sulamith), New York; **197** Getty Images RF (Photodisc), München; **197** Corel Corporation Deutschland, Unterschleissheim; **198** Klett-Archiv (Meyle + Müller), Stuttgart; **202** iStockphoto (David Hughes), Calgary, Alberta; **204** shutterstock (Iurii Konoval), New York, NY; **207** Thinkstock (Photodisc/James Woodson), München; **211** shutterstock (ary718), New York, NY; **213** MEV Verlag GmbH, Augsburg; **214** Alamy Images (Expuesto - Nicolas Randall), Abingdon, Oxon; **214** Avenue Images GmbH (CorbisRF), Hamburg; **216** BBC Information and archives, London; **217** Alamy Images (Adams Picture Library t/a apl), Abingdon, Oxon; **219** Corbis (Harms), Düsseldorf; **223** Thinkstock (iStockphoto), München; **223** iStockphoto (Anita Patterson-Peppers), Calgary, Alberta; **223** iStockphoto (makkayak), Calgary, Alberta; **224** shutterstock (Yuri Arcurs), New York, NY; **227** iStockphoto (Zorani), Calgary, Alberta; **228** Mercedes Benz, Niederlassung, Stuttgart; **228** MEV Verlag GmbH, Augsburg; **228** iStockphoto (RF/Maier), Calgary, Alberta; **236** BBC Information and archives, London; **237** Thinkstock (Digital Vision), München; **240** Mauritius Images (Simone Fichtl), Mittenwald; **241** creativ collection Verlag GmbH, Freiburg; **242** creativ collection Verlag GmbH, Freiburg; **244** Thinkstock (Comstock), München; **253** Klett-Archiv, Stuttgart; **COVER** shutterstock (StockLite), New York, NY; **COVER** iStockphoto (ricardoazoury), Calgary, Alberta; **COVER** Avenue Images GmbH (Fancy), Hamburg

Textquellennachweis

173/174 Heather Timmons: In a sinking world economy, outsourcing proves resilient. From The New York Times © 06/03/2009 The New York Times All rights reserved. Used by permission and protected by the Copyright Laws of the United States. The printing, copying, redistribution, or retransmission of the Material without express written permission is prohibited.